Canon Law Society of America

Proceedings
of the Seventy-Fourth
Annual Convention

Chicago, Illinois
October 8-11, 2012

Canon Law Society of America

© Copyright 2013 by the Canon Law Society of America

ISBN 1-932208-34-8
ISSN 0277-9889
SAN 237-6296

The Canon Law Society of America's programs and publications are designed solely to help canonists maintain their professional competence. In dealing with specific canonical matters, the canonist using Canon Law Society of America (CLSA) publications or orally conveyed information should also research original sources of authority.

The views and opinions expressed in this publication are those of the individual authors and do not represent the views of the CLSA, its Board of Governors, staff or members. The CLSA does not endorse the views or opinions expressed by the individual authors. The publisher and authors specifically disclaim any liability, loss or risk, personal or otherwise, which is incurred as consequence, directly or indirectly, of the use, reliance, or application of any of the contents of this publication.

Unless otherwise noted, all canons quoted are from the *Code of Canon Law, Latin-English Edition* (Washington, DC: Canon Law Society of America, 1999) and the *Code of Canons of the Eastern Churches, Latin-English Edition* (Washington, DC: Canon Law Society of America, 2002).

Printed in the United States of America.

Canon Law Society of America
Office of the Executive Coordinator
3025 Fourth Street, NE
The Hecker Center, Suite 111
Washington, DC 20017-1102

TABLE OF CONTENTS

Foreword vii

Keynote Address
Vatican II and the Parish 50 Years Later: A Bishop's Perspective
    Most Reverend Gregory M. Aymond 1

Major Addresses
The Parish: 50 Years Into the Future
    Reverend Monsignor Roch Pagé 13

Lay Ecclesial Ministry in Parishes: Diverse Services in Varied
    Settings and Circumstances
    Sister Katarina Schuth, OSF 32

Seminars
Diocesan Reorganization in Boston and Detroit: The Good, the
    Bad, and the Ugly
    Reverend Monsignor Ricardo Bass & Very Reverend Mark O'Connell .. 44

Going Global with *The Charter* and *Essential Norms*
    Most Reverend R. Daniel Conlon 62

Latin Parishes and Eastern Catholics
    Chorbishop John Faris 77

The 21st Century Catholic Parish
    Mark M. Gray 89

The Establishment of a Religious Institute: Where the Rubber
    Meets the Road
    Doctor Eileen C. Jaramillo 117

Happily Never After: Some Reflections on Rotal Jurisprudence
    Concerning the *Bonum Sacramenti*
    Reverend Monsignor John G. Johnson 140

The Quest for Truth in Consensual Incapacity Causes: *Dignitas Connubii* and the Use of Psychological Experts
   Deacon Gerald T. Jorgensen 192

New Models of Parish Schools
   Reverend Monsignor Patrick R. Lagges & Sister Mary Paul McCaughey, OP 221

The Sacramental Life of the Parish: An Encounter with Justice?
   Reverend Bruce Miller 249

Modern Family Life and the Exclusion of Openness to Children
   Doctor Lynda Robitaille 290

Tribunal Advocacy on the Parish Level
   Sister Marilyn R. Vassallo, CSJ 307

A Diocese, a Parish, a Religious Institute, a Member: An Exploration of Canon and Civil Law
   Reverend Daniel J. Ward, OSB 312

Officers' Reports
President
   Rita F. Joyce 321

Treasurer
   Reverend Gregory T. Bittner 327
   Independent Auditor Report
      Linton Shafer Warfield & Garret, P.A. 331
   Fiscal Year 2012-2013 Budget 345

Executive Coordinator
   Sister Sharon A. Euart, RSM 356

Committee Reports
Constitutional Committees
   Nominations 363
   Resolutions 364
   Resource and Asset Management 365
   Professional Responsibility 367

Standing Committees
    Church Governance..368
    Clergy..369
    Convention Planning..370
        General Convention Chairperson..372
        Convention Liturgies...374
    Institutes of Consecrated and Apostolic Life 375
    Laity 376
    Publications Advisory Board...377
    Research and Development..384
    Sacramental Law..385

Varia
Business Meeting Minutes
    Zabrina R. Decker 388

Reflection After Communion
    Rita F. Joyce 400

Role of Law Award Citation
    Rita F. Joyce 402

Role of Law Award Response
    Reverend Patrick Cogan..404

Tribunal Statistics 2011..408

Contributors 419

2012 Convention List of Participants 421

Foreword

The Canon Law Society of America (CLSA) is pleased to present the Proceedings of the seventy-fourth annual convention held in Chicago, Illinois, October 8-11, 2012. The CLSA annually publishes for its members, and others in the canonical community, the major addresses, seminars and reports presented at the annual meeting.

We are grateful to the presenters who provided their final texts in a timely fashion. Texts have been edited for consistency in conformity with the CLSA Style Sheet and Publication Guidelines including capitalization, use of footnotes, gender-inclusive language, and citation of canons. Included in this edition of *CLSA Proceedings* are the Tribunal Statistics collected from participating (arch) dioceses and (arch)eparchies along with a listing of the participants who attended the convention in Chicago.

The CLSA, established on November 12, 1939 as a professional association dedicated to the promotion of both the study and the application of canon law in the Catholic Church today, numbers over 1,400 members who reside in the United States and 37 other counties. *CLSA Proceedings 74* (2012) should take its place among previous volumes as a professional resource. Additional copies of this volume may be purchased from the CLSA website: www.clsa.org.

For information on how to become a member of the CLSA, please visit the CLSA website (www.clsa.org) or contact the Office of the Executive Coordinator.

Sr. Sharon A. Euart, RSM
Executive Coordinator
Canon Law Society of America
3025 Fourth Street, NE
The Hecker Center, Suite 111
Washington, DC 20017-1102

Keynote Address

Vatican II and the Parish 50 Years Later: A Bishop's Perspective
Most Reverend Gregory M. Aymond

For this presentation I will include five parts.

- A comparison of the parish fifty years ago and what it is today.
- A definition of the parish as it was defined in Vatican II and in other church documents since then.
- Some statistics regarding the parish of today.
- Some challenges in parish life today.
- Some specific suggestions for renewal in the parish of today.

Section One: The Parish Fifty Years Ago and Today

Let us take a look at what the church and our parish life looked like fifty years ago and some of the ways in which it compares to today. While comparisons are never fully accurate or fair, let us give it a shot nonetheless.

Fifty years ago, the church parish was the center of activity for the Catholic family. It was, in many ways, their home away from the family home. The parish was a place of faith and worship, socialization, and community.

Fifty years ago, Sunday was considered a very sacred and important day. It was to be used primarily for family and for church and the attire was always going to church in "Our Sunday Best." Now we compete with soccer games, football games, school activities, and numerous other events planned for Sunday.

Before Vatican II, as we all know, Mass was celebrated in Latin. It had a mystical dimension and there was no need for people to participate, in fact, many people read their own prayers and prayed the rosary. It was a more passive participation and silence in church before Mass and after Mass was the order of the day. In today's church, we are called to active participation and to put our focus on the Eucharist and to participate in a very deliberate way.

Fifty years ago and more, parishes were designated for ethnic groups. In many cities within a short distance, there was a church for the Spanish community, one for the German community, one for the French community and they celebrated Mass in those languages. Because of church closures and the need for consolidation, many of those ethnic churches have been closed, which has caused great pain among many people. Now some parishes offer Masses in multiple languages on any given Sunday.

In the past five decades, the only ministers at the Mass were the priests, altar boys, and ushers. There were no permanent deacons, no lay ministers.

Daily Mass was celebrated. Now in many parishes throughout the United States there is a Communion service in the absence of a priest.

Parish life has changed significantly as has the role of the priests and other ministers in the church. Prior to Vatican II, "Father was in charge" and many pastors had associates. Religious sisters and brothers had very specific ministries and were well respected. The priest was trusted and put on a pedestal. Father and sister always knew best. There was no finance council and no pastoral council. Lay ministries were limited. The laity volunteered, but had no real authority. They did share often as catechists in the parish under the direction of the pastor or the sisters. In comparison, fifty years later, lay ministry is an integral part of parish life. Many lay people have degrees in theology or in pastoral ministry and we gratefully and respectfully call them co-workers in the vineyard of the Lord. Years ago, we would not have equated lay people with ministry.

Years ago, there were many devotions in the church. For example, "Forty Hours Devotions" was a popular one in many parishes. First Communions and confirmations were important events both for the family and for parish life. Novenas, Way of the Cross, and First Fridays were a part of the fabric of what it meant to be an active parishioner. Fifty years later, I do not believe you will find many parishes with "Forty Hours Devotions." Sometimes at confirmations, I wonder where the family and the parish are because the church seems to be half empty. Some devotions have fallen by the wayside.

In the past, in some dioceses, there was truly a Catholic culture that was developed in many neighborhoods. Holy days of obligation, fasting for Lent, and meatless Fridays were a part of what it meant to be Catholic.

Five decades ago, people knew parish boundaries and respected them. In today's church, people shop for the parish of their choice, where they will feel at home and where they enjoy the liturgy and the preacher.

In the past, we had a strong Catholic school system; in fact, sometimes there was a division between the public school students and the Catholic school students. I know that in my own my life, there were different first Communions, one for the public school children and one for the Catholic school children. While we cannot necessarily justify that division, Catholic schools did give energy and a family spirit to the parish. Today, many Catholics cannot afford Catholic schools and the enrollment within the schools is diminishing. This does affect parish life.

Lastly, in the 1960's and before, church teaching was respected and if there was disagreement it was something spoken about quietly and respectfully. Today, people are very vocal as to what church teachings they accept and which ones they openly reject.

I know that comparisons are never fully accurate or fair, but I hope that this gives some description of what we have seen and the changes within the last fifty years. With that as our back drop, it is evident that our Catholic faith is lived out through the parish community and finds within it a true center. Therefore, for this discussion, it is important for us to seek some descriptions and definitions of the parish as proclaimed in Vatican II and enhanced since then.

Section Two: A Definition of the Parish

Before looking at the 1960's, let us go back to the Acts of the Apostles. I suggest that Luke in Acts 4:32-35 gives a very accurate description of what the parish community was intended to be. He says, "The community of believers were of one heart and one mind none of them ever claimed anything as his own; rather, everything was held in common. With power, the Apostles bore witness to the resurrection of the Lord Jesus, and great respect was paid to them all; nor was there anyone needy among them, for all who owned property or houses sold them and donated the proceeds. They used to lay them at the feet of the Apostle's to be distributed to everyone according to his need."

Using that description from Acts of the Apostle as a foundation, let us now move to Vatican II. In the *Decree on the Apostolate of the Laity* it states, "...the parish in as much as it brings together the many human differences found within its boundaries and draws them into the universality of the Church...as far as possible, the laity ought to collaborate energetically in every apostolic and missionary undertaking sponsored by their local parish" (#10). In the *Constitution on the Sacred Liturgy* it states, "...parishes set up locally under a pastor who takes the place of the bishop are most important: for in a certain way they represent the visible Church as it is established throughout the world" (#41-42).

More recently, in 1997, Pope John Paul II spoke about the basic elements of the parish community when he addressed the Bishops of France during their *Ad Limina* visit. He said: "It is essentially the parish which gives the Church concrete life... (the Church) must be a home where the members of the body of Christ gather together, open to meeting God the Father full of love and the Savior his son, incorporated into the Church by the Holy Spirit at the time of their baptism and ready to accept their brothers and sisters with fraternal love whatever their condition and origins. The parish is not merely a geographical territory or an administrative unit of the diocese but a fundamental ecclesial community, a portion of the people of God that make up a particular Church."

In his synodal exhortation *Christifideles Laici*, John Paul II says the Church "...finds its most immediate and visible expression in the parish. It is there that the Church is seen locally. In a certain sense, it is the Church living in the midst of the homes of her sons and daughters... the parish is not primarily a structure, a territory, or a building, but rather the family of God... a familial and welcoming home, the community of the faithful" (#26).

In *Ecclesia in America* it states "...the parish must continue to be above all a Eucharistic ministry... parishes are called to be welcoming and fraternal, places of Christian initiation, of education in and celebration of the faith, open to the full range of charisms, services and ministries, organized in a communal and responsible way, capable of utilizing existing movements of the apostolate, attentive to the cultural diversity of the people, open to pastoral projects which go beyond the individual parish, and alert to the world in which they live" (#41).

Ecclesia in America also states that the parish must be renewed and in so doing it "can be the source of great hope. It can gather people in community, assist family life, overcome the sense of anonymity, welcome people and help them to be involved in their neighborhood and in society."

Most recently, on December 10, 2010, in a Sunday Homily in a parish, Pope Benedict XVI stated, "Here, as in every parish, it is necessary to start with those who are "close" in order to reach out to those who are "distant" so as to bring an evangelical presence to the milieus of life and work. All must be able to find in the parish an adequate means of formation and must be able to experience that community dimension which is a fundamental characteristic of Christian Life."

From all of these statements, the parish can be defined as God's people gathered in a community related to the universal church and to the bishop of the local church. It is truly a home for people as they are formed into God's family. There is a sense of belonging and welcome. Central to the parish community is the Eucharist. Nourished by the Eucharist, the family of God is sent to be Christ in the world carrying on the mission of Christ. Through the parish, the clergy, religious, other ministers, and the laity are called to be active and to share in the mission of Christ and to offer their gifts and charisms.

Section Three: Statistics of Parishes Today

Let us now take a look at what parish life looks like in the world today. As some of you may know, CARA, that is the Center for Applied Research in the Apostolate at Georgetown University, conducted a series of surveys on parishes nationwide. The particular survey which I will make use of collected data from March 2010 to December 2010. Eight Hundred Forty-Six parishes responded (15.3% of U.S. parishes).

The major findings show that registered households in U.S. parishes is 1,168 (median of 761). A third of the parishes have more than 1,201 registered *households*. United States parishes average 3,277 *individual registered parishioners*. Forty percent of all growth in registered parishioners in the United States parishes from 2005 to 2010 was among Hispanic and Latinos. Obviously, from diocese to diocese this differs. Some parishes are larger, others smaller. We must recognize and take into account differences that rural communities embrace. They also recognize through this survey that many parishes have closed in the last couple of years; nevertheless, the number of Catholics continues to increase in the United States.

Twenty-nine percent of the parishes celebrate Mass in a language other than English. This is an increase from twenty-two percent of parishes in 2000. Most of these Masses, eighty-one percent, are in Spanish. Overall, about six percent of all Masses, weekday and weekend, are celebrated in Spanish.

Smaller parishes tend to have more sacramental activity per registered parishioner than larger parishes. Parishes in the South and West are more racially and ethnically diverse than those in the Midwest and the Northeast.

Regarding programs and ministries, this survey shows that parishes are most likely to have programs and ministries for sacramental preparation, religious education, and for the infirm and homebound. Seventy-six percent have youth ministry, sixty-four percent have ministry to seniors, fifty-nine percent social services to meet individual needs, and fifty-four percent ministry to the bereaved. Fifty percent of the parishes, a majority, report some sort of a commitment to a Catholic school. Twenty -our percent indicate that they have a Catholic school.

Regarding the staff in our parishes; the total number of people on parish staffs in the United States is estimated to be 168,448. The survey indicates that the average parish has a total staff size of about nine to ten members with about five to six of those individuals in ministry positions. Ninety-three percent of the parishes indicate that they have a pastoral council and ninety-seven percent say that they have a finance council.

More than one in four parishes, that is twenty- seven percent, are utilizing multi-parish ministry where the parish is most often "clustered" or "linked" to another parish. A third of those parishes, that is thirty-three percent, indicate that this is a relatively new development, beginning sometime after 2004.

Using this profile, we are reminded that there are fewer priests available to serve in these parishes. Although the average number of priestly ordinations in the United States has been about 500 per year, there are fewer men being ordained than what is needed to replace an aging clergy population. The number of diocesan priests in the United States has declined by eleven percent in the last decade. Women religious and laity provide significant leadership and ministry in United States parishes today and we are grateful to them.

Section Four: Challenges in Parish Life Today

I propose for our consideration a number of specific challenges that do affect parish life at this time. This is not meant to be an exhaustive listing, but gives us some indication of some of the tensions that we feel as we minister to God's people within the parish community.

Parish priests have complex responsibilities and are often overworked. Priests are not as available to meet the needs of the people given the fact that they are overworked. Nonetheless, recent surveys show that the majority of priests are happy in their ministry.

In our culture today, people gather less in community. People tend to be more independent and have greater anonymity. This has an effect on parish life. Furthermore, people are very busy, usually overbooked, and on the run, especially many families. Because of this and other attitudes, people volunteer less and do not seriously consider formal service in the parish. Family life has also changed and, in some families, I have heard them express that when they finally have free time they want to spend it alone with their families and not with others.

As we know, a challenge today is providing liturgies and homilies that relate to the spirituality of the people. When this challenge is not fulfilled, it causes people to shop for the parish of their choice where they will be fed. Sunday is not a day for family and church. We are in competition with many other activities, sports, community events, and family celebrations. It is estimated that twenty-three percent of Catholics attend Mass each week.

As we know, many parishes strive towards a bilingual community. People in general do not have a great tolerance for other languages and cultures. Another factor that is challenging to parish life is that some people think that the church is outdated and not in touch with reality. Some have had a negative experience of the parish. And, of course, there are still those who remember the hurt of the sex abuse crisis, and have distanced themselves from the church because of a lack of healing. Divorced and remarried Catholics sometimes feel alienated and not a part of the parish family. In a parish community we are in competition with the social media. Within our parishes, we tend to use technology because it is helpful, but very often technology does not come across in a personal way and sometimes the church is not perceived as caring or personal. In some parishes, it takes three to five minutes on the phone to reach a live person. These are but a few of the challenges that we face today as we recommit ourselves to renewing parish life.

Section Five: Suggestions for Renewal of the Parish Today

The parish is the center for New Evangelization in the church today. On June 28, 2010, Pope Benedict XVI renewed the church's call for the New Evangelization. He mentioned that we must evangelize those who are still awaiting a first evangelization, as well as to those regions where the roots of Christianity are deep, but have experienced a serious crisis of faith due to secularization. He clarified that the New Evangelization is new, not in its content, but rather in its inner thrust. It should be new in its methods that must correspond to the signs of our times. It is new because it is necessary to proclaim the Gospel to those who have already heard it. He has emphasized the use of social media regarding the work of evangelization. As quoted earlier, Pope Benedict XVI, in his visit to a parish in 2010, stated that "the parish is to serve those who are close in order to reach out to those who are distant so as to bring evangelical presence to daily life and to our daily work." He went on to say that "people should be able to expect to find in the parish a means of spiritual formation and experience, a sense of community, which is a fundamental characteristic of Christian Life." He points out that by listening to the word of God and the celebration of the sacraments, particularly the Eucharist that we are sent to evangelize the world. Therefore, it is our responsibility to be the evangelizers of today and to do our best within our local parish and within the diocese at large to work towards the renewal of parish life.

In order to discuss the renewal of parish life I would like to divide my comments into four areas.

1. Parish renewal through pastoral governance
2. Renewal in our approach to religious education and formation
3. Renewal in liturgical life
4. Renewal in witness and outreach: the work of evangelization

1: Let us take a look now at pastoral governance and a renewal that is needed within.

In order for a parish to evangelize and be renewed, the pastor must be committed to a collaborative ministry with deacons, religious, and lay ministers. It is his responsibility to look for, recognize, and invite people to use their charisms. Likewise, certain ministry responsibilities should be full-time and it is our responsibility to pay people a just wage as we recognize their gifts and use their talents.

For renewal, the parish *must have an active pastoral council and finance council.* The pastor must consult these groups and take them seriously. The priest must be transparent and trustworthy.

Though technology is a gift in ministry, it can also become an obstacle and make it seem as though the priests and others in ministry are less available and impersonal. This challenges our ability to use technology and to still provide a pastoral touch. The personal contact with individual priests and others in ministry is essential to parish renewal and evangelization.

The parish must be a home for the people of God. We often use the word "parish family" but it must be a place where people gather and feel a sense of welcome and belonging. This is accomplished through many people, including the ushers at Mass, the secretary at the pastoral office, the attitude of people in ministry, and our availability. The attitude of pastoral care and concern must be evident and must create in the minds and hearts of people that it is their home and not our workplace.

Parish policies and guidelines should be consistent within a diocese. In so doing, this will eliminate "shopping" from parish to parish for minimal requirements regarding the celebration of the sacraments. We should always be faithful to the church, to the teachings of the church, and to canon law. We must live out this fidelity in a pastoral way. We should never require more than the church requires. As ministers of the church, we should not make it difficult for people to be a Catholic and to be a member of the family. I have seen some parishes that have little or no guidelines for sacramental preparation and others who have such a long list that it makes it difficult for people to celebrate the sacramental life of the church. In examining some of those lists, they do not represent the teachings of the church or the requirements of canon law, but a pastor's own wish and whim for his parishioners. Parish policies and guidelines should be consistent and should reflect fidelity to the church and pastoral sensitivity.

We should clarify in a pastoral way who belongs to the parish family. Obviously, parishioners are all those within the boundaries. How can we allow people to choose their own particular parish, to register within a parish and be an active member? This can cause tension between pastors. Nevertheless, this needs our attention.

Ministry to hospitals, nursing homes, prisons, and accepting emergency phone calls has become a tension in many parishes and dioceses today. In order to renew the parish and to be serious about the New Evangelization, we must have a plan that people are not left without ministry, especially in critical times of need and their nearness to death.

It is important for the bishop to make pastoral visits to the parish. Some do this by a formal pastoral visit, others by confirmations, anniversaries, or special events. But it is important that the shepherd of the diocese be seen by the people and that they feel a relationship to him and through him to the universal church.

2: Renewal in our approach to religious education and formation

Parishes are blessed with many people who volunteer to do lay ministry. They are people of deep faith and good will but they must also be prepared spiritually, theologically, and pastorally in order to do ministry. This includes all those who share in the ministry in the parish, especially those in religious education, liturgical ministry, social justice, and outreach. These are important dimensions of parish life. For these people, we must provide theological education and formation. They become formed, not only in their own faith life, but become richer in what they can share with others in ministry.

We know that good catechesis must exist from the womb to the tomb. We must be committed within the parish community to educate and inform our children, our youth, and our adults. We tend to give more attention to children and youth and less to our young adults and to the adults. We must serve them in a particular way as we strive to renew parish life. We must give them opportunities for ongoing conversion and growth in the spiritual life. We also realize that adults can often be educated and formed as we take good advantage of opportunities as we prepare them for the baptism of their children, first Communion, confession, and confirmation. These are opportunities that sometimes we overlook and do not take good advantage of. Another challenge for religious education is addressing children with disabilities. Certainly it is impossible for all parishes to provide such services, but we should be able to connect families with parishes that can provide religious education for children with disabilities.

New Evangelization includes enriching marriage and family life. In marriage preparation, many parishes successfully train married couples and use them in this important time of preparation for couples. We, as a church, are also very good at ministering to those whose marriages are in trouble and providing assistance to those divorced and seeking annulments. Perhaps, as we renew parish life, we could provide many more opportunities to enrich good marriages in order that the domestic church at home becomes more directly related to the parish family.

In sacramental preparation, specifically marriage, baptism, first Communion, confession, confirmation, and RCIA, we need to see these as unique moments of evangelization and not just as a duty or another program in the parish.

The New Evangelization, I believe, calls for a renewed commitment to the sacrament of penance. This could challenge us to make the sacrament of penance and reconciliation more available. Most parishes offer confessions on Saturday night or an hour or so before Mass. Is that really the most convenient time for people to take advantage of this healing opportunity of Christ through the church?

In parish life, we are to model a life of prayer and discipleship. Very often the prayer offered before a meeting or an event is a quick prayer or a formal prayer like the Our Father. If we are to model a life of prayer, could we not begin with a brief prayer service that gives us time to truly pray and reflect together as a community of faith? Retreats and parish missions for renewal are often used in parishes. Eucharistic adoration is growing and helping people to develop a deeper prayer life. Sometimes we take for granted that people know how to pray. We need to ask them what their needs are and how they believe they need to grow in the spiritual life. Also, in modeling prayer and discipleship, we are called to respect the various movements in the church, to make them feel welcomed, and to give them opportunities to live out the charism of their movement within the parish community. By so doing, this can enrich the parish and eliminate the fear of competition.

In order for evangelization to be more deeply rooted, we need to use the opportunities of Advent and Lent. During the special times of the church year, we can call people to prayer, to family, and to witness. These are opportunities where we can provide suggestions for family programs. I have found a good practice is to choose a book on sacred Scripture, the Mass, or aspects of the Catholic faith and to ask people to read and to discuss these within the family, within the neighborhood, or gatherings sponsored by the parish itself. People are hungry for an understanding of their faith and for a deeper knowledge of the scriptures. These opportunities can help to satisfy that hunger and to enhance the new evangelization.

3: Renewal in liturgical life
In order for renewal to take place, those involved in presiding and preaching must be committed to prayer, continuing education, and genuine preparation. Liturgy committees can be used to provide insights and suggestions as how the liturgy can more effectively address the culture of the parish community. Though many pastors fear obtaining feedback from the parishioners, it is an opportunity to discover how true renewal and the liturgical life of the parish can be fostered.

A few elements that we must be attentive to in liturgical life are making sure that our liturgies focus, not only on the parish, but on the world. Pope Benedict XVI says that we must serve those near in order to reach those that are far. Our general intercessions, our homilies, and other announcements should be outwardly directed also. It may seem foolish to mention this, but I have heard people say that they do not feel welcomed in a parish community for Mass on Sunday because there is no cry room or no child care that is provided.

4: Renewal in witness and outreach

Some other Christian denominations and religions do a door-to-door invitation. Can we learn from them? Perhaps, if we had lay coordinators in neighborhoods, they could arrange for a visit to homes simply to drop off information about the Catholic faith or to see if our neighbors have any needs. This could move us to true renewal.

The health of a parish is determined by its reaching out to those who are in need and this begins, obviously, with the poor and the needy in the parish by providing a soup kitchen or a specific ministry to the poor. We very often supply monetary or physical assistance, but all of these actions, if we are to truly evangelize, should also have a spiritual dimension. Charity begins at home but does not end there. The poor parishes in the diocese must be considered for twining and for assistance. We must develop in our people a true sense of home mission within the United States. Equally important is fostering in our people an understanding of the global Church, in mission lands so that our sisters and brothers in developing countries are truly part of this family of God. We do bear responsibility for their lives and for their growing in faith.

The parish must teach, promote, and live social justice. Obviously, we must model this within a parish community and challenge people when they are not living the social justice message of the gospel. Within every parish, there are opportunities to find those who do not have the respect that God has intended for them. We must find opportunities to educate our people, to reach out to them in the name of the compassionate Christ.

The list of those whom we have to reach out to is long and complex. But, in a particular way, we must extend open arms and a sense of belonging to families with disabilities, to those with addictions, to those struggling in marriage, and to those recently divorced. In doing so, we fulfill an important dimension of evangelization. But we must give special attention, if we are to truly renew parish life, to those who are away from the church or those who have been hurt by the church and specifically by church leaders. To find them and to invite them by name is a genuine way for parish renewal to become effective. In so doing, we remind them that the parish is indeed a family and around our table there is an empty chair with their name inscribed on it.

Conclusion:

I humbly submit these reflections to you and ask all of us to do our best within our own dioceses and parishes to renew parish life. By taking this on as a particular mission, we will have to become more committed to the New Evangelization that Pope Benedict XVI speaks about today.

In conclusion may I ask us to:

- Pray for renewal of our parishes,
- Actualize a plan for renewal,
- Witness renewal so that the parish becomes an evangelizing community.

I share with you a dream. I dream that within a diocese all of the pastors, diocesan staff, and lay ministers could agree upon one renewal program for parish life that will be used in every parish throughout the diocese. That program would include opportunities in every parish for prayer, education and formation, and action. If every parish within the diocese embraced and was committed to the same renewal program, it would certainly speak strongly of our universality as a church, but also of our desire for parish renewal and evangelization.

Thank you very much for this opportunity to share these reflections with you. Parish renewal can happen as we follow the guidance of the Holy Spirit and commit ourselves to the work of the New Evangelization.

Major Address

The Parish: 50 Years Into the Future
Reverend Monsignor Roch Pagé

After accepting the invitation of the planning committee to treat this topic, I began to wonder whether I was not a bit naive. I probably was. Convinced that much of my future is behind me, and that fifty years from now, many among us will be evaluating the relevance of my conclusions from heaven, I was imprudent enough to accept to give this presentation, which is not so much the result of my imagination, but of time spent considering the various issues to be discussed. I am not a prophet to predict the future, nor a politician to promise what I know I will be unable to accomplish.

I know that I owe your kind invitation to a number of articles I published on the future of the parish system. This even led one other author to write that "Roch preaches a gospel of death."

Nevertheless, I am grateful to those who invited me and to you whose presence honors me.

Introduction

In his apostolic exhortation, *Christifideles laici* of 1988, Pope John Paul II wrote these beautiful words about the parish: "the ecclesial community, while always having a universal dimension, finds its most immediate and visible expression in the parish. In a certain sense, "[the parish] is the Church living in the midst of the homes of her sons and daughters."[1] These are words pregnant with deep meaning.

Ten years after *Christifideles laici*, the same pope recognized the fact that, "Today in America as elsewhere in the world the parish is facing certain difficulties in fulfilling its mission. The parish needs to be constantly renewed on the basis of the principle that the parish must continue to be above all a eucharistic community."[2] This important principle will lead the coming development.

Given that the parish is the second localization of the church after the diocese—the third one being the Christian family, also called the Domestic Church—one

---

1 *Origins* 18 (February 9, 1989) 573, n. 26.
2 *Origins* 28 (February 4, 1999) 578, n. 41.

can conclude that the difficulties faced presently by the parish—and the family—are a reflection of the difficulties experienced by the church herself.

The purpose of this presentation is not to show that the parish, as the basic institution of ecclesial organization, is a privileged witness to the degree of vitality of the church, whether particular or universal. This seems quite evident. As suggested by the pope, one cannot isolate the parish from the church, as one cannot consider a means without taking into account the goal.

Christian communities began to be called parishes by the fourth century, but it did not happen everywhere at the same time. In the same way, the difficulties, and their causes, faced by the parish today do not exist everywhere and at the same time. They are not the same everywhere and their solutions should vary accordingly.

I would like to be clear. Since the problems faced by the parish are not universal, although quite common, any observation or solution or assumption I will submit will not necessarily apply everywhere in the church or in all dioceses of America. While some parishes are suppressed or merged in different dioceses, some parishes are erected in others. And while some priests are imported from other countries to supplement the lack of priests in certain dioceses, there are ordinations in some others. Most dioceses experiencing problems for any kind of reasons as regards the parish or the recruitment of candidates to the priesthood, for example, were most probably flourishing a few decades ago.

Commenting on one of the important surveys led by CARA, Georgetown University's Center for Applied Research in the Apostolate, Mark Gray, a senior research associate and director of CARA Catholic Polls (CCP), never looks further than twenty-five years ahead when he analyzes the recent trends concerning the parish and the decline of ordinations to priesthood.[3] For him, a projection is only as good as its underlying assumption.[4] I will try to found my assumptions not only on the present situation of the parish but on the recent past. If "it is also important to look back before one looks forward," as Gray says,[5] there is also the danger to opt for the restoration of a past whose historical environment will never be the same, while we could opt for a renewal within a new historical environment.

Let me quote Gray again: "Many compare the Church today in the United States with the way it functioned in the 1950s and 1960s, when, indeed, there were large number of priests. Yet these two decades are really the exception

---

3   See M. Gray, "Facing a Future with Fewer Catholic Priests," in *Our Sunday Visitor* (June 27, 2010) 6.
4   Ibid., 4.
5   Ibid.

rather than the rule, and in no other span in Church history in the United States has this country experienced such an abundance of clergy. If you start from the highest point, you will always notice the steepest decline."[6]

Who am I to predict how the parish will look like fifty years from now when the CARA senior research associate, with all the scientific data he can refer to, does not dare predict how the Catholic Church in the United States might look like twenty-five years from now? Nevertheless, considering the recent past and the present situation of the parish in America and in Europe, a certain future is predictable; let me say, into the next twenty-five years. The remaining twenty-five years of my "mandate" lie under the second part of this presentation: the unpredictable future.

I. The Predictable Future of the Parish

As recalled earlier, Pope John Paul II mentioned in 1998 that the parish today, in America and elsewhere in the world, is facing certain difficulties in fulfilling its mission and that it "needs to be constantly renewed." Not by any means though, but "on the basis of the principle that the parish must continue to be above all a eucharistic community." How can a community be eucharistic without a priest? In canon law, a parish without a priest is called a "vacant parish."

This means that any solution brought to the difficulties faced by the parish must include the presence of a priest—in one way or another. The parochial office and, eventually, the office holder as "proper pastor," belong to the nature of the parish according to the code.

Therefore, even if it is not the unique cause, the lack of priests is the main one that led many dioceses in North America to proceed with a reorganization of parishes; the second cause being the decline in religious practice. This is also true for different dioceses in Canada, but for CARA it may be different in the United States: "the expanding parish sizes have been caused by both the current Catholic population migrating—particularly to the South and the Southwest—and an influx of Catholic immigrants in those same areas." Gray adds, "Now the Catholic population isn't closely aligned with where parishes are, so that's why you've had parish closures, and you haven't had enough parishes created in the areas where there is growth in the Catholic population. So, what you end up with is larger parishes."[7]

No reason is given why not enough parishes are created in those areas. One can assume that it is because of the lack of priests since, according to CARA, in

---

6   Ibid., 4-5.

7   Quoted in Scott Alessi, "Study shows the rise of Catholic megaparishes," in *Our Sunday Visitor* (August 7, 2011) 1.

2035, in the United States, "the assumptions and projections lead to the estimate that there will be 12,500 active diocesan priests and 14,825 parishes."[8]

Gray continues, "If no additional parish closings or mergers occurred and the Church maintained the same number of parishes in 2035 that it had in 2009, the number of active diocesan priests per parish would fall to 0.7%."[9] The conclusion is evident, "Staffing parishes with priests in the future will likely require continued parish closings and mergers as well as some combination of more parish assignments per priest, increasing the use of international priests and maintaining as many assignments to religious priests as possible."[10] Those statistics concern the number of diocesan priests and not parish priests. Not all diocesan priests are assigned to parishes.

The parish being a eucharistic community, its future depends essentially on the availability of priests, which means that closings and mergers of parishes will continue. "Given recent trends, this is a future that can be expected to have fewer priests."[11] These priests will be entrusted with the pastoral care of larger and larger parishes.

The reports of CARA, like the majority of studies concerning the state of the parish and of the church, do not deal explicitly with the shortage of priests in relation with the decrease in religious practice. This link is clear in dioceses of the Province of Québec and elsewhere in Canada, where important decline in religious practice has been noticed in recent years, especially among teenagers and young adults.[12] Therefore, we may ask ourselves how the absence of faith education and sacramental practice can incite young people to devote themselves to priestly ministry. In several parishes, priests are entrusted with the pastoral care of elderly parishioners who were young parishioners of the past. Where are the elderly parishioners of tomorrow?

---

8   M. Gray, "Facing a future with fewer Catholic priests," Ibid., 1. "In 2009, according to CARA, there was slightly more than one active diocesan priests per parish (1.05) in the United States. If the number of parish closings and mergers continue in future decades at the same rate that these occurred from 2000 to 2009 (a loss of 6.2 percent of parishes for the decade), the number of active diocesan priests per parish will still likely fall well below 1.0% and is estimated to reach 0.84% in 2035."

9   Ibid., 1-2.

10 Ibid., 2.

11 Ibid., 1.

12 In my own diocese, whose Catholic population is about one quarter million people, and which is located far from large cities, the regular religious practice is between five and seven percent. This is most probably representative of the religious practice elsewhere in Québec.

The code itself does not make a connection between the religious practice and the shortage of priests, mentioned three times in the chapter on the parish. The first two are related to this study. They introduce exceptions to the principle "one parish-one pastor" in canon 517 §2 and canon 526 §1. The first one allows a bishop who is unable to confer the office of pastor on a priest as "proper pastor," to appoint a deacon or a non-ordained member of the faithful on condition he also appoint a priest provided with the powers and faculties of a pastor. The second mention of a *sacerdotum penuria* is found in canon 526 §1, which permits that the pastoral care of several neighboring parishes be entrusted to the same pastor "because of a lack of priests or other circumstances," without mentioning what those circumstances might be. They could include the decrease in religious practice or simply a significant reduction in the number of parishioners because of any sociological reason, or, as mentioned in the report of CARA, because of the current Catholic population "migrating to the South and the Southwest and an influx of Catholic immigrants in those same areas." Is this the main cause of the reorganization of parishes everywhere in the United States and in Canada? I doubt it, at least in Canada.

Of the two solutions to the shortage of priests already mentioned, the multi-dicasterial instruction of 1997 on *Some Questions Regarding Collaboration of Non-Ordained Faithful in Priests' Sacred Ministry*[13] prefers the second one. The reason is easy to presume: in the case of the application of canon 526 §1, the same priest is the pastor of each of the clustered parishes which retain their juridic personality and their proper identity, while in the case of canon 517 §2, the parish is vacant since there is no "proper pastor." Moreover, the same instruction insists on the exceptional character of resorting to lay people in the event of a shortage of priests. For this reason, the instruction explains, "before employing them, other possibilities should be availed of, such as using services of retired priests still capable of such service."[14]

Before establishing mixed pastoral teams of canon 517 §2 or clustering parishes of canon 526 §1, some dioceses in Europe, Canada, United States, Australia, and New Zealand have freely accepted or have recruited priests from well provided countries, like Poland, certain countries of Africa, South America, and Asia.

A. The Parish Structure

The presence of laity and permanent deacons on parish pastoral teams in the absence of a resident priest or of a proper pastor constitutes a radical change in the traditional leadership of the parish, but those solutions concern only the parish personnel and, therefore, they remain open to the situation we experienced

---

13 *Origins* 27 (November 27, 1997) 397-409.
14 Ibid., 404.

in a rather recent past. Actually, they do not concern the traditional structure of the parish, leaving intact the juridic existence and the autonomy of each parish in expectation of an eventual priest to be the proper pastor of each parish.

In several dioceses of Europe, the United States, and Canada, apart from a decline in religious practice and a lack of priests, the population decrease in certain parishes has led to more and more radical solutions as the union of one or more parishes to another one, and the merger of two or more parishes to create an entirely new one. Contrary to the establishment of a mixed pastoral team of canon 517 §2 and to the clustering of canon 526 §1, both the union and the merger of parishes have a more or less irreversible character, implying sometimes the closing of churches.

The union or the merger of parishes, even caused by pastoral considerations, is a mere juridical operation, made in accord with general norms on juridic persons. Actually, the parish is a determined community of Christ's faithful that is granted juridic personality when it is legitimately erected (canon 515 §3). In a letter to the president of the USCCB of March 2006, the Prefect of the Congregation for the Clergy recalls that in the case of a union or of a merger, it is the juridic person that disappears and not the community. This is why the assets and financial obligations should follow the community whose juridic personality has been suppressed and not go to the diocese.[15]

This is the present situation of the parish in many dioceses of America. The choice of either solution involving the pastoral personnel or the structure of the parish may vary from one diocese to another and even from one parish to another in the same diocese. Much depends on the circumstances of places and persons, and among others, on the diocesan bishop.

B. The Pastoral Personnel

The main question to be raised now is: are those solutions final? In other words, what is the future of the parish with regard to the present solutions? It depends on the reasons why, or the purpose of the solutions that are being applied. Whatever the reasons or the purpose, any solution so far respects the principle that "the parish must continue to be above all a eucharistic community," which means that any solution should take into account the presence of a priest—in one way or another.

---

15 See the letter of the Prefect of the Congregation for the Clergy to the President of the USCCB "concerning the distinction to be made between a merger of a parish with another parish or parishes and the suppression of a parish," of March 3, 2006, N. P. 20060481, in *Roman Replies and Advisory Opinions 2006*, 13-14. Among others, referring to canon 121, the Prefect recalls that "the goods and liabilities should go with the amalgamated juridic person and not to the diocese" (14).

1. The Laity

Pursuant to these words of the pope and in the light of the theology of the parish,[16] we can say that the "parish-eucharistic-community" is a key for reading and interpreting the norms of the code on the parish and its reorganization. Since the ministry of the laity in the parish is referred to as a "participation in the exercise of the pastoral care" of a eucharistic community, it follows easily that it is often viewed as the laity substituting for the absent priest. Moreover, when the ministry of the laity comes out of the rectory or the sacristy, it perpetuates a clerical model of ministry. And despite the learned discourses that could be given to establish the theological foundations for the pastoral involvement of laity, it would still bear the mark of its concrete origin, namely, the lack of priests.

We are used to seeing lay ministers substituting for the priest due to his sacramental ministry being overextended, but the day might come when the pastor will be seen as doing what the laity cannot do. The next decades will certainly see the canonical status of the laity be conformed to its theology. But do we have already a fully developed theology of the laity? This will probably be the most important evolution in the next fifty years. It will bring with it a major change not only in the parish system and in the diocesan organization, but above all in a new approach to the priestly ministry—as it has already begun—and to the formation of the future clergy.

Regardless of the reasons which led to the full-time involvement of lay persons and their participation in the exercise of the bishop's pastoral office, it is better to presume that they are here to stay and, therefore, we should act accordingly. A bishop was once asked what he would do if he were now to receive ten more priests. After briefly considering the question, he replied that none of them should replace the lay persons involved full-time in various offices in his diocese. And yet, is it not true that these same lay persons were originally employed because of a shortage of priests?

The code did not anticipate the rapid growth of lay involvement in pastoral structures. Had it foreseen the great decline in the number of priests that we experience, it is not certain that the law would have gone any further than it did, given its purpose which is not to deal with projections and probabilities, eventual facts, or activities in ecclesial society. In fact, it did, to a certain extent, when it presumes a shortage of priests in the two examples we have examined earlier.

The least we can say is that the code is very cautious when we compare its norms with the tasks lay faithful assume in reality, whether in parishes, tribunal, diocesan organisms, teaching institutions, or others. This caution is found in the

---

16 Karl Rahner established the existence of a close bond between the parish as localized community, the universal church and the Eucharist, in K. Rahner, "Theology of the Parish," in *The Parish - from Theology to Practice*, (Westminster, MD: Newman, 1958) 24.

norms regarding involvement in ministry, as well as participation in the various structures of government. We all know the doubt concerning the possibility for a lay chancellor to be delegated to grant dispensations from diriment impediments of marriage.[17] And what about a lay judge, who is not less a judge than a cleric but cannot exercise his/her office as a sole judge?

The lay persons involved full-time in pastoral activities are, in practice, associated with the bishop's power of teaching and sanctifying in virtue of their baptism, confirmation, and an appropriate mandate. Therefore, what prevents them from being somehow associated to the power of governance, assisting the bishop in making decisions regarding the exercise of the offices of teaching and sanctifying that I consider as the subject matter of the power of governance?[18]

Actually, among the mandatory organisms of the diocesan government, not one of them must necessarily include lay faithful among their members. For example, the presbyteral council and the college of consultors are mandatory, and their composition includes only priests. The finance council, which is also mandatory, could be composed entirely of clerics if the bishop so desires. On the other hand, the only institutes which must include necessarily Christ's lay faithful—the diocesan synod and the pastoral council—are not mandatory. This means that a bishop could, in practice, govern his diocese without ever having, by law, to consult the laity. Even if this is not the *mens legislatoris*, this is the law. This absence of lay involvement, by itself, shows the limits currently placed on lay persons in their role of assistants to the bishop's power of governance and in their role of leadership in pastoral activities at any level. How long can this situation last?

Regardless of the observations we might make to support the code's hesitancy regarding the laity, we must not be led to believe that there would automatically be significant changes if the code were revised today.[19] On the other hand, one cannot blame the legislator for believing that only a priest can replace a priest, that the present situation can only be temporary, and that it cannot be made official by a legislation that would normalize the exceptional or the temporary.

---

17 See, for example: F. J. Urrutia, "Delegation of the Power of Governance," in *Studia canonica* 19 (1985) 339-355.

18 See R. Pagé, "Full-Time Lay Ministers and Diocesan Governance," in *Louvain Studies* 26 (2001) 166-179.

19 Fifteen years after the promulgation of the code, the multi-dicasterial instruction referred to earlier, in its content, in the number of signing dicasteries (eight), and with the *in forma specifica* approval by the pope, leaves no doubt as to the legislator's intention in the present code. He was not overcome by the rapid and considerable involvement of laity in diocesan and parish pastoral activities, no more than he was at the time of the promulgation of the code or in the period thereafter.

2. Deacons

The multi-dicasterial instruction of 1997 refers to canon 517 §2 by insisting on the exceptional character of resorting to lay people in the event of a shortage of priest: "In any event, says this instruction, the preference which this canon gives to deacons cannot be overlooked."[20] In fact, where the permanent diaconate has been restored, deacons are assigned to teams participating in the exercise of the pastoral care of one or more parishes. "However, under the pressure of the shortage of priests, in more and more places deacons are often entrusted with the actual leadership of the parish."[21]

In certain teams constituted according to canon 517 §2, the priest moderates the participation in the exercise of the pastoral care, but a permanent deacon carries out not just the day-to-day pastoral care of the parish, but also the coordination of the administrative aspects of pastoral care, such as personnel, finances, temporal goods, etc.[22]

We can add that the deacon acts less as supply for the priest than does the lay minister. But every consideration on this subject and on that of the lay pastoral worker leads inexorably to the conclusion mentioned above: only a priest can replace a priest. Thus, the conclusion of the multi-dicasterial instruction is completely logical: "Solutions addressing the shortage of ordained ministers cannot be other than transitory."[23] Transitory to what?

3. The Recruiting of Imported Priests

The importation of priests from other countries well supplied with vocations is presently among those transitory solutions to the extent that those priests serve to maintain a cultic ministry. According to the author of a study entitled *Europe Without Priests* published in 1995: "These priests who have been provisionally imported are not always prepared to devote themselves to a completely different cultural milieu, in contrast to members of the great missionary institutions of the

---

20   Instruction, *Some Questions Regarding Collaboration of Non-Ordained Faithful in Priests' Sacred Ministry*, Origins 27 (November 27, 1997) 404.

21   J. Kerkhofs and P. Zulehner, "Where Now? – Possible Scenarios," ("Where Now?"), J. Kerkhofs, *"Europe Without Priests?"* (London: SCM Press, 1995) 169.

22   "This person, sometimes called pastoral or parish coordinator, parochial minister, pastoral administrator, pastoral leader, parish director, resident pastoral minister, etc., is appointed by the diocesan bishop." (S. Euart, "Parishes Without a Resident Pastor: Reflections on the Provisions and Conditions of Canon 517, §2 and its Implications," *The Jurist* 54 (1994) 379. In their research on the applications of c. 517 §2, B. Cusack and T. Sullivan point out that "the law does not provide a well-defined plan for applying and implementing this canon. This is well and good!" (*Pastoral Care in Parishes Without a Pastor - Applications of Canon 517, §2*)X. Further on (XI), the authors make another observation: "The personnel involved in this new model have no consistent name or title."

23   Instruction, *Some Questions Regarding Collaboration of Non-Ordained Faithful in Priests' Sacred Ministry*, Conclusion (*Origins* 27) 407.

past."[24] One of those priests told me one day that it is actually a kind of return of history, meaning that after having sent our priests as missionaries to their countries, the time has come for them to send back their own priests to re-evangelize our faithful. It would be great if it were that simple. We cannot deny, though, that they are temporarily filling some of the gaps and doing a marvelous job.

On the other hand, there are some institutions in the United States, two of them for seminarians in Chicago, which offer programs for future priests and priests who come from other countries. They spend some time in formation, do ministry in parishes, and work on their English language skills to facilitate their inculturation.[25] And this also is great.

In its recent survey, CARA dealt with the question of international pastors. Gray comments: "Many Catholics today worship in parishes that have international priests. In CARA surveys, 34 percent of adult Catholics indicate that a priest from outside the United States has come to their parish to serve regularly in the past five years. Most have been pleased with the ministry provided. Fifty-three percent of those who have been in these parishes say they are "very" satisfied with the ministry of this priest, and 34 percent indicated they were "somewhat" satisfied. If current trends continue," Gray says," international priests may become even more common in parishes in the United States. Yet, the irony is that this may exacerbate priest shortages elsewhere in the world."[26]

4. The Shortage of Priests
One can discuss the real cause that led to the restructuring of parishes in many dioceses. It depends on local circumstances. It may be the emigration of the Catholic population as mentioned by Gray. It may be, like in many Canadian dioceses, a serious decline in religious practice. Whatever the cause, were it not so closely linked to the decrease in the number of priests, the remodeling of parishes would most probably have been different, if it had been made at all. The emigration of population and the decline in religious practice did not begin recently.

Actually, we must admit that it is the shortage of priests that urged the reorganization of parishes. This is a fact that proposes a courageous question and

---

24 J. Kerkhofs, "Where Now?" 164.
25 "There are a couple of seminaries that do inculturation pieces: in Chicago, we have two formation houses (Casa Jesus for Hispanic seminarians and Abramowicz seminary for Polish seminarians). They accept students from Latin America and Poland prior to their entering the college or graduate seminary in Chicago. [...] There is a seminary near Detroit in Orchard Lake that is for Polish seminarians. [...] There is also a program down at the Oblate School of Theology in San Antonio. I think that is for priests who are coming from other countries" (Particular correspondence).
26 "Facing a future with fewer Catholic priests" 6.

probably a more dauntless answer or at least a serious reflection: what does it mean when canons 517 §2 and 526 §1 speak of a lack of priests that leads to the two exceptions to the principle "one parish-one pastor"?

This expression is relative and may be understood from at least three points of view:

> a) If we think of the absolute number of priests we used to have in certain dioceses in the recent past, obviously there is presently a shortage of priests. However, we must go further and dare ask ourselves: were there not too many priests then? Without passing judgment on decisions made in a given context, when we see in some areas two or three bell towers not far from each other, we may wonder today if each and all parishes erected in the past were always answering real needs of the faithful? Entrusting the pastoral care of a parish to a priest was not an issue. But the constant condition was that a new parish could support its pastor's "subsistence." The great number of priests available certainly contributed to the creation of new parishes.
>
> Since priests used to fulfill all the tasks in a parish—according to canon 1306 §2 of the 1917 Code, "Purificators, palls, and corporals, which were used in the Sacrifice of the Mass are not to be washed by lay persons, even religious, until they have first been washed by a cleric in major orders"[27]—to what extent did an excessive number of priests contribute to the delay in giving laity their place in the exercise of pastoral care of a parish?
>
> In the church, we must admit that we often have functioned with the mentality that her mission was achieved in a place to the end of time. Just think of the hundreds of bishops in the North of Africa at the time of Saint Augustine. Even if in the fourth century the distinction between diocese and parish and, accordingly, between the bishop and the parish priest was not yet well defined; it nevertheless remains true that the church and particular churches were flourishing in that part of the world. We can say that the church of Christ was temporary in North Africa, as it can also be here. The mission is not the object of quiet acceptance but, rather, it should be a cause of constant worry.
>
> b) The second point of view concerning the shortage of priests is a consequence of the preceding one. It concerns the needs created

---

27 T. L. Bouscaren and A. C. Ellis, *A Text and a Commentary*, (Milwaukee, WI: The Bruce Publishing Company, third revised edition, 1957) 711.

in the past that can no longer be filled. Those parishes are often the first victims of the reorganization of parishes, after spending a lot of energy in trying to continue to exist as if nothing had changed or should change.

c) This consideration leads me to the third viewpoint. Without diminishing the importance of the preceding two viewpoints, I think that the real problem is the lack of priests disposed and prepared to be pastors in the present circumstances, considering the capacities needed to be pastors of two, three, or more parishes. There was a time when a parish had a pastor with two or three parochial vicars; presently, this is an endangered species in most dioceses. The present situation is an energy killer. As W. J. Bausch writes, "The clergy shortage cuts across all lines and the remaining and graying priests themselves are shouldering heavier burdens with less help."[28] How many of them dream of their retirement or at least of submitting their resignation from a responsibility that is too heavy for them and for which they were not prepared? Most of them would probably be willing to assist a younger parish priest named to replace them.

II. The Unpredictable Future of the Parish

After giving such a picture of the parish in the present time and in a predictable future, I think we must seriously wonder if the parish will survive. Even though shocking, the question must be asked. I am not the first one to raise it.

A. The Demise of the Parish System?

Even if the parish has existed for more than sixteen centuries, even if it was and continues to be an excellent means to localize the church, it remains a means. And as a means, it should not be confused with its final goal, which is to gather faithful in communion. "For the goal of apostolic endeavor is that all who are made children of God by faith and baptism should come together to praise God in the midst of his Church, to take part in the sacrifice and to eat the Lord's Supper."[29]

Being a eucharistic community, the parish, as it is, will continue to depend on the presence of a priest as an essential element. And if or when there will be no more priests available for the parish ministry, what will happen?

---

28 W. J. Bausch, *The Parish of the Next Millenium,* (Mystic, CT: Twenty-third Publications, 2000) 51.

29 *Sacrosanctum concilium*, 10.

For Paul McPartlan, "parishes were an eventual arrival on the scene, a convenient solution to a practical problem as numbers of Christians hugely increased, particularly in the fourth century, but not by any means essential; a device, we might even say. It would be wrong historically to think of them as fundamental and needing to be sustained at all costs." He goes further in saying, "that system is becoming increasingly unsustainable because of falling numbers of priests," and he finally writes, "I suggest both historically and theologically that we do not need to cling on, we can let it go."[30] But since it is a theological study founded on a historical approach, McPartlan is content with that conclusion, without suggesting any replacement.

At the 2005 plenary session of the Pontifical Council for Laity, a theologian spoke of the obsolescence of the "tridentine parish."[31]

I also think that the parish system, as we have known it so far, is probably going to die—it is less and less the same anyway—since the solutions brought so far, being exclusively based on the presence of priests, are necessarily limited, temporary, or transitory.

When I say that the parish system might be called to disappear, I do not mean that this will happen everywhere and at the same time. And where it will survive, it will necessarily not be the same as we have known it in the past. Just think of the increase in the number of "Sunday Worship Without a Priest" (SWAP), also called "Sunday Eucharist Without a Priest." We are all aware of the possible confusion between a "communion service" and a Eucharist. "In the United States, however, the bishops of Kansas spoke for many of us when they declared [...] that 'they have come to judge that holy communion regularly received outside of Mass is a short-term solution that has all the markings of becoming a long-range problem'."[32]

The involvement of non-ordained faithful has already changed the picture of the parish ministry and its leadership. Whatever their title may be, "pastoral associates," "pastoral leaders or directors," or "parish coordinators," they are usually full-time, appointed by the bishop, and responsible for the effective day-to-day pastoral care of the parish. Since these people are not ordained, a priest must visit the parish(es) to provide the sacraments; moreover, most of the time he will be unknown to those he comes to serve. He is less and less the "proper pastor" described in canon 515 §1. The notion of a "vacant parish" will have to

---

30 Paul McPartlan, "Presbyteral Ministry in the Roman Catholic Church," in *Ecclesiology*, 1.2 (2005) 24.

31 S. Lanza, "La parrocchia in un mondo che cambia: les grandi sfidi socio-culturali et religiose", dans *Riscoprire il vero volto della parrocchia*, (Libreria Editrice Vaticana, 2005) 15.

32 Bausch, 49.

be revisited, given the impossibility to foresee the time when a priest will be appointed as its "proper pastor." If the bishop cannot foresee that possibility, this community will, in fact, no longer be a parish, subsisting only in regard to its juridic personality that is perpetual by law.[33]

Would it be possible that married men would be ordained to the priesthood in the future? I thought that the opened door to the ordination of married men would naturally be married permanent deacons. That could be true, but the ordination to the priesthood of former Anglican bishops and ministers who are married could constitute an experience which should be carefully observed by faithful and ecclesiastical authorities. On the other hand, we note that among parish staffs in the United States, only twenty-one percent are laymen, compared to forty-nine percent of lay women.[34] The cohort of women is much larger, but we all know that the ordination of women is no longer an issue for the Holy See.

B. Conformity of Canonical Parish with Civil Law

Over the next decades, I believe that most if not all parishes in the United States and Canada, whatever their profile, will become civilly incorporated. Of course, I realize that, in a number of States, this is already the case. But where it is not so, this changeover will occur for two reasons: first to enable the parishes to exercise their autonomy as public non-collegial juridic persons and, secondly, to protect their assets.

As for the first reason, we know that "a legitimately erected parish possesses juridic personality by the law itself."[35] The same wording is used in canon 373 in regard to the diocese. As public juridic persons, both the parish and the diocese are autonomous and, therefore, according to canon 1255, each of them should enjoy the right to acquire, retain, administer, and alienate its own ecclesiastical goods.

However, as we know, this presently is not the case for many parishes in the United States and in Canada. It follows, as John Foster notes, that, "the diocese [should] not own the ecclesiastical goods acquired and administered by its parishes. Similarly, the diocesan bishop [...] is not the administrator of ecclesiastical goods belonging to public juridic persons subject to him. The diocesan bishop is the administrator of the diocesan public juridic person only."[36] Canon 393 tells us that "the diocesan bishop represents his diocese in all juridic affairs," and canon

---

33 See c. 120 §1.

34 See CARA, Mark M. Gray, Mary L. Gautier, and Melissa A. Cidade, *The Changing Face of U.S. Catholic Parishes* (http://emergingmodels.org) 57.

35 Canon 515 §3.

36 John. J. M. Foster, "Canonical Issues Relating to the Civil Restructuring of Dioceses and Parishes," in *The Jurist*, 69 (2009) 317.

532 states that the pastor does it in his parish, but "according to the norm of law." This last clause reminds us that autonomy does not mean independence. The parish is not an entity separated or independent from the author of its establishment, who is the diocesan bishop. The same applies to the diocese which, as a juridic person, is autonomous, but which is not independent from the Holy See in the exercise of its rights as juridic person.

As a matter of fact, canon 1276 states that, "it is for the ordinary to exercise careful vigilance over the administration of all the goods that belong to public juridic persons subject to him [...]" (§1). On the other hand, the same canon provides that, "with due regard for rights, legitimate customs, and circumstances, ordinaries are to take care of the ordering of the entire matter of the administration of ecclesiastical goods by issuing special instructions within the limits of universal and particular law" (§ 2). The parish priest exercises his office "under the authority of the diocesan bishop."[37]

There is no need to go further. The question has thus been raised: to what extent, if any, do most parishes in dioceses in America exercise their autonomy as public juridic persons in acquiring, retaining, administering, and alienating their own ecclesiastical goods?

The second reason why I think that most parishes in the United States and Canada will eventually become civilly incorporated is the protection of their assets. Actually, according to canon 1284, "All administrators are bound to fulfill their function with the diligence of a good householder. Consequently they must take care that the ownership of ecclesiastical good is protected by civilly valid methods." Civil incorporation is certainly one of those methods.

This idea is not new in the United States. Indeed on July 29, 1911, the American bishops requested the Congregation of the Council establish appropriate norms for the care and preservation of temporal goods in the country. In its reply, the Congregation recommended the separate incorporation of parishes. It wrote: "Among the methods which are now in use in the United States for holding and administering church property, the one known as Parish Incorporation is preferable to the others, but with the conditions and safeguards which are now in use in the State of New York. The bishops, therefore, should immediately take steps to introduce this method for handling property in their dioceses, if the civil law allows."[38] In passing, we can note the use of the term "immediately." One hundred and some years later, we are still considering the matter! It is often said that the church moves slowly.

---

37   Canon 519.

38   "Methods of Holding Title to and Administering Church Property in the United States [Private]," in *Canon Law Digest* 2: 444-445.

We all know that as a consequence of liability issues arising from many causes, numerous lawsuits have been launched against individual dioceses in the United States and in Canada in recent years, eventually placing in jeopardy all of the assets of those dioceses, including those of their parishes.

A reflection on this worrisome and distressing situation led the Holy See to wonder how, if possible, similar situations could be prevented in the future.

Quite naturally, when faced with this issue, people were immediately inclined to refer to the civil status of the diocese and/or of the office of the bishop as a corporation sole, since according to this status, the civil ownership of all the assets of the diocese, including those of each parish, was vested in the diocesan corporation. Therefore, this particular civil status, whereby all assets are registered under the same corporation, should well be questioned, since at first sight it seems incompatible with the autonomy granted to the parish by canon law. However, it seems to me that this conclusion may be too simplistic.

For instance, in a letter sent to the Apostolic Nuncio in Canada in 2005, the then Prefect of the Congregation of Bishops raised the matter "of the real conflict between c. 515, § 3, which grants juridical personality to a lawfully established parish by virtue of the law itself, and the Canadian civil law concept of a diocesan *corporation sole*, which removes the legal and economic autonomy of the individual parish, granted by the Code, and places it in the hands of the bishop." The letter goes on by saying, "Therefore, since the *corporation sole* is in fact incompatible with the canonical autonomy of the parish, it appears necessary that all dioceses having their bishop holding the civil status of a *corporation sole* look seriously into changing it."[39]

With all due respect, I do not think that the problem is directly related to the concept of corporation sole. Rather, it lies in the manner in which it is applied. In theory, there is nothing preventing a diocese from being a corporation sole; what causes problems is the fact that all diocesan and parish assets in the territory are registered under this one corporate title. Of course, we have to take the civil law of the place into consideration, and, when incorporating parishes, structure the corporate charter of the parish in such a way that it would recognize the canonical relationship that exists, on the one hand, between the parish and the diocese and, on the other, between the diocesan bishop and the parish priest. Therefore, if it is correctly structured, the parish corporation would not be able to carry out validly certain acts of administration without the advice or the consent of the parish finance council and, in certain more important or extraordinary acts of administration, without the permission of the diocesan bishop. If this were the case, then there would be no incompatibility between the diocese as a

---

39 Apostolic Nuntiature, Ottawa, December 14, 2005, N. 6088/05.

corporation sole and the canonical autonomy and civil status of the parishes as separate civil law entities.[40]

Indeed, in all dioceses of the Province of Québec, Canada, where the bishop has the status of a corporation sole, all parishes that are not "religious parishes" according to canon law, are civilly incorporated. All that is required is that notice of their establishment be given to the relevant government department. This system has worked well for decades. Note that the board of trustees consists of six parishioners and the parish priest.

On the other hand, in the neighboring Province of Ontario, directly concerned by the Nuncio's letter, opinions differ with regard to the advisability of incorporating parishes. The civil lawyer representing one important diocese in Ontario has held that changing the status of the bishop as a corporation sole in order for the parish to be incorporated separately would not be possible, given the present civil legislation. But the diocesan lawyers in other circumscriptions disagree with him. The jury is still out!

C. What Replacement for the Parish?

Jesus did not found a parish, but a community of believers that developed as a movement and structured itself step by step to form the parish system. One must not forget that the parish is a means and the community is a goal. Energies dedicated to some restoration or maintenance of the parish should not make us lose sight of the renewal of the church that, most probably, will not be reached by the means of larger and larger parishes which weakens the sense of belonging to a community.

Actually, I believe that the real eucharistic communities are presently, and will be in the future, associations of Christ's faithful of different kinds and names, such as movements, basic ecclesial communities or, like the Directory for the Pastoral Ministry of Bishops says, "groups of Christians who gather together to assist each other in the spiritual life and in Christian formation and to discuss shared human and ecclesial problems related to their common goal."[41]

Speaking to representatives of church movements and new communities gathered in Rome in 1998, Pope John Paul II remarked: "their advent and diffusion have brought something new and unexpected, sometimes even explosive to the life of the Church."[42]

---

40 See R. Pagé, "The Difficulties Faced by the Parish: Some Solutions (a response to Joseph Fox, O.P., "The Parish in the Code of Canon Law")," in *Chicago Studies* 46 (2007) 79-82.

41 *Apostolorum successores*, n. 215, e.

42 John Paul II, Address to representatives of ecclesial movements and new commun-

The terminology used to define these groups has followed their explosion in number and diversity.[43] I mean that very few of them are called "associations." They exist in virtue of the fundamental right to associate of canon 215, and they devote themselves to apostolic activities or the promotion and fostering of a more perfect life.

It may be easily assumed that faithful that are attracted to different associations or movements are all parishioners somewhere and that they do not find in their parish what their association or movement offers and brings them in terms of spiritual growth, dedication to the apostolate, and, above all, a sense of belonging to the church. In other words, their association or movement has become their "eucharistic community–their real parish. I believe that those who will return to religious practice will do so through an association rather than through a parish.

If for many faithful, now and in the future, their movement might replace their parish, would it mean that the parish system eventually will be replaced by groupings of Christ's faithful of any kind? I do think that we should now look in that direction while keeping an eye on the evolution of the parish.

I am not glorifying the associations at the expense of the parish system. I think that parishes will grow in size at the same time as different groupings will grow in number and in purpose. And I think that the recruitment of priests will come from the practical needs of associations. It is not unthinkable to see some international associations becoming like parallel dioceses, having some characteristics of a particular church, with their own clergy supported by some sympathetic bishops, members or not, ordaining and incardinating some of their members. I am just suggesting that if the parish system continues to evolve in the present line, I do not see how its goal could be reached otherwise than by the associative system, whose forms are for the moment unpredictable. Given the present emergence of associations and the disaffection for the parish, one could conclude that Christ's faithful are presently more attracted by the charismatic dimension of the church than by its institutional one. This is an excellent condition for her renewal.

Conclusion

Having reached the end of this presentation, I remain personally optimistic; if not for the parish, at least for the church. I am conscious that the analysis and opinions I have expressed might be provocative and, who knows, even irritating.

---

ities, "This day is the day the Lord has made" ("This day is the day"), in *Osservatore Romano*, Weekly edition in English, N. 22 (1544) June 3, 1998, p. 2.

43 See M. Casey, *Breaking from the Bud: New Forms of Consecrated Life* (Sydney, Australia: Sisters of St. Joseph NSW, 2001) 188.

I am firmly convinced that the parish is, as Pope John Paul II said, a eucharistic community, although in practice it is not always evident. Its goal can be reached by other means.

I am conscious that it is not easy for the church, as for any of us, to figure out how such an immemorial institution might disappear. Once again, if it does, it will not be a sudden event, most probably not everywhere, and if everywhere, not at the same time.

The temptation will probably be strong to spend much of one's energy in the survival of the parish. The real challenge should not be to preserve the past, but to welcome the future and assure a real renewal. For this renewal to occur, the parish, the most immediate and visible expression of the church, should not be understood as the only way and place to live the Gospel.

Finally, one should remember that the parish is not the church. The church has lived before the parish existed; she will not disappear if the parish system, as we have known it, ceases to exist. Nor will the particular churches, although what is presently happening with parishes might happen with particular churches in some areas, as it took place in the history of the church. Just think of the number of former dioceses now called *in partibus infidelium*, which disappeared under the influence of Islam in Eastern Europe and in North Africa.

The fifty years of my mandate have already begun. I believe that the movement is irreversible. It follows the trend of the Second Vatican Council and of the ongoing Synod in Rome on New Evangelization. Not that the Gospel needs to be rewritten, but made palatable for our time. So also the structures of the church in the coming decades will have to be adapted to the needs of the future. Our church does not have to be the church of past centuries. We live today, and it has to be in a church for today.

MAJOR ADDRESS

LAY ECCLESIAL MINISTRY IN PARISHES: DIVERSE SERVICES IN VARIED SETTINGS AND CIRCUMSTANCES
Sister Katarina Schuth, OSF

Introduction

On the anniversary of the very day of the opening of Vatican II it is a great privilege to speak to you about important matters in the church related to your vocation. As I was preparing this talk, it came to my awareness what a crucial role each of you in your profession as canon lawyers performs for the church. You significantly affect the formation of the consciences of all Catholics and you meaningfully guide the direction of pastoral care. For fulfilling so well that demanding and spiritually important role, I thank you.

The world of October 11, 1962, was a very different one in matters pertaining to so many aspects of church life. Significant among them was the role of lay people before and after the council. Your interest in and desire to examine the impact of lay ecclesial ministry in parishes is timely and perceptive. Lay ministers are essential to evangelization—the mission of the church in our times—and thus deserving of careful consideration.

Background

Although much remains, much has been done to appreciate more fully what the greater involvement of lay people means to Catholics today. The documents of Vatican II created a somewhat dualistic view of the role of laity in the church. For the most part it emphasized their work in the "secular world," their priestly mission in the lay apostolate. At the time the council fathers issued "The Decree on the Apostolate of the Laity," *Apostolicam Actuositatem,* (November 18, 1965), few lay people were working directly for the church in professional "churchly" ministry, so the concept was not addressed in a direct way. Other Vatican II documents discussed the laity, importantly in *Lumen Gentium* ("The Church in the Modern World"), especially Chapters 2 and 4, and in other places too numerous to mention. Chapter 2 of *Lumen Gentium,* #10, makes reference to the threefold office of Christ. In the book, *Keys to the Council* (Richard Gaillardetz and Catherine Clifford, pp. 84-85), the authors say, "For centuries this threefold office (of Christ as priest, prophet and king) had been applied to the ministry of the ordained as it is on the decree on the priesthood. However, the council would teach that all the baptized participate in this threefold office." The question not thoroughly addressed at the council was how the laity would live out that common priesthood of the faithful. Cardinal Leo Suenens, in his 1968 book, *Co-Responsibility in the Church*, laid out his view that the council had taken up the role of laity in the *world*, but did not give direction about their responsibility in the *church*. During the intervening years, this question continues to call for attention, as you have done at this meeting.

Other forms of recognition of the laity came as well, but did little to clarify or amplify the role lay people might play in working within church structures. In 1988, following 1987 Synod of Bishops, Pope John Paul II issued the Post-Synodal Apostolic Exhortation *Christifideles Laici*, (On the Vocation and the Mission of the Lay Faithful in the Church and in the World). Critics of the document pointed to the fact that Pope John Paul II disapproved of using the term "ministry" in relation to the laity. In response, by 1995, the U.S. bishops generally used the term "mission" rather than "ministry" when referring to the work of the laity in the church. Meanwhile, the number of lay people working within church structures grew tremendously. Finally, after twenty years the number of professional lay ministers more than doubled from about 15,000 to 30,000 by 2005, prompting the U.S. bishops to issue "Co-Workers in the Vineyard of the Lord, A Resource for Guiding the Development of Lay Ecclesial Ministry." This document addressed the formation and education needed for various ministerial roles, and encouraged lay people to take an active role in church ministry.

Your own Board of Governors in 2009 established the Committee on Laity, as recommended by the Future Initiatives Project Committee, which was to assume all functions currently assigned to the Lay Canonists Committee and the Lay Ministry Handbook Project Committee. The functions, which you know well, are as follows: to initiate as needed any projects pertinent to the study of canon law pertaining to the life and ministry of lay persons or the implementation thereof, including, but not limited to, the following: (a) lay ecclesial ministry; (b) collaboration with clergy; (c) rights of the lay faithful. The committee was charged: 1) to oversee projects referred to the committee by the Board of Governors; 2) to oversee its subcommittees working on projects concerning the laity; (and) 3) to collaborate with national organizations and other groups dealing with the role of the laity in the church.

When I read about the functions of the Committee on Laity, my estimation was that you have probably thought of everything on the topic I might suggest as a result of my research. Nonetheless, I will plow ahead with the hope that I might introduce a new idea or two. Therefore, in this presentation, I will attempt to relate three topics: changes in church personnel, resultant changes in the role of lay ecclesial ministers, and changes in the Catholic population. I will suggest how these factors affect the situation of parish ministry today and relate to your profession as canon lawyers, especially those of you who serve on diocesan tribunals.

I will begin by examining the situation of parish ministry, including changes in the composition of parish personnel from the mid-1960s to 2012, and then I will look at how those changes have affected parish organization and leadership. Also of great importance, I will consider who comprises the Catholic population—its generational and ideological differences, as well as its ethnic and cultural diversity. As we delve into these topics, I will attempt to identify the potential effects of these changes in parish life on the practices, approaches, and functions of diocesan tribunals and the growing mutuality of relationships between lay ecclesial ministers and canon lawyers. I look forward to being further enlightened by your insights on these matters.

Who Ministers in the Church Today and How Structures Have Changed

I will not go into great detail since the facts about the numbers of vocations of various church ministers are fairly well known and the patterns of change are clear-cut, but here are a few basics statistics to keep in mind:

- The Catholic population is presently 68.2 million, 23 million more now than it was in 1965;
- The number of parishes and missions has declined slightly from 22,184 to 20,688, resulting in many larger parishes;
- The number of permanent deacons (17,816) and lay ecclesial ministers (about 40,000) increased greatly—from no deacons and few lay ministers to at least 55,000 in 2012;
- The number of priests, sisters, and brothers has declined greatly during those years – a combined reduction of nearly 150,000; and
- The number of diocesan priests declined by about 9,000 and religious priests by 10,000 since 1965.

At the same time that the number of American-born priests declined, many more priests and seminarians came from other countries. According to CARA research, about 17 percent of priests serving in U.S. dioceses in 2004 were foreign-born, and 87 percent of them were diocesan priests. Some 30 percent were educated in U.S seminaries; all others came already ordained and, in most cases, entered directly into ministry after only a brief orientation to U.S. religious practices. One of the major implications for canon lawyers is that most priests coming from other countries need special assistance in handling issues related to canon law since they are unfamiliar with U.S. diocesan policies and procedures.

Other personnel changes also are relevant to parish ministry. The number of ordinations in recent years has averaged just under 500, while the replacement rate would require more than 1,000 priests per year. From 1965 to the present, the number of sisters has declined by 125,000 and the number of brothers by 8,000. What is the impact of these cumulative changes? The ecclesial status of those ministering in parishes is radically different, especially in the past twenty years. Sisters working in parishes have declined by 25 percent, while lay women have increased by 20 percent and lay men by 6 percent. As a result of these changes, new relationships are evolving and new understandings of collaboration are developing. At issue are the theological education and preparation of those now ministering in parishes and their understanding of the responsibilities related to their roles.

Basic Statistics: United States

	1965	1985	2005	2010	2012
Catholics	45.6 m.	52.3 m.	64.8 m.	68.5 m.	68.2 m.
Priests: Dioc. & Rel.	58,432	57,317	43,422	40,788	39,718
Lay Ecclesial Ministers	Less than 3000 est.	15,000 est.	30,632 (DeLambo)	37,929	40,000 est.
Sisters	179,954	115,386	69,963	58,724	55,045
Permanent Deacons	None	7,204	15,027	17,165	17,816
Parishes/ Missions	22,184	22,793	22,198	21,052	20,688

Data from *The Official Catholic Directory* in the years indicated

Preparation and Ministry Skills

With what degrees are lay people being prepared for ministry? Two degree types are common: the Master of Divinity (MDiv) is the usual highest degree requiring about three years of study; the other Masters' degrees, requiring two years of study, are variously named as Master of Arts in Pastoral Studies (MAPS), Master of Arts in Pastoral Ministry (MAPM), and Master of Arts in Ministry (MAM). About one-fourth of those in church ministry earn one of these degrees. Most others earn a certificate from dioceses in a wide variety of specialized areas. Those with academic degrees take a limited number of courses in canon law. Those earning an MDiv degree are generally required to take one course, a few take two, and others may choose a canon law course as an elective. The first course is usually "Introduction to Church Law" or "Principles of Canon Law" (or Church Law); if a second course is taken it is called "Canon Law: Sacraments and Marriage," "Marriage Law," or some similar title. The other Masters degrees seldom require any study of canon law (only two do), but if an MDiv is offered in the same school, other Master-level students may elect to take a course in canon law. Except in rare circumstances, those in certificate programs do not study canon law. The bottom line is that lay ministers working in parishes are almost never versed in the use of canon law in parish settings.

A second consideration is what the understandings of pastors and of lay ecclesial ministers are about the most and least important skills and qualifications in providing lay ministry in parishes. In a thorough study of the state of the question, *Lay Parish Ministries,* (New York, NY: National Pastoral Life Center, 2005), David DeLambo found some differences in the views of the two groups. Lay ecclesial ministers believe that the five most important ministry skills are: communicating one-on-one, recruiting volunteers, planning, collaborating, and facilitating events/meetings. They believe that the five least important ministry skills are: counseling, visiting (e.g., homes, hospitals), accessing social services, spiritual direction, and preaching. None of the items suggests anything related to issues of canon law; although counseling could involve such concerns, it is listed among the least important.

Pastors have a slightly different set of qualifications that they believe to be most and least important. Among those they consider important are: that the person has good relational skills, is prayerful, has experience in ministry, has a similar ecclesiology, and has a degree in a ministry-related field. The least important qualifications from the pastors' viewpoint concern personal attributes rather than actual qualifications: it is not important whether the person is married or not, that the person's ethnic background matches the parishioners, or that the person is bi-lingual; they also express no preference for a woman or man to hire as a minister. The desire for both experience in ministry and a degree suggest that the pastor might expect the lay minister to be knowledgeable about issues related to canon law, though they do not indicate such specifically. In this context, no other reference is made to skills or qualifications that would indicate an awareness of the importance of canon law issues in the parish.

Adaptations in Parishes Resulting from Changing Church Personnel

In countless ways, priests and others ministering in parishes have inconspicuously and generously adapted to the immense cultural and demographic shifts in parishes. More priests than ever are serving more than one parish, parishes have merged and been closed, parish sizes have expanded, and the numbers and roles of those who serve in parishes, especially permanent deacons and lay ecclesial ministers, have shifted. At present at least 50 percent of parishes are served by a priest who is responsible for more than one parish; in turn, some 30 percent of priests serve in such a situation (see *Priestly Ministry in Multiple Parishes* by Sr. Katarina Schuth, O.S.F., Collegeville, MN: Liturgical Press, 2006). In the absence of priests living in every parish, lay ecclesial ministers have adapted their roles to accommodate the temporal and spiritual needs of parishioners. This task is exacerbated as the sizes of parishes grow in urban settings and the number of parishes served by one priest increases in rural areas. Thus, the proportion of larger parishes (over 1,200 parishioners) has grown from 50 percent to 61 percent from 2000 to 2010, and the number of smaller parishes has declined from 50 percent to 39 percent. The bulk of smaller parishes are, of course, in rural areas.

Specific tasks stemming from these changes require a new approach to ministry. This means that both pastors and lay ecclesial ministers must:

- acquire an understanding of the effects on parishes and parishioners of changing personnel,
- engage more conscientiously in social analysis to uncover real and perceived pastoral needs,
- be willing to accept the reality of diversity without destroying essential unity,
- bring into compatible working relationship those with ideological differences and those with varied preparation who minister together, and
- equip both spiritually and intellectually all those who minister, so that they are prepared to work collaboratively for the salvation of all.

Further, the results of these changes may well affect the work of diocesan tribunals. Since parish priests are serving a larger number of parishioners and/or several parishes, these more complicated arrangements may require canonical opinions/interventions, for example, in the process of combining parishes and in hiring or letting go parish personnel. Additionally, as lay ministers and permanent deacons assume a wider range of pastoral responsibilities, especially those involving parish administration and business transactions such as property and personnel matters, more interactions with diocesan offices, including tribunals, are likely. Yet these ministers usually are not as familiar with canon law policies and procedures as are priests. Foreseeing the issues that may develop, procedural handbooks might be prepared to assist those who will work with such situations.

Additionally, apart from these local matters, the entire Catholic population is shifting. Significant movement from rural to urban and suburban areas continues and even more pronounced is the movement from the north and northeast to the south and southwest. As a consequence, the demand increases to develop personnel, facilities, and services in areas of the country with a recent higher density of Catholic population. Careful resource assessment will help these developing dioceses serve the burgeoning church membership more effectively.

U.S. Latin Rite <u>Parishes</u> Served by a Priest with Multiple Parishes

2005	44% (9,109 of 22,668)
2010	between 50% and 60%

U.S. Latin Rite <u>Priests</u> Serving Multiple Parishes

2005	20% (4,408 of 22,302)
2010	at least 30% of parish priests

Parish Sizes of All Parishes

Type of Parish	Percent 2000	Percent 2010	# Registered Parishoners	# Registered Households
Mega Parishes	25%	33%	more than 3,000	more than 1,200
Corporate Parishes	25%	28%	1,200-3,000	550-1,220
Community Parishes	26%	24%	450-1,199	201-549
Family Parishes	24%	15%	fewer than 450	200 or fewer

From *National Parish Inventory of 2000 and 2010* (CARA)

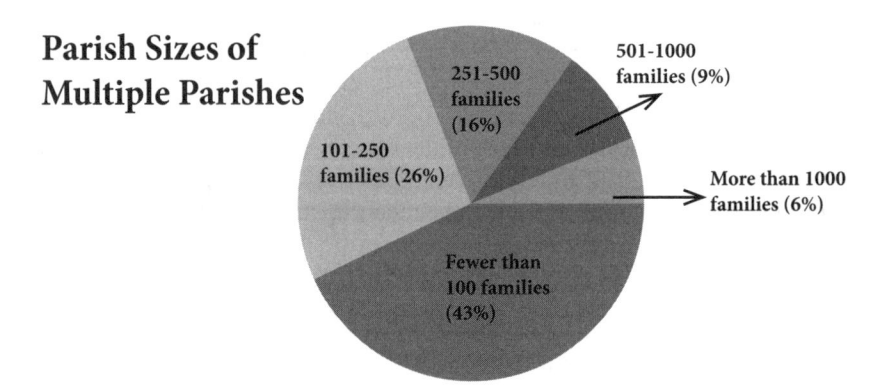

Parish Sizes of Multiple Parishes

- 251-500 families (16%)
- 501-1000 families (9%)
- 101-250 families (26%)
- More than 1000 families (6%)
- Fewer than 100 families (43%)

Generational, Ethnic, and Cultural Differences in the Catholic Population

As the number of years since Vatican II increase and as the "Catholic culture" grows thinner, generational differences stand out more significantly than ever before. Moreover, the ethnic composition of the Catholic population also has shifted dramatically in recent years. Both of these factors have a tremendous impact on church personnel and the ministry they are expected to provide.

Generational Differences

The diminishing strength of Catholic identity represents the gravity of concerns about the church's future. Research reported in *American Catholics Today* conveys the seriousness of the problem of weakening commitment through four generations.

Strength of Catholic Identity by Generation, 2005

	Low %	Medium %	High %	Generational % 1987	Generational % 2005
Total Catholics	29	46	24	100	100
Pre-Vatican II	22	45	33	31	17
Vatican II	31	44	25	47	35
Post-Vatican II	27	50	24	22	40
Millenials	47	46	7	0	9

Adapted from: *American Catholics Today,* D'Antonio, Davidson, Hoge, Gautier. Rowman & Littlefield Publishers, Inc., 2007. (Top chart pp. 11 and 21; text pp. 18-19)

The strongest sense of identity is found among **Pre-Vatican II Catholics**, those born before the mid-1940s. For them, being Catholic was a central facet of their life. The content of the faith was as clear as a bell and obeying church teachings was a given. They saw Catholicism as distinct from, and truer than, other faiths. Catholics were economically poor and trying to "make it" in society. For about a third of them, being Catholic was highly significant to their understanding of who they were, and for nearly another half it was moderately significant. A low sense of Catholic identity was reported by only about one in five of the Pre-Vatican II group.

The strength of identity of the **Vatican II cohort** is weaker than the Pre-Vatican II group, but stronger than the Millennial generation, thus situating in the medium range. These Catholics were born from the mid-1940s to early 1960s and came of age when the church was changing, opening up, and updating as a result of Vatican II. The church adopted a more ecumenical attitude and Catholics were gaining acceptance in the larger society as they grew more prosperous. Their identity as Catholics underwent change as they began to question the centrality of Catholicism in their lives and wondered about the content of the core of the faith.

The profile of **Post-Vatican II Catholics**, born from the mid-1960s to 1978, is similar to the Vatican II cohort in terms of the strength of their Catholic identity. Like their older counterparts, uncertainties about the centrality of their Catholicity began to emerge. Similarities, not differences, between Catholics and Protestants were emphasized. This cohort saw their commitment as voluntary as they became more autonomous in their thinking about issues of faith and morals. Catholic laypeople were increasingly willing to disagree with the church on what some viewed as optional teachings. Meanwhile, the hierarchy was trying to restore order in what it perceived as a chaotic church. At the same time Catholics were moving into the middle class as they advanced educationally and socially, thus feeling secure enough to lessen their dependence on the church.

Unlike any of the three older cohorts, the **Millennial Generation** is characterized by a significant loss of Catholic identity. Born between 1979 and 1987, only a small percentage of the group sees itself as highly committed to the Catholic Church. Many of them raise questions about the importance of being Catholic, the substance of the faith, and the porous boundaries they see between Catholics and others. Not only did this group suffer from a sense of insecurity after the tragedy of 9/11, they also were coming of age in the midst of the most unsettling news of widespread clergy sexual abuse. The sex abuse scandal was a traumatic shock for these young people, some of whom responded with disgust and removed themselves from the church. At the same time a more conservative climate was permeating the larger society and gravitation toward a conservative direction was present in the church as well. Not only did ideological differences create a split, but many Catholics now firmly in the upper middle class were clashing with a stream of new immigrants, many of them poor, who greatly augmented the Catholic population. This youngest generation is clearly not the same as the older cohorts. How the church responds to their needs will make all the difference in their future association with the church and its vitality.

The research on this younger generation categorizes them in distinct groups: religiously disconnected, unschooled in Catholicism, and schooled in more conventional Catholicism (for more information on the religious affiliation and practices of this generation see the writings of Sister Patricia Wittberg and Christian Smith). We might add a small but significant group of those schooled in more progressive Catholicism. Each segment brings its own challenge to those in ministry who are concerned about future participation in parish life. The religiously disconnected, for example, are reluctant to impose their beliefs on anyone else. The unschooled have not experienced Catholic education in any depth and so are unlikely to know the content of Catholic doctrine and, if they do, they are less likely to think it is important. The two smaller groups—those who are more conventional and those who are more progressive—hold distinct views. The former desire a more traditional spirituality and prefer a conservative self-contained community; the latter see their faith as somewhat important, but not essential, and they prefer a more participative worship and a community that emphasizes outreach. What they hold in common is a spiritual hunger. Determining the most effective approach to meet their spiritual needs requires careful observation and extensive interaction with each group.

Ethnic and Cultural Diversity

Diversity extends beyond generational differences to include an array of ethnic and cultural groups. Church membership mirrors the nation in its move toward an equal number of Anglo/Caucasians and all other ethnic groups. At present, the percentages indicate the following distribution of Catholics: Latino/a Hispanic (35-40%); Anglo/Caucasian (50-55%); Native American (1%); African & African American (3%); and Asian/Pacific Islanders (4-5%). The numbers and characteristics of each group require ministry that addresses specialized needs. In some cases educational and economic development are important, especially for those who have immigrated recently to the U.S. In all cases the character of the liturgy and other spiritual concerns are crucial in sustaining close ties with the church. Some examples follow.

The sheer numbers of Latino/a Hispanic Catholics and the rather high proportion of recent immigrants indicate the necessity of providing extensive parish programming. Hispanics are present in practically every diocese of the United States and more than 20 percent of parishes have some form of Hispanic ministry. More than 80 percent of all (arch)dioceses have diocesan staff coordinating Hispanic ministry. As for the future, more than 50 percent of all Catholics in the United States under age twenty-five are of Hispanic descent, and they have contributed 71 percent of the growth of the Catholic Church in the United States since 1960 (sources: usccb.org/hispanicaffairs; U.S. Census Bureau; Center for Applied Research in the Apostolate).

Despite the widespread presence of Latino/Hispanic Catholics, their practices of popular piety are unfamiliar to many North Americans and some may view them as unacceptable for use in official liturgical celebrations. In these cases, canon lawyers may be asked to render opinions about what is permissible in liturgical and devotional services, so it is imperative to know about the nature of these practices in order to make religiously and culturally appropriate judgments. In light of the prevalence of Latino and other *ethnic communities, diocesan officials should seek involvement of these members on committees of the diocese and perhaps as consultants to diocesan tribunals.* Further, those serving in dioceses with a growing Spanish-speaking population need to make available documents, policies, and directives in Spanish—all for the sake of making possible greater inclusivity and participation in parish life.

A second example involves a smaller and more recent immigrant group of Catholics from Southeast Asia. They have proven to be extraordinarily faithful and involved parishioners who have provided more than their share of priestly vocations. Vietnamese Catholics, for example, have preserved their faith and made significant and steady progress in evangelization while adjusting to U.S. culture. They were able to make these advances because of the development of pastoral activities that embraced their own culture. These efforts at inculturation have resulted in strong family unity and sound academic achievement by their children; more and more, they are participating in and contributing to the life of the local community. Their involvement as lay members in parishes is exemplary and has implications for all Catholics. Canon lawyers, in collaboration with liturgists and those who understand other cultures, might be proactive in studying these religious and spiritual practices and encourage those who minister among these groups to incorporate the ceremonies and practices that are legitimate according to church laws and practices and also helpful to various ethnic groups.

Conclusion

The purpose of this presentation was twofold: to examine how the experience of lay ecclesial ministers might assist canon lawyers and how canon lawyers might assist lay ecclesial ministers in their ministry in a changing church. To address this mutual relationship, the paper identifies some of the main areas related to church personnel and structures, and church membership including generational differences and the ethnic, cultural make-up of Catholics in the U.S. Suggestions for effective ways of working within the church organization are made throughout the paper. In addition, four other ways that lay ministers might assist canon lawyers are:

- to provide firsthand knowledge of the joys and challenges of marriage and all that that commitment requires,
- to offer insight into the beliefs and preferred religious practices of young people,
- to help develop a greater appreciation for the variety of cultural traditions represented in the church, and
- to represent the need of lay ministers to learn the basics of canon law so that they can assist parishioners in their relationship with diocesan officials.

In turn, canon lawyers might contribute to parish ministry by:

- authoring an "essential elements" of canon law for parish settings,
- preparing guidelines that outline the steps needed to complete commonly

used forms in parishes,
- translating all pertinent documents into the languages of various cultural groups, and
- initiating a study of cultural practices that can be incorporated into devotional and liturgical life.

In a recent article on the impact of Vatican II and what remains to be done, Ladislas Orsy, S.J., wrote with great specificity about the role of canon law and the laity. In *"A Time to Harvest: The Second Vatican Council was the Sower,"* he says:

> Last, but truly not least, the church needs to bring the laity into its organizational and governmental operations far more than it has done thus far. Among them immense and diverse gifts of nature and grace are lying fallow and so do not benefit the Christian community. This is all because of a doctrinal position taken unnecessarily by the drafters of canon 129: "Lay members of the Christian faithful can cooperate in the exercise of the power [of governance] according to the norm of law." Note the canon says "cooperate," not "participate"—a world of difference. The former calls for passive obedience, the latter for active contribution. This view has no justification in tradition beyond the basic rule that a layperson cannot participate in the sacramental power given by ordination. For many activities in church government no anointing is necessary. Radical exclusion of the laity is a novelty in the church's 2,000 years of history. The best witnesses against the new rule would be the Byzantine emperors and empresses (surely not ordained); they called all the ecumenical councils in the first millennium. This was participation in church governance if ever there was any." (*America*, October 8, 2012, Vol. 207, #9)

The task ahead is immense and, as Fr. Orsy points out, crucial for the church as it faces a future drastically different from the past. In order to benefit from the collaborative and mutual effort that lies ahead, some important qualities and virtues come to mind that may be useful in working together with parish staff on issues pertinent to canon law parish life and ministry:

- Humility—willingness to learn from others;
- Openness to new approaches, challenges, and opportunities;
- Generosity—readiness to reach out to help those who are forgotten or neglected; and
- Trust in collaborative working relationships with lay ecclesial ministers that will result in "a future filled with hope."

SEMINAR

DIOCESAN REORGANIZATION IN BOSTON AND DETROIT: THE GOOD, THE BAD, AND THE UGLY
Reverend Monsignor Ricardo Bass
Very Reverend Mark O'Connell

Introduction

When we were asked by the Board of Governors to make this presentation, we were aware that there would be a pre-convention workshop regarding the canonical aspects of diocesan reorganization. In order not to repeat the same material, we decided to offer a brief overview of some of the canonical aspects but also to present a historical perspective on the experience of diocesan reorganization in the archdioceses of Boston and Detroit. Our presentation is in four parts: 1) a brief overview of the canonical aspects of diocesan reorganization; 2) the first diocesan reorganization in the Archdiocese of Detroit; 3) the diocesan reorganization in the Archdiocese of Boston; and, 3) the ongoing diocesan reorganization in the Archdiocese of Detroit. Each of the last three sections is accompanied by our personal observations of the good, the bad, and the ugly aspects of the processes which were initiated in each of our archdioceses.

Part One [O'Connell]

I think that most dioceses I am familiar with have a need for some kind of reorganization of parishes. The most obvious two reasons are that there are fewer Catholics that go to church now and the fact that in many areas Catholics used to be living in the cities and now many Catholics have moved to the suburbs. Canonically, the problem is that there is no section of canon law that is dedicated to this situation of the need to reorganize dioceses. There is a lacuna that is filled by scant canons that deal with parishes and others that address public juridic persons, but none of them are truly adequate to the needs of bishops to most effectively serve the people of God.

Over the past decade, what is possible and not possible with the existing legislation has become clearer, but it is admittedly trial and error that has helped to define what is possible and what is now forbidden.

The Archdiocese of Boston attempted to reorganize itself in 2004. Decisions were made in good faith interpreting the laws and based upon what had worked in the past. What took place in 2004 is no longer possible based upon feedback from the Congregation for Clergy and the Apostolic Signatura, but this is all in hindsight now that the resultant appeals have run their course and that bishops of the United States have been specifically clarified on the matter. Nevertheless, what actually happened canonically should be recorded. At this point this is written not so much as a "how-to" but as a lesson in what to avoid in the future.

I want to say personally that this has been a learning process for me. Back in 2004 I was a relatively new canon lawyer relying upon the experience of others. I hope that what I have learned over this time will assist others to continue to help clarify how best to reorganize dioceses to better serve the people of God.

First, a review of the most relevant canons; since there are no specific canons as stated above the first canon to be reviewed is that canon dealing with parishes, canon 515:

> §1. A parish is a certain community of the Christian faithful stably constituted in a particular church, whose pastoral care is entrusted to a pastor (parochus) as its proper pastor (pastor) under the authority of the diocesan bishop.
>
> §2. It is only for the diocesan bishop to erect, suppress, or alter parishes. He is neither to erect, suppress, nor alter notably parishes, unless he has heard the presbyteral council.
>
> §3. A legitimately erected parish possesses juridic personality by the law itself.

Relevant first in this canon is the definition in paragraph one which begins "a certain community of the Christian faithful." This becomes key to the understanding of the current interpretation of what it means to suppress a parish. More specifically, the parish is not a church building that ceases to exist when the building is closed but a portion of the people of God that ceases to exist when the people no longer exist. More on this later, but it is a good distinction to remember for now because back in 2004 this was not as clear based upon practice.

Second, the next paragraph indicates that "it is only for the diocesan bishop" to make these decisions as long as he consults with his presbyteral council. This, of course, needs to be paired with other canons to be discussed, but based upon only this canon it would seem that the diocesan bishop has great discretion to do what he feels is necessary. This paragraph reflects what is contained in the Vatican II document *Christus Dominus* paragraph 32:

Finally, the same concern for souls should be the basis for determining or reconsidering the erection or suppression of parishes and any other changes of this kind which the bishop is empowered to undertake on his own authority.

Third, the canon uses the words "erect," "suppress," and "alter." The word "merge" is not used, however it is common practice that to merge a parish is to alter a parish (but not necessarily the other way around).

Finally, paragraph 3 of canon 515 states that parishes are public juridic persons. Because of this, the canons that deal with public juridic persons are thus relevant to the fate of parishes.

Concerning the relevant canons with regard to public juridic persons, canons 120 to 123 need to be highlighted. These canons once again do not address the reorganization of dioceses which is the ultimate topic of this, but they need to be honored when parishes are up for scrutiny.

Canon 120 deals with suppressions of juridic persons:

>§1. A juridic person is perpetual by its nature; nevertheless, it is extinguished if it is legitimately suppressed by competent authority or has ceased to act for a hundred years. A private juridic person, furthermore, is extinguished if the association is dissolved according to the norm of its statutes or if, in the judgment of competent authority, the foundation has ceased to exist according to the norm of its statutes.
>
>§2. If even one of the members of a collegial juridic person survives, and the aggregate of persons (*universitas personarum*) has not ceased to exist according to its statutes, that member has the exercise of all the rights of the aggregate (*universitas*).

The concept of suppression indicates that something ceases to exist. Here it is most relevant that it must be "legitimately suppressed." The question is what constitutes legitimacy. Based upon canon 515, it certainly means that the bishop must consult his presbyteral council. Other canons that would be relevant would be canons dealing with singular acts of administration, most especially canon 50 (to be discussed later in this paper).

Following upon the suppression of a juridic person, it would appear (but is not necessarily so as will be shown) that canon 123 most logically follows:

>Upon the extinction of a public juridic person, the allocation of its goods, patrimonial rights, and obligations is governed by law and

its statutes; if these give no indication, they go to the juridic person immediately superior, always without prejudice to the intention of the founders and donors and acquired rights. Upon the extinction of a private juridic person, the allocation of its goods and obligations is governed by its own statutes.

Since most parishes do not have individual statutes, it would seem that the goods of parishes go to the "juridic person immediately superior," in other words, the diocese; however, this needs to be further explained and balanced with other canons and with the principle of temporal goods whereby money donated for a specific purpose must be used for that specific purpose.

Canon 121 speaks of "joining" juridic persons which is more commonly known as "merging":

> If aggregates of persons (*universitates personarum*) or of things (*universitates rerum*), which are public juridic persons, are so joined that from them one aggregate (*universitas*) is constituted which also possesses juridic personality, this new juridic person obtains the goods and patrimonial rights proper to the prior ones and assumes the obligations with which they were burdened. With regard to the allocation of goods in particular and to the fulfillment of obligations, however, the intention of the founders and donors as well as acquired rights must be respected.

The canon is perfectly clear as regard to the distribution of the assets after the merger; namely, all of the goods and obligations stay with the newly merged entity.

The last canon is canon 122 which speaks of division of juridic persons. Note that the canon begins with a very clear description of the two cases that are considered divisions:

> If an aggregate (*universitas*) which possesses public juridic personality is so divided either that a part of it is united with another juridic person or that a distinct public juridic person is erected from the separated part, the ecclesiastical authority competent to make the division, having observed before all else the intention of the founders and donors, the acquired rights, and the approved statutes, must take care personally or through an executor:
>
> 1° that common, divisible, patrimonial goods and rights as well as debts and other obligations are divided among the juridic persons concerned, with due proportion in equity and justice, after all the circumstances and needs of each have been taken into account;

2° that the use and usufruct of common goods which are not divisible accrue to each juridic person and that the obligations proper to them are imposed upon each, in due proportion determined in equity and justice.

Here too, the distribution of the goods and obligations are clear with their being distributed in "due proportion determined in equity and justice." Practically speaking, when it comes to the division of parishes the goods follow in the same proportion as the division of the people involved.

To understand fully the relevant factors used in Boston in 2004 one last canon needs to be highlighted which speaks about the role of consulting the people affected:

Canon 50: Before issuing a singular decree, an authority is to seek out the necessary information and proofs and, insofar as possible, to hear those whose rights can be injured.

The church in Boston in 2004 was in very serious difficulty. These difficulties were exacerbated by the clergy sexual abuse crisis no doubt, but the situation with the parishes predated these other troubles. The demographics clearly showed that where most Catholics lived in 1950 had changed dramatically at the turn of the Millennium. In addition to empty churches in some areas, there was an enormous amount of deferred maintenance and debt in the parishes, and finally, many of the personal parishes built to handle the large number of Catholic immigrants were no longer needed for their original mission.

A plan was needed to "reconfigure" the archdiocese but the canons were not adequate to the goals set forth. If the options are only to merge, suppress, or divide parishes this does not address the more macro needs. Up to that time the Archdiocese of Boston relied most often upon merging parishes in accord with canon 121. The problem with merging is twofold: first, it deals with the micro situation in that decisions end up being only local decisions whereby parishes join with the parishes next to them. This works locally but it does not address the problem with moving populations. Second, the problem with merging is that merging two poor parishes results in one large doubly poor parish, while merging two rich parishes results in one large doubly rich parish. What was needed was for the entire archdiocese to help each other so that the rich parishes help the poor parishes. Merging was rejected as not adequate for the massive macro changes that were judged to be needed.

Canon 122 concerning divisions was rejected as well due to the precise wording of the canon in that it begins with a description of the two cases whereby the canon applies; namely either dividing a large parish into two parishes or taking a portion of a large parish and giving that portion to another parish. In both cases the result is not fewer parishes; therefore, it was deemed (incorrectly) that the canon did not apply to what was needed.

This leaves canons 120 and 123 dealing with suppressions. The archdiocese chose to use this method during its "reconfiguration" fully conscious that any goods and obligations from the parish would flow up to the archdiocese as the juridic person immediately superior, but that these would also flow right back into parishes; first to where the people went and second to other needy parishes in the archdiocese. Two other things are extremely important to note and that is that the obligations (i.e., debts) were not given back to the parishes but absorbed by the central administration and also that none of the money from this reconfiguration went to non-parish obligations and so, therefore, none of the monies went to the costs connected with the sexual abuse of minors by priests.

In order to honor the stipulations of canon 50, the Archdiocese of Boston held extensive consultations with the people effected, eliciting the feedback of the parishioners themselves, the pastors, the vicars forane, the regional bishops, a special panel of mostly laypeople who analyzed the feedback, and, finally, the advice of the vicar general with a final decision made by the archbishop. All of this consultation was difficult and ultimately stood the test of scrutiny by the Vatican during the appeal process but this consultation was, in the end, flawed. The major flaw was that down at the very local level it is extremely difficult for parishioners who love their parish to look at the situation from where they stand in relation to all the other parishes in the diocese. The only way this was done effectively was when a parish was led by extraordinary priests who helped the parishioners truly discern with open minds. The Archdiocese of Boston was blessed with many such priests, but there were also some priests and deacons who immediately took sides and immediately turned the discernment into a fight akin to survival of the fittest; spending their energies plotting other parishes' demise rather than aiding objectivity. Note also that this "taking sides" was not always against the plans of the archbishop. In some circumstances, the priests and deacons involved alienated the objectivity of the parishioners by force feeding what was thought to be the will of the archbishop upon the people. The lesson learned is that the priest and deacon must both express the will of the bishop to the people and express the will of the people to the bishop and in this way lead the people to true discernment.

Ultimately, eighty parishes were suppressed in reconfiguration and the people were assigned to places of worship that accepted them and assimilated them into their parishes, bolstered by the assets of the closed parishes but bearing none of the debt of the closed parishes. What monies remained was given to other needy parishes in the archdiocese. Some seventeen parishes appealed the decision and the process of appeal took multiple years and had many twists and turns.

There are many lessons learned from the appeal process. Clearly the most important lesson learned was that system created in the Archdiocese of Boston, although done in good faith to help redistribute the assets of the entire archdiocese to better serve the people of God, was flawed in that the Congregation for Clergy has clearly ruled that all of the assets (and it would seem obligations) must follow the people to their new parishes as in accord with the canon concerning divisions (canon 122). As was explained prior, the archdiocese did not utilize canon 122 precisely because it begins with an explicit explanation of when it applies and the archdiocese never thought it was doing either of those scenarios. However, the Vatican explained very clearly, both to the archbishop of Boston and subsequently to all the dioceses in United States, that as long as there are people that remain from the suppressed parish, the parish in some sense still exists and therefore the money must follow them completely.

Another lesson learned from the appeal process is that the Vatican dicasteries have a very broad definition of who can have recourse against the action of the bishop. It speaks to the power of each member of the people of God to have their voice heard when they feel unfairly treated by a member of the hierarchy. Practically, this meant for the archdiocese that recourse could come in rather late by strict canonical standards and still be accepted, and it meant in these cases that the definition of the people affected, or of those who can claim rights, is much more inclusive than was anticipated.

The final major lesson which is still being learned and understood is that the Congregation for Clergy now holds a clear separation between the process to suppress a parish and the process to relegate a church building to profane use. As with the process of reconfiguration, the archdiocese is currently engaged in the process of relegating some churches to profane use, and is doing so in as open and transparent a method as possible. From what we have learned from our experience and the experience of other dioceses, the emphasis for the action must be due to clearly defined grave reasons.

Part Two [Bass]

The date was January 10, 1989. Detroit's Roman Catholic Cardinal Edmund Szoka ordered thirty-one inner-city parishes closed by June 30 and gave twenty-five additional parishes one year to boost membership and income or risk a similar fate. The move, the largest mass closing of parishes in the history of the U.S. Catholic Church, was prompted by the flight to the suburbs by large numbers of ethnic Catholics in recent decades and dwindling support for the parishes they left behind.[1]

---

1 "Catholic Cents," a blog written by Donald Wittmer, 20 February 2012 (www.catholicjournal.us/catholiccents).

On January 10, 1989, many of these fifty-six parishes were aware of their fate, others were not.

The Timeline

In his Pastoral Letter, "Dying and Rising Together With Christ," which was sent to every registered Catholic household in the Archdiocese of Detroit in 1989, Cardinal Edmund Szoka wrote:

> When I first arrived in the Archdiocese of Detroit in the spring of 1981, I became immediately concerned about the presence and ministry of the Church within the City, both in parishes and in schools.... It became evident to me that we had more very small parishes in the City which found it difficult, if not impossible, to live a full parish life in carrying out the mission of the Church. Furthermore, some had to expend so much time and energy simply to survive that they were not able to develop the full range of parish life and ministry.[2]

To address this situation, Cardinal Szoka initiated a process to address this very real ministerial concern. The timeline for that process from its beginning to its conclusion is as follows:

> December 1978–Cardinal Szoka appoints Auxiliary Bishop Patrick R. Cooney head of a task force for pastors, religious, and lay with the responsibility for determining the presence and ministry of the church in the cities of Detroit, Highland Park, and Hamtramck.
>
> Late 1984–Preliminary self-assessment tool developed.
>
> March 1985–Vicariate meetings held to discuss data.
>
> October 1985–Task force makes tentative proposals.
>
> June-October 1986–Parish meetings encouraged to discuss tentative proposals.
>
> October 1986–Vicariate meetings obtain feedback from parish meetings.
>
> June 1987–Self-study questionnaire of all parishes in archdiocese.
>
> July 1987–Task force recommendations presented to Cardinal Szoka.

---

2 Cardinal Edmund Szoka, "Dying and Rising Together With Christ: A Pastoral Letter on the Church," (15 January 1989) 34.

January 1988–As per task force recommendations, Urban Advisory Board and Implementation Committee established to study new data and make recommendations.

September 1988–Urban Advisory Board and Implementation Committee make public in an archdiocesan wide teleconference. Bishop Cooney states that in making judgments about parishes the following nine (9) areas were included: pastoral activity (per the June 1987 self-study), sacramental activity, geography, accessibility, finance, condition of buildings, history, and city planning.

September 1988–Office for the Church in the City established.

September-December 1988–Hearings before Bishop Cooney and members of the Urban Advisory Board and the Implementation Committee.

December 1988–Final recommendations of the Urban Advisory Board and the Implementation Committee.

January 15, 1989–Cardinal Szoka publishes his pastoral letter entitled, "Dying and Rising Together with Christ" and writes: "In total, eighty-two of the original 112 parishes in the City will remain open…with twenty-five of these being questionably viable."[3]

June 1989–Scheduled closing date of thirty-one parishes.

Reflections and Observations

The Good:

1. Laity coming to understand more about their own parish than they had in the past. In 1983, many of the laity had little or no clear understanding about the ministry, the finances, or the basic pastoral "health" of their parish. This process provided many of them with their first opportunity to come to an understanding of the many facets and aspects to their parish. In other words, this provided them with an opportunity to learn the inner workings of their own parish. The education of the people regarding matters concerning their own parish became central to this process going forward

2. Need for laity to lay claim to responsibility for the life of the parish. Many began to understand that for their parish to continue into the future (for it to

---

3 Ibid., 37.

be "viable") they would need to take a more active role in the ministry and life of their parish than they had in the past.

3. Pastors being held accountable for the parish. Pastors now found themselves educating their parishioners about their parish and having to answer sometimes difficult questions about its governance, its finances, and its ability to sustain itself (remain "viable").

The Bad:

1. Focus only on "inner city" parishes. "Inner city" was a term frequently used at that time, a term which was often accompanied with negative connotations. The memories of the 1967 Detroit riots were still fresh in the minds of many and recalled a very painful chapter in the history of the city.

2. Process and decisions coming from the top down. Although a concerted effort was made to involve a cross-section of persons in this process, there was a perception by many that decisions had already been made by those in positions of authority. Many people became frustrated with waiting to hear the results of the process and how their own parish would be affected.

3. One-way communication. Many of those involved were suspicious that few if any of those in authority were listening to their frustrations, to their aspirations for their parish, and to the need to support the church in the city. When the decision was finally made as to which parishes would close, it was communicated through a one-time closed circuit television presentation to the affected parishes. This necessitated the need for members of these faith communities to find a location where they could watch what the outcome of this process was for their own parish.[4]

The Ugly:

1. Charges of racism. It was very clear that this diocesan reorganization was to be concerned almost exclusively with the parishes in the city of Detroit and two of its closest communities, Hamtramck and Highland Park. Since the 1967 riots, the demography of these areas had been in flux and all three were beginning to be populated by a larger and larger African-American population. Many living in those communities thought that they were being "targeted" by a church structure which was largely Caucasian.

---

4 "If you explain the situation to people, they understand. But when you go in and announce it over closed-circuit TV, it's like GM closing an auto plant. It really gives the church a black eye," said Jay Dolan, a Catholic historian at Notre Dame University. ("Church Closings Stun Catholics in Detroit," Tom Hundley, *Chicago Tribune*, 16 October 1988.)

2. City pastors vs. all other pastors. Many of the pastors of parishes in the city were very vocal about the fact that they saw this process as the church abandoning the city. They did not believe that those in authority had a clear understanding of the importance of church ministry in the city of Detroit.

3. Ongoing distrust of the "downtown offices." The "downtown offices"– where the majority of the administrative offices for the archdiocese were/ are located–have always had a rather tenuous relationship with the parishes throughout the archdiocese. This process further eroded the relationship between these faith communities and the "downtown offices" which were meant to assist them.

Part Three [O'Connell]

Sometimes only the worst news gets publicity, and when it comes to the reconfiguration of the Archdiocese of Boston beginning in 2004, this was certainly the case; however, it also provided an opportunity to show the good things along with the bad ... and the ugly.

The Good:

1. The need to "reconfigure" the Archdiocese of Boston in 2004 can be highlighted with a comparison to the Archdiocese of Los Angeles. The Archdiocese of Los Angeles is made up of at least twice as many Catholics as the Archdiocese of Boston, yet when the plan to reconfigure the parishes in Boston began, Los Angeles actually had far fewer parishes that Boston. Not only is that context demonstrative of the real problem of maintaining and staffing too many churches, but the truth is that many of our parishes were built specifically where the Catholic populations were in the mid-1900s. Since then, many of our Catholics have moved. Once upon a time in a particular section of Boston, there were twelve parishes that were full but now, years later, were mostly running dry. In other sections of the archdiocese a few churches were bursting at the seams. The reconfiguration of the Archdiocese of Boston managed to successfully close some sixty-three parishes. This was absolutely needed.

2. The level of consultation was extremely broad and comprehensive–at least on paper. This topic appears below in a more negative light, but let it not be underestimated the multiple levels of consultation that the archbishop demanded prior to closing a parish. These levels included the parishioners and the parish pastoral councils, the pastors, the neighboring parishes, the vicar forane, the regional bishop, a central committee made up of a majority of lay people that analyzed all parishes equally, a smaller committee that included the archbishop, then a comprehensive review by the presbyteral council,

followed by a new review of the central committee, and a final view by the archbishop. Then, after the announcements, there were multiple levels of appeals and an independent review committee re-looked at every contested closing. Clearly, the infrastructure of consultation was in place.

3. One very successful aspect was the two manuals created for the archdiocese: the "Closing Manual" and the "Welcoming Manual." These manuals were given to every parish affected, both those parishes that were asked to close and those that were slated to receive new parishioners. The manuals were in binder form and each binder contained a CD of the same. The manuals created by the central administration contained all aspects of the issues including: checklists for closing, rationale for closing, extensive financial spreadsheets to aid the parish staffs, liturgical suggestions for final Masses or welcoming Masses, information on how parishioners could appeal the closings, explanations of things that the pastor could sell or give away, and clear information as to what needed to remain or be appraised.

4. Sacred goods were all invoiced and transferred in a clear pecking order: first to the welcoming parish, second to the other Boston parishes using an extensive internet website with pictures and closed church halls for housing and viewing, then to other Catholic parishes in the country, and some things to missionary territories. Prominent among these carefully indexed and stored items were many stained glass windows that have now served to beautify other parishes, most especially new and renovated Boston parishes.

5. The canonical process of recourse against the archbishop's actions was absolutely and fully respected and advertised, and it is should be noted that not a single closing was subsequently overturned by Congregation for Clergy or the Apostolic Signatura. In addition, not a single civil lawsuit has been successful against the actions of the archbishop.

6. The majority of the parishes closed without incident and with an extremely generous spirit by the people of God. One such stewardship oriented parish was particularly remarkable, where the parishioners chose to build a new church in the Dominican Republic with the same patron saint and even brought many of the items from the closed church down for the opening ceremony. So many good and holy stories happened where parishioners who were led by faithful pastors and parish staffs understood the real issues and closed for the greater good.

The Bad:

1. Part of the problem was the system of consultation with the local parishes. The bottom line is that parishioners had a very difficult time looking at their

own parish objectively. Unless each parish is carefully guided by the counsel of their parish leaders they will naturally look to self-preservation rather than where they fit into the greater archdiocese. The consultation in Boston began with local clusters of parishes gathering together and answering the following questions: "If one of these parishes should close, which would it be? And if two should close, which would they be?" These questions proved ineffective in many cases where it seemed to pit parishes against each other. This type of consultation was especially unsuccessful when the pastors joined in the chorus or allowed the chorus of unfairness. Local consultation must happen but these were the wrong questions.

2. There should have been at least two rounds of consultation rather than just one. The archdiocese chose to inform every parish of their fate on the same day at the same hour (via FedEx) and then to set in motion the process of the closings right away. The archbishop was actually advised to do this by the presbyteral council who stated that it would be best to use the "rip off the bandage quickly approach" rather than a slower drawn out process. Hindsight shows clearly that there should have been an initial plan given to the people and another round of consultation after. This would have avoided multiple complaints and would have saved time in the long run when considering appeals.

3. Some pastors who were supposed to welcome the new parishioners did not do this effectively. This was especially highlighted when parishioners of a closed parish thought that it was their new receiving pastor who had sealed their fate in closing. In cases where there were contentious consultations a new pastor should have been chosen for the welcoming parish.

4. Some parishes were able to almost opt out of the process by ignoring it. Led by pastors who normally do not participate in things of the archdiocese, they simply did not consult or comply with the archdiocese's requests and in some cases avoided the entire matter. Each vicar forane and regional bishop should have been more insistent upon full participation by all.

The Ugly:

1. Some priests and deacons actively led the parishioners into rebellion against the decisions of the archbishop. This was a small yet loud minority of parishes. Pastors and deacons should be able to represent the views of the bishop to the people and the views of the people to the bishop, and then allow for the greater good in light of the information. There were few priests and deacons, however, who sided immediately with the people against the bishop, thereby misleading the people and giving them a one-sided view. In other cases, the opposite happened whereby the priest and deacons did not

listen to the parishioners but forced the situation falsely representing the bishop as not willing to listen. Both approaches pushed to the extreme, and consequently did more harm than good.

2. Some groups of parishioners chose to stage sit-in vigils in the closed churches rather than peacefully closing them. These "vigils" have been successfully avoided by careful planning in subsequent closings since that time.

3. It is impossible to avoid negative publicity as emotions can run high when closing a parish and news stories thrive on emotions. One quick example to this was a parish closing Mass where five media outlets set up their cameras outside church to capture the people leaving. All the people were positive and happy with how the final Mass went and none of the stations aired the story.

Part Four [Bass]

It soon became clear that the closing of the thirty parishes in 1989 had ongoing effects in the life of the church in the Archdiocese of Detroit. Those parishes which had not been closed but were termed "questionably viable" kept waiting with bated breath to hear if they would remain open or not. Even the parishes which were termed as being "viable" were suspect that the archdiocese might suddenly decide to close them. Morale of all church employees (lay, clergy, and religious) was at an all-time low.

This concern had been reinforced by the fact that after the announcement that thirty of the parishes were to close by 1 July 1989, fourteen of them appealed to the Sacred Congregation for the Clergy and all fourteen appeals were rejected. Eighteen of the parishes pursued action through the civil courts that there be an injunction against the closing but that too was rejected.

A pall hung over the Archdiocese of Detroit which has never completely lifted. Church life continued but it was clear that a decision which came from the top down left many feeling discouraged and disconnected. It was decided that from this point forward, a parish would only close if the pastor of that parish, in consultation with and with the approval of his finance council and his parish pastoral council, would request the archbishop in writing that the parish be closed. It was also important to establish a new process which would involve a larger number of the people of God who would share an active role in the decision making process for the future life of each parish.

Together in Faith, which began in 2001, responded to that need. All of the parishes in the archdiocese were sent an extensive questionnaire about their parish (percentage of various ethnic groups, percentage of various age groups, questions about the mission of each parish, the various staff members, the various sacramental statistics, etc.). Once that material was submitted to the archdiocese it was combined with other information provided by the archdiocese (demographic changes [both present and projected], numbers of active priests [both present and projected], finances of the parish according to archdiocesan records, etc.). The pastors were then asked to discuss the material in these packets with their various consultative parish groups–especially the parish pastoral councils–and to develop a five-year plan for their parish based upon the facts presented to them.

As one of the members of the coordinating committee for this process, I (along with the other members) was asked to review the reports submitted. Each member was responsible for reviewing and reporting on the parishes within two of the twenty-five vicariates and make a presentation of the reports to the committee as a whole (including any questions or concerns that the reports raised). The members were then to provide feedback to each of the parishes as to how realistic their five-year plans appeared to be based upon the facts specific to their parish. For many of the participants at the parish level, this was the first time they were made aware of projections regarding available priests in the future and finances of their own parish. A second committee was then formed to follow-up with the five-year plan of each of the parishes.

The changes that were simultaneously taking place within the archdiocese and within the city during the years of 2008-2009 could not have been anticipated when *Together in Faith* began. Detroit's population plunged by more than 25% by 2010, to just 714,000 residents. Much of the former tax base was gone. The enrollment in the Detroit public schools continued to decline to less than 60,000 students from 170,000 students in 2000. In the Archdiocese of Detroit in the year 2000, there were 414 priests. In 2010 there were 286 and by 2015, the number will continue to decline to 243. Most of the current priests are between the ages of fifty and sixty-nine (with one active pastor who is presently ninety-three!!). Archbishop Vigneron asked in 2010 for the pastoral plan generated by *Together in Faith I* be "refreshed."

So began *Together in Faith II* in 2010. From January-June 2011, forty planning groups were formed. Each parish in the archdiocese was asked to send four representatives to their assigned group to discuss the strengths and weaknesses of each parish and to project how they might work cooperatively with one another in the future. Planning groups met to study data, statistics, and maps for their parishes. Eventually, each parish was asked to select a "cluster partner"– that is, a parish with whom the parish would cluster in the future when there would not be priests and/or financial resources to allow each parish to exist by itself. The reality of "clustering" was already being implemented along with the reality of "merging." Whereas in "clustering" each parish would retain its own identity but pastoral services would be offered in a new way – in a "merging" one parish (or more) would only be available for occasional liturgical services or might be used as a Christian Service Center for the area. Those parishes would operate under one name (often a new name chosen by members of the parishes involved). From July-August 2011, Archdiocesan Pastoral Council (APC) members reviewed the strategic plans submitted for each vicariate and responded with comments and recommendations. The parishes responded and from September-December 2011, the APC sent comments and requests for clarification to the planning groups for their response and final plans. In January 2012, the archbishop approved and presented the overall plan to the Catholic faithful. This included the fact of two parishes which would close, eight other parishes which will merge into four by the end of the year, and the rest which will merge, cluster, or close in coming years, depending on various factors including debt repayment and priest availability. The APC now monitors the implementation of these plans. On 1 July 2012, each parish and its cluster partner(s) were to submit to the archbishop strategic plans for its clustering and/or merging and or closing.

Reflections and Observations

The Good:

1. Raising the consciousness of the people of God regarding the realities of the future and the challenges facing the archdiocese and each person's parish by providing them with good information and having them discuss that information. Through prayer, study, and discussion, laity and clergy involved with this process began to develop a more realistic view of the future of their parish. They began to discuss new ideas: sharing of facilities with other parishes, sharing of personnel with other parishes, combining liturgical services (e.g., communal penance services) with other parishes, etc.

2. Involving the laity in the decision-making process of the future of their parish. The laity definitely became more empowered in setting the future course of their own parish. Through directed discussions, prayerful reflections, and new understandings about parish finances they began working with their respective pastors and other parish communities on setting a vision for the future of their own parish.

3. Having parishes ultimately determining their future. The question ultimately became: in the future, should we cluster with another parish or merge with another parish or close? An often painful process began to yield to new ideas and new life which had not been present before. The recommendations of each were to be brought to the archbishop for his final decisions.

4. It can be argued that the crowning achievement, under the leadership of Archbishop Vigneron, is that for the first time a pastoral plan for the

Archdiocese of Detroit is being developed which is the cooperative effort of all the members of the Archdiocese of Detroit: lay, religious, and clergy.

The Bad:

1. Only three options available: cluster, merge, or close. These are the three options with which the Archdiocese of Detroit is presently working. They do not preclude the possibility of other options in the future but, at the moment, these are the only three being presented for the consideration of every parish in the archdiocese (not just the city parishes). A very important question remains as to what other models might be available for parishes. This will take further study as to options being used by other dioceses (e.g., the Archdiocese of Vienna is moving from 610 parishes to 150 parishes in the next ten years) and creative thinking on the part of those involved with this process.

2. The toll that clustering is taking on some of the priests. It is too early in the process to say anything definitive about this, however, on a purely anecdotal basis it is clear to many priests and laity alike that some of our pastors are "wearing out" physically or emotionally or spiritually because they are often on a much more demanding way of ministering than has been used in the past. Some pastors are now responsible for two or more parishes, each with its own parish pastoral council and set of commissions. Some pastors have had little experience in parish ministry when they assume the role of pastor, sometimes as little as two or three years. Some pastors are just not able to handle the administration of more than one parish at a time.

3. Lack of a significant role for the Archdiocesan Pastoral Council in this process. The Archdiocesan Pastoral Council is still lacking a clear understanding of its role in this process and many of the parishes and pastors have little idea what the purpose of this council is or how it may assist the parishes in moving forward.

The Ugly:

1. Lack of support of parish communities losing their present identity. Clustering, merging, and closing are all "death experiences" for the members of a parish community. Oftentimes this is overlooked and many of the people are left feeling a real sense of loss or a real sense of anger and are not sure how to address those feelings. The parish is often the place where all of their sacraments have taken place–as well as the sacraments of their family members (especially their children)–and now they are informed that they must move on to a new or different parish. For many this is very, very difficult and for others it is impossible and they leave in anger or frustration.

2. The role of the presbyteral council. The question becomes: if all of the ground work has been done–decisions have been arrived at–and a given parish is ready to cluster or merge or close, what then is the role of the presbyteral council? By law, it must be "heard" but what, if anything, does it have to offer to a process which seems to have been concluded before it is presented to the presbyteral council for its consideration and ideas?

SEMINAR

GOING GLOBAL WITH *THE CHARTER* AND *ESSENTIAL NORMS*
Most Reverend R. Daniel Conlon

Everybody's Problem

The fairly recent travails at Penn State University are very real, very painful and, from our perspective as Catholic insiders, very predictable. Twenty-five years ago I was shocked to learn that youngsters had been abused by priests. I am still deeply pained by every new revelation, but I am no longer shocked.

For a while I held my breath, thinking that maybe this problem truly was an American one. Then came other English speaking countries: Ireland, England, and Australia. The Continent joined the ranks of the afflicted next. Not much has been heard from Latin America, Africa, Asia and Oceania. Is that yet to come? Is there more tragedy hidden beneath the surface? Does the Holy See, with its vast network of diplomatic missions, Curia contacts and globetrotting hierarchs and religious, sense that the scandal has by no means run its course? Is there recognition that a universal issue requires a universal response?

On May 3, 2011, the Congregation for the Doctrine of the Faith (CDF) took a significant step to expand the Church's commitment to protect her youngest members and to respond to instances of abuse. Through the instrumentation of a circular letter, the congregation intended "to assist episcopal conferences in developing guidelines for dealing with cases of sexual abuses of minors perpetrated by clerics." The circular letter was for the whole church, for every episcopal conference, no matter how small, no matter how remote.

The circular letter laid out many criteria for the guidelines. Two things it did not do: it did not require episcopal conferences to develop guidelines, and it set no deadline for submitting guidelines. I heard no reference to these points at the Gregorian symposium. (The *ad limina apostolorum* for our episcopal region was taking place at the same time as the symposium. So, I was not present every minute of the symposium.) Yet, at the Anglophone Conference[1] on child protection in Rome also last February, Monsignor Charles Scicluna, CDF's Promoter of Jus-

---

1 For the past several years, representatives from the episcopal conferences of English-speaking countries in the developed world have met annually to discuss among themselves issues related to the sexual abuse of minors and the safeguarding of minors in the church.

tice, gave the distinct impression that the congregation expected every episcopal conference to produce guidelines and deliver them to Rome by this past May.

There is much more to say about the criteria for the guidelines laid out in the circular letter. For now, a reasonable inference may be drawn from the issuance of the circular letter a year and a half ago: in Rome a narrow, localized view of the child abuse problem no longer holds sway. That is good news for children and young people everywhere.

The sexual exploitation of minors is not an American problem, or an English-speaking problem, or one only in the developed world. It is not a Catholic problem, nor only a clerical one. Children are abused everywhere and at every stratum of society, in institutions and in families. It is good news that the kind of response reflected in the United States' "Charter for the Protection of Children and Young People" and the "Essential Norms" is going global.

Gregorian Symposium

Someone, I have to assume at the Congregation for the Doctrine of the Faith, determined that, in order to facilitate a response to the circular letter, an informational program for episcopal conferences ought to be provided. The resources of the Pontifical Gregorian University in Rome were enlisted, and hence came about the symposium, "Toward Healing and Renewal," in early February 2012.

Each episcopal conference was invited by the CDF to send one bishop. Cardinal Timothy Dolan, President of the United States Conference of Catholic Bishops, asked me, as Chairman of the Committee on the Protection of Children and Young People, to represent our conference. With this background, I assumed that the symposium participants would be mostly bishops. As it turned out, of the approximately two hundred participants, about half were bishops, while the other half were not. There were general superiors of men and women religious, most of them Rome-based, as well as academics, child protection experts, including representatives from Virtus and Praesidium, and a smattering of others, among them the Executive Coordinator of our Society, Sr. Sharon Euart, RSM.

We met in the modern, tiered conference room in the Gregorian's basement over a period of three days. Immediate translation was provided in the major modern languages. The program consisted mainly of plenary sessions, with a few small workshops in nearby rooms. Security was tight, although there was ready access to the media in a building across the piazza from the university's main building.

I intend to summarize the major presentations. First, though, I feel compelled to share some of my personal sense of the gathering. It is not often that a hundred bishops from around the world are convened by the Holy See. I never expect to attend an assembly of the Synod of Bishops or a conclave! At the same time, the addition of other members of the Christian faithful on an even footing contributed a dimension of broad collaboration. Although the majority of presenters were clerics, lay men and women took their turns. After listening to a weighty speech, followed by equally ponderous questions, we adjourned for coffee and sweets. Everyone had to wait patiently at the coat check, from curial cardinals to diminutive Spanish sisters. The overall atmosphere was one of seriousness mixed with informal cordiality.

The church approaches the issue of child abuse from many perspectives and using many disciplines. This was the case at the Gregorian symposium. Only two major presentations contained substantial canonical material, and I will accord them fuller treatment this morning. Other contributions covered theology, sociology and psychology, seminary training, ongoing clerical formation and best practices for dealing with abuse. Symposium participants were also invited to join in two moving liturgical celebrations in nearby churches.

Cardinal Levada
After some brief introductions, including the reading of a message from the Vatican Secretary of State, Cardinal Tarcisio Bertone, on behalf of Pope Benedict XVI, Cardinal William Levada, then the Prefect of the Congregation for the Doctrine of the Faith, set the stage for the symposium with a talk titled, "The Sexual Abuse of Minors: A Multi-faceted Response to the Challenge."

Although his presentation was largely a commentary on the circular letter of the previous May, he began with a quotation from Pope Benedict when speaking about priests who "twist the sacrament [of Holy Orders] into its antithesis, and under the mantle of the sacred profoundly wound human persons in their childhood, damaging them for a whole lifetime." Said Cardinal Levada: "I chose this phrase to begin my remarks this evening because I think it important not to lose sight of the gravity of these crimes as we deal with the multiple aspects [of] the Church's response."

Levada's context is important. The guidelines to be developed by episcopal conferences relating to the sexual abuse of minors obviously must represent sound canonical principles, as must the work of the CDF, diocesan curias and penal tribunals in dealing with specific cases. But the "gravity of these crimes" and their devastating effects must be kept in front of us. As the cardinal also told the symposium participants in the first paragraph of his talk, "...the question is both delicate and urgent."

Levada began the core of his speech with an analysis of the impact of Blessed John Paul II's *motu proprio Sacramentorum sanctitatis tutela* (*SST*), promulgated on April 30, 2001. Besides revising the definition and pertinent norms of certain delicts, *SST* required all cases involving the sexual abuse of minors by clergy to be reported to the Congregation for the Doctrine of the Faith for further determination. A year later the bishops of the United States adopted the "Charter for the Protection of Children and Young People" and, with the support of the then-Prefect of CDF, Cardinal Josef Ratzinger, their "Essential Norms" received the *recognitio* of the Holy See allowing them to become particular law.

Cardinal Levada explained that, because of the media coverage, especially in the United States but also in other countries, the congregation saw a "dramatic increase" in the number of cases reported, more than 4000 in the past decade. "In studying these cases we see, on the one hand, the inadequacy of an exclusively canonical (or canon law) response to this tragedy, and on the other, the necessity of a truly multi-faceted response. While the Congregation's primary responsibility is the application of equitable norms in the discipline of guilty clergy, it has necessarily made its own the expanded view of how best to assist in the healing of victims, of promoting programs for the protection of children and young people, of urging bishops to provide for the education of communities of faith to responsibility for their youth, and of working with other Dicasteries of the Holy See and Episcopal Conferences in ensuring the proper formation of today's priests, and the priests of the future, in the various aspects related to the issues of sexual abuse of minors."

At this point Cardinal Levada skipped forward to the spring of 2010 and the promulgation by Benedict XVI of modifications to *SST* proposed by his former congregation, "in the light of her experience in dealing with the thousands of cases presented from various parts of the world." We canonists know that the revision of the church's law, at least through promulgation by the Supreme Pontiff, occurs at a measured pace. Yet, within ten years, the penal code has been revised twice, largely because of the child abuse scandal and largely because of the United States, not only on account of the abuse itself but also the vigorous if tardy response.

Among the major 2010 affirmation of practices for CDF, mentioned by Levada, are "the right to derogate from the prescription of these crimes, the faculty to dispense from judicial trial in order to allow an extra-judicial process in cases where the facts seemed clear, the faculty to present cases directly to the Holy Father for dismissal from the clerical state in cases of extreme gravity, and the addition of the delict of possession and/or distribution of child pornography (regarding minors of 14 years)...."

Yet, as he had already mentioned, a canonical response alone is not sufficient. By 2010 other countries had followed the U.S.'s example and adopted broader guidelines, even norms, to offer a uniform response to this complex issue throughout the territory of their respective episcopal conferences: Australia, Belgium, Brazil, Canada, France, Germany, Great Britain, Ireland, New Zealand, and South Africa. As with the United States, these provisions were generally adopted in the wake of media revelations. It was time, in the view of the CDF, for a proactive approach by the remainder of the episcopal conferences. Hence, in May, 2011 came the "Circular Letter to assist Episcopal Conferences in developing Guidelines for dealing with cases of sexual abuse of minors perpetrated by Clerics."

Before commenting on specific points of the letter, Cardinal Levada itemized the key elements that such guidelines need to address elements that mirrored the wider approach to the problem that the CDF had already come to appreciate. "[Episcopal conferences] must pay due attention to the canonical discipline of the clergy who are guilty of such crimes; they must have standards to evaluate the suitability of clergy and other persons who minister in Church institutions and agencies; they should oversee education programs for families and Church communities to ensure the protection of children and young people from the crime of sexual abuse in the future; and they must be pastors and fathers to any victims of sexual abuse among their flocks who may appeal to them for remedy or help."

The prefect pointed out to his audience that the circular letter is divided into three parts: general considerations; a summary of canonical legislation; and suggestions for ordinaries on procedures. Since other presenters would address the canonical portions of the letter, the balance of his presentation focused on the "general considerations."

I want to cover two important points that Cardinal Levada made before addressing the "general considerations." Then, I would like at least to enumerate those considerations.

The guidelines to be developed by the episcopal conferences in response to the circular letter are to be "for the diocesan bishop members of the Conference, and for the Major Superiors of Religious residing in the territory of the Conference, in their response to cases of sexual abuse by clerics, and in taking necessary steps to eliminate such abuse from Church and society." Furthermore, "the Congregation considers it an obligation for Bishops and Religious Major Superiors to participate in the development of these guidelines, and to observe them for the good of the Church once they have been approved by the Congregation for the Doctrine of the Faith. No bishop or major superior may consider himself exempt from such collaboration."

Many believe that one weakness of the Dallas Charter is the exclusion of male institutes of consecrated life, both in the drafting of the Charter and in those covered by it. Besides the men religious feeling excluded from such a significant moment in the life of the church, an exclusion which might well be understood considering the circumstances in which the Charter was born, there has been confusion and sometimes hard feelings resulting from the confusion for ten years. Despite their not being covered by the Charter, the institutes in our country have worked hard to develop their own methods to assure the same standards as have dioceses, both in addressing abuse cases and in creating safe environments. They have crafted a process for accrediting the institutes for compliance with those standards, and, one could safely argue, given the communal life of religious, that they have been generally more effective at helping their members fulfill a life of prayer and penance.

However, as we move forward toward another revision of the Charter starting in 2013, CDF's circular letter and Cardinal Levada's comments on it provide us with an opening to remedy a shortcoming in the original Charter. I do not know, though, whether consecrated men will welcome such a readjustment, precisely because of their accomplishments over the past ten years and because of the recognition of the uniqueness of their way of life. If CDF wants a universal approach, we will need to move with great care, honesty and respect.

The other important point is the cardinal's reference to approval of the guidelines by the CDF and no bishop or major superior being exempt from "such collaboration." The circular letter makes no reference to approval by the Apostolic See in any form, and Cardinal Levada was not promulgating law in the aula of the Gregorian University last February. So, what form will these guidelines have? Will they be like our Charter, without the force of law? Or will they be like the "Essential Norms"? Will the former prefect's admonition be only that, leaving a loophole for the occasional reluctant or recalcitrant bishop or religious superior?

As for the "general considerations" in the circular letter, they are the victims of sexual abuse, the protection of minors, the formation of future priests and religious, support of priests, and cooperation with civil authority. Here I would like to point out that, while care for victims, protection of minors and cooperation with civil authorities are central features of the "Charter for the Protection of Children and Young People" and the "Essential Norms," the other two areas are not. The formation of future clergy and support for those who already are were two significant areas of recommendation recently from the National Review Board. The NRB drew its recommendations largely from the John Jay College *Causes and Contexts Study* of the abuse crisis. My guess is that the CDF came to the same conclusion from its work on abuse cases and found affirmation from the John Jay study. If we are serious about preventing the sexual exploitation of children by clergy, these are areas that we will need to work on even more deliberately.

Monsignor Scicluna
Besides Cardinal Levada, the only other presentation at the Gregorian symposium with major canonical significance was the one given by Monsignor Charles Scicluna, CDF's Promoter of Justice, and just recently appointed auxiliary bishop in his native Malta. His address was titled, "The Quest for Truth in Sexual

Abuse Cases: A Moral and Legal Duty." For a framework, he used the 1994 Rotal address of Blessed John Paul II that focused on truth as the basis of justice. Monsignor Scicluna developed five principles arising from the Holy Father's address.[2]

The first principle is that "*Love for the truth* must be expressed in *love for justice* and in the resulting commitment to establishing truth in relations within human society." Justice and law must serve truth.

The first implication of this principle in abuse cases is the need to establish the facts with a spirit of fairness. This task of seeking the facts objectively, beginning with the preliminary investigation and continuing through every successive step, is essential. The victim, the accused and any witnesses must be heard, and the right of the parties to hear arguments and respond to them must be assured. The accused must be able to defend himself, to know the reasons for the decision, and to review a decision. Likewise the victim, in addition to presenting the complaint, also has the right to act as the injured party (*pars laesa*) in a penal judicial trial.

The second implication, conversely, is the damage that silence, to say nothing of lying, does to truth and, hence, to justice. Trying to protect an individual or an institution's reputation by withholding pertinent information is ultimately a form of injustice.

Scicluna's second principle is that justice based on truth evokes a response from the individual's conscience. In 1994, John Paul II said, "…if well formed, conscience naturally assents to truth and perceives within itself a principle of obedience compelling it to conform to what the law commands."

I found it interesting that Monsignor Scicluna applied this principle to the perpetrators and victims of sexual abuse but not to those who administer justice in these cases. Of course, issues of conscience are paramount for offenders, both in the commission of their crimes and then coming to terms with them afterward. Even with the victim/survivors, as Monsignor pointed out, honest self-awareness, often so difficult for them to achieve, is important in bringing their allegations forward and in the process of healing. Obviously the role of an active, well-formed conscience in those of us who have an official duty in the administration of justice is critical. Quoting from the address to the Roman Rota, as did Scicluna, "As a participation in truth, *justice too has its own splendor* that can evoke a free response in the subject—one not merely external but arising from the depths of one's conscience."

---

2   The quotations of the English translation of the Rotal address used by Msgr. Scicluna were taken from W.H. Woestman, *Papal Allocutions to the Roman Rota, 1939-2002,* Ottawa, 2002.

"Respect of the truth generates confidence in the rule of law, whereas disrespect for the truth generates distrust and suspicion." That is the third principle. Here, Monsignor Scicluna briefly summarized the developments in ecclesiastical law pertaining to sexual abuse over the past eleven years. His point is that the law in this matter is clear. Its consistent, fair application must also be clear.

Such an application creates a "truth," by which, in the mind of John Paul, "the faithful will remain convinced that ecclesial society is living under the governance of law; that ecclesial rights are protected by the law; that in the final analysis, the law is an opportunity for a loving response to God's will."

The fourth principle holds that the protection of rights is implemented within the context of the concern for the common good. The truth that justice demands must look beyond the narrow application of law to a specific situation. Since all law is ordered to the common good, the real circumstances of the common good must be weighed in making concrete judgments, and the rights of the individual must be tempered by the rights of the many.

It is from this principle that the church is able to designate the safety of children as a paramount concern and justify the curtailment of the rights of individuals to function as her agents when they have abused minors or give indication that they could. Regard for the common good extends to compliance with civil law and cooperation with civil authorities, since the sexual abuse of children is a state crime. This reality creates a legitimate interest on the part of the state, another "truth" if you will, that the church must honor in the exercise of her justice.

The fifth principle involves avoiding distortions of the "pastoral" nature of church law. Scicluna again referred to John Paul II's 1994 address: "You are well aware of the temptation to lighten the heavy demands of observing the law in the name of the mistaken idea of compassion and mercy.... If the rights of others are at stake, mercy cannot be shown or received without addressing the obligations that correspond to these rights.... One is also duty-bound to be on guard against the temptation to exploit the proofs and procedural norms in order to achieve what is perhaps a 'practical' goal, which might perhaps be considered 'pastoral,' but is to the detriment of truth and justice."

In the view of both the Holy Father and the Promoter of Justice, conscientious adherence to the truth is inherently pastoral and serves the good of souls. No more is this so than in dealing with the painful, uncomfortable subject of sexually exploited children within the church. Citing another pope, Benedict XVI when speaking to the Irish bishops in 2010, Monsignor Scicluna came toward the conclusion of his own address with these words: "Only decisive action carried out with complete honesty and transparency will restore the respect and good will of the Irish people towards the Church to which we have consecrated our lives."

Monsignor Rossetti

The remaining addresses to the plenary assembly of the Gregorian symposium and the workshops did not contain major canonical material. With that in mind, and given the limitations of today's seminar, I will only summarize some of those presentations.

Although I mention it only in passing, one was perhaps the most emotionally profound presentation of the symposium, given in tandem by Mrs. Marie Collins, a victim of childhood sexual abuse inflicted by a priest in Ireland, and a therapist from England, Lady Sheila Hollins. These two women reminded the audience of the damage done when a victim is not believed and treated with respect.

Monsignor Stephen Rossetti, with a clinical background as former director of the St. Luke Institute in Maryland, drew attention to those who commit sexual offenses against young people in the church. As a framework, he identified six frequent mistakes we have made and suggested remedies.

The first mistake is not listening enough to victims and allowing ourselves instead to be manipulated by offenders. The solution is to listen first to those making allegations and allowing professionals to handle the investigations. The second mistake is underestimating the prevalence of child abuse, including among clergy. The remedy is to determine the truth about child sexual abuse in each country and develop and implement a comprehensive prevention program. The third mistake is believing that perpetrators can be cured and live risk-free, which can be countered by assuring that offenders undergo a proper treatment program that addresses their pathologies but also promotes for them a healthy, virtuous life. The fourth mistake is considering the sexual abuse of minors by priests an internal ecclesiastical matter and something that can be readily forgiven. We now understand that allegations must be reported to civil authorities, that offenders must be restricted from ministry and access to children and be subjected to an appropriate safety plan. The fifth mistake is an insufficient human formation of priests, including the area of sexuality. The remedy includes extensive formation in the seminary and afterward in healthy chaste psychosocial and psychosexual living, plus a psychosexual screening of seminary candidates. The sixth mistake is "missing the red flags." These include grooming behaviors, boundary violations or other indications that an adult may be at risk of abusing a child. The remedy is for church leaders to become educated about "red flags" and to intervene appropriately when they appear.

Reverend Nair

When Father Desmond Nair of South Africa spoke, I was surprised to learn that the experience in southern Africa almost paralleled ours in the United States chronologically. The Southern African Council of Priests expressed concern about child abuse at its general meeting in 1994. In response the Bishops' Conference of Southern Africa produced a "Protocol for Church Personnel in regard to the Sexual Abuse of Children" early in 1999. This document has been revised three times since and contains most of the same standards as our Charter. One exception is that letters of suitability are only "encouraged."

Father Nair reported that the Professional Conduct Committee of the bishops' conference has recommended a special program of formation for priests during the first five years after ordination, support for and supervision of newly ordained priests, psychological assessment of seminary candidates, and human development for seminarians, especially with regard to celibacy and chastity, leadership, responsibility, service, and accountability. The committee also continues to explore the possibility of a house of wellness for priests, a facility that would offer spiritual and psychological support.

Reverend Valle, SVD

The next presenter allows us to remain south of the Equator. Father Edenio Valle is a Divine Word missionary and psychotherapist from Brazil. In presenting "A Dialogue between Religion, Society and Culture," he laid out two objectives: to place child abuse in the church into a social and cultural context and to awaken the listeners to an awareness that this question goes beyond the frontiers of the church and religion and challenges it in an especially new way.

Radical shifts are occurring in Brazilian society due to rapid urbanization and a breakdown of the colonial ecclesiastical model. There is a growing trivialization of the sacred, an absence of sensitivity to misery, and an increase in violence. All of these factors are reflected in the increase of child abuse, including within the church.

Although the Catholic Church in Brazil has had a significant role in helping to strengthen civil laws protecting women and children, it has been slow to address the issue of child abuse in its midst. Most efforts have been in the form of imposing canonical penalties. In 2011 the Brazilian Episcopal National Assembly did issue directives for dealing with accusations of sexual abuse against minors. There have been surveys sponsored by the national Presbyteral Council to gage the satisfaction of priests, and there have been some sociological studies attempting to measure various types of sexual misconduct by priests and any underlying psychological pathologies.

Father Valle concluded his contribution to the symposium by offering some suggestions for Brazil, most of which are in place in our country. His last suggestion for Brazil is not in place in the United States, so far as I know, at least not quite as he described it. He recommended that the bishops' conference encourage the creation of a "*Study Centre on Human Sexuality* which, bearing in mind the Christian anthropological focus and Brazil's social and cultural specificities, may provide an advisory committee for Church intervention in cultural and politically controversial matters and for the training of clergy, of Consecrated life and of the Catholic lay community in general."

Bishop Patrón Wong

The screening and formation of seminarians and candidates for religious life was a frequent topic at the symposium. Bishop Jorge Carlos Patrón Wong of Mexico focused on that topic, bringing to bear his experience as a former seminary rector. He began by emphasizing the importance of permanently forming the *formators*, a new emphasis that the Organization of Latin American and Caribbean Seminaries (OSLAM) has called a "Copernican revolution." Said Patrón Wong: "Moving from an environment which is solely institutional to one which is a genuine family environment is essential in order to achieve real changes in the way seminarians live and think. Paternal, filial, fraternal relations, the common good, service to others, and placing all this before one's own personal interests or preferences, can only be experienced in a family atmosphere." In such an environment the psychological and spiritual restructuring of the person can be woven before the call of God's grace.

The seminary program is structured to allow the candidate to advance along a path that is gradual and internal, from being a man to a Christian to a true disciple and then a good shepherd. Conversion must occur to truth, goodness and love and involve the whole person. The common attributes of child abusers—narcissism, self-sufficiency, and self-fulfillment—must be confronted. The seminarian must develop an authentic affectivity toward people, a real connection with people's hearts and minds.

At the same time, there must be a comfort with solitude. In many ways a relationship with Mary serves to strengthen the candidate's inner life and his affectivity toward others, especially women. Ultimately a transcendent experience of God and a Christocentric life option are indispensable.

Archbishop Tagle

We move across the Pacific to the Philippines and an address from His Excellency, Luis Antonio Tagle, Archbishop of Manila, who spoke about clergy sexual misconduct from an Asian perspective. In his view the crisis involves theological, spiritual, anthropological, and pastoral dimensions.

So far in Asia, the known cases of sexual misconduct among the clergy mostly involve other adults. There are surely cases of child abuse, but the culture values honor and dignity so highly, especially within the family and community, that silence is maintained out of fear of shame. There are other outlooks that color the way this issue is understood. Sexuality tends to be seen in a more holistic and personalistic way. Touching is very common in the Philippines. Adults are accorded great authority and deference, with clergy perceived as almost superhuman.

It was of interest to me that Archbishop Tagle's call for a deeper understanding of celibacy would resonate with the ancient Asian religions. His other suggestions for a pastoral response to the crisis also came with an Asian twist. Compassion for the suffering is a cultural trait that should infuse pastoral care for victims and their families. With regard to working with communities affected by abuse, care must be taken to strive for real healing, not just the appearance of quickly restoring "harmony," so valued in Asian culture. Since dishonor affects an entire family, attention should be given to the family of clerics who have offended. The same holds for the entire presbyterate. To conclude, the speaker addressed, as did other symposium speakers, the need for better seminary formation and ongoing formation of the clergy.

Father Carola, SJ, Father Rotsaert, SJ, Doctor Tenace, Father Yáñez, SJ
A team of three Jesuits and one laywoman presented "Theological and Moral Reflections on Child Sexual Abuse in the Catholic Church." Their thesis was that the link between child abuse and celibacy is less significant than the link between child abuse and deterioration of the family environment. As the traditional understanding of marriage and human sexuality retains less hold on contemporary society, human relationships, and sex in particular, no longer reflect the life-giving love of God.

As part of an extensive analysis of King David's sin involving Bathsheba and Uriah, the speakers stressed the need to acknowledge the reality of sin, to educate people about the dignity of the human person and the integrity of human sexuality, and to recognize human authority as a sign of God's presence among his people.

Toward the end, the speakers pointed out that "a transparent legislation that allows [sic] to proceed quickly and effectively in these unfortunate situations is key." In reference to seminarians, they said, "…the candidates must be aware of the responsibility that they themselves have in their own training. One must create a climate of trust and responsibility to ensure that the trainee may expose his problems without too much difficulty before his educators, asking for their help." As a conclusion to their opening thesis, they noted, "He who can really open up to love, will live his sexuality as an expression of his *altruism*…. The more intense the love, the more effective the renunciation. He who truly loves does not care about renouncing that which opposes the object of his love."

Cardinal Marx
Cardinal Reinhard Marx, a successor to Josef Ratzinger as Archbishop of Munich and Freising, chose as his topic, "Church, abuse and pastoral leadership." He began by asking if the current challenge can be accepted as a spiritual opportunity, especially by bishops. He framed the answer as one of holiness, understood as Jesus understood it, "the unison between the interior and the exterior of people's lives." As the church reflects the Incarnation, it must interact with the

world in honesty and transparency, cooperating with society and the state, and thinking and acting globally.

Cardinal Marx carried the reality of the Incarnation into the realm of abuse cases, advising that the church's mystical and temporal dimensions must both be at work. These dimensions were reflected in the concentrated response of the Conference of German Bishops in 2010. Research was done and made available to the public, liturgical observances were held, and opportunities for collaboration with other groups were organized.

In the end, the abuse crisis is a call to spiritual renewal. "At its centre is not the survival of the Church or its outward significance and its political influence, but the question of whether it fulfills its mission of showing people the way to communion with the Triune God." Our attention to children and young people should be expansive, incorporating the promotion of strong families, education, and catechesis.

Toward the middle of his talk, and no doubt speaking from his actual experience as a diocesan bishop, Marx commented that the complex role of the bishop can be perceived as "structural overload." I can echo from my own experience, both as a bishop and a canonist, that balancing the various responsibilities of a diocesan bishop in the area of child abuse and protection is indeed structural overload. How does one person serve as the primary leader in the effort to protect young people in the local church, give credible witness to the public that the church is committed to making progress in this area, serve as father and brother to the clergy of the diocese, oversee the local canonical processes involved in investigating and adjudicating cases, implement any directives from the Holy See in this regard, and assure that victim/survivors *and* offenders are handled appropriately? Although current norms may provide some ways for mitigating this situation (e.g., delegation), I doubt that any truly workable solution is available. Yet, in my view, both to assure the safety of our young people and to heal the church's wound, the labor somehow needs to be divided.

Doctor Liebhardt, Reverend Zollner, SJ
During his address, Cardinal Marx referred to a collaborative project sponsored by the Archdiocese of Munich and Freising, the Pontifical Gregorian University, and Ulm University Hospital's Department for Child and Adolescent Psychiatry and Psychotherapy. A more thorough presentation of the project was given by Doctor Hubert Liebhardt from the Ulm University Hospital and Father Hans Zollner of the Gregorian University.

The Centre for Child Protection was established to provide e-learning in four languages (English, Spanish, Italian and German) to "partners" in eight countries initially. Eventually the training program will be open to other interested users, in the Catholic Church and beyond. The training will be provided primarily to parish leaders and will include segments on recognizing, understanding and preventing abuse. This program will be especially helpful in developing countries.

Virtus Team

Most of you know Virtus as a service of the National Catholic Risk Retention Group that provides various resources to assist organizations, especially the church, in creating safe environments for children and adolescents. Several representatives of Virtus addressed the Gregorian symposium on the issues of the internet and pornography, the abuse of vulnerable adults, and the cost of the abuse crisis.

The Internet should be viewed as a gift that holds the potential for better communication for the world and better evangelization for the church. However, it is more complex and more rapidly evolving than any technological advance that humankind has heretofore devised. Because it is available even to children, the role of parents as the first and primary educators of their own children requires attention. This is a challenge, since often children are more adept with the electronic technology than their parents. Specifically, with human sexuality, parents must be alert not to allow the Internet to become their children's first teachers, with the risk of malformed attitudes for life.

Acknowledging that all us in our ordinary lives are *vulnerable adults*, even by opening ourselves to the will of God, the church has a special responsibility toward those who are vulnerable because of physical, mental or emotional conditions or an illness that renders them unable to defend themselves from abuse or get help when they suffer abuse. Those who abuse vulnerable adults—sexually, physically, emotionally, financially—use many of the same grooming and isolating strategies as those who abuse minors. The presenters also referred to adults in a relationship with another adult where there is a presence of "unilateral power," such as student-teacher or spiritual director-directee.[3]

Is there anyone in this room who does not already appreciate the *cost* that the sexual abuse crisis has brought, the cost to victims and their families, the cost to those who continue to labor in the vineyard, the cost to treasuries, the cost to the church's stature as a moral teacher, the cost to people's faith and adherence to the church? Perhaps the Virtus presenters wanted to help attendees from countries where the issue has not yet surfaced significantly to understand how costly an inadequate response can be. They did end on a hopeful note, reminding the audience that with Christ as her Lord and the Holy Spirit as her guide and strength, the church has endured other severe tests.

---

3 It is important to remember that, for application of the "Essential Norms" and the "Charter for the Protection of Young People," "vulnerable adult" is defined narrowly in *Sacramentorum sanctitatis tutela,* art. 6 as "a person who habitually lacks the use of reason."

Conclusions

From what has already been said, conclusions from the Gregorian symposium are not difficult to draw.

1. The Congregation for the Doctrine of the Faith's circular letter has expanded the Catholic Church's insistence that attention to child sexual abuse within the church be taken seriously in every corner of the church. Pro-action is far superior to reaction.
2. Significant developments have already occurred in the developed world that can be shared with other churches; many of the developing countries have already taken steps; and in many underdeveloped countries, little has been accomplished.
3. Similarly, large numbers of cases have surfaced in many developed countries, some in the developing countries and relatively few in the underdeveloped countries. Misconduct with adults among clerics is more common in the latter, but that does not mean that the sexual exploitation of minors has not occurred. Cultural conditions may make reporting more unlikely.
4. While the focus is still clearly on priests and those preparing to become priests, the emphasis is more positive, that is, to build programs and structures designed to form healthy, holy, properly motivated priests and to support them as true servants of God's people.
5. It remains to be seen what impact the circular letter will have on the canonical life of the church. Will all episcopal conferences be required to develop guidelines and enforce them? Will particular law be enacted with the *recognitio* of the Holy See? If these developments occur, will the current universal law of the church be adjusted, as seems to have occurred because of developments in the major English-speaking countries?

The Gregorian symposium was a historic moment in the life of the church, a concrete response to a pressing pastoral need. A long time has passed since *The Boston Globe* exposed the difficulties in that part of the world. Even more time has passed since shocking news emerged from the bayous of Louisiana. The whole world came to know that the Catholic Church in the United States had an awful problem. Now the entire church recognizes that she must be prepared everywhere to respond well to those who come forward to tell painful stories and to keep safe the children who dwell in her house.

SEMINAR

LATIN PARISHES AND EASTERN CATHOLICS
Chorbishop John Faris

Inter-Ecclesial Norms on Ascription and Parish Life

State of the Question
The standard fare of the "Eastern topic" in CLSA convention programs generally treats ascription to a Church *sui iuris* and/or the administration of sacraments with a focus on inter-ecclesial[1] issues, that is, when the case involves a member of the Latin Church *sui iuris* and a member of one of the twenty-two Eastern Catholic Churches *sui iuris*. Such presentations are appropriate and, indeed, necessary for Latin Church ministers and canonists who are unfamiliar with the Eastern Catholic Churches[2] and the provisions of the *Codex Canonum Ecclesiarum Orientalium*[3] (henceforth "Eastern code" or *CCEO*) especially in the area of ecclesial ascription.

However, at some point, it becomes necessary to stand back and examine these norms critically to ascertain their canonical effects. This presentation will be a critical examination of the norms on ecclesial ascription and their effect on Eastern and Latin parishes. A noted and respected canonist and scholar recently characterized the norms on ecclesial ascription as "crucial to the survival of the Eastern communities in the diaspora."[4] Is this true? At best, are we expecting too

---

[1] Quite often such norms are called "inter-ritual" norms. However, in consideration of the reality that we are dealing with the relations between churches (see *CCEO* c. 27 with its definition of *Ecclesia sui iuris*), we shall use the term "inter-ecclesial."

[2] A significant number of Latin Catholics are unaware of the existence of the Eastern Catholic Churches. Even if there is an awareness of their existence, their "Catholicity" is in doubt ("Are you under the pope?"). One author notes that Eastern Catholics are not rarely referred to as "Orthodox Catholic faithful." See Marco Dino Brogi, "Obblighi dei Vescovi Latini verso i Fedeli di una Chiesa Orientale Cattolica Inseriti nella loro Diocesi," in *Cristiani Orientali e Pastori Latini*, ed. Pablo Gefaell (Milan: Giuffrè Editore, 2012) 5, n. 2.

[3] Codex Canonum Ecclesiarum Orientalium auctoritate Ioannis Pauli PP. II promulgatus (Vatican City: Libreria Editrice Vaticana, 1990).

[4] ". . .cercherò sempre limitarmi ad esporre solo le questioni che a mio avviso sono più cruciali per la sopravvivenza delle comunità orientali della diaspora." Péter Szabó, "L'Ascrizione dei Fedeli Orientali alle Chiese *sui iuris*. Letture dello *Ius Vigens* nella Diaspora," in *Cristiani Orientali e Pastori Latini*, ed. Pablo Gefaell (Milan: Giuffrè Editore, 2012) 154.

much from these norms and ignoring—possibly more effective—methods? At worst, are we ignoring their failure?

Inter-Ecclesial Norms

The current norms on ecclesial ascription are found in canons 111 and 112 of the *Codex Iuris Canonici*[5] (henceforth "Latin code" or *CIC*) and canons 29-38 of the Eastern code.

We can begin with the ecclesial ascription of non-baptized children under the age of fourteen. It is important to keep in mind that the Church *sui iuris* in which the baptism was celebrated does not determine the ascription status of the child. *CCEO* c. 683 (which has no counterpart in the *CIC*) states: "Baptism must be celebrated according the liturgical prescripts of the Church *sui iuris* in which in accord with the norm of law the person to be baptized is to be ascribed."[6] The ascription status of the parents (or parent, if only one is Catholic) determines the ascription status of the child and the Church *sui iuris* in which the child is to be baptized.

It is interesting that when a doubt arises regarding the ascription status of someone who approaches a parish—Latin or Eastern—for sacraments, the first question posed is "where were you baptized?" No matter the response, it does not result in a clarification of the doubt. The appropriate question (which admittedly might lead to a dead end) is: to what Church(es) do your parents belong?

Regarding the ascription of a child under the age of fourteen who is born of two Catholic parents the Latin code makes the following provision: [7]

- If the father is a member of the Latin Church and the mother is a member of an Eastern Catholic Church, the child is to be ascribed in the Latin Church. The determination of the rite of baptism follows.

- If the father is a member of an Eastern Catholic Church and the mother is a member of the Latin Church, the mutual agreement of the parents can allow for the child to be ascribed in the Latin Church.

---

5   *Codex Iuris Canonici auctoritate Ioannis Pauli PP. II promulgatus* (Vatican City: Libreria Editrice Vaticana, 1983).

6   "Baptismus celebrari debet secundum praescripta liturgica Ecclesiae sui iuris, cui ad normam iuris baptizandus ascribendus est."

7   *CIC* c. 111 §1: "Ecclesiae latinae per receptum baptismum adscribitur filius parentum, qui ad eam pertineant vel, si alteruter ad eam nonpertineat, ambo concordi voluntate optaverint ut proles in Ecclesia latina baptizaretur; quodsi concors voluntas desit, Ecclesiae rituali ad quam pater petinet adscribitur."

A careful reading of the canon does not provide for a child born of a Latin father and an Eastern Catholic mother to be ascribed in the Eastern Catholic Church of the mother.[8] This limitation will remain in place until 1 October 1991, when the canons of the Eastern acquired the force of law. Given that children baptized in 1990 are now beginning to enter into marriage, this fact is of canonical significance.

CCEO c. 29 §1 completes the provisions of on ecclesial ascription: A child under the age of fourteen is to be ascribed, and, therefore, to be baptized in the Church *sui iuris* of the Catholic father or the Catholic mother if the father is non-Catholic or if both parents agree.[9] The Eastern code also provides for other specific cases: a child under the age of fourteen born of an unwed mother is ascribed and is to be baptized in her Church *sui iuris*; a child under the age of fourteen born of unknown parents is ascribed and is to be baptized in the Church *sui iuris* of the legal guardian; an adopted child is to be treated canonically as a natural child; a child under the age of fourteen born of non-baptized parents is to be ascribed to and baptized in the Church *sui iuris* of the one who is responsible for his / her faith formation.[10]

It is interesting that when we critically examine the norms, our modern sensibilities are attentive to any inequalities between the ascription status of the father and mother; the provisions of the 1917 *Codex Iuris Canonici* gave preference to the status of the father.[11] However, predecessors of these canons were concerned more with *rite* than *gender*: Preference was given to the Latin rite, which was presumed as superior to any Eastern rite. This presumption found expression in the inter-ecclesial norms of the times. The pattern began in the fifteenth century with Nicholas V, who issued a prohibition against members of the Latin Church adopting the Greek rite.[12] In the eighteenth century, the premise of the superiority

---

8   See *CIC* c. 1: "Canones huius Codicis unam Ecclesiam latinam respiciunt."

9   "Filius, qui decimum quartum aetatis annum nondum explevit, per baptismum ascribitur Ecclesiae sui iuris, cui pater catholicus ascriptus est; si vero sola mater est catholica aut si ambo parentes concordi voluntate petunt, ascribitur Ecclesiae sui iuris, ad quam mater pertinet, salvo iure particulari a Sede Apostolica statuto."

10 *CCEO* c. 29 §2: "Si autem filius, qui decimum quartum aetatis annum nondum explevit, est: 1° a matre non nupta natus, ascribitur Ecclesiae sui iuris, ad quam mater pertinet; 2° ignotorum parentum, ascribitur Ecclesiae sui iuris, cui ascripti sunt ii, quorum curae legitime commissus est; si vero de patre et matre adoptantibus agitur, applicetur §1; 3° parentum non baptizatorum, ascribitur Ecclesiae sui iuris, ad quam pertinet ille, qui eius educationem in fide catholica suscepit."

11 17 *CIC* c. 756 §2: "Si alter parentum pertineat ad ritum latinum, alter ad orientalem, proles ritu patris baptizetur, nisi aliud iure speciali cautum sit." This canon has no counterpart in the pre-conciliar Eastern legislation since the section on canons was never promulgated.

12 *Pervenit ad aures*, 6 September 1448: *Collectio Lacensis*, 2:601c.

of the Latin rite was officially sanctioned by Benedict XIV[13] and found concrete and practical expression in the constitution *Etsi pastoralis* which provided the following norms regarding ascription of infants:

- Infants born of Greek parents were to be baptized in the Greek rite unless the parents, having received the consent of the Ordinary, wished to do otherwise.[14]
- Infants born of a Latin father and Greek mother were be baptized in the Latin rite.[15]
- A Greek father and Latin mother are free to have their offspring baptized in the Greek or the Latin rite with the consent of the Greek father.[16]

We can pause with bemusement at norms of earlier times, but let us critically examine a few aspects of the current provisions.

With regard to the ascription of a child under the age of fourteen, the child is to be ascribed by "default" in the Church *sui iuris* of the father, but the parents are given the option of agreeing to ascribe the child in the Church *sui iuris* of the mother. We all enjoy having options, but such a freedom will contribute to ambiguities regarding the ascription status of the Christian faithful. For example, a Melkite father and Latin mother took their infant child to be baptized in a Latin parish in a locale lacking a Melkite parish on 1 January 1991. Should this action be construed as an agreement for the child to be ascribed to the Latin Church ("if both parents are of the same mind in requesting it, to the Church of the mother") or, lacking an express indication of an agreement, is the child to be regarded as ascribed to the Melkite Church?

Given that there is no prescription (or "statute of limitations" in Western civil law parlance) in this matter,[17] let us consider another situation. Under the provi-

---

13 Benedict XIV, the great canonist Prospero Lambertini, at first sanctioned the superiority of the Latin rite over the Greek rite: ".quod sit ritus Sanctae Romanae Ecclesiae omnium Ecclesiarum Matris, et Magistrae, sic supra Grecum ritum prevalet" (Constitution *Etsi pastoralis*, 26 May 1742 §2, 13: Pietro Gasparri, *Codicis iuris canonici fontes cura emĩ Petri Card. Gasparri editi,* 9 vols. (Rome: Typis Polyglottis Vaticanis, 1923-1939) 1:739). He later extended this superiority of the Latin rite over all Eastern rites: "Cum Latinus Ritus is sit, quo utitur Sancta Romana Ecclesia, quae Mater est et Magistra aliarum Ecclesiarum, reliquis omnibus Ritibus praeferri debet." Encyclical letter *Allatae sunt*, 26 July 1755, n. 20: Gasparri 2:459.

14 "Infantes nati ex Patre, et Matre Graecis, ritu Graeco, nis aliter Parentes, accedente Ordinarii consensus, voluerint, baptizari debent." §2, 9.

15 "Nati vero ex Patre Latino, et Matre Graeca, latinis sunt caeremoniis baptizandi; proles enim sequi omino debet Patris Ritum, si sit Latinus." §2, 9.

16 "Si vero Pater sit Graecus, et Mater latina, liberum erit eidem Patri, ut Proles, vel ritu Graeco baptizetur, vel etiam ritu Latino, si Uxor Latina praevaluerit, idest si in gratiam Uxoris Latinae, consenserit Graecus Pater, ut latino ritu baptizetur." §2, 10.

17 Prescription is a means of resolving ambiguities involving rights and obligations

sions of the 1917 *Codex Iuris Canonici*[18] c. 756 §1[19] and *Cleri Sanctitati*[20] c. 6 §2,[21] Mary, the child of an Armenian Catholic father and Latin Catholic mother, was baptized in a Latin Catholic parish in a locale where there was no Armenian Catholic Church. Mary, though canonically ascribed to the Armenian Catholic Church, was reared in the Latin Catholic Church and rite. A few decades later, Mary married Sam, a baptized Protestant. They took their child to a local Latin parish for baptism. There is no discussion regarding ecclesial ascription and the baptism was administered in the Latin Church. Under the provisions of *CCEO* c. 29 §1, the child of Mary and Sam was ascribed to the Armenian Catholic Church, even though there has not been any connection with that Church for two generations.

CCEO c. 37[22] requires that the baptismal registers of both Eastern and Latin parishes contain information about the ascription status of a person who is baptized, transfers from one Church *sui iuris* to another or who is received into full communion with the Catholic Church. With great confidence, I would conjecture that this canonical provision is observed more in the breach than the observance. How many certificates of baptism refer to ascription status? Recall that we are emphasizing that it is not the rite of the baptism that is the determinant factor in ecclesial ascription.

The problem is more than poor record keeping. The ambiguity resulting from canonical provisions of the twentieth century legislation have resulted in untold numbers of Catholics presuming that they are members of one Church *sui iuris* when, in fact, they are members of another. They are unwittingly acting in contravention of canon law.

---

through the mere passage of time (cf. *CCEO* c. 1540 / *CIC* c. 197). It is grounded in the need of society for good order. In the case of ecclesial ascription, prescription could resolve ambiguities by providing that a person who in good faith (cf. *CCEO* c. 1541 / *CIC* c. 198) has participated in the Church *sui iuris* of his / her parents and grandparents is now canonically ascribed to that Church *sui iuris*.

18   *Codex Iuris Canonici Pii X Pontificis Maximi iussu digestus Benedicti Papae XV auctoritate* promulgatus (Rome: Typis Polyglottis Vaticanis, 1917).

19   Proles ritu parentum baptizari debet.

20   Pius XII, Motu proprio *Cleri Sanctitati*, de Ritibus Orientalibus, de personis pro Ecclesiis orientalibus, 2 June 1957: *AAS* 59 (1957) 433-603.

21   "Si baptismus a ritus diversi ministro vel ob gravem necessitatem cum sacerdos proprii ritus praesto esse non potuit, vel ob aliam iustam causam de licentia proprii Hierarchae, vel ob fraudem collatus fuit, ita baptizatus illi ritui adscriptus habeatur cuius caeremoniis baptizari debuit."

22   "Omnis ascriptio alicui Ecclesiae sui iuris vel transitus ad aliam Ecclesiam sui iuris in libro baptizatorum paroeciae, etiam, si casus fert, Ecclesiae latinae, ubi baptismus celebratus est, adnotetur; si vero fieri non potest, in alio documento in archivo paroeciali parochi proprii Ecclesiae sui iuris, cui ascriptio facta est, asservando."

Let us now look at the norms on the transfer from one Church *sui iuris* to another, treated in *CIC* c. 112 and *CCEO* cc. 32-33. We note that *CCEO* c. 31 prohibits the inducement of anyone to transfer to another Church *sui iuris*;[23] the prohibition is accompanied by a penal sanction in *CCEO* c. 1465 that extends also to Latin Catholic faithful.[24] This norm is clearly an attempt to protect ecclesial minorities in the midst of the Latin Church. However, I have never heard of the imposition of this sanction.

While transfers of laity from one Church *sui iuris* (to use modern nomenclature) to another were handled at the local level in the eighteenth century,[25] permissions for all such transfers are now exclusively in the competence of the Apostolic See.[26] This permission is presumed when the two eparchial/diocesan bishops are in agreement.[27] In the case of the transfer of spouses, it is now possible for a Latin rite spouse to transfer at any point during the marriage to the Church *sui iuris* of the other spouse and for an Eastern Catholic wife to transfer to the Church *sui iuris* of her husband.[28] Again, modern sensibilities are attentive to the imbalance between the husband and the wife,[29] but in the eighteenth century,[30] the "swing of the pendulum" was not between *husband* and *wife*, but

---

23 "Nemo quemvis christifidelem ad transitum ad aliam Ecclesiam sui iuris ullo modo inducere praesumat."

24 "Qui officium, ministerium vel aliud munus in Ecclesia exercens, cuicumque Ecclesiae sui iuris, etiam Ecclesiae latinae, ascriptus est, quemvis christifidelem contra can. 31 ad transitum ad aliam Ecclesiam sui iuris quomodocumque inducere praesumpsit, congrua poena puniatur."

25 See Benedict XIV, constitution *Etsi pastoralis*, 26 May 1742, §2, 14: Gasparri 1:739.

26 *CCEO* c. 32 §1: "Nemo potest sine consensu Sedis Apostolicae ad aliam Ecclesiam sui iuris valide transire." Cf. *CIC* c. 112 §1, 1°.

27 *CCEO* c. 32 §2: "Si vero agitur de christifideli eparchiae alicuius Ecclesiae sui iuris, qui transire petit ad aliam Ecclesiam sui iuris, quae in eodem territorio propriam eparchiam habet, hic consensus Sedis Apostolicae praesumitur, dummodo Episcopi eparchiales utriusque eparchiae ad transitum scripto consentiant." Cf. *CIC* c. 112 §1, 1°. A *correctio iuris* was issued in the form of a rescript indicating when the consent of the Apostolic See can be presumed. Secretariat of State, 26 November 1992: *AAS* 85 (1993) 81.

28 *CIC* c. 112 §1, 2°: "Post receptum baptismum, alii Ecclesiae ritualis sui iuris adscribuntur coniux qui, in matrimonio ineundo vel eo durante, ad Ecclesiam ritualem sui iuris alterius coniugis se transire declaraverit; matrimonio autem soluto, libere potest ad latinam Ecclesiam redire;" *CCEO* c. 33: "Integrum est mulieri ad Ecclesiam sui iuris viri transire in matrimonio celebrando vel eo durante; matrimonio autem soluto libere potest ad pristinam Ecclesiam sui iuris redire."

29 Preferential consideration was given to the ascription status of the husband because of the social contexts of the Church in the Middle East. See *Nuntia* 28 (1989) 25-26.

30 The preference for the Latin rite was found in the sixteenth century instruction of Pope Clement VIII: "Maritus Latinus uxoris Graecae ritum non sequatur. Latina uxor non sequatur ritum mariti Graeci. Graeca vero uxor sequatur ritum Mariniti Latini. Quod si id fieri non possit, quisque coniugum in suo ritu, catholico tamen, manere permitta-

between the *Latin* and *Eastern* rites. Regarding transfer from one rite to another, one baptized in the Latin rite could not transfer to the Greek rite.[31] It was possible for individuals or communities only to transfer from the Greek rite to the Latin rite, not from the Latin rite to the Greek rite.[32] A Latin spouse could not follow the rite of the Greek spouse.[33] A Greek husband could follow his Latin wife; a Greek wife could follow a Latin husband, but after his death, could not return to the Latin rite.[34]

One can conclude that equality between rites has been achieved in the provisions regarding transfer of persons from one Church *sui iuris* to another. However, the freedom accorded to persons to transfer leads to ambiguity.[35] One should again refer to the requirement of *CCEO* c. 37 that "Every ascription...or transfer...is to be recorded in the baptismal register where the marriage was celebrated." If is it not recorded, the presumption can be made that a transfer, with all the canonical effects, did not occur.

Canonical Effects of Ecclesial Ascription

We have examined how ecclesial ascription is determined in specific cases. We have also examined how a member of the Christian faithful can transfer from one Church *sui iuris* to another. Let us now examine the canonical effects of ecclesial ascription. The theological consequence of baptism is incorporation into the Church, the Body of Christ (*CCEO* c. 675 §1); the canonical effect is that one acquires *canonical personality*, the possessor of rights and obligations. It is the task of law to determine what rights and obligations are to be assigned to what persons and the first step in the process of determination is ecclesial ascription. A

---

tur." Pope Clement VIII, *Instructio Super Aliquibus Ritibus Graecorum*, 30 August 1595: *Bullarium Pontificium Sacrae Congregationis de Propaganda Fide*, 5 vols. and 2 App. (Rome: 1839-1841)1:1-4.

31 "Quem ritum semel in baptism sunt professi, sive Latinum, sive Graecum, in eo instituti, et educari debent, nec ad alium possunt transpire, si Latinum semel susceperint;" §2, 13.

32 "Adultis autem, si quidem sunt Ecclesiastici, in quocumque Ordine minori, vel etiam maiori constitui, Saeculares, vel Regulares, a Ritu Graeco ad Latinum sine express Sedis Apostolicae licentia transpire non liceat; si Laici, ut ad ritum latinum transire possint, Episcopus Diocesanus pro sua prudentia permittere valeat; non tamen Communitate Graecorum, sive Albanensium huius modi, sine Sedis Apostolicae licentia, sed solum privates personis, attenat uniuscuiusque necessitate." §2, 14.

33 "Maritus Latinus Uxoris Graecae ritum non sequatur." §8, 7: Gasparii 1:750. "Latina Uxor non sequatur ritum Mariti Graeci." §8, 8: Gasparri 1:750.

34 "Gaecus Maritus potest, si velit, ritum Uxoris Latinae sequi. Item Graeca Uxor potest, si velit, sequi ritum Mariti Latini, post cuius obitum, ad ritum Graecum redire nequeat." §8, 9: Gsasparri 1:750

35 The faithful usually simply participate in the life of a parish or Church *sui iuris* where they feel comfortable or transfer from one to another for a variety of reasons. No one adverts to canonical requirements or consequences.

person is never a Catholic "at large," but is ascribed to the Latin Church or one of the twenty-two Eastern Catholic Churches. Ecclesial ascription determines the code of canons the person is obliged to observe, i.e., the *Code of Canon Law* for Latin Catholics or the *Code of Canons of the Eastern Churches* for all Eastern Catholics. Such a determination is important in areas such as marriage law where the requirements for the canonical form of marriage differ significantly. Ecclesial ascription also determines the hierarchy to which one is subject. In the United States, there are eighteen Eastern Catholic jurisdictions in the United States,[36] all of which are co-territorial with Latin jurisdictions. Ascription status determines which of the nineteen possible jurisdictions (i.e., eighteen Eastern and one Latin) one belongs. The determination of a hierarchy also on the determination of one's pastor.

With regard to one's relationship to a Church *sui iuris* and observance of a *rite*, ecclesial ascription articulates a specific set of rights and obligations. One of the rights is to worship God according to the prescriptions of their own Church *sui iuris*,[37] a right that establishes and concomitant obligation on the part of bishops and pastors to provide the means for such worship.[38] With regard to *rite*, a member of the Christian faithful also has an obligation to foster the knowledge and appreciation of their own rite and are bound to observe it everywhere.[39] With regard to the Church *sui iuris*, the Christian faithful are to fulfill their obligations to the universal Church and the Church *sui iuris*.[40]

The exercise of these rights and obligations presupposes clarity and awareness of one's ascription status. To put it otherwise, the Christian faithful cannot observe a rite and support a Church *sui iuris* if they are mistaken or unaware of their ascription status.

Freedom to Observe Another Rite
Despite the rigorous details regarding ascription to a Church *sui iuris*, both codes are quite liberal in provisions for the observance of another rite on an occasion or for a prolonged period.

---

36   The Armenian, Syro-Malabar, Syro-Malankara and Syrian jurisdictions extend into Canada. *Annuario Pontificio* 2012

37   *CCEO* c. 17: "Ius est christifidelibus, ut cultum divinum persolvant secundum praescripta propriae Ecclesiae sui iuris utque propriam vitae spiritualis formam sequantur doctrinae quidem Ecclesiae consentaneam." Cf. *CIC* c. 214.

38   *CCEO* c. 674 §2: "The minister should celebrate the sacraments according to the liturgical prescripts of his own Church *sui iuris*, unless the law establishes otherwise or he himself has obtained a special faculty from the Apostolic See." Cf. *CIC* c. 846.

39   *CCEO* c. 40 §3: "Ceteri quoque christifideles proprii ritus cognitionem et aestimationem foveant eumque ubique observare tenentur, nisi iure aliquid excipitur."

40   *CCEO* c. 12 §2: "Magna cum diligentia obligationes impleant, quibus tenentur erga universam Ecclesiam et propriam Ecclesiam sui iuris."

Lay persons are free to participate actively in the liturgical celebrations of any Church *sui iuris* whatsoever.[41] "Active participation" means not only attendance but serving in various capacities such as lector or cantor.[42] There is no time restriction, but the canonical obligation to fulfill one's obligations to the proper Church *sui iuris* (*CCEO* c. 12 §2) should be kept in mind. Families with members belonging to different Churches *sui iuris* can accommodate themselves to the calendar of one Church *sui iuris*.[43] The provisions of *CCEO* c. 883 §1 are somewhat awkward: "As regards feast days and days of penance, the Christian faithful who are outside the territorial boundaries of their own Church *sui iuris* can adapt themselves fully to the norms in force where they are staying." One should not conclude that Eastern Catholic faithful residing in the United States are free to adapt themselves to the calendar of the Latin Church, because the local norms to which the canon refers are the Eastern Catholic jurisdictions in the region.

Norms and Values

Every law has as its object the promotion of a certain value; a law that does not pursue a value is a misguided effort.[44] So often we comment on a law by delineating its precedents and explaining the proper implementation of the norms without offering any reflection on the values the law intends to uphold.[45] We have a five-hundred year history of inter-ecclesial norms. What values are being upheld? It is appropriate that we articulate the values intended to be upheld by these norms. Have the underlying values always been the same? And, finally, have the norms been effective?

Norms regarding ecclesial ascription enacted from the sixteenth through the nineteenth century were enacted within the context of a presumed superiority of the Latin rite over all other rites, a presumption that was officially sanctioned by Pope Benedict XIV in the eighteenth century. The norms reflect this presumption

---

41   *CCEO* c. 403 § 1: "Firmo iure et obligatione proprium ritum ubique servandi laici ius habent actuose in celebrationibus liturgicis cuiuscumque Ecclesiae sui iuris participandi secundum praescripta librorum liturgicorum."

42   Cf. *CIC* c. 230 §3.

43   *CCEO* c. 883 §2: "In familiis, in quibus coniuges diversis Ecclesiis sui iuris ascripti sunt, circa dies festos et paenitentiae praescripta unius vel alterius Ecclesiae sui iuris observare licet."

44   Ladislaw Örsy, *Theology and Canon Law. New Horizons for Legislation and Interpretation* (Collegeville, MN: The Liturgical Press, 1992) 28.

45   "In practice, however, the habit of the post-Tridentine centuries still tends to prevail: critical questions about values are scarce, and the need for such an inquiry is by no means universally accepted. Many commentaries stay with the text of the law, without offering any reflection on the values the law intends to uphold. Yet, no vigorous, healthy, and well balanced development of the law and of its interpretation is possible without our canon lawyers gradually entering into the new horizon of the value oriented evaluation of the norms." Ibid., 28.

in a variety of ways: in the case of baptism, options were always provided for an infant to be baptized in the Latin rite; transfers from the Greek rite to the Latin rite were possible, but the opposite was prohibited. These norms were not intended to preserve the Eastern rites. The Eastern rites were considered as inferior and tolerated for the sake of the unity of jurisdictions. Norms were enacted primarily to prevent the contamination of Latin Catholics by an inferior rite. Despite legislation that prohibited inducement of Eastern Catholics to the Latin Church,[46] the overall effect of legislation in this area was an *increase* in the flow of faithful from these ecclesial minorities to the Latin Church. One must admit the value, i.e., the superiority of the Latin rite and the prevention of its contamination by Eastern rites, was effectively upheld by the norms of the time.

With Pope Leo XIII, the Eastern Churches were accorded rightful recognition.[47] Later in the century, the Second Vatican Council opened its decree on the Eastern Catholic Churches, *Orientalium Ecclesiarum*, with praise and esteem for the Eastern Churches.[48] Because of the economic, political, religious, and social upheavals in the lands of their origin, the Catholic Church now became concerned about the survival of the Eastern rites.[49] One finds in the decree phrases such as, "The Catholic Church wishes the traditions of each particular church or rite to remain whole and entire, and it likewise wishes to adapt its own way of life to the needs of different times and places" (*OE* 2) and "All members of the Eastern Churches should be firmly convinced that they can and ought always preserve their own legitimate liturgical rites and ways of life, and that changes are to be introduced only to forward their own organic development" (*OE* 6).

---

46 Benedict XIV, constitution *Demandatam* 26 December 1743: This constitution was addressed to the Melkite Greek Catholic patriarch. Pope Leo XIII, with *Orientalium dignitas Ecclesiarum* extended the prohibitions with respect to all Eastern Catholics with the apostolic letter *Orientalium dignitas Ecclesiarum*, De Disciplina Orientalium conservanda et tuenda, 30 November 1894: *Acta Sanctae Sedis* 27 (1894-1895) 257-264.

47 "The Churches of the East are worthy of the glory and reverence that they hold throughout the whole of Christendom in virtue of those extremely ancient, singular memorials that they have bequeathed to us. For it was in that part of the world that the first actions for the redemption of the human race began, in accord with the all-kind plan of God. They swiftly gave forth their yield: there flowered in first blush the glories of preaching the True Faith to the nations, of martyrdom, and of holiness. They gave us the first joys of the fruits of salvation. From them has come a wondrously grand and powerful flood of benefits upon the other peoples of the world, no matter how far-flung. When blessed Peter, the Prince of the Apostles, intended to cast down the manifold wickedness of error and vice, in accord with the will of Heaven, he brought the light of divine Truth, the Gospel of peace, freedom in Christ to the metropolis of the Gentiles." Leo XIII, apostolic letter *Orientalium dignitas Ecclesiarum*, De Disciplina Orientalium conservanda et tuenda, 30 November 1894: *Acta Sanctae Sedis* 27 (1894-1895) 257-264.

48 "The Catholic Church values highly the institutions of the Eastern Churches, their liturgical rites, ecclesiastical traditions and their order of Christian life." *OE* 2.

49 The situation has only deteriorated since the 1964 promulgation of *Orientalium Ecclesiarum*.

Emigration of Eastern Christians from their homelands has increased in the past fifty years and posed even greater challenges to the preservation of the Eastern Churches and rites. With foresight, the Second Vatican Council adverted to the issue:

> Provision must be made therefore everywhere in the world to protect and advance all these individual churches. For this purpose, each should organize its own parishes and hierarchy, where the spiritual good of the faithful requires it. (*OE* 4)

Eastern Catholic hierarchies multiplied. In 1962, in the United States, there was only the six jurisdictions of the Ukrainian and the Ruthenian metropolias. Today, there are eighteen jurisdictions.

Hierarchies have been established. The norms of ecclesial have been in place, with greater liberty accorded to the faithful in virtue of the post-conciliar codes. However, can we—should we—rely on the norms of ecclesial ascription to provide for the preservation of the Eastern Catholic Churches in the diaspora? Have we been relying on these norms to provide "canonical fences" that members of the Christian faithful cannot jump?

The numbers are somber and disturbing. (In considering these statistics, we are mindful of the phrase popularized by Mark Twain that there are "lies, damned lies, and statistics.")

Let us examine the demographics.[50]

- In 1972 the Ukrainian metropolia (archeparchy and two eparchies) reported the number of Christian faithful as 284,159. The number of Christian faithful for the archeparchy and three suffragan sees is reported in 2012 as 49,184.
- In 1972, the Ruthenian metropolia (archeparchy of Munhall [Pittsburgh] and two eparchies) reported the number of Christian faithful as 272,786. The number of Christian faithful for the archeparchy and three suffragan sees is now reported as 85,881.
- The Melkite eparchy reported a population of 55,000 in 1972. In 2012, the Melkite Eparchy of Newton reported a the number of Christian faithful as 25,000.
- The Maronite eparchy reported 152,000 faithful in 1972. Today, the two eparchies report a total population of 84,500.
- The largest Eastern Catholic community in the United States is that of the two Chaldean eparchies with a population of 164,000. The Eparchy of St. Thomas (in metropolitan Detroit) was founded as an exarchate in 1982 and elevated

---

[50] The source for the 1972 population is *Annuario Pontificio 1972*; for 2012 figures, the source is *Annuario Pontificio 2012*.

to an exarchate in 1986. The Eparchy of St. Peter (California) was established in 2002.
- The second largest jurisdiction, the Syro-Malabar Eparchy of St. Thomas, is one of the newest, established in 2001.

Conclusion

This brief presentation might be construed as a call for the abolition of norms on ecclesial ascription and for unfettered freedom of ritual worship, but this is not the case. It is not a cry that the emperor has no clothes, but a call that the emperor might not be properly dressed. The norms do provide for a certain good order, but we would be wrong to expect more from them. Reliance on them to preserve our communities simply does not bring the expected results. Like most parochial territorial boundaries today, the faithful are ignorant of or choose to ignore such strictures.

Families whose member speak only English or are of mixed ethnic backgrounds might feel uncomfortable in a parish that employs a foreign language for most of its liturgical worship. They will involve themselves in the parish life of a community where they feel more comfortable. In a society that places much on convenience, individuals and families may succumb to the temptation of attending Mass in a nearby Latin parish rather than travel to their own (at least canonically) Eastern Catholic parish.

Young men who, during the process of vocation discernment, discover that they are ascribed to an Eastern Catholic Church, might feel some attraction, but more often than not, consider to pursue their vocation in the Latin Church.

On the other hand, one finds Latin Catholics who are dissatisfied with the liturgical life of the Latin Church and attracted to the rituals of an Eastern Catholic Church and the sense of family and community that pervades some parishes. Again, the canons provide that they can worship according to another rite for as long as they desire, with no effect on their ascription status.

The preservation of the Eastern Catholic Churches is not open to debate; it is a mandate of the Second Vatican Council. From an ecumenical perspective, the flourishing of the Eastern Catholic Churches is critical in order to demonstrate to the Orthodox world that it is indeed possible to be *Eastern* and *Catholic*. Nevertheless, Eastern Catholic pastors must not depend on the norms of ecclesial ascription to retain the faithful. The borders are too porous and the flow is evidently in one direction. Other more effective means must be sought to maintain the integrity of the Eastern Catholic parish communities and thereby preserve and protect the Eastern rites.

SEMINAR

THE 21ST CENTURY CATHOLIC PARISH
Mark M. Gray

Introduction and Background

In 2009, the Emerging Models of Pastoral Leadership project, a Lilly Endowment Inc. funded collaboration of five Catholic national ministerial organizations, commissioned the Center for Applied Research in the Apostolate (CARA) at Georgetown University to conduct a series of three surveys in parishes nationwide. The first of these was a single informant survey sent to parishes to develop a portrait of parish life in the United States today. This was followed by surveys of parish leaders in a sub-sample of these parishes as well as in-pew surveys with their parishioners.

The parish survey was based on a partially stratified random sample of 5,549 U.S. parishes. The stratification of the first 3,500 parishes sampled was based on weighting by the arch/diocesan averages of the percentage of the Catholic population *and* the percentage of the number of Catholic parishes in the United States in each arch/diocese as reported in *The Official Catholic Directory* (*OCD*). This stratification ensured that parishes representing the full Catholic population were included rather than a sample dominated by areas where there are many small parishes with comparatively small Catholic populations. CARA also sampled an additional 2,049 parishes using simple random sampling. These parishes were selected to ensure that the survey included at least 800 responses. Following a series of reminders and a field period spanning from March 2010 to December 2010, a total of 846 parishes responded to the survey for a response rate of 15.3 percent. The margin of sampling error for the survey is ±3.3 percentage points.

The second survey for the project included responses from 532 parish leaders (e.g., parish staff, finance and pastoral council members, other parish leaders) in 246 of the parishes from the first survey (margin of sampling error of ±4.2 percentage points). This survey was in the field from May 2011 to April 2012. Parish leaders include all staff—ministry and non-ministry, paid or volunteer—in the parish as well as all parish finance council members, pastoral council members, and up to ten other individuals identified by the pastor or parish life coordinator (a deacon or lay person entrusted with the pastoral care of a parish under canon 517 §2) "who exhibit leadership in the parish community."

These parish leaders were drawn from a subset of parishes completing the first phase survey as well as in-pew surveys of parishioners for the overall project.

Additionally, a random sample of 930 parish leaders, identified by their pastors and parish life coordinators from the first phase, were also invited to respond. Another 100 pastors and parish life coordinators from the first survey were asked to distribute surveys to all of their parish finance council members. It is not possible to calculate a response rate as we cannot be certain how many finance council members were given the survey. As an estimate, it is likely that no more than 2,500 parish leaders in total were invited to take the survey. Note: due to the number of responding leaders it is only possible to report on differences between non-Hispanic white leaders (i.e., Anglos) and non-Anglos (all other respondents) as well as results for Hispanics/Latino(a)s specifically for parish leaders.

The third survey for the project, still in progress, currently includes 13,614 parishioners surveyed in-pew in a subset of parishes from the first phase. It is technically not possible to calculate a margin of error for this survey as these are not randomly selected Catholic Mass attenders nationally and are instead all Mass attending, participating adults in the pews at an Emerging Models study parish on a given Sunday. However, as a rule of thumb consistent with statistical inference using survey data we use a difference of 6 percentage points between sub-groups to establish an indication of real difference.

The Context
Parish life in the United States has been undergoing significant changes in the last decade. A number of evolving trends have combined to alter the ways in which parishes operate. Church leaders must generally try to balance a delicate equation: On one side, they must provide worship sites—each of which has its own seating capacity and number of Masses. These parishes must be staffed by a sufficient number of priests, deacons, and/or lay ecclesial ministers (LEMs). On the other side, church leaders must consider the demands on these parishes in terms of the local size of the Catholic population, its frequency of Mass attendance, and needs for sacraments. In the last decade, through a combination of closing and mergers, church leaders have reduced the number of Catholic parishes in the United States by 1,359 parishes (a decline of 7.1 percent). In 2000, the church had more than 19,000 parishes nationally and by decade's end it had fewer than 17,800, almost the same number it had in 1965.

These parish closures are concentrated in areas of the United States where waves of Catholic immigrants created parishes in the 19th and 20th centuries. These parishes were often erected in urban areas and met the needs of specific populations and languages. Now in the 21st century the distribution of the Catholic population is no longer closely aligned with these parishes. In the post-World War II era the Catholic population began to shift. Many Catholics moved to the suburbs out of the urban ethnic enclaves. They also moved away from the Rustbelt areas of the Northeast and the farming communities of the Midwest into the Sunbelt. New waves of Catholic immigration from Latin America have led to even more growth in the South from coast to coast.

The Catholic population has realigned itself in the course of a few generations. People move, parishes and schools do not. Many of the parish closures and mergers have been in inner cities of the Northeast and Midwest where Catholic population has waned. At the same time, it is also the case that several states in the South have seen a significant number of new parishes being created where population has grown.

There are also fewer priests available to serve in these parishes. Although the average number of priestly ordinations in the U.S. has been about 500 per year in the last 25 years, there are fewer men being ordained than what is needed to replace an aging clergy population. The number of diocesan priests in the United States declined by 11 percent in the last decade and many of these men are now retired or plan to retire in the next decade. Without an increase in the number of priestly ordinations these declines are expected to continue in the decades ahead.

The number of religious priests, religious brothers, and religious sisters is also declining. However, the number of permanent deacons is increasing. Together, the total number of clergy and vowed religious in the United States in 2010 was 117,080. By comparison this totaled 197,172 in 1980. This change represents a decline of 41 percent in the last three decades.

The analysis of the Emerging Models survey data reveals a number of findings that are linked to these changes in the number of parishes, clergy, and vowed religious, including an increasing number of lay ecclesial ministers (i.e., those lay persons in paid parish ministry for 20 or more hours per week), larger parish sizes, and an increasing number of Masses per parish.

Parishes must get bigger in the U.S. because the number of Catholics continues to grow and is expected to continue to do so in the future. Since the end of World War II, on average, 25 percent of the U.S. adult population has self-identified in national surveys as Catholic (±2 to 3 percentage points attributable to margin of sampling error). This spans many trusted sources from commercial polling by Gallup and others, news media polls, exit polls, and academic surveys such as the General Social Survey and the World Values Survey.

In the last 40 years, the Catholic population has grown by about 75 percent and numbers about 77.7 million in 2011. If the Catholic population grew at the same rate in the next 40 years, it would be 136 million in 2050 and represent about 31 percent of the projected U.S. population at that time. This, however, is an unlikely scenario as overall population growth has slowed in the United States and is expected to slow more as the Baby Boom, and the "echoes" from it, fade.

CARA estimates that the Catholic population in 2050 will be between 95.4 million and 128 million depending on patterns of immigration, fertility, and Catholic retention and conversion rates. CARA's mid-range prediction is 109.8 million.

Although Mass attendance has declined in the long-term since the 1950s, there has been no recent decline or increase in attendance in the last decade in more than 20 CARA national surveys (averaging about 23 percent "weekly attenders" and 32 percent of self-identified Catholics attending in any given week). As Mass attendance remains steady and the Catholic population grows, this suggests increasing demands on parishes as the real number of Catholics attending and needing sacraments increases.

Types of Parishes

In addition to the results for all parishes, CARA prominently presents results for four other sub-groups of U.S. parishes. These sub-groups include multicultural parishes, parishes that are involved in multiple parish ministry, parishes that have recently undergone consolidation, and PLC parishes (where the pastoral care of the parish has been entrusted to a parish life coordinator who is a deacon or lay person under Canon 517 §2). Additionally, where statistically significant differences exist, CARA reports on differences by region and parish size as measured by the number of registered households.

Distribution of Responding Parishes:

	Number	Percentage
All parishes	846	100%
Multicultural parishes	323	38
PLC parishes	40	5
Consolidated parishes	59	7
Multi-parish ministry	230	27

Multicultural Parishes

Multicultural parishes are defined here as meeting at least one of three criteria: 1) regularly celebrating Mass in a language other than English (or Latin); 2) the percentage of parishioners who are non-Hispanic white is less than 40 percent; and/or 3) the diversity index is 33 percent or higher (the diversity index measures the probability that two randomly selected parishioners would be of a different race or ethnicity). In many cases the parishes identified as multicultural met more than one of these criteria.

PLC Parishes

Parishes were asked to indicate how their parish is administered and one of the options was that the pastoral care of the parish is entrusted to a parish life coordinator (parish life director, pastoral coordinator, etc.) appointed by the bishop or his delegate according to Canon 517.2. Respondents who indicated this are defined as PLC parishes.

Consolidated Parishes

Parishes recently experiencing consolidation indicated that one or more of the following had happened since January 1, 2005: 1) the parish was created (erected) as the result of a merger with at least one other parish; or 2) parish membership or territory was affected by the closing or suppression of a parish.

Multi-parish Ministry

Parishes experiencing multi-parish ministry indicated that the parish is clustered, linked, yoked, twinned, paired, or are sister parishes with at least one other parish.

Parish Life and Structure

The average seating capacity of U.S. parishes is 537 (median of 471). A third of U.S. parishes (32 percent) have a seating capacity of 630 or more. Less than one in five (19 percent) has a seating capacity under 270 seats. Among the parish sub-groups, PLC parishes are much more likely than others to have a small seating capacity (47 percent have fewer than 270 seats). Multicultural parishes have, on average, the largest seating capacities, with 40 percent of these parishes seating 630 or more individuals. Comparing to CARA's 2000 National Parish Inventory (NPI), the number of parishes with seating capacities of less than 270 has declined from 25 percent in 2000 to 19 percent in 2010. The number of parishes with 630 or more seats has grown to 32 percent of all parishes—up from 25 percent in 2000. This change in seating capacity has not occurred because parishes have added more seats. Instead, it is a function of parish closures being more common among the smallest parishes.

Church Seating Capacity (Main Parish Church Only):

	All Parishes	Multi-cultural Parishes	PLC Parishes	Consolidated Parishes	Multi-parish Ministry
269 or fewer	19%	17%	47%	21%	33%
270 to 419	25	20	37	18	30
420 to 629	24	23	13	28	23
630 or more	32	40	3	33	14
Average	537	585	296	544	393
Median	471	513	275	500	350

The average number of registered households in U.S. parishes is 1,168 (median of 761). A third of parishes (33 percent) have more than 1,200 registered households. Among the parish sub-groups, multicultural parishes and consolidated parishes are most likely to report larger numbers of registered households. PLC parishes and those using multi-parish ministry are much more likely to indicate that they have fewer than 550 registered households. The average number of registered households increased from 855 in 2000 to 1,168 in 2010. The percentage of parishes with 200 or fewer households dropped from 24 percent in 2000 to 15 percent in 2010. Parishes with more than 1,200 registered households now make up a third of all U.S. parishes. These changes again are related to the disproportionate numbers of small parishes closing and/or merging in the last decade.

Number of Registered Families/Households:

	All Parishes	Multi-cultural Parishes	PLC Parishes	Consolidated Parishes	Multi-parish Ministry
200 or fewer	15%	9%	51%	13%	32%
201 to 549	24	21	41	24	34
550 to 1,200	28	31	0	27	21
1,201 or more	33	39	8	36	13
Average	1,168	1,445	382	1,236	566
Median	761	983	200	850	325

On average, U.S. parishes have 1,100 Mass attenders at all Saturday Vigil and Sunday Masses on a typical Sunday in October. The median attendance as a percentage of all registered parishioners is 38 percent and the median capacity used (seating capacity multiplied times the number of Masses) is 47 percent.

Total number of persons (adults and children) attending Sunday/Saturday Vigil Masses on a typical weekend in October:

	All Parishes	Multi-cultural Parishes	PLC Parishes	Consolidated Parishes	Multi-parish Ministry
344 or fewer	25%	18%	73%	30%	48%
345 to 749	25	19	16	16	30

750 to 1,399	24	26	3	32	15
1,400 or more	26	37	8	22	7
Average	**1,110**	**1,482**	**352**	**972**	**499**
Median	**750**	**1,000**	**190**	**793**	**350**
Median attenders as a % of registered	38%	40%	53%	38%	44%
Median attenders as a % of capacity*	47%	47%	47%	42%	50%

*Capacity is seating capacity of the main church multiplied by the number of Sunday/Saturday Vigil Masses

In 2000, the average number of Mass attenders per parish was 966. The 2010 average of 1,110 is 15 percent larger. Whether measured by surveys or *OCD* data, the U.S. Catholic population is estimated to have grown by 9 percent during this period. With Mass attendance growing slightly more quickly than the population overall this is an indication of a slight uptick in Mass attendance in the last decade.

Total number of Sunday/Saturday Vigil Masses each week:

	All Parishes	Multi-cultural Parishes	PLC Parishes	Consolidated Parishes	Multi-parish Ministry
One	10%	6%	41%	12%	22%
Two	13	9	36	9	24
Three	26	17	10	24	27
Four	23	23	0	24	16
Five	12	14	3	17	4
Six	9	16	5	5	5
Seven or more	7	15	0	9	2
Average	**3.8**	**4.5**	**2.3**	**4.1**	**2.8**
Median	**4.0**	**4.0**	**2.0**	**4.0**	**3.0**

On average, parishes celebrate about four Sunday/Saturday Vigil Masses per week (an average of 3.8 and a median of 4.0). Only one in ten parishes has a single weekend Mass and 16 percent of parishes have six or more Sunday/Saturday Vigil Masses.

Multicultural parishes are more likely than other sub-groups of parishes to celebrate five or more weekend Masses per parish. This is in part due to celebrations of Mass in multiple languages. PLC parishes are much more likely than other parishes to celebrate only one weekend Mass. This is in part due to the limited availability of priests at these parishes. The average number of weekend Masses per parish has increased from 3.5 in 2000 to 3.8 in 2010. There are fewer parishes indicating they celebrate only one or two of these (-6 percentage points) and more reporting that there are five or more of these each weekend (+4 percentage points).

As parishes have been closed and merged in the last decade, while the Catholic population has grown and Mass attendance remained stable, parishes have responded by adding more Masses.

About three in ten parishes (29 percent) indicate that they celebrate at least one Mass a month in a language other than English. This is equivalent to more than 5,000 parishes. Four percent of all parishes celebrate Masses in three or more different languages (including English) at least once a month. In 2000, 22 percent of parishes indicated that they regularly celebrated Mass in a language other than English. Even with fewer parishes in 2010 than 2000 there is still a significant increase in the number of parishes (approximately 1,000 more) regularly celebrating at least one Mass in a language other than English. Most of the Masses celebrated in a language other than English in the United States are celebrated in Spanish (81 percent). Other languages used include Portuguese (6 percent), Latin (4 percent), Vietnamese (2 percent), sign language (1 percent), Italian (1 percent), and Polish (1 percent). In 2000, 76 percent of parishes regularly celebrating Mass in a language other than English reported that these were in Spanish. Six percent at that time reported Polish language Masses and 3 percent Italian.

In a typical parish in 2009, there was one sacrament or rite celebrated for every 18 members. The most frequent celebrations are related to entry into the faith, with 67 of these celebrated in the average parish each year (including infant, child, and adult baptisms, and receptions into full communion). These are followed in frequency by first communions, of which a typical parish celebrated 58 in 2009. On average, there are 44 confirmations, 14 weddings, and 29 funerals celebrated in the typical parish.

Indicate the total number of sacraments or rites celebrated in the parish in each category during 2009:

Average numbers celebrated per parish, by parish type

	All Parishes	Multi-cultural Parishes	PLC Parishes	Consolidated Parishes	Multi-parish Ministry
Baptisms up to age 7	56.6	95.1	24.8	42.1	24.7
Baptisms age 7+	6.0	10.4	2.6	5.1	2.8
Receptions into full communion	4.3	5.7	2.1	3.5	1.9
First Communions	57.6	82.5	26.6	47.2	23.3
Confirmations	43.6	54.4	18.0	36.8	20.2
Marriages between Catholics	8.9	12.9	3.7	8.3	4.0
Inter-church marriages	3.5	3.9	1.1	5.1	2.1
Inter-faith marriages	1.1	1.4	0.5	1.5	0.4
Funerals	29.0	34.2	8.8	42.4	17.7
All celebrations	**207.9**	**294.9**	**84.0**	**189.4**	**95.2**
Registered parishioners per celebration	17.7	16.2	19.7	17.7	17.5

Among sub-groups of parishes, multicultural parishes report the largest numbers of sacraments celebrated. PLC and multi-parish ministry parishes indicate lower levels of activity. These differences remain even after controlling for the number of parishioners in the parish. In multicultural parishes there are 16.2 parishioners for every sacrament or other celebration. By comparison there are 19.7 for each of these in PLC parishes.

On average, 78 percent of parishioners in U.S. parishes are non-Hispanic white and 13 percent are Hispanic or Latino(a). Four percent are Black, African American, or African, 3 percent Asian, Native Hawaiian, or other Pacific

Islander, and 1 percent are American Indian or Alaskan Native. In CARA's most recent national survey of the adult Catholic population 60 percent of self-identified Catholics are estimated to be non-Hispanic white and 33 percent Hispanic or Latino(a). The disparities between the findings from the national survey for these two groups and what respondents perceive may be related to several factors. These may include differences in frequency of Mass attendance, concentrations of specific racial and ethnic groups in parishes, and differences among these groups in the likelihood of registering with the parish.

Estimate the percentage of registered parishioners in each category (should sum to 100%):

Average percentages within responding parishes

	All Parishes	Multicultural Parishes	PLC Parishes	Consolidated Parishes	Multi-parish Ministry
White	78%	51%	74%	82%	87%
Hispanic or Latino(a)	13	30	18	11	7
Black, African American, or African	4	9	3	5	3
Asian, Native Hawaiian, or other Pacific Islander	3	7	1	1	1
American Indian or Alaska Native	1	1	2	0	1
Other	1	2	2	1	1

Of *all* registered parishioners reported by parishes, 74 percent were estimated to be white, 16 percent Hispanic or Latino(a), 5 percent Asian, Native Hawaiian, or Pacific Islander, 3 percent Black, African American, or African, 1 percent some other race or ethnicity, and less than 1 percent American Indian or Alaska Native. The racial and ethnic composition of registered parishioners in parishes regularly celebrating Mass in languages other than English is very similar to the race and ethnicity percentages found in CARA's national surveys.

Race and Ethnicity of Parishioners: Averages

	Only English Masses	Multi-lingual Masses
White	88.2%	55.7%
Hispanic or Latino(a)	3.7	34.4
Black, African American, or African	4.3	3.5
Asian, Native Hawaiian, or Other Pacific Islander	2.4	5.2
American Indian or Alaska Native	0.9	0.3
Other	0.5	1.4

Parishes that only celebrate Mass in English are significantly less racially and ethnically diverse than other parishes. On average, 88 percent of parishioners in these parishes are non-Hispanic white and no other average for any other race or ethnicity group attains 5 percent.

In the average American parish, the total operating revenue of about $695,000 exceeds expenses of $626,500. The average surplus is 4.3 percent of revenue. However, 30 percent of parishes indicate that their expenses exceed their revenue. Of those parishes reporting a deficit, the average size for the shortfall is 15.8 percent of revenue. Total weekly offertory is about $9,200 or $9.57 per registered household. Offertory has grown in the last five years, on average, by more than 14 percent.

Parish Budget and Offertory Collections
Average per parish (excluding schools), by parish type

	All Parishes	Multi-cultural Parishes	PLC Parishes	Consolidated Parishes	Multi-parish Ministry
Annual operating revenue	$695,291	$756,605	$248,555	$578,943	$346,317
Annual operating expenses	$626,589	$723,442	$272,008	$551,871	$313,422
Deficit/surplus as a % of revenue	+4.3%	-1.2%	-6.8%	+0.4%	+2.8%
Total weekly offertory collection	$9,191	$10,070	$3,216	$7,617	$4,258
Weekly offertory per registered household	$9.57	$8.72	$10.61	$9.96	$9.58
Change in avg. total weeky offertory in last 5 years	+14.5%	+16.1%	+11.0%	+0.9%	+9.3%

PLC parishes are more likely than others to report a deficit. The average revenue in PLC parishes is smaller than average expenses. On average, these parishes report a deficit that is 6.8 percent of revenue. At the same time, PLC parishes collect more in offertory per registered household than all other types of parishes. Smaller parishes are more likely than larger parishes to indicate a budget deficit. The largest parishes, those with more than 1,200 registered households, report the largest average budget surpluses.

Parish Lay Ecclesial Ministers

In 1992, Msgr. Philip J. Murnion conducted a survey of 1,163 parishes in 43 randomly selected dioceses. The pastor (or a person designated by the pastor to respond) listed parish staff, their positions, salaries, hours per week, and other demographic information. From these data Murnion estimated that there were 21,569 lay ecclesial ministers (LEMs) in the United States. These were defined as paid, non-ordained parish ministry staff working at least 20 hours per week. These LEMs were 42 percent vowed religious and 58 percent other lay persons. Overall 85 percent were female and 15 percent male. In 1997, Murnion and David DeLambo replicated the 1992 study with a survey of 949 parishes in the same 43 dioceses. This study estimated that the number of LEMs had grown to 29,146. These LEMs were 29 percent vowed religious and 71 percent other lay persons. Overall 82 percent were female and 18 percent male. In 2005, David DeLambo replicated the 1992 and 1997 studies with a survey of 929 parishes in the same

43 dioceses. This study estimated that there were 30,632 LEMs in ministry in the United States. These LEMs were 16 percent vowed religious and 84 percent other lay persons. Overall 80 percent were female and 20 percent male.

The data used in the Emerging Models study are from a national random sample survey conducted in all U.S. territorial dioceses rather than a selection of 43. However, the study also utilized a grid design that was very similar to that used by Murnion and DeLambo to request information from respondents about the parish staff. In addition to using the data provided by respondents, CARA and NACPA researchers also verified staff lists using secondary sources—primarily parish websites and online parish bulletins. It immediately became evident that many parishes did not always include their full staff as instructed. In some cases pastors listed themselves and perhaps a deacon and left off lay staff members.

There are many possible reasons for this omission. Some may have not had the information about their lay staff members, others simply may have not taken the time to completely fill out this section, others expressed concerns about confidentiality and providing this information for their staff. Regardless, relying on survey data alone would have provided an undercount of LEMs.

This study estimates that the number of LEMs has grown to 37,929. They are 14 percent vowed religious and 86 percent other lay persons. Overall 80 percent are female and 20 percent male. The trend over time since 1992 indicates that, on average, about 790 new LEMs are added to U.S. parish ministry staffs per year in the last two decades.

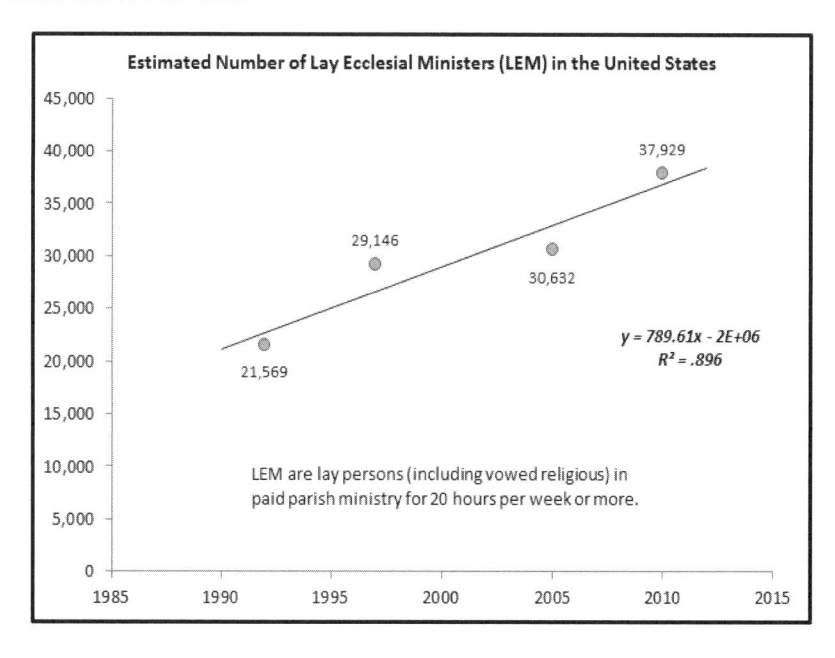

Estimated Number of Lay Ecclesial Ministers (LEM) in the United States

Data points: 21,569; 29,146; 30,632; 37,929

$y = 789.61x - 2E+06$
$R^2 = .896$

LEM are lay persons (including vowed religious) in paid parish ministry for 20 hours per week or more.

Between 1992 and 1997 (i.e., five years), Murnion and DeLambo estimated an increase of LEMs by 35 percent. However, between 1997 and 2005 (eight years), Delambo estimated that the number of these ministry professionals increased by only 5 percent. The current study estimates that LEMS have grown by 24 percent in the last five years. It is possible that the DeLambo estimate from 2005 slightly underestimates the number of LEMs. It is likely that respondents to the 2005 survey behaved similarly to those in the current study and left off some of their LEM staff members. This may have become more likely in recent years as pastors, LEMs, and Americans in general have become more aware and concerned about the collection of personal information.

Overall, we expect that the growth in LEMs has slowed a bit from the 5-year pace between 1992 and 1997 but that there is still continued substantial growth as the number of priests and vowed religious in the U.S. available for ministry becomes smaller each year. Given the expected continued decline in numbers of priests and vowed religious in the U.S. we expect LEMs, as well as deacons, to become more numerous on parish staffs in the future.

In the current study we estimate a total staff size in U.S. parishes of 168,448. This total includes ministry staff and volunteers as well as non-ministry staff and volunteers (including parish bookkeepers, groundskeepers, cooks, etc.). This results in an estimated staff size of 9.5 members per parish.

Excluding those in non-ministry positions, the total number of paid and volunteer ministers in parishes (including pastors and deacons) in 2010 is estimated to be 95,951 or 5.4 ministry staff members per parish. Restricting this further to lay persons only (including vowed religious)—volunteer and paid—the total number of parish ministers in the U.S. is 50,298 (2.8 per parish). Restricting this further to those paid and in ministry at least 20 hours per week results in the 37,929 total of LEMs (2.1 per parish), the number that is most comparable to the Murnion and DeLambo studies.

Sixteen percent of LEMs work 20 hours a week, on average, and no more. One in four (26 percent) work more than 20 hours but less than 40 hours per week. Forty-nine percent work forty hours on average per week. One in ten (9 percent) work more than 40 hours per week. Eighty-eight percent of LEMS (unchanged from DeLambo's 2005 estimates) are non-Hispanic white. Nine percent are Hispanic or Latino(a). Less than 2 percent are black, African American or African (1.6 percent). A similar percentage is Asian or Pacific Islander (1.7 percent). Less than 1 percent is Native American or Native Alaskan (0.2 percent). Seven percent of LEMs are under the age of 30. Eleven percent are in their 30s and 22 percent in their 40s. Thus, four in ten LEMs are estimated to be under the age of 50. Three in ten are between the ages of 50 and 59 and 22 percent are in their 60s. Seven percent are age 70 or older.

Characteristics of All Parish Leaders (i.e., staff, volunteers, council members)

The average age of parish leaders is 59. A majority, 54 percent, are members of the Vatican II Generation (those born 1943 to 1960). One in five is of the Pre-Vatican II Generation (those born before 1943). Nearly one in four is of the Post-Vatican II Generation (those born 1961 to 1981) and only 3 percent are Millennials (born 1982 or later). The average age when parish leaders say they first felt the call to ministry in any setting (e.g., parish, school, hospital) is 29.

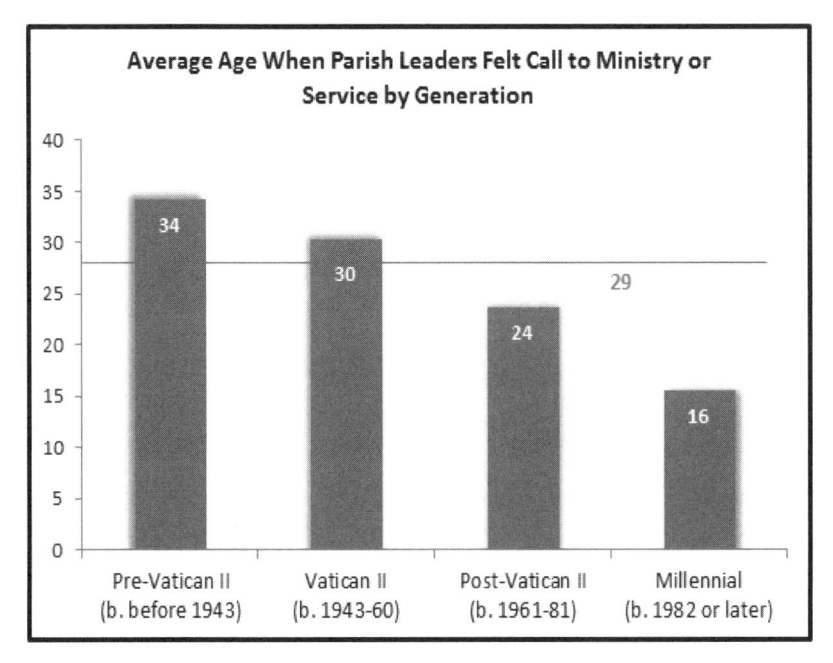

Average Age When Parish Leaders Felt Call to Ministry or Service by Generation

Pre-Vatican II (b. before 1943)	34
Vatican II (b. 1943-60)	30
Post-Vatican II (b. 1961-81)	24
Millennial (b. 1982 or later)	16

Current parish leaders of the Millennial Generation have answered a call to ministry a bit *before* the norm of previous generations. Those in ministry now are "early adopters." If the past repeats itself we can expect many Millennials to be called to ministry in this decade.

Nearly nine in ten parish leaders self-identify their race and ethnicity as Non-Hispanic white. Six percent self-identify as Hispanic/Latino(a), 2 percent as Asian or Pacific Islander, 2 percent as Black, African American, African, or Afro-Caribbean, and 1 percent as Native American. This distribution is strongly related to the age of parish leaders and the racial and ethnic composition of the Catholic population within these generations. In parishes identified by the project as multicultural (i.e., those with more racial and ethnic diversity among parishioners) there are greater numbers of non-Anglo parish leaders.

About one in 20 parish leaders were born outside of the United States. One in ten reports their mother was born in another country and a similar number report their father was. Thirty-eight percent have at least once grandparent who immigrated to the United States.

Nearly all parish leaders—98 percent—say they use English in their ministry. One in ten also uses Spanish. One percent indicates use of Latin. Two percent report some other language such as French, Creole, Italian, Tagalog, Polish, Czech, German, or Portuguese.

Eighty-five percent of responding parish leaders are lay persons (excluding men and women religious in ministry). Fifty-seven percent overall are female (including lay women and women religious).

Leaders are very highly educated. Nine in ten have attended college or university at some point in their life and more than a third have graduate degrees (35 percent) and two-thirds have an undergraduate degree (67 percent). This high level of education may be part of why 97 percent of leaders agree "somewhat" or "very much" in the survey that they feel adequately prepared now for ministry and three in four said, similarly, that that they were adequately prepared for their ministry at the time they began it.

Leaders are most likely to say they feel "very much" prepared for the following aspects of parish life: communicating (56 percent), facilitating events and meetings (51 percent), administration and planning (50 percent), collaborating (48 percent), and providing ministry to others (45 percent). Leaders are *least* likely to indicate they are "very much" prepared for managing conflict (24 percent), working in a multicultural environment (19 percent), and counseling (18 percent).

Fifty-one percent say they earn a salary or wage for their ministry or service to their parish. Of those that do, the median annualized earnings for this are $31,000. Respondents with higher education degrees in ministry, religion, or theology earn more, on average, than those without these. Eighty-four percent of those who are paid say there are "somewhat" or "very much" satisfied with what they earn.

Of those who are paid for their ministry or service, nearly one in five have other employment outside of their parish as well. Among those volunteering for their parish, half have paid employment elsewhere. Parish leaders provide, on average, 23.2 hours of ministry or service to their parish weekly. Lay ecclesial ministers provide an average of 40.6 hours. Sixteen percent of parish leaders provide ministry and service to at least one other parish as well.

Most feel secure in their parish role. Nine in ten agree "somewhat" or "very much" that they have sufficient job security in their ministry. Most also indicate they have access to what they need. Ninety-three percent agree at least "somewhat" that their parish provides them with the resources needed for their ministry. However, Hispanic/Latino(a) parish leaders are among the least likely to agree with this statement (76 percent). Anecdotally, this may be related to needs for bilingual and Spanish-language resources.

Answering the Call to Ministry

Most leaders, 76 percent, indicate they began their ministry or service to the church in the same year they felt the call to do so. Others indicate more of a lag time—most often for acquiring formation or accreditation, as well as placement. Overall, the average time between when one feels the call to ministry and begins ministering is 1.2 years.

Seven in ten parish leaders were members of the parish they began ministry in. Lay ecclesial ministers are less likely to report this (52 percent). Two-thirds of leaders were recruited initially as volunteers. However, those who are *currently* paid for their ministry or service are less likely to report this (49 percent). Younger parish leaders are less likely to indicate being recruited as volunteers. This may reflect their coming of age during a period in which paid ministry is more of a norm whereas previous generations may have begun ministry in a time where volunteering was more prevalent.

Respondents were most likely to say the following first led them to enter ministry:

- To be of service to the church (75 percent)
- As a response to God's call (56 percent)
- A desire to be more active in parish life (55 percent)
- To enhance their spiritual life (51 percent)

Lay ecclesial ministers were especially likely to say they did so in response to God's call (73 percent). Those *not* involved in any pastoral ministry were especially likely to emphasize they entered ministry at the invitation of their pastor or the parish life coordinator (50 percent).

A majority of leaders indicate they entered ministry after being encouraged by a priest (53 percent). Others noted encouragement from fellow parishioners (34 percent), friends (29 percent), and spouses (27 percent). Millennials are less likely than others to note encouragement from a priest (39 percent) and were more likely to note receiving this from friends (54 percent) or a teacher or professor (46 percent).

One in four parish leaders say they were inspired to enter ministry by a specific movement or program within the church. This was most often reported by men (31 percent) and Millennials (33 percent). Among the movements and programs most often cited by respondents are RCIA, Cursillo, Knights of Columbus, RENEW, and Teens Encounter Christ.

Three in four leaders (75 percent) agree "very much" that their ministry or service to their parish is a calling or vocation rather than just a job. Lay ecclesial ministers were especially likely to respond as such (89 percent).

Evaluations of Parish and Ministry
Half of all parish leaders (50 percent) evaluate their overall satisfaction with their parish as "excellent." Another 41 percent say this is "good." Non-Anglo parish leaders were more likely to evaluate their parish overall as "good" rather than "excellent' (48 percent compared to 36 percent) and more in this group provided "fair" (13 percent) and "poor" evaluations (4 percent). Just three in ten leaders (31 percent) in the smallest parishes, those with 200 or fewer registered households, evaluate their parish overall as "excellent."

Leaders are most likely to evaluate their parishes as "good" or "excellent" for the following aspects: celebration of the sacraments, Masses and liturgies, efforts to educate parishioners in the faith, and promoting important church teachings and causes.

What Parishes Do Best
Percentage of parish leaders responding
that their parish does "good" or "excellent"

Celebration of the Sacraments	90%
Masses and liturgies	89
Efforts to educate parishioners in faith	89
Promoting important Church teachings and causes (e.g., protecting life, helping the needy)	86
Encouragement of parishioners to share time, talent, and treasure	85
Sense of community	85
Hospitality and sense of welcoming to all	83
Vision provided by parish leaders	79
Spreading the Gospel and evangelizing	69

The area where respondents were *least* likely to provide a "good" or "excellent" or evaluation is in their parish's effort to spread the Gospel and evangelize.

Leaders in multi-parish ministry parishes (i.e., those formally sharing ministers and/or ministries) were especially likely to provide an "excellent" evaluation for their parish's sense of community (55 percent). Hispanic/Latino(a) parish leaders were among the most likely to give their parish only "fair" or "poor" marks for this aspect of parish life (22 percent). At the same time, leaders in Midwestern (51 percent) and Southern (48 percent) parishes were more likely than those in the Northeast (37 percent) and West (28 percent) to evaluate the sense of community in their parish as "excellent."

Others differ on their parish's sense of hospitality. Only 38 percent of Millennial leaders and 41 percent of Hispanic leaders provide an "excellent" evaluation for their parish's hospitality and sense of welcome. A majority of Millennials (54 percent) say this is "poor" or "fair" (46 percent "fair" and 8 percent "poor").

Younger leaders—those of the Millennial Generation—are much more positive about a central aspect of parish life. They are among the most likely to provide an "excellent" evaluation for their parish's Masses and liturgies (69 percent).

Others are more pessimistic about sacraments in their parish. Non-Anglo and PLC parish (i.e., Canon 517 §2) leaders are among the least likely to evaluate their parish as "excellent" for the celebration of sacraments (58 percent and 55 percent, respectively). In PLC parishes, this may be due to these parishes having a lack of priests in residence.

Turning to more specific aspects of parish life, leaders are most likely to say their parish is "somewhat" or "very much" successful at managing parish finances, recruiting and retaining ministers and staff, communicating with parishioners, and educating parishioners in the faith.

What Parishes Are Most Successful At

Percentage of parish leaders responding that their parish has "somewhat" or "very much" success with each aspect

Managing parish finances	90%
Recruitment and retaining ministers/staff	89
Communicating with parishioners	89
Educating parishioners in the faith	86
Welcoming new parishioners	85
Promoting ministry opportunities	85
Listening to parishioner concerns and input	83
Effectively using committees and councils	79
Providing social activities and programs	77
Providing accessibility for persons with disabilities	77
Ministering to the elderly	76
Ministering to families	75
Ministering to those who are grieving	75
Ministering to those in financial need	66
Collaborating with other parishes	61
Providing cultural, ethnic, or national celebrations	59
Celebrating cultural diversity	56
Providing mass in preferred languages	56
Ministering to young adults	56
Outreach to inactive Catholics	43
Ministering to recent immigrants	45

Leaders are least likely to indicate their parish is at least "somewhat" successful at celebrating cultural diversity, providing Mass in preferred languages, ministering to young adults, outreach to inactive Catholics, and ministering to recent immigrants.

Millennial leaders are among the more negative in evaluating some of these aspects. They are among the least likely to say their parish is at least "somewhat" successful at: communicating with parishioners (69 percent), welcoming new parishioners (54 percent), listening to parishioner concerns and input (54 percent), ministering to young adults (40 percent), celebrating cultural diversity (39 percent), collaborating with other parishes (39 percent), and outreach to inactive Catholics (25 percent).

Non-Anglo leaders are among the most likely to say their parish is "very much" successful at celebrating cultural diversity (50 percent), providing cultural, ethnic, or national celebrations important to parishioners (53 percent), providing Masses in preferred languages (52 percent), and ministering to recent immigrants (21 percent).

There are several sub-group differences in parish evaluations of these aspects related to parish structure:

- Leaders in parishes that have been consolidated are the least likely to say their parish is "somewhat" or "very much" successful in recruiting and retaining ministers and staff (50 percent). On the other hand, these leaders are among the most likely to say their parish is at least "somewhat" successful at ministering to those in financial need (76 percent) and outreach to inactive Catholics (64 percent).
- Those in multi-parish ministry parishes are the most likely to say their parish is "somewhat" or "very much" successful at welcoming new parishioners (95 percent).
- Leaders in PLC parishes are among the least likely to indicate their parish is at least "somewhat" successful at listening to parishioner concerns and input (77 percent), effectively using committees or councils (68 percent), ministering to the elderly (63 percent), providing social activities and programs (61 percent), and collaborating with other parishes (53 percent).
- Those in multicultural parishes are among the most likely to say their parish is "somewhat" or "very much" successful at celebrating cultural diversity (71 percent), providing cultural, ethnic, or national celebrations (75 percent), and providing Mass in preferred languages (67 percent).

About half of all leaders agree "very much" that their parish has undergone significant changes in the last five years. However, most do not see this as a change for the worse with just 13 percent of leaders agreeing "very much" that things were *better* in their parish five years ago.

Leaders in PLC parishes are most likely to agree "very much" that significant changes have occurred in their parish (67 percent). Yet only 4 percent of these leaders agree "very much" that things were better in their parish five years ago.

Half of all respondents agree at least "somewhat" that their parish is multicultural. As one might expect, this is more common in parishes identified as being multicultural by the study (73 percent). Non-Anglo (74 percent) and Hispanic/

Latino(a) (75 percent) leaders are also very likely to agree at least "somewhat" that their parish is multicultural. More than half of leaders (55 percent) agree at least "somewhat" that parishioners of different cultures participate in parish life together. Leaders in multicultural parishes (65 percent) and PLC parishes (67 percent) are more likely to respond as such.

Parish Restructuring

Leaders in parishes that have experienced reorganization in the last five years (i.e., transition to multi-parish ministry or consolidation) were provided with a separate set of questions specific to these events. Of these leaders, 63 percent had experienced the reorganization themselves and responded to these questions.

Only 22 percent indicated that their role in ministry changed before or after the transition. Remarkably, these respondents also reported relative stability in a variety of different aspects of parish life. As shown in the table below, however, some reported less support from their diocese. Some also note a decrease in the willingness of parishioners to volunteer and to generally be involved.

How did the following change after the reorganization?

	Decreased	Stayed the same	Increased	Not applicable
Arch/diocesan support for this parish	10%	51%	8%	31%
Willingness of parishioners to volunteer	9	65	17	9
Parishioner involvement	9	60	19	11
Arch/diocesan support for your ministry	8	47	8	37
Your total hours of ministry per week	7	57	21	14
Sense of community among parishioners	6	48	40	6
Your time spent on administrative responsibilities	4	36	36	35
Collaboration of parish leaders and staff	4	50	37	10
Your time spent on your primary ministry	2	58	27	13
Your time spent on planning and coordination	2	47	27	24
Your effectivesness	2	61	28	9

| Expectation of parishioners toward your ministry | 0 | 69 | 19 | 13 |
| General effectiveness of the parish staff | 0 | 69 | 19 | 13 |

Yet, many reported increases in the sense of community among parishioners and collaboration among parish leaders and staff. More personally, nearly three in ten reported an increase in their personal effectiveness. However, this may have led to working longer hours for some who noted increases in time spent on administrative responsibilities, their primary ministry, and on planning and coordination.

Few indicate they received any specialized training before these reorganizations. However, those that did tend to consider this to have been useful. In an open-ended question about best practices they could recommend the second most common recommendation were related to preparation, of which a common sub-topic was training (the most common topic noted in responses was about the need for communication).

In considering what was difficult about the reorganization, leaders were most likely to agree at least "somewhat" that the following have been an issue since reorganization: unhappiness of parishioners (50 percent), finding enough volunteers (43 percent), and interaction of parishioners from other parishes (38 percent). A majority, 54 percent agree only "a little" or "not at all" with the statement that there was little opposition to the changes brought by the reorganization (just 7 percent agree "very much").

Parishioners In-pew
It is important to note at the outset of this section that every respondent in our surveys has in some sense *chosen* to be a part of the parish they are evaluating (i.e., many are not attending at their territorial parish). With more than 1,000 CARA in-pew surveys conducted in the past decade, the results of the Emerging Models project presented below are generally consistent with what we see in this much broader sample (367,000+ completed surveys). Overall, 60 percent of in-pew respondents are in traditional parishes, 19 percent in MPM parishes, 18 percent in PLC parishes, and 4 percent in consolidated parishes.

Pastors and parish life coordinators surveyed in the first phase of the Emerging Models project were able to fairly accurately estimate the racial and ethnic composition of their parishioners. They slightly overestimate the non-Hispanic white percentage of parishioners (74 percent versus 70 percent self-identification). Pastors and parish life coordinators underestimated slightly the percentage of parishioners who self-identify as Asian or Pacific Islander (5 percent versus

10 percent self-identification). Generally, differences were within or near the surveys' margins of sampling error.

Recall that Mass attenders are not representative of the Catholic population at large. Many young Catholics of the Post-Vatican II and Millennial generations are not Mass attenders even on a monthly basis. It is these two youngest generations that are also the most racially and ethnically diverse. Given that the surveys are conducted in-pew within parishes, responses reflect Mass attenders rather than the total Catholic population.

None of the pastors or parish life coordinators requested CARA to translate surveys into a language other than English or Spanish (translations into other languages was offered). However, CARA did ask respondents to indicate the primary language they use at home. About 8 percent said they primarily use Spanish at home and the same percentage chose to take the survey in Spanish. Others, who primarily speak languages other than English at home (e.g., Tagalog, Vietnamese, Polish, Portuguese), chose to take the survey in English.

Consistent with other research, Mass attenders are disproportionately female. Overall, 64 percent of parishioners surveyed are female and 36 percent are male. The median age for parishioners is 52. One in ten respondents is a ten or adult Millennial (born after 1981). Nearly four in ten (39 percent) are members of the Post-Vatican II Generation (born 1961 to 1981) and a third (33 percent) are of the Vatican II Generation (born 1943 to 1960). Seventeen percent are of the Pre-Vatican II Generation (born before 1943).

Three in four respondents describe themselves as an active Catholic since birth. One in ten respondents (11 percent) is a "returned Catholic" and the same number is Catholic converts (11 percent). Two percent are inactive Catholics and another 2 percent are non-Catholic.

Eight in ten or more of Mass-attending parishioners at traditional and MPM parishes are registered with their parish. Those in PLC and consolidated parishes are less likely to be registered (62 percent and 72 percent, respectively). As shown in the next figure, parish registration is least common among Hispanic/Latino(a) (60 percent) and Asian and Pacific Islander parishioners (63 percent). This is consistent with what pastors and parish life coordinators reported in the first phase survey regarding unregistered groups in their parish.

Eight in ten or more respondents say that the parish is their primary place of worship. Ninety three percent of those in traditional parishes indicate this as do 92 percent of those in MPM parishes. Eighty-six percent of those in consolidated parishes indicate the parish is their primary place of worship as do 82 percent of those in PLC parishes. Parishioners in MPM parishes report the longest time, on

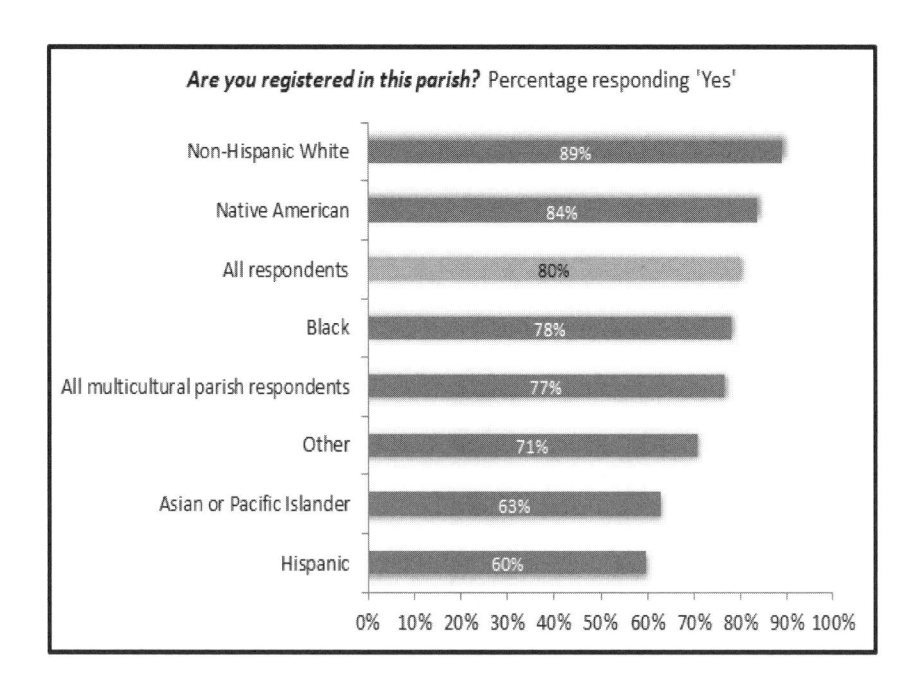

Are you registered in this parish? Percentage responding 'Yes'

Group	Percentage
Non-Hispanic White	89%
Native American	84%
All respondents	80%
Black	78%
All multicultural parish respondents	77%
Other	71%
Asian or Pacific Islander	63%
Hispanic	60%

average, of attending their parish at 22.6 years. Those in consolidate parishes report attending their parish for an average of 18.2 years. Those in traditional parishes say they have attended their parish for an average of 12.8 years. Those in PLC parishes report the shortest average length of attendance at the parish (9.1 years).

As shown in the next figure, three in ten Catholics (29 percent) attending a traditional parish drive by a parish closer to their home. A third of those in MPM parishes report this (34 percent). Those attending PLC and consolidated parishes are the most likely to indicate they drive by another parish to attend the parish in which they took the survey (45 percent each).

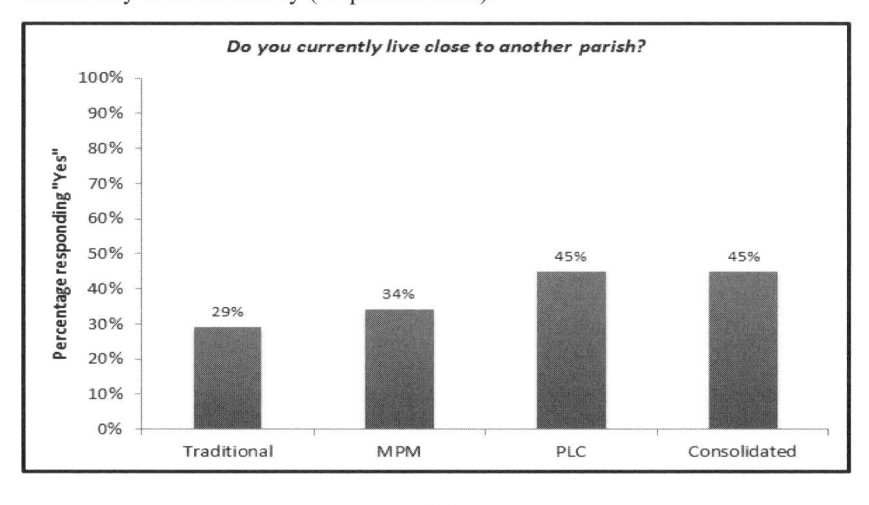

Do you currently live close to another parish? Percentage responding "Yes"

Parish Type	Percentage
Traditional	29%
MPM	34%
PLC	45%
Consolidated	45%

Nearly seven in ten of those in traditional parishes and MPM parishes attend Mass at least once a week. Fewer in PLC and consolidated parishes (64 percent and 60 percent, respectively) attend this often.

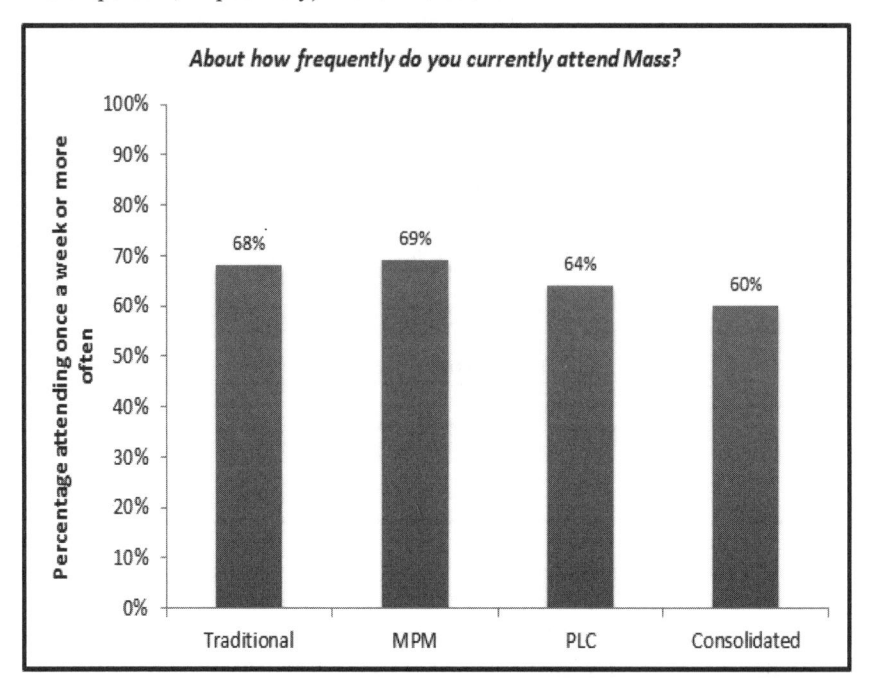

About how frequently do you currently attend Mass?

Parish Type	Percentage attending once a week or more often
Traditional	68%
MPM	69%
PLC	64%
Consolidated	60%

Overall, 68 percent of respondents say they attend Mass every week. This is most common among non-Hispanic white respondents (70 percent) and least common among African American respondents (54 percent). Sixty-three percent of Hispanic/Latino(a) parishioners attend Mass every week as do 64 percent of Asian Pacific Islanders, and 56 percent of Native Americans.

Seven in ten parishioners evaluate the celebration of sacraments in their parish as "excellent" with nearly all saying this is at least "good" (97 percent). Parishioners are also likely to provide positive evaluations for their parishes hospitality and sense of welcome (91 percent at least "good"), and promoting important teachings or causes (94 percent at least "good"). Nearly six in ten (58 percent) provide an "excellent" overall evaluation for their parish (94 percent at least "good").

Please evaluate these aspects of parish life:

	"Excellent" only	"Good" or "Excellent"
Celebration of the Sacraments	70%	97%
Hospitality or sense of welcome to all	62	91
Promoting important Church teachings/causes	61	94
Your overall satisfaction with the parish	**58**	**94**
Masses and liturgies in general	58	94
Encouragement of parishioners to share their time, talent and treasure	58	92
Efforts to educate parishioners in the faith	55	92
Vision provided by parish leaders	49	90
Sense of community within the parish	46	87
Spreading the Gospel and evangelizing	44	88

Respondents are less likely to evaluate their parish as at least "good" for the sense of community (87 percent) or the parish's spreading of the Gospel or evangelizing (88 percent).

Parishioners in PLC and consolidated parishioners are slightly less likely than others to give their parish an "excellent" overall evaluation of satisfaction (51 percent and 52 percent, respectively). Hispanic and Asian or Pacific Islander respondents are more likely than others to give their parish "excellent" marks for spreading the Gospel or evangelizing (50 percent and 55 percent, respectively).

Recall that many Catholics are not attending their territorial parish and are drawn to another by some other aspect. Parishioners were asked about what attracts them to their parish. The number one reason is their perception of their parish as having an open and welcoming spirit. Two-thirds of parishioners (67 percent) said this drew them to their parish "very much" and more than nine in ten (93 percent) said this attracted them at least "somewhat." Other aspects that attract a majority of parishioners "very much" include the quality of the liturgy (62 percent), the quality of the preaching (62 percent), the quality of the music (53 percent), the sense of belonging they feel there (52 percent), and the beauty of the church (51 percent).

How much do the following attract you to this parish?

	"Very much" only	"Somewhat" or "Very much"
Its open, welcoming spirit	67%	93%
The quality of the liturgy	62	93
The quality of the preaching	62	92
The quality of the music	53	83
The sense of belonging you feel here	52	90
The beauty of the church	51	82
Its opportunities for spiritual growth	50	88
Its religious education/formation for children and youth	47	79
Its respect for your cultural traditions	47	81
The program and activities of the parish	42	83
Its character as a diverse community	42	79
Its commitment to social justice	41	80
Its programs in your native language	41	68
Its faith formation for adults	39	77
Its programs for young adults	37	72

African American and Asian or Pacific Islander respondents were more likely than others to be "very much" attracted by their parish's open and welcoming spirit (75 percent and 73 percent, respectively). Non-Hispanic white respondents are among the least likely to say they are "very much' attracted to their parish because of its commitment to social justice (36 percent) or its character as a diverse community (35 percent).

Millennial Generation Catholics (those born after 1981) are less likely than the oldest Catholics, those of the Pre-Vatican II Generation (born before 1943), to say they are "very much" attracted to their parish for its program for young adults (35 percent compared to 47 percent). Millennials are also among the least likely to say they are "very much" attracted to their parish by its religious education and formation program for children and youth (41 percent). Pre-Vatican II Catholics are more likely than others to be "very much" attracted to their parish by the sense of belonging they feel there (70 percent).

Seminar

The Establishment of a Religious Institute: Where the Rubber Meets the Road
Doctor Eileen C. Jaramillo

I. Parameters of this Seminar

This presentation concentrates on the establishment of forms of consecrated life that fit into the current canonical structure of the church. Canon law identifies four forms of consecrated life. The two individual forms are hermits (c. 603) and consecrated virgins (c. 604 §1).[1] The two corporate forms are religious institutes (c. 607 §2) and secular institutes (c. 710). The code then states that societies of apostolic life "resemble institutes of consecrated life" (c. 731 §1). This seminar focuses only on groups of individuals who want to form a new religious institute, a new secular institute, or a new society of apostolic life. Therefore, the term "new," as used in this seminar, refers to a "new religious community" or a "new foundation" that the church can recognize in accordance with the existing canonical system.

Why is it important to be careful about the word "new?" The central reason stems from the fact that the code uses the word "new" when it speaks about new forms of consecrated life in canon 605.[2] Such a canon really leaves room to go beyond what exists in our current canonical system. It envisions new forms of consecrated life not contemplated or established in the present set of norms. These new forms would be separate from those forms contained in the current code. Therefore, in having a canon like 605 in the code, the legislator acknowledges that the Holy Spirit can contribute to the life and holiness of the church in ways not envisioned by the current code. This seminar is not addressing these "new movements" or "new experiments."

The chart on *Corporate Forms of Consecrated Life* provides greater clarity about the differences between a religious institute, a secular institute, and a society of apostolic life.[3] It gives a breakdown of eleven different areas as well as citing examples. Since it also refers to various canons, it might be useful when

---

[1] For practical details about living the individual calling of a hermit, see M. Weisenbeck, "Guide Book for The Vocation to Eremitic Life," Diocese of LaCrosse (1997). Elements of living the singular life of a consecrated virgin can be found at http://consecratedvirgins.org.

[2] See M. Casey, "Breaking from the Bud: New Forms of Consecrated Life," (Sydney: Sisters of St. Joseph, 2001), for a thoroughly researched study of this canon.

[3] E. Jaramillo, *Corporate Forms of Consecrated Life Chart*.

working on the statutes for a particular group. For the most part, this seminar addresses religious institutes. The information, however, applies equally to secular institutes and societies of apostolic life unless a distinction makes it evident that it only applies to one of them.[4] This author hopes that the chart will be helpful to canonists in assisting a particular group in discerning the form of consecrated life that it desires to embrace.

An additional parameter of this seminar pertains to the two codes. This seminar cites canons from the *Code of Canon Law* for the Latin Church. It references the *Code of Canons for the Eastern Churches* in the footnotes when there is a significant difference.

With this foundation in mind, this author moves to the pivotal elements for establishing a religious institute.

II. Principles and Criteria
Primarily, consecrated life is a "charism." In its various identifiable forms, this visionary gift has been present from the earliest of times.[5] It has played a very strong prophetic role whenever there have been struggles and hardships in the secular world or in ecclesial life. In *Evangelica testificatio* (1971), Paul VI uses the word "charism" to describe consecrated life (§11). Like all charisms, the charism of consecrated life stands out as a manifestation of the Holy Spirit given to individuals for the sake of others. It is a particular configuring with Christ. It signifies communion as arising from the relationship among the persons of the Trinity. The word "charism," however, never made its way into the *Code of Canon Law*. Nevertheless, canon 573 clearly asserts that consecrated life is a fruit of the Holy Spirit. The code also uses terms such as "spiritual patrimony" or the "sound traditions of an institute" as a way of conveying the life-giving breath of "charism" (cc. 577, 578, 631).[6]

Other documents of the church that explicitly address the issue of discerning charism and have as their purpose the establishment of new institutes of conse-

---

4   For even greater clarity about the distinctions see S. Holland, "Title III: Secular Institutes" in *New Commentary on the Code of Canon Law*, ed. John P. Beal et al. (New York/Mahwah, NJ: Paulist Press, 2000) [hereafter *New Commentary*] 878- 891 and P. Brown, "Societies of Apostolic Life: The Evolution of a Canonical Institute" in *Essays in Honor of Sister Rose McDermott*, ed. Robert Kaslyn (Washington, DC: The Catholic University of America, 2010) 201-234.

5   See N. Foley, "The Ecclesial Identity of Religious Life," in *Leadership Conference of Women Religious [LCWR] Occasional Papers*, Fall (1996) 3-10 and F. Morrisey, "The Development of Consecrated Life," in *Origins* 36 (April 19, 2007) 718-723 for excellent overviews of the history of consecrated life.

6   For a more thorough understanding of the charism of religious life see W. Hogan, "Canonical Room for Charisms," in *The Church and Consecrated Life*, eds. David L. Fleming and Elizabeth McDonough (St. Louis: Review for Religious, 1996) 144-149.

crated life remain an invaluable resource for us. Several significant documents from Vatican II address this issue. One of them is the Dogmatic Constitution on the Church, *Lumen Gentium* (1964). Chapter 2, "The People of God," speaks about charisms that are very remarkable or more simple, and indicates that those who have charge over the church should judge the genuineness and proper use of these gifts (§12). When the charism of an institute of consecrated life appears to be authentic, canon 579 then recognizes that the diocesan bishop has the right to erect both religious institutes and secular institutes. However, consultation with the Apostolic See needs to occur before making such a decision.[7] Canon 732 applies the norm of canon 579 to the establishment of societies of apostolic life.

Chapter 6 of *Lumen Gentium,* "Religious," refers to those who profess the vows of chastity, poverty, and obedience or other sacred bonds in a stable form of life approved by the church. Hence, the term "religious," as used in that chapter, includes not only members of religious institutes, but also members of secular institutes and societies of apostolic life. That chapter acknowledges the place of consecrated life in relation to the hierarchical structure of the church (§43) and makes statements about the nature of consecrated life (§44). It also comments on the relationship between consecrated life and the hierarchy (§45), notes the special consecration effected through the profession of the evangelical counsels (§46), and urges religious to persevere (§47).[8] These concepts are evident in canon573 as well as other canons throughout the code.

One of the conciliar decrees of Vatican II, *Perfectae Caritatis* (1965), centers itself upon the original inspiration or charism as the reason why institutes of consecrated life should come into existence. Being faithful to that original inspiration means continually returning to it because it is the foundation from which everything else flows (§2). That decree reminds everyone that before all else, religious life is ordered to the following of Christ and union with God through the profession of the evangelical counsels.[9] Institutes exist for the good of the church

---

7   While the 1983 *Code of Canon Law* for the Latin Church uses the term religious institutes to refer to both orders and religious congregations, the *Code of Canons of the Eastern Churches* maintains the distinction between monks, orders and congregations. Canons 506-510 clarify the role of the Patriarch, the Exarch, and the Holy See in the erection of orders and congregations. See J. Abbass, *The Consecrated Life, A Comparative Commentary of the Eastern and Latin Codes* (Ottawa: St. Paul University, 2008) 298-301 for more details.

8   See E. McDonough, "Lumen Gentium's Chapter 6," in *The Church and Consecrated Life*, eds. David L. Fleming and Elizabeth McDonough (St. Louis: Review for Religious, 1996) 22-28 for a more complete development of these concepts.

9   See M. Allen and M. O'Brien "The Decree on the Appropriate Renewal of Religious Life, *Perfectae Caritatis"* in *Vatican II, Renewal Within Tradition,* (New York: Oxford University Press, 2008) 251-270 and S. Robert "To Live Here Below from the Beyond: Religious Vows and Apostolic Life," [hereafter *To Live Here Below from the Beyond*], in *Review for Religious* (2011) 70.3,234-246 for a more thorough understanding.

and the world. Therefore, *Perfectae Caritatis* states that when new religious institutes are proposed, it must be asked whether they are necessary, whether it will be possible for them to increase and if they have sufficient resources (§19). If such questions are not the central part of the process, it may be imprudent to establish a new institute.[10] Such questions do not have immediate responses. Rather, it takes time to assess the workings of the Holy Spirit. As we will see, the code puts this into practice by having various stages in such a process.

Additionally, *Perfectae Caritatis* also makes other significant points (§11). It indicates that while secular institutes are not religious institutes, they are a true and full profession of the evangelical counsels in the world. The profession of vows confers a specific consecration on people who are living in the world. This can include men and women, lay people and clerics. These institutes ought to preserve their own distinct secular character so that they can carry their apostolate into the world. Added at the end of the debate, this particular paragraph clarifies that the charism of secular institutes is distinct from religious institutes.

The post-conciliar documents also provide important points. *Mutuae Relationes* (1978) recognizes that the Holy Spirit can indeed inspire individuals to embark on certain works for the good of the church. These apostolic works are subject to the authority and supervision of the bishop.[11] It also says that in its surroundings such a charism might appear troublesome and may even cause difficulties because it is never easy to recognize it as originating in the Holy Spirit (§12). Such a statement speaks about the inevitable relationship between the cross and charism. As a sign of a valid charism, this same document presents the following norms: a) a distinctive inspiration that comes from the Holy Spirit, b) a desire to be conformed to Christ, c) a deep love for the church, and d) an experienced spiritual life as well as a founder that is docile to the hierarchy (§51). An example from the past provides an understanding as to why this document says what it says.

At the beginning of the thirteenth century, Bishop Diego of Osma, Spain along with his companion, Dominic Guzman, journeyed into southern France and met with the widespread success of the Albigensian preaching. Albigensians,

---

10 The church has raised the issue of multiplying institutes in the past. The Fourth Lateran Council, the Second Council of Lyons, and the First Vatican Council addressed this issue. For example, in "Between Charism and Institution: The Approval of the Rule of Saint Clare in 1253," in *Studia Canonica* 31 (1997) 431, A. McGrath says, "At the Fourth Lateran Council (1215), the bishops were anxious to have some control over the emerging forms of religious life. Consequently, it was decided that any new group of men or women seeking to lead a religious life in the Church had to adopt one of the ancient and approved Rules. In effect, this meant the Rule of St. Benedict or the Rule of St. Augustine."

11 See R. Joyce and S. Euart "The Relationship between Bishops and Religious: Specific Working Scenarios," in *Legal Seminar*, (Legal Resource Center for Religious [LRCR], 2004) for a more extensive treatment of this dynamic.

also known as Cathars, held that matter was evil and only the spirit was good. Bishop Diego and Dominic also witnessed the very inadequate response of the clergy regarding this heresy. In order to counter it, both believed that simplicity of lifestyle, poverty, and preachers who were educated in the truths of the faith were the responses to such heretical teaching. However, this plan met with much failure. When Bishop Diego died, for example, most of the men who had joined him and Dominic left. Furthermore, people were converting from such a heresy out of fear rather than conviction. Therefore, it looked like this new charism was not an authentic one.

In the midst of these circumstances, Dominic entered into the meaning of the cross and continued with his vision. He received encouragement from Bishop Fulk of Toulouse and, eventually, the Dominican Order was established. However, once that event transpired, Dominic made another decision. He was going to disperse the brethren throughout the world. For its day and time, this was very unusual because the accent was on stability not mobility. Bishop Fulk and Bishop Narbonne knew about such an emphasis, and thought that Dominic had gone mad. In spite of such conflict with those bishops who were also his friends, Dominic remained convinced of the inspiration of the Holy Spirit for the Order and said, "I know what I am doing."[12] Eventually, the vision of this saint took shape.

This brief look at the beginnings of the Dominican Order shows that discerning a charism has never been an easy task for either the founder or the local bishop. With such an example in mind, this author now returns to the current century.

The Apostolic Exhortation *Vita Consecrata* (1996) affirms that the essential identity and purpose of any institute exists in its original charism. Charisms come from the Holy Spirit. A founder or foundress mediates the gift. The members live it. Church authority discerns the authenticity and gives it juridic status. It is also important to remember that no one should think of consecrated life as solely existing to fulfill a pastoral need. Rev. Arnaldo Pigna, OCD explains it by saying,

> This helps us to remember once more that the ultimate sense and the most profound identity of consecrated life lies not in accomplishing a particular service (even though it might be useful and necessary according to the differing vocations) but in living and proclaiming the absolute primacy of the love of God. This is why consecrated life will always remain valid and necessary to the Church and to the world.[13]

---

12 T. Heath, "St. Dominic's Failure" in *Spirituality Today*, Autumn, Vol. 32 (1980) 3:215.

13 A. Pigna, "New Charisms of Consecrated Life—The Role of the Founder" in *Consecrated Life*, Vol. 24, No. 2, (Institute on Religious Life, 2002) 238. Also see D. Gotte-

Furthermore, Bishop Joseph Galante speaks about this dynamic when he says that he believes that in the past, some bishops brought religious institutes into existence without a specific charism.[14] He states this began to occur at the end of the last century and the beginning of this century when there was a concern about meeting the needs of immigrants. He even suggests that some bishops might still be operating in this way. To prevent such a disservice to the church, especially to the laity, he indicates that it is vital that a religious institute have "a gospel charism that transcends and buttresses and is the foundation of the local apostolate."[15]

Even *Vita Consecrata* stresses this important issue when it says,

> In recent years following the Second Vatican Council, new or renewed forms of consecrated life have arisen. In many cases, these institutes are similar to those already existing, but inspired by new spiritual and apostolic impulses. Their vitality must be judged by the authority of the church, which has the responsibility
> of examining them in order to discern the authenticity of the purpose of their foundation and to prevent the proliferation of institutions similar to one another, with the consequent risk of a harmful fragmentation into excessively small groups (§12).

With such fundamental principles and criteria in mind, this author now turns to the process or stages for becoming a diocesan or pontifical institute.

III. Stages of the Process

In the canons on consecrated life (cc. 573-746), the code never mentions how to establish a new religious institute. Hence, we have to go to another part of Book II, "The People of God," to find canons. It is not surprising that our journey takes us to Part I of Book II, "The Christian Faithful," because that section provides the groundwork for a lived ecclesiological perspective. With such a foundation, it continues by establishing the rights and obligations of the Christian faithful. Then it treats Associations of the Faithful in a body of thirty-two canons (cc. 298-329). They stand as the canonical framework that will establish the juridic status of these associations.

These canons on Associations of the Faithful fall into various sections. The first fourteen canons (cc. 298-311) present basic norms. They are common to any

---

moeller, "Vita Consecrata: The Post-Synodal Exhortation on Consecrated Life," in *CLSA Proceedings* 58 (Washington, DC: Canon Law Society of America, 1996) 176-186.

14 J. Galante, "The Relationship of the Diocesan Bishop and Institutes of Pontifical Right," in *CLSA Proceedings* 56 (Washington, DC: Canon Law Society of America, 1994) 90-96.

15 Ibid., 92.

association that has status in the church. Canons 312-320 address Public Associations of the Faithful while canons 321-326 pertain to Private Associations of the Faithful. The remaining canons (cc. 327-329) form special norms.

Many types of associations exist in the church. These groups have a variety of functions. Usually, they have a charitable, social, liturgical, or spiritual purpose. They differ in many ways from religious institutes formally established by church authority. While the canons on associations were not originally envisioned as the process for becoming a new religious institute, they do offer a structure that appears to be suitable for discerning whether a group should be established as a religious institute.[16] Having a process is not a new practice. Long established religious institutes will find in their history a phase such as a "pious union" or something else before recognition as a religious institute. At the same time, however, there are dynamics involved in the process of becoming a new religious institute that need addressing because the canons do not cover them.

A group that envisions becoming a new religious institute begins without any formality. The founder or foundress desires to promote the charism and others are joining with that individual. They often have a spiritual director or a religious institute is guiding them. Hence, they begin as a purely private endeavor or what the code calls a *de facto* association by living their experience and determining their purpose. This type of association has no recognition and no juridical existence in the diocese, other than by virtue of the right of association recognized by the church (c. 299). In accordance with canon 298 §1 they might discern that one or more of their purposes is: a) to strive in a common endeavor to foster a more perfect life, b) to promote public worship, or c) Christian doctrine, or d) exercise other works of the apostolate such as evangelization, works of piety or charity, or works that animate the temporal order with a Christian Spirit.

Having lived their purpose and desiring to be more specific about it, they draw up statutes (cc. 94, 299, 304).[17] During this period, it is advisable to seek the help of competent persons (cc. 310, 605). It is at this time that they need to discern their orientation. In other words, they need to begin thinking about whether they intend to be a religious institute, a secular institute, or a society of apostolic life. They also should intensify their dialogue with the diocesan bishop.

---

16 An excellent resource is E. Gambari, *The Canonical Establishment of a Religious Institute, Process and Procedures*, a private work translated from the Italian by M. Armato and T. Blessin (1999).

17 Statutes and any changes are one of the most important aspects of the association. Accomplishing this work takes time. See J. Hite, "Canons that Refer to the Constitutions and Proper Law of Institutes of Consecrated Life and Societies of Apostolic Life," Appendix 2, in *A Handbook on Canons 573-746*, (Collegeville, MN: The Liturgical Press, 1983) 371-381 for more details about the contents of the statutes. Also, see L. Jarrell and D. Ward, "Procedures for Changing the Constitutions and Secondary Norms," in *Procedures and Documents for Canonical and Civil Administration*, (LRCR, 2007) 29-33.

The next step would be recognition as a Private Association of the Faithful. The bishop has the responsibility to judge when it would be opportune to praise the new group, give formal approval of the association, and review its statutes. As Sister Sharon Holland, IHM notes, "The praise or recommendation of ecclesiastical authority will be of significant encouragement to this new association."[18] Recognition is given by a decree from the diocesan bishop (c. 322 §1). He may grant this Private Association juridical personality if its statutes have been approved (cc. 310, 322 §2). While this type of association possesses autonomy (c. 321), it is subject to the vigilance of the diocesan bishop according to the norms of canon 305 §1. The diocesan bishop also watches the association so that dissipation of energies is avoided, and so that the exercise of the apostolate is ordered to the common good (c. 323§1).

There are other aspects to the private association. It can freely choose a spiritual advisor, if it desires one, from among the priests exercising ministry legitimately in the diocese. He needs the confirmation of the diocesan bishop (c. 324 §2). The association freely administers those goods it possesses according to the prescripts of its statutes without prejudice to the right of the diocesan bishop to exercise vigilance, so that the goods are used for the purpose of the association (c. 325 §1). It is subject to the authority of the diocesan bishop according to the norms of canon 1301 in what pertains to the administration and distribution of goods which have been donated or left to it for pious causes (c. 325 §2). If its activity causes grave harm to ecclesiastical doctrine or discipline or is a scandal to the faithful, the diocesan bishop may suppress it (c. 326 §1).

After spending a number of years as a Private Association of the Faithful, this group might be ready to proceed to the next step in the process: establishment as a Public Association of the Faithful in a particular diocese. Written consent of the diocesan bishop is required for the valid establishment of an association in the diocese (c. 312 §3). In this decree, the public association is constituted a "juridic person." Its statutes are approved and, to the extent required, it receives a mission that it pursues in the name of the church (cc. 313, 315). The decree establishing the public association should include the phrase "in view of being erected in the future as a religious Institute of Diocesan Right." This phrase clarifies the specific status of the association and the members begin to live "as if they are religious." The group can have houses in other dioceses as long as the bishop of the diocese gives his consent, but no new establishment of the association is required.

At this time, the association imitates the spirit and structure of a religious institute. This means that it has a novitiate, its members pronounce private vows

---

18   S. Holland, "New Institutes, Mergers and Suppression," in *Procedural Handbook for Institutes of Consecrated Life and Societies of Apostolic Life*, (Washington, DC: Canon Law Society of America, 2001) 37.

(cc. 1191-1198),[19] and they can wear a religious habit. It also means that they have their own superiors, councils and chapters, and temporary and perpetually professed private vowed members. The statutes of each public association and their revision or change need the approval of the diocesan bishop who is competent to establish the association in accordance with canon 312 §1. Normally, a group spends a number of years in this stage of development.

There are other aspects to this type of an association. Usually, the diocesan bishop confirms the election of the superior, installs the one presented or appoints one in his own right (c. 317 §1). The diocesan bishop also appoints the chaplain or ecclesiastical assistant after having heard the major officials of the association when it is expedient (c. 371 §1). He can remove this person according to the norms of canons 192-195 (also see c. 318 §2). In associations that are not clerical, laypersons are able to exercise the function of superior. If the diocesan bishop appointed or confirmed the superior, he can remove the person for a just cause after hearing the individual and the major officials of the association and in accordance with the statutes (c. 318).

Additional dynamics also pertain to the Public Association. Unless other provisions have been made, a legitimately established association administers the goods it possesses according to the norms of the statutes under the higher direction of the diocesan bishop (c. 319 §1). It must render an account of administration to the diocesan bishop each year (c. 319 §2). It must also give him a faithful account of expenditures of offerings and alms that it has collected (c. 319 §2). For a grave cause, the diocesan bishop can suppress the association that he decided to establish (c. 320 §2). He is not to suppress it unless he has heard its superior and other major officials (c. 320 §3). Additionally, it is during this stage that there should be some initial contact with the Congregation of Religious Institutes and Societies of Apostolic Life (CICLSAL) in Rome.

Concerning associations that are clerical, it is important to note that the term "clerical" pertains not only to those directing the association, but also to the specific form of the exercise of pastoral ministry. In other words, there is explicit reference to a particular apostolic mission. This is part of its founding charism. It has a direct relationship to church authorities, especially as it applies to the selection and preparation of candidates for orders. Canon 302 indicates three conditions for using the title of clerical. It must be under the direction of clerics. It must exercise sacred orders and be acknowledged as such an association by church authority. Other issues regarding clerical associations need consideration. They are: a) incardination into a diocese, prelature, institute, or society,

---

19 J. Huels makes important points about a public and a private vow in "Chapter I, A Vow" in *New Commentary*, 1417. Canon 731 §2 indicates that for members of societies of apostolic life who assume the obligation of the evangelical counsels, the nature of such bonds is defined in their constitution. Canon 712 requires that "sacred bonds" bind members of secular institutes.

b) dimissorials for ordination, c) faculties for ministry, d) clerics who leave the association, e) healthcare issues, and f) senior priest status. These dynamics can be addressed in the statutes or in some other document.[20]

It is worth noting that while this author has mentioned the various canons that pertain to Public Associations of the Faithful, the statutes of these groups will not always follow all the particular norms for associations. The reason is that they are to live as closely as possible to the type of institute they want to become (cc. 573-704, 710-746). Consequently, their statutes will look more like the constitution of a religious institute rather than like the statutes of a group that will remain an association of the faithful. This author has mentioned the various canons on associations because it is important to have an awareness of them.

This writer also believes that the bishop of the diocese where the group was erected needs to be vigilant about the dynamics operating within the group. In the experience of this author, the areas of finance, short and long term, the spirituality of the group, and admittance procedures need to be watched very closely. Furthermore, having exhausted the various alternatives, an association might have to be suppressed. In more than one situation, this author has been a part of a team that advised suppression of an association of the faithful to the bishop of a diocese. Great care was taken by the various team members regarding a number of issues when making such a recommendation.

The next step in the process would be to discern whether this Public Association is ready to be erected as an Institute of Diocesan Right. Recognizing that the association is the work of the Holy Spirit and that it has provided sufficient indications to warrant its erection into an institute of consecrated life falls within the competency of the diocesan bishop in accordance with canon 579. Since its existence will become a part of the patrimony of the universal church, it is not surprising that CICLSAL needs to be consulted. Once the *nihil obstat* is given, the diocesan bishop can erect the group as an Institute of Diocesan Right through a formal decree. Is the *nihil obstat* required for validity? Some authors would say "yes" because the word *dummodo* (provided that) is used in canon 579. However, not all authors agree about this matter. Some point to canon 10. They state that nothing in canon 579 expressly states that the act would be null if CICLSAL was not consulted. If CICLSAL chose not to grant the *nihil obstat* and the bishop erected the group as an Institute of Diocesan Right, the establishment would not be invalid.[21] This author believes that the observations by the Holy See about the

---

20 See F. Morrisey, "Canonical Associations Destined to Become Religious Institutes," in *Consecrated Life*, Vol. 26, No. 1, (Institute on Religious Life, 2006) 87-108 for an excellent treatment of issues pertaining to clerical associations.

21 When Jesus Torres was undersecretary of the Congregation, he considered this consultation unnecessary for validity and cited canon 10. Also see V. D'Souza, "Erection of A Religious Institute of Diocesan Right: Law and Praxis," in *Studies in Church Law*, St. Peter's Pontifical Institute, 1 (2005) 78-81.

constitution are more important than the issue of validity because they are often very vital for the identity and rightful autonomy of the group.

The list of required documents that must be sent to the CICLSAL includes the following elements: a) the names of the founder and the first superior general along with a *curriculum vitae* of each, b) a historical-juridical account of the association from its beginnings including the decree of erection as a Public Association of the Faithful, c) the constitution and the directory of the institute revised in accordance with the *Code of Canon Law*, d) where applicable, a picture of the religious dress of both a professed member and a novice, e) up to date statistics of the membership, including the year of birth and of temporary and perpetual profession[22], the place and diocese where houses are located, and the works of the institute,[23] f) an account of the financial patrimony of the institute including debts, g) statements regarding any extraordinary experiences or particular devotions and whether in the diocese of origin there already exists another institute with the same purpose and name, and h) testimonial letters from the diocesan bishops of those dioceses in which the institute is represented; such letters are to be sent directly to the Holy See giving the opinion of the bishops about the following matters: usefulness, stability, discipline of the institute, formation of members, government, administration of goods, liturgical and sacramental dimensions, a sense of being with the church, particularly in regard to the observances of ecclesiastical discipline as expressed in the common law of the church and in the diocesan directives, and i) the "deposit" of 500 euros equivalent to $682 (checks are made out to CICLSAL).[24]

From experience, this author can attest to the fact that putting together this package is not an easy task. Great care must be taken regarding the various requirements in order to prevent delays and exchange of letters. The testimonial letter from the bishop(s) stands out as very significant. The matters that he must address describe concisely the important issues for founders and bishops in founding and guiding a new institute.

At CICLSAL, at least two consultors examine the entire file. They give a written *votum* or an opinion. Then everything is sent to the *Congresso* or meeting of

---

22 For erection as an Institute of Diocesan Right, the required number is about 40 members who have professed perpetual private vows. For erection as an Institute of Pontifical Right, the number is about 100. For a monastery of canon 615, the number is 8-12 members in perpetual private vows.

23 For secular institutes there is no listing of houses as there is for religious institutes since there is no obligation to common life or corporate works.

24 Even though the amount of the deposit continues to increase a) through i) can be found in S. Holland "New Institutes, Mergers and Suppression" and in L. Jarrell and D. Ward, "Procedures for Establishing an Institute/Society" in *Procedures and Documents for Canonical and Civil Administration in Institutes of Consecrated Life and Societies of Apostolic Life*, (LRCR, 2007) 5-6.

the higher officials of CICLSAL including the Prefect and/or Secretary. Before CICLSAL makes a decision, the file might be forwarded to the Congregation for the Doctrine of the Faith to ensure that nothing is improper regarding doctrine, prayers, devotions, visions, miracles, etc. When granting the *nihil obstat* or the "go ahead" CICLSAL usually sends certain remarks about the proposed constitution. Sometimes it also grants special faculties to the diocesan bishop (i.e., appointing the first superior general). When the *nihil obstat* is received, the diocesan bishop, through a formal decree, approves the constitution and erects the group as an Institute of Diocesan Right. At this time it is the usual practice that the superior pronounces her vows, now as public vows in a diocesan institute, before the bishop, and the rest of the religious pronounce their vows in the hands (or presence—according to their formula of the particular institute) of the superior. In the future all vows are received by the superior.

The last stage, establishment as an Institute of Pontifical Right, is an option but not a requirement. However, it might be wise to consider this option if the Institute of Diocesan Right has spread into different dioceses or around the world. If so, this option would better reflect its identity. The documents and information that are sent to the Holy See are the same as they were for the erection as a Diocesan Institute. However, the number of members needs to be about one hundred. The bishop of the principle house, at the request of this Institute of Diocesan Right, sends the petition and required documents. The Holy See issues the decree.

It might seem that the work of a canonist is now completed. All the paper work can be filed in the appropriate places and the canonist can move on to other canonical work. Such a statement might be true. On the other hand, there might be more work to do. It depends on some important relationships. Therefore, this author now turns to those dynamics in an effort to offer some insight into them.

IV. Aggregates
Canon 580 speaks about how aggregation may pertain between one institute and another one. What does this mean? It refers to a relationship between institutes of consecrated life that respects the rightful autonomy of the individual institutes. Aggregation pertains to the spiritual bond or connection between first, second, and third orders of mendicants such as Dominicans, Franciscans, or Carmelites, for example. It can also pertain to the relationship between Benedictine monasteries of women religious with the men. These institutes not only share a common spirituality, they also support one another. Furthermore, some secular institutes are also aggregated to religious institutes. This author has been instrumental in facilitating the process for a group of women religious.

In the latter stages of their erection as a Public Association of the Faithful, at the very least, the group should begin developing a firmer bond with the group that will make a decision about aggregation. For example, if the group intends to be Dominican, they should converse with the Master of the Order and find out what is required for aggregation to the Dominican Order. Once erected as an Institute of Diocesan Right, they may petition for aggregation. The act of aggregation rests with the competent authority, for example the superior general or the general chapter of the aggregating institute in accordance with proper law. While the aggregating authority has no jurisdiction over the aggregated institute, this bonding allows for collaboration that is more extensive as well as the sharing of resources.

Having addressed how aggregation pertains to the process, this author now turns to the studies about groups that hope to become a religious institute.

V. The CARA Study: A Look at the United States
There have been numerous studies conducted about new institutes. In 1993, Sister Rose McDermott, SSJ published a study.[25] In 1996, Sister Marlene Weisenbeck, FSPA gave a presentation at one of our annual conventions on emerging expressions of consecrated life.[26] In 1999 the Center for Applied Research in the Apostolate (CARA) at Georgetown University compiled the first ever directory of new and emerging communities that had been established in the United States since 1965. They had a follow-up directory that was published in 2006.[27] All of these studies looked at the dynamics transpiring in the approved forms of consecrated life as well as the new movements. This author limits herself to looking at the 2006 CARA study as it pertains to what is transpiring in the approved forms of consecrated life.

CARA began its study in the fall of 2004 by contacting the 195 dioceses and eparchies whose bishops and eparchs are members of the United States Conference of Catholic Bishops. The center asked for the names and addresses of any new or emerging religious communities and lay movements. The criterion was: a) good standing in the diocese, b) having at least three or four members, and c) founded since 1965 in the United States. After sorting through the responses, it gathered information from 165 communities of consecrated life and lay movements across the country in eighty-eight dioceses and eparchies in forty states and territories. CARA discovered that 120 new communities have been founded within the last twenty-five years.[28] The study contains the following statistics: a)

---

[25] R. McDermott, "Recent Developments in Consecrated Life," in *Bulletin on Issues of Religious Law*, Vol. 9, Fall, (Washington, DC: Canon Law Society of America, 1993).

[26] M. Weisenbeck, "Emerging Expressions of Consecrated Life in the United States: Pastoral and Canonical Implications," *CLSA Proceedings* 58 (Washington, DC: Canon Law Society of America, 1996) 368-390.

[27] M. Bendyna (Editor), *Emerging Communities of Consecrated Life in the United States*, Second Edition, Center for Applied Research in the Apostolate [CARA],(Georgetown University, 2006).

[28] Ibid., 2.

thirty-eight (23%) are Private Associations, b) forty-eight (29%) are Public Associations, c) twenty-five (15%) are Religious Institutes, d) two (1%) are Secular Institutes, c) three (2%) are Societies of Apostolic Life and e) forty-nine (30%) did not give a response when asked about their canonical status.[29]

The CARA study indicates that some of these new communities broke off from an institute that had already been in existence. Thirty-three groups fall into this category. They include Franciscans, Carmelites, Dominicans, Benedictines, Augustinians, Sisters of Mercy, Society of St. John, Marists, and the International Families of Nazareth. Three out of the thirty-three were either a "pious union" or a "religious institute *ad experimentum* for five years" prior to formally being established as a religious institute.[30] The others experienced the stages that have been described in this seminar. In the history of consecrated life, there is also a documented example of a group of women religious who broke off from their original institute, and many years later, they decided to get back together and reunite into one institute.[31] The letter petitioning the Congregation for a reuniting of their two institutes says, "The causes of the separation are no longer issues."[32] In preparation for this seminar, this author spoke with a number of the communities that have broken off as well as the original institute. Additionally, this writer read a substantial amount of information from various archives. In some cases, there is hope for reuniting at some point in time. In other cases, the groups have engaged in cooperative ventures but do not see a reuniting at this time. Other patterns are also evident.

The CARA study also revealed common themes about the new groups that are forming. This includes groups that broke off from a religious institute and groups that began their existence without ever having been a part of a religious institute. In one-fourth to one-third of these groups, characteristics include devotion to Mary and the Eucharist, simple lifestyle, fidelity to the pope, and evangelization. Ten percent of these same communities also embrace other devotions, a charismatic spirituality, orthodoxy, and working with youth. Very few groups mention engaging in one of the traditional ministries that has been characteristic of religious institutes (i.e., teaching, nursing, or social work). The communities list contemplation, conducting retreats, parish missions, prayer groups, or doing catechetical work as their primary apostolate.

---

29 Ibid., 5. In addition to the statistics, the information includes the average year they attained their canonical status. Generally, it was after the 1983 code.

30 C. Darcy, *The Institute of the Sisters of Mercy of the Americas, The Canonical Development of the Proposed Governance Model*, (Lanham, MD: University Press of America, 1993) 166-171.

31 Sacred Congregation of Religious and Secular Institutes, 20 January 1986, Procedures for the Reunion of two Religious Institutes, *Canon Law Digest* Vol. XII (Washington, DC: Canon Law Society of America, 2002) 372-374.

32 Ibid., 372.

Additionally, those communities that wear habits are more likely to attract new members and to have more than seven members in formation. Communities that emphasize adherence to orthodox teaching are less likely to have numerous candidates than groups that do not put on emphasis on orthodoxy. Communities having Marian devotion have a large number of entrants. However, the same thought is not true regarding a devotion to the Eucharist. Groups living a simple lifestyle and working with the poor have people in formation. Benedictine, Franciscan, and Carmelite spiritualities remain attractive to prospective members.

With the United States in mind, this author now turns to other countries to see if there are similarities.

VI. A Brief Look at Other Countries

The May 2009 Colloquium in Montreal, *The Consecrated Life in Contemporary Canada,* had a conference about emerging religious communities in Quebec.[33] While the presenter, Rev. Rick van Lier, OP indicated that an in-depth sociological and demographic study has not been conducted and analyzed, he was able to provide some statistics.

He stated that more or less twenty new communities have emerged in Quebec since Vatican II. As a group, one fourth of them imitate the classical forms of consecrated life. He gave the following examples: the Congregation of St. John, the Monastic Fraternities of Jerusalem, and the Petits Frères de la Croix. The other three-fourths seem to bear features of something new (c. 605). In the rest of Canada, he said that the Companions of the Cross have emerged in Ottawa as a Society of Apostolic Life.

He also identified main characteristics. They have a strong prayer life, and they define themselves as monastic or semi-contemplative. There is a visibility by their own personal witness, and many are choosing to wear a habit. Their apostolate centers itself on evangelization, faith education, and spiritual experience. They have common apostolic projects rather than individual apostolates.

This brief overview of the Canadian experience looks very similar to what is transpiring in the United States and elsewhere. While neither the United States nor Canada is experiencing a lot of growth in the approved forms of consecrated life, major features found in both countries are alike. These dynamics also appear to be true in other countries. Sister Sylvie Robert, SA spoke eloquently about such traits at her presentation on consecrated life in Rome at the 2011 Theological Seminar.[34]

---

[33] R. van Lier, "New Emerging Religious Communities in the Catholic Church in Quebec." Conference documents can be found online at: http://www.crc-canada.org/en/documentation/leadership.

[34] See S. Robert, *To Live Here Below from the Beyond.*

Sister Vera Bombonatto, FSP verbalized these same vibrant issues in a presentation regarding what is transpiring in Latin America.[35]

Having looked at what is emerging in such groups, this author will now explore how these dynamics apply to the life of the Christian faithful.

VII. Relationship to Parish Life
Some of the questions that surface in parishes about these groups and often make their way to the ear of the bishop or the vicar for religious are: Who are these groups? Are they really sisters or brothers? Are they a religious order? As canonists, we can be helpful by making certain that the status of these groups is clear to the faithful and the various people who work at a diocesan level. For example, this might mean writing an article in the diocesan newspaper about associations of the faithful or placing a commentary in the parish bulletin where the group seems to be the most well known.

Another issue that surfaces is their capacity to raise funds from the faithful. When the group is not a public juridic person, it needs the permission of the diocesan bishop before it can begin to ask for money. Prior to making a decision about granting such permission, the bishop would need to know the financial situation of the group. Additionally, they need to indicate to him how they intend to use the funds that they raise. There needs to be a clear distinction between money going to the association itself and money that would go to the works of the group.

Other issues might arise. While the code gives the group the right to exist as a *de facto* association, it asks the bishop to be vigilant about what is transpiring in these groups. For example, if they are doing something to alienate the faithful from parish life and refuse to correct the situation, the bishop has the right to act for the sake of the common good. Another example would be groups promoting unhealthy devotions. They fail to cooperate with diocesan authorities. They only want to do things their own way. These dynamics are signs that the group is influencing the faithful in detrimental ways.

On the other hand, however, these communities can give a vibrant witness in the midst of many troubling situations in our world that affect parish life in one way or another. When they live an intense spiritual life that renders them sensitive to the cries of the needy, they give witness to a life that counters the secularism that is so prominent in our world. Such a witness can beckon the people in our parishes to give of themselves, their time, and their talent to the central mission of the church.

---

35 V. Bombonatto, "Theological Reflection on the New Experiences of Apostolic Religious Life," Unione Superiori Generali, http://www.fmi-adele.org/files/Bombonatto_2011_en.pdf. Even though she might be including new movements (c. 605), many of the dynamics are similar to what is transpiring with new foundations.

We also live in a world where there is a great deal of isolationism and individualism. By the profession of vows or other sacred bonds, these groups commit themselves to fostering communion by living a strong community life. Therefore, they have the potential to give witness to a radical living of the gospel message in a world that centers itself in consumerism, applauds freedom at any cost, and advocates unhealthy sexual desires and selfishness. Indeed, such a witness is the very foundation of religious life. Its essence is expressed very concisely by Sister Nadine Foley, OP when she says that addressing the issues of any particular moment in time means that each institute "adapts and grows and grafts new things into its old self, for the sake of gospel mission."[36]

Having made these general remarks about how new foundations can affect parish life, this author now turns to some concluding remarks.

VIII. The Critical Tasks

This seminar has addressed a number of central points and very practical issues. The key consists in discerning the authenticity of the charism of the founder/foundress, if is such a person is already evident, or the charism of a new foundation. Even though the canons on Associations of the Christian Faithful need more development because they do not always seem to address all the issues, they do provide a viable structure that is workable and foundational for any group that desires to begin the process of establishing itself as a religious institute. The journey involves a path marked by stages designed to help the group and church authority in this discernment process. In most instances, the statutes of such a group will look more like the constitution of a religious institute rather than the statutes of other associations that might exist in the diocese. When we, as canonists, serve as the bridge that facilitates this process, we will be contributing to the transformation of our church and our world. Indeed, that transformation is an urgent task in our time.[37]

---

36 N. Foley, "The Ambiguity of Religious Life: Does It Evolve?" in *Review for Religious* 56 (1997) 1:6-13.

37 This author gratefully acknowledges the following canonists for making suggestions and/or reviewing seminar material: Sisters Dominica Brennan, OP, Sharon Holland, IHM, Marlene Weisenbeck, FSPA and Ms. Siobhan Verbeek.

Appendix A

The Establishment of a Religious Institute

RELIGIOUS INSTITUTES	SECULAR INSTITUTES	SOCIETIES OF APOSTOLIC LIFE
1. *Definition:* A religious institute is a society in which members, according to proper law, pronounce public vows, either perpetual or temporary which are to be renewed, however, when the period of time has elapsed, and lead a life of brothers or sisters in common. (Canon 607 §2)	A secular institute is an institute of consecrated life in which the Christian faithful, living in the world, strive for the perfection of charity and seek to contribute to the sanctification of the world, especially from within. (Canon 710)	§1. Societies of apostolic life resemble institutes of consecrated life; their members, without religious vows, pursue the apostolic purpose proper to the society and, leading a life in common as brothers or sisters according to their proper manner of life, strive for the perfection of charity through the observance of the constitutions. §2. Among these are societies in which members assume the evangelical counsels by some bond defined in the constitutions. (Canon 731)
2. 2. *Proper Law:* Constitutions and other norms. (Canon 587)	Constitutions and other norms. (Canon 587)	Constitutions and other norms. (Canons 587 and 732)
3. 3. *Commitment:* Profess the three evangelical counsels: poverty, chastity, obedience (Canons 559-601)	Assume the three evangelical counsels: poverty, chastity, obedience (Canons 559-601)	α. All members embrace celibacy. (Canons 739 and 277) β. In some: members embrace the evangelical counsels. (Canon 731 §2) χ. Personal Property (Canon 741 §2)

RELIGIOUS INSTITUTES	SECULAR INSTITUTES	SOCIETIES OF APOSTOLIC LIFE
4. *Bond:* Public Vows (Canons 607 §2 and 1192 §1)	Determined in the Constitutions (Canon 712); sacred bonds, oath, promise, other.	Determined in the Constitutions; some bond if the evangelical counsels are assumed
5. *Community Living:* Fraternal life in common (Canons 602, 665, 668 §3, 670)	Fraternal life but not normally in common. (Canons 602, 714)	Fraternal life in common. (Canons 731, 740, 741 §2)
6. *Witness:* Public witness to Christ and the Church and a certain separation from the world. (Canon 607 §3)	Living in the world like a leaven endeavoring to permeate everything with an evangelical spirit. (Canons 710, 713)	Pursue the apostolic purpose proper to each one. (Canon 731 §1)
7. *Apostolate:* apostolate in the name of the Church and of the Institute. (Canons 675 §3, 665 §1, 671)	Ordinarily members are engaged in their own professions or avocations in the world. (Canon 731)	Apostolic purpose proper to the society (Canon 731 §1)

RELIGIOUS INSTITUTES	SECULAR INSTITUTES	SOCIETIES OF APOSTOLIC LIFE
8. *Status:* Clerics are incardinated in the institute. (Canon 266 §2)	a. Lay members retain their own status. (Canon 711) b. Clerics normally incardinated in the diocese. (Canons 266 §3, 715 §1, 713 §3)	Clerics are incardinated into the Society unless Constitutions say otherwise. (Canons 266 §2, 736 §1)
9. *Admission:* a. See canons 643, 656, 657 b. 17 years complete c. First Profession: at least 18 years old d. Final Profession: at least 21	a. See canons 721-723 b. Majority Age (canon 97) c. First Commitment: after at least 2 years d. Final Commitment: after at least 5 years	a. See canons 735 §2 (cc. 642-645); 643 b. 17 years complete c. First and Final Commitment: determined in proper law.
10. *Ordination:* Studies: Universal and Proper Laws (Canon 659 §3) Pontifical Clerical Institute Superior Issues Dimissorials (Canon 1019)	Same as secular clergy (Canon 1019 §2)	Program of Studies same as Secular Clergy (Canon 736 §2) Pontifical Clerical Society Superior issues Dimissorials (Canon 1019 §1)

RELIGIOUS INSTITUTES	SECULAR INSTITUTES	SOCIETIES OF APOSTOLIC LIFE
11. *Government:* Superiors have authority according to universal law and Constitutions (Canon 596 §1) In Pontifical Clerical Religious Institutes: power of governance (Canons 596 §2, 134)	Superiors have authority according to universal law and Constitutions (Canon 596 §§1 and 3)	Superiors have authority according to universal law and Constitutions (Canon 596 §§1 and 3) Clerical Societies: power of governance (Canons 134, 596 §2, 732)

APPENDIX B
THE ESTABLISHMENT OF A RELIGIOUS INSTITUTE

The list of required documents that need to be sent to CICLSAL in view of erecting a Religious Institute of Diocesan Right includes the following elements:

1. The names of the founder and the first superior general along with *curriculum vitae* of each.

2. A historical-juridical account of the association from its beginnings including the decree of erection as a Public Association of the Faithful.

3. The constitution and the directory of the institute revised in accordance with the *Code of Canon Law*.

4. Where applicable, a picture of the religious dress of both a professed member and a novice.

5. Up to date statistics of the membership, including the year of birth and of temporary and perpetual profession,[1] the place and diocese where houses are located, and the works of the institute.[2]

6. An account of the financial patrimony of the institute including debts.

7. Statements regarding any extraordinary experiences or particular devotions and whether in the diocese of origin there already exists another institute with the same purpose and name, and

8. Testimonial letters from the diocesan bishops of those dioceses in which the institute is represented; such letters are to be sent directly to the Holy See giving the opinion of the bishops about the following matters: a) usefulness, b) stability, c) discipline of the institute, d) formation of members, e) government, f) administration of goods, g) liturgical and sacramental dimensions, h) a sense of being with the church, particularly in regard to the observances of ecclesiastical

---

1 For erection as an Institute of Diocesan Right the required number is about forty (40) members who have professed perpetual private vows. For erection as an Institute of Pontifical Right, the number is about one hundred (100). For a monastery of canon 615, the number is eight to twelve (8-12) members in perpetual private vows.

2 For secular institutes there is no listing of houses as there is for religious institutes since there is no obligation to common life or corporate works.

discipline as expressed in the common law of the church and in the diocesan directives.[3]

9. Establishment as an Institute of Pontifical Right is an option but not a requirement. However, it might be wise to consider it if the Institute of Diocesan Right has spread into different dioceses or around the world. The documents and information sent to CICLSAL are the same as they were for erection as an Institute of Diocesan Right.

10. The "deposit" of 500 euros equivalent to around $682 (checks are made out to CICLSAL).[4]

---

[3] The testimonial letter from the bishop(s) describes concisely the important issues for founders and bishops in founding and guiding a new institute.

[4] Even though the amount of the "deposit" continues to increase, 1 through 10 can be found in S. Holland "New Institutes, Mergers and Suppression" in *Procedural Handbook for Institutes of Consecrated Life and Societies of Apostolic Life* (Washington, DC: Canon Law of America, 2001) 37 and in L. Jarrell and D. Ward, "Procedures for Establishing an Institute/Society" in *Procedures and Documents for Canonical and Civil Administration in Institutes of Consecrated Life and Societies of Apostolic Life*, LRCR (2007): 5-6.

Seminar

Happily Never After:
Some Reflections on Rotal Jurisprudence Concerning the *Bonum Sacramenti*
Reverend Monsignor John G. Johnson

Once a year Tribunal administrators busy themselves preparing the Roman report on the activities of their courts. A few months later bishops receive letters from the Signatura, acknowledging receipt of the report and reacting to it. These letters express sometimes curiosity and sometimes alarm over the large number of cases American Tribunals routinely decide on psychological grounds. The statistics easily stoke suspicion that the majority of the population of the United States is at least slightly mad. Although bishops and Tribunal officials could shrug off the Signatura's correspondence as just an annual annoyance, a more prudent reaction is to see it as an invitation to think more broadly about potential grounds of marital nullity. A wider use of more traditional grounds tends not to attract such guarded Roman scrutiny.

Among the traditional grounds of nullity exclusion of the *bonum sacramenti* is increasingly worth a look. When civil divorce was unavailable—as was the case in Italy or Ireland a generation ago—it might not have made much sense to inquire whether Titius entered marriage with Bertha intending to retain the right to divorce her if the marriage proved to be unhappy. When civil divorce was available only for flagrant adultery or violent spousal abuse, it might not have made much sense to inquire whether Bertha intended to enter a dissoluble marriage with Titius. Nowadays, at least in the United States of America, the civil dissolution of a marriage is readily and easily available; and it is no longer fanciful to wonder whether Bertha and Titius both meant to marry "until death do them part."

Nearly forty years ago Larry Wrenn published an essay about the attitudes marriageable young adults had towards marriage.[1] "One percent of the respondents said that, if the values most important to them were not realized after a year or two, they anticipated, not that they would try harder or make the best of it, but that they would separate; and 13.7% of the respondents expected to do the same if their most important values were not realized after five years."[2] "If they actu-

---

1   Lawrence G. Wrenn, "A New Condition Limiting Marriage," *The Jurist* 34 (1974) 292-315.
2   Ibid., 310.

ally planned or intended to divorce after five years if their values were not being met," Wrenn pointed out, "that of course would constitute an intention against the substance of marriage, namely against the perpetuity of marriage."[3] It is difficult to believe that people approaching marriage in the United States around the turn of the century were more strongly committed to the indissolubility of marriage than were the young people whom Wrenn studied in the early 1970's. Unless what Wrenn observed was an aberration, it does not stretch credulity to suppose that there are a lot of broken marriages out there, one or both parties to which excluded the *bonum sacramenti*. Sciacca's observation that "The... grounds of exclusion of the good of permanence (*bonum sacramenti*)... occurs these days hardly less often than the allegation of consensual incapacity"[4] indicates that canonists everywhere are more sensitive to this possibility.

In the light of the Signatura's recurring request that American canonists think more about traditional grounds of nullity, and in light of the possibility that there may be many cases which could be investigated fruitfully under the heading of exclusion of indissolubility, I propose to reflect today on how Rotal Auditors have been dealing with this ground recently.

Consent as the Efficient Cause of Marriage
Rotal analysis of most marriage cases involving deficiencies of consent begins with a discussion of that all-important act. Sentence after sentence points to the spouses' act of consent as the efficient cause of marriage. For example, Funghini, cites *Gaudium et spes*, n. 48, in recognition that the spouses' "covenant or irrevocable personal consent" establishes the conjugal community of life and love. The auditor continues:

> Consent, which makes a marriage between legally capable persons and which no human power can supply (c. 1057, §1), is an act of the will by means of which a man and a woman by means of an irrevocable covenant mutually give and accept each other (c. 1057, §2) for the purpose of establishing between them a partnership of the whole of life.... From this it is evident that the constitutive element of the matrimonial contract is consent, or an act of the will, which is a human act understood in the philosophical sense, and [which] therefore presupposes a previous knowing on the part of the intellect and a free determination of the will, which therefore should have mastery of its own acts.[5]

---

3 Ibid., 312.

4 *Coram* Sciacca, 1 June 2007, *Rotal Jurisprudence: Selected Translations*, ed. Victoria Vondenberger, RSM (Washington, DC: Canon Law Society of America, 2011) 228-229. The presentation will cite this volume as *RJ*, p.

5 *Coram* Funghini, 19 January 2001, *Rotae Romanae Tribunal Decisiones seu Sententiae* (in future references, *RRTDecisiones*) 93 (2009) 61.

Caberletti writes, "Marriage arises only through the consent of the spouses."[6] "The spouses' consent gives birth to marriage or creates it.... Matrimony cannot arise if the subject is held incapable or if the object is missing or vitiated."[7] Sciacca observes, "Matrimonial consent—as everyone in fact knows and unanimously proclaims it—makes the marriage.... consent pertains to the essence of marriage so that, in its absence, marriage itself cannot exist."[8] Pena identifies consent as "the essence of *matrimonium in fieri*. Therefore, when such consent is lacking the marriage cannot be valid."[9] Ciani waxes poetic, "Just like a soul without a body, so marriage without consent cannot exist, for consent is the soul of the contract."[10] Huber is more sober: "the consent of the contracting party is the efficient cause of marriage...."[11] Defilippi uses the same language: "...the sole, adequate and entirely necessary 'efficient cause' of marriage as they say '*in facto esse*' is the personal consent of the spouses...."[12]

This Rotal unanimity about the function of marital consent is not surprising: it expresses, sometimes literally, the provision of canon 1057 §1 of the 1983 Code of Canon Law: "The lawfully expressed consent between legally capable parties makes a marriage. It cannot be supplied by any [other] human power." I tax your patience with so many statements of this obvious principle both because it serves as the basis for any discussion of simulation and because it gives rise to a conundrum. If genuine matrimonial consent is the efficient cause of any marriage, and if only the spouses can give that consent, it should follow that if the consent of either party is absent, no marriage can come into being. The citation from Sciacca expressed this conclusion in virtually the same words: "...consent pertains to the essence of marriage so that, in its absence, marriage itself cannot exist."[13] Nevertheless, Rotal Auditors are emphatic that the mere absence of consent cannot warrant an affirmative decision on grounds of simulation.[14] Canon 1101 §2 prescribes that a spouse "contracts [marriage] invalidly" only if he or she "by a positive act of the will excludes marriage itself or some essential matrimonial element or some essential [matrimonial] property." A prerequisite

---

6   *Coram* Caberletti, 5 April 2000, *RRTDecisiones* 92 (2007) 294.

7   *Coram* Caberletti, 10 April 2003, *RRTDecisiones* 95 (2012) 214.

8   *Coram* Sciacca, 22 October 2002, *RJ*, 146.

9   *Coram* Pena, 15 December 2000, *RRTDecisiones* 92 (2007) 723.

10   *Coram* Ciani, 21 May 2003, *RRTDecisiones* 95 (2012) 320.

11   *Coram* Huber, 27 January 2000, *RRTDecisiones* 92 (2007) 118.

12   *Coram* Defilippi, 9 February 2000, *RRTDecisiones* 92 (2007) 141.

13   *Coram* Sciacca, 22 October 2002, in *RJ*, 146.

14   For example, *coram* Lopez-Illana, 30 April 2003, *RRTDecisiones* 95 (2012) 259: "...only he invalidly contracts who by a positive act of the will excludes some essential property, or unity or indissolubility, but by no means [he] who does not accept by a positive act of the will unity or indissolubility."

for an affirmative decision on grounds of simulation, whether total or partial, is sufficient proof of the existence of this "positive act of the will."[15]

Before one attempts to discern the meaning of a *positive act of the will*, however, it may be worthwhile to examine the object of matrimonial consent, because what a simulator will be excluding by his or her "positive act of the will" is something essential to the object of consent. In the course of a very long sentence dealing with multiple grounds of nullity Caberletti writes, "The spouse most certainly is, through [his] act of consent, the agent or the author of the conjugal covenant, but the essence of marriage, that is [*scilicet*] the object of consent, in no sense depends on the human subject of the marriage, because 'Only God himself is the author of marriage endowed with various goods and ends.'"[16] Elsewhere the same auditor says,

---

15 This is not to say that a marriage cannot be invalid if there is insufficient proof of the "positive act of the will" excluding either marriage itself or something essential to marriage. *Coram* Lopez-Illana, 30 April 2003, *RRTDecisiones* 95 (2012) 252-270 provides an example. Ursula met Urbanus in 1968 at the house of a common friend. Ursula's father, a rich and severe man, disapproved of their relationship from the outset. While living with her brother Michael, Ursula occasionally saw Urbanus. When she became pregnant, the couple eloped and celebrated a civil marriage; and Ursula gave birth to a son (p. 252). "At that time they were not legitimately spouses even though they were living together either with the man's parents or with friends. Therefore Ursula, unhappy about this unstable relationship, expressed her desire for their son to be baptized and for her to celebrate a religious marriage with Urbanus" (p. 253). "Many were the problems in both the civil and the religious marriage. Urbanus treated his wife improperly—he was even unfaithful—and often violent" (p. 253). Long after they divorced Ursula petitioned for annulment "on ten grounds" (p. 253). Against the first instance negative decision, Ursula appealed; and the second instance court heard the case on grounds of her grave lack of discretion of judgment and on grounds of her having simulated. She received an affirmative decision only on grounds of a grave lack of discretion of judgment. The case thereupon came before the Rota, and her advocate induced the turnus to add "subordinately, and as if in first instance, … exclusion of the indissolubility of the bond on the part of the woman Plaintiff" (p. 254). The turnus ultimately could find no evidence of "a positive act of the will… whereby the indissolubility of the marriage was excluded by the Plaintiff" (pp. 269-270). On the other hand, the Auditors were favorably impressed with the Rotal expert's finding that for Ursula "the religious rite was superfluous and was justified only as the necessary means of fulfilling a promise she had made" (p. 268). In their judgment "the Plaintiff could not give present consent if she was indeed convinced that the first merely civilly expressed consent was valid" (p. 268). "… the Plaintiff thought nothing about the essential rights and duties of marriage because of her grave lack of discretion of judgment, for she was in fact destitute of that discretion of judgment which is demanded for valid consent" (p. 270). On her part the consent that was necessary for a valid marriage to come into being was lacking, but not because, by a positive act of the will, she excluded anything essential to marriage, but because "there was lacking in her, while she approached the altar,… the will to contract, for she was of the opinion that she had already contracted perfectly" (pp. 268-269).

16 *Coram* Caberletti, 12 June 2003, *RRTDecisiones* 95 (2012) 365.

Marriage arises only through the consent of the spouses... But still consent, indeed an act of a subject, should receive an object established by the Divine Founder of marriage: "When consent is present, the marriage is valid. Since however the nature of matrimony does not depend on the will of the spouses, but has been constituted by God himself, it is necessary that the consent be truly matrimonial, or that it embrace everything which pertains to the essence of marriage, not indeed in the sense that someone should have all of this expressly before his/her eyes, but that he/she intends to enter a true marriage, just as other human beings [do], and he/she excludes no constitutive element' (*coram* Heard, 22 July 1944...).[17]

Bottone finds, "for it to be possible to establish marriage the contracting parties should accept all and every essential property of marriage, not to mention its ordering to the good of the spouses and to children; besides they should enjoy the capacity of assuming and fulfilling the essential obligations [of marriage] and be free from impediments."[18] Pinto agrees: "...the matrimonial sacrament is always the same, because God established it in its nature and grace...."[19] "Marriage has its own objective structure which specifies it and distinguishes it from every other institution," insists Defilippi.[20] "Consequently, whoever intends to contract marriage cannot depart from the essential objective elements and properties of marriage..., although the sole, adequate and entirely necessary 'efficient cause' of marriage as they say '*in facto esse*' is the personal consent of the parties."[21] Funghini likewise asserts, "Conjugal consent... cannot deviate from the essential objective elements and properties of the conjugal covenant, with which God adorns [marriage] and which the magisterium of the Church faithfully interprets and declares and teaches."[22]

The non-canonist might find both quaint and unjustifiably dogmatic this Rotal insistence that marriage has a nature independent of the parties' preferences. There was a time, however, when the most forceful of these Rotal *dicta* would have seemed a commonplace. Some evidence of this is what the Scots jurist, Viscount Stair, by no means a man of Catholic sensibilities, published in 1681:

> Obligations arising from voluntary engagement take their rule and substance from the will of man and may be framed and composed at his pleasure... but so cannot marriage, wherein it is not in the power

---

17 *Coram* Caberletti, 5 April 2000, *RRTDecisiones* 92 (2007) 294.
18 *Coram* Bottone 8 June 2000, *RRTDecisiones* 92 (2007) 453.
19 *Coram* Pinto, 14 January 2000, *RRTDecisiones* 92 (2007) 14.
20 *Coram* Defilippi, 9 February 2000, *RRTDecisiones* 92 (2007) 139.
21 Ibid., 141.
22 *Coram* Funghini, 19 January 2001, *RRTDecisiones* 93 (2009) 61-62.

> of the parties, though of common consent to alter any substantial… marriage arises from the law of nature and it is given as the very example of the Natural law.[23]

This opinion expressed by a Protestant common law jurist might be inserted into a randomly-selected Rotal sentence and no one would find it alien.

The conclusion towards which these observations tend is that marriage is not simply the creation of the spouses. It is true that a spouse must be free to choose whether to marry or not.[24] It is also true that, while respecting the freedom of the partner, a spouse has the right to choose whom he or she will marry. But the spouse is *not* free to fashion a relationship in accordance with his/her preferences and to demand that others recognize it as "marriage." Marriage has its own nature, its own structure, its own essential characteristics; and to enter marriage one must embrace these with one's act of consent.[25] What Defilippi said above bears repeating: "…whoever intends to contract marriage cannot depart from the essential objective elements and properties of marriage…."[26]

Pena, however, approvingly cites a qualification offered earlier by Stankiewicz (19 May 1998):

> "…in order to enter marriage validly it is not required that the contractants accept the indissolubility of the bond [or, for that matter, the other essential properties or essential elements of marriage] by a positive act of the will. For the actuation of this essential property of marriage is not immediately caused by the will of the spouses, but by the divine will. Therefore for the validity of consent it is not required that the contractants positively intend indissolubility, but it is enough that this property is not excluded by a positive act of the will."[27]

---

23 This excerpt from *Institutions of the Laws of Scotland* is cited in John Haldane, "Against Erotic Entitlements," *First Things* 222 (April 2012) 20.

24 Cf. canon 219: "All Christ's faithful have the right to immunity from any kind of coercion in choosing a state in life." Also canon 1103: "A marriage is invalid which was entered into by reason of force or of grave fear imposed from without, even if not purposely, from which the person has no escape other than by choosing marriage."

25 *Coram* Sciacca, 1 June 2007, *RJ,* pp. 229-230 helpfully cites Pope John Paul II's 21 January 1999 allocution to the Rota: "They [viz., the spouses] are free to celebrate matrimony after choosing each other in a completely free way but at the very moment that they posit this act they establish a personal state in which love becomes a kind of duty that is also endowed with a juridic character."

26 *Coram* Defilippi, 9 February 2000, *RRTDecisiones* 92 (2007) 141.

27 *Coram* Pena, 17 October 2003, *RRTDecisiones* 95 (2012) 590.

If, in order to marry validly, the spouse had to grasp fully and to choose explicitly everything essential to marriage, only canon lawyers and theologians would be apt subjects for marriage. Canon law is far less exacting. In order to posit valid matrimonial consent, according to canon 1096 §1, "it is necessary that the contractants not be ignorant that marriage is a permanent partnership between a man and a woman ordered to the procreation of children by means of some kind of sexual cooperation."[28] The law presumes that a person acquires at least this much knowledge of the nature of marriage by the time he or she has reached puberty (canon 1096 §2). If a person knows what marriage is, and if he/she undergoes a ceremony by which people become married, it is reasonable to presume that he/or she intends, at least implicitly, to enter the kind of relationship that marriage is. Pena expresses the matter succinctly: "Canon law presumes, whenever the baptized appear before the Church to exchange nuptial consent, that they cherish the true internal intention to bind themselves by a sacred bond until the completion of their whole lives, and that they sincerely assume the obligation of preserving mutual fidelity and generously accepting the heavenly gift of children (cf. can. 1101 §1)."[29]

Canon law does recognize, however, that a person might undergo a ceremony of marriage while intending not to become married or while intending to establish a relationship that does not have "some essential element of marriage or some essential property" of marriage (canon 1101 §2).[30] Pinto offers a sage comment: "Although the matrimonial sacrament is always the same, because God established it in its nature and grace, ... it is nonetheless received by the human person, who on the contrary changes under the influence of emotions which very often oppose Catholic doctrine and indeed the natural law founded by God...."[31] This peculiar double intention—on the one hand, to participate in a marriage ceremony, and, on the other hand, not thereby to establish "a permanent partnership between a man and a woman ordered to the procreation of children"—is what canonists denote by *simulation*. Such *simulation* is *total* if the party intends

---

28 This description of marriage might once have been non-controversial. Nowadays, almost every element is subject to dispute. For example, judges and politicians emphatically deny that marriage is, by definition, a relationship between a man and a woman. Opinion makers might concede that this particular couple or that one might want to welcome children into their family, but they by no means "know" that an openness to children is an essential characteristic of marriage. On the other hand, a couple desirous of having children might opt to do so without "some kind of sexual cooperation" (they might opt for *in vitro* fertilization), or they might use a "surrogate mother."

29 *Coram* Pena, 17 October 2003, *RRTDecisiones* 95 (2012) 588.

30 Pena continues, "Nevertheless the law cannot pass over in silence the case in which the spouse, while he says he adheres to marriage just as the Church proposes, really in his inmost heart totally rejects marriage or embraces it only in accordance with his own intention. This he does through the exclusion of some essential element or essential property of the natural covenant just as the Church has received it (cf. can. 1101, §2)." Ibid., 588.

31 *Coram* Pinto, 14 January 2000, *RRTDecisiones* 92 (2007) 14.

not to become married at all or *partial* if the party intends to become married, but not in every essential. And because indissolubility is an essential property of marriage (canon 1056), intending to enter a marriage that is not indissoluble is a species of partial simulation.

When deciding cases involving the exclusion of the *bonum sacramenti*, some Rotal Auditors stress the theological roots of indissolubility. For example, Monier writes:

> Indissolubility is a property of marriage which in Christian marriage obtains firmness and special significance by reason of the sacrament (cf. c. 1056). The Second Vatican Council in its Pastoral Constitution *Gaudium et spes* receives traditional doctrine and successively teaches: "This intimate partnership of married life and love has been established by the Creator and qualified by His laws. It is rooted in the conjugal covenant of irrevocable personal consent. Hence, by that human act whereby spouses mutually bestow and accept each other, a relationship arises which by divine will and in the eyes of society too is a lasting one. For the good of the spouses and their offspring as well as of society, the existence of this sacred bond no longer depends on human decisions alone" (n. 48). For this reason no one can change the object of marriage because it was established as such by the Creator.... Indissolubility is necessary for the building up of the community of persons as the Supreme Pontiff teaches (*Familiaris consortio*, n. 20)....[32]

Civili, too, finds inspiration in *Familiaris consortio*. Because God has established indissoluble marriage as a sign of his love for human beings, and because the indissoluble marriage is also a sign of the unbreakable union of Christ and the church, he writes,

> ...indissolubility is a consequence of grace, which makes it possible. Nowadays many say that it is not possible for a person to conjoin himself/herself to only one person for a lifetime. These people reject the indissolubility of marriage declaring that it is not consistent with the human person. To all of this the Supreme Pontiff objects that the law of indissolubility flows from the intimate nature of the gift: with God's help, it concerns a person's gift of a person to a person. In truth the spouses do not mutually and fully give and accept each other, unless this gift includes their temporal condition as well. For if one or the other party retains for himself/herself the faculty of

---

[32] *Coram* Monier, 16 February 2001, *RRTDecisiones* 93 (2009) 155. The translation from the citation of *Gaudium et spes* comes from *The Documents of Vatican II*, ed. Walter M. Abbott (New York: Crossroad, 1989) 250.

deciding otherwise afterwards, for that reason he/she is not already giving himself/herself totally.[33]

Huber observes:

> ...despite some texts of difficult interpretation and examples of indulgence, the magisterium of the Church has always taught that marriage between baptized [persons] is indissoluble.... The bond of marriage arises from a free and conscious human act. This act, by which the man and the woman mutually give and receive each other for the purpose of establishing marriage, requires their indissoluble unity. The indissolubility of marriage is therefore not an invention of the Church, but [is rooted] in the intimate disposition of a man towards a woman, that is to say in their gift of each to the other, without either's becoming the possession of the other. The matrimonial bond, founded in God's will and engraved in creation itself, is irrevocable, that is, not dependent on human will and beyond posited human power, consequently intrinsically indissoluble.[34]

A faithful sexual relationship that lacks indissolubility may look like marriage in many respects, but it will not be marriage as the church understands marriage. If someone should intend to establish such a relationship with his/her spouse, that person would not be intending to enter marriage.

What Is Excluded When Someone Excludes the Bonum Sacramenti?
Serrano has observed that technical precision in specifying the object of a court's investigation greatly facilitates the gathering of proof.[35] The better judges know exactly what question they are attempting to answer, the more likely they are to know what evidence they will need, where they are likely to find it, whether they have found it, and whether further digging is likely to unearth anything of value. Conversely, when judges do not know what question they are attempting to answer, they may well spend lots of time and energy heaping up irrelevancies.

In cases involving allegations of exclusion of the *bonum sacramenti* Rotal Auditors have devised precise, although perhaps somewhat cumbersome, formulations of the object whose occurrence the court is attempting to verify or falsify. With characteristic incisiveness Huber notes that "The object of proof" in such cases "is the existence or inexistence of the act of the simulator."[36] The specific "act of the simulator" is the exclusion of indissolubility. Hence, it is important for the court to know exactly what such an act contains. Stankiewicz

---

33 *Coram* Civili, 14 December 2000, *RRTDecisiones* 92 (2007) 715.
34 *Coram* Huber, 30 April 2003, *RRTDecisiones* 95 (2012) 240.
35 *Coram* Serrano, 3 August 2001, *RRTDecisiones* 93 (2009) 601.
36 *Coram* Huber, 30 Huber 2003, *RRTDecisiones* 95 (2012) 242.

writes, "that person excludes the *bonum sacramenti* or indissolubility who reserves to himself, absolutely or relatively, that is if something should happen, the freedom [*licentiam*] or power [*arbitrium*] of recovering his pristine status of freedom, breaking off and dissolving by his own efforts or through the intervention of public authority, whether civil or canonical, the conjugal bond [which is] perpetual by its very nature...."[37] Elsewhere Stankiewicz describes exclusion of indissolubility as "a subjective reservation on the part of the simulating party of resuming his status with full freedom through vindicating for himself the faculty of dissolving, not only the civil, but also the canonical conjugal bond."[38] "Or, in other words, 'he directly and properly excludes indissolubility who reserves to himself the right of radically dissolving the matrimonial bond...'."[39] Monier agrees, "In other words the spouse, who values himself as a source of law, elicits consent for his own advantage, and whether in every case or in only some accidental circumstance reserves to himself the faculty of dissolving the bond so as to be able to recover his entire freedom" excludes the *bonum sacramenti*.[40] "Certainly a marriage is considered null if it has been proven that by a positive act of the will the spouse reserved to himself the right of destroying the bond in the case of an unhappy outcome of the marriage...."[41] The same Auditor elsewhere adds that "it is not necessary that the spouse by a positive will intends to get a divorce in any case"; it is sufficient "'that he reserves to himself the faculty... to recover his full freedom from the bond' (c. Faltin, 19 February 1992...)."[42]

It may be helpful here to draw a distinction between what the simulator intends—the reservation to himself/herself of the faculty to become free from the obligations of marriage—and the means the simulator may use to realize his/her intention. Pena has observed,

> ...the essential property of indissolubility is excluded by the spouse who reserves to himself the power—or rather the decision [*arbitrium*]—of dissolving the bond and recovering his freedom, to wit of breaking the bond at will. This happens when the spouse cherishes a plan concerning the dissolution of the personal bond, nor is it required that he himself intends the seeking of a civil divorce or the introduction of a nullity action, in order to enter a new marriage: for it suffices that he should consider the marriage, celebrated with such

---

37   *Coram* Stankiewicz 26 January 2001, *RRTDecisiones* 93 (2009) 95.

38   *Coram* Stankiewicz, 25 October 2001, *RRTDecisiones* 93 (2009) 697.

39   This citation of *coram* Stankiewicz, 26 November 1998, is found in *coram* Funghini, 19 January 2001, *RRTDecisiones* 93 (2009) 64.

40   *Coram* Monier, 16 February 2001, *RRTDecisiones* 93 (2009) 155.

41   Ibid., 155.

42   *Coram* Monier, 26 January 2001, *RRTDecisiones* 93 (2009) 108.

a positive limitation, as non-existing, and himself as bound by no bond (cf. *coram* Palestro, 24 March 1993...).[43]

Pena's point appears to be that a judge might conclude that one of the spouses had simulated even if the simulator had not determined by the time of the marriage exactly *how* he/she would recover the freedom to marry. "The object of the exclusion of indissolubility is not the will of divorcing civilly, but the reservation of the right or the faculty of somehow dissolving the entire bond...."[44] It might be easier for a court to conclude that someone had excluded the *bonum sacramenti* if the simulator had clearly and emphatically stated on the very day of the wedding, "If x happens, I will obtain a divorce and remarry"; but the predetermination of the means he/she will use to recover his/her freedom is not the point at issue. The point at issue is the reservation of the right to dissolve the bond, however he/she proposes to accomplish that.

Keeping this distinction in mind is important, in part, because of the ambiguity of the term *divorce*. It is true that some Auditors, who are anything but unsophisticated or linguistically challenged, view a spouse's intention to seek a divorce as the basis for a presumption that he/she excluded indissolubility from his/her marriage;[45] but Huber urges caution:

> To designate exclusion of indissolubility, the parties and witnesses often [*haud raro*] employ the word *divorce*. But these writings are read: "Where the parties or the witnesses use the word *divorce*, the Judge should proceed cautiously. By no means from this common word is it permitted to conclude in favor of a positive act of the will against indissolubility. For in the field of canon law the term *divorce* does not have an accurately circumscribed meaning. For this reason, in the concrete case it must always be investigated, in what sense the term is employed, whether it is a case of [*agatur de*] an intention of breaking off the conjugal life or of an intention of vindicating freedom for other [people], or an intention of rescinding the matrimonial bond" (*coram* [Huber], 16 June 1994...). This diverse meaning of the word *divorce* also shines forth from *The Catechism of the Catholic Church*, when it teaches: "If civil divorce remains the only possible way of ensuring certain legal rights, the care of the children, or the protection of inheritance, it can be tolerated and does not constitute a moral offense." ... In these cases the word *divorce*

---

43 *Coram* Pena, 17 October 2003, *RRTDecisiones* 95 (2012) 589.

44 This citation of *coram* Huber, 28 September 1995, is from *coram* Turnaturi, 10 April 2003, *RRTDecisiones* 95 (2012) 199.

45 This position is ably argued *coram* Sciacca, 9 May 2003, *RRTDecisiones* 95 (2012) 286-287. In support of this position Sciacca cites Massimi (a heavyweight, if ever there was one) and Grazioli.

means a separation of the spouses or a separation from bed, board, and habitation, while the matrimonial bond remains.[46]

Ridding oneself of the matrimonial bond rather than achieving separation form bed and board is the real object of exclusion of the *bonum sacramenti*. Because someone might use the term *divorce* to indicate only the latter, the ecclesiastical judge prudently probes beneath the language to determine the meaning.

One should also bear in mind that a spouse can exclude the *bonum sacramenti* without indicating beforehand exactly how he/she proposes to regain freedom. Defilippi writes about a young Plaintiff who "either in her judicial declarations or in her extrajudicial declarations… said nothing about [her] intention of taking recourse to divorce, which in Italy already for many years was considered as the customary concrete means of recovering [one's] liberty."[47] The turnus was nevertheless certain that she had "really made the continued existence [*perseverantiam*] of the connubial bond depend on her own will," or, in other words, that "she had reserved to herself the power, that is [*seu*], the right of disposing of the property of the indissolubility of the marriage."[48] The real object of the court's investigation in a case involving exclusion of the *bonum sacramenti* is, not whether the alleged simulator used the word *divorce*, but whether he/she "at the time of the marriage reserved to himself/herself the faculty of *somehow* dissolving the entire bond, even though he/she did not decide to which legal means he/she would have recourse to obtain this concrete end."[49]

Absolute and Hypothetical Exclusions

The reservation of the right to dissolve the marriage can be either absolute or hypothetical. Caberletti explains the former: "the perpetuity of marriage is *absolutely* spurned, if the spouse intends the dissolution of the marriage, without himself deciding on any circumstance as necessary…."[50] Stankiewicz is of the opinion that the *absolute* exclusion of the *bonum sacramenti* is not a frequent occurrence "because no one of sound mind intends to enter a marriage which at the very same time he, with an absolute will, has decided to dissolve."[51] Opera lovers know that such behavior is not unimaginable, though: moments before "marrying" Butterfly, Lieutenant Pinkerton confesses to the consul his firm intention of escaping the entanglement so that he can marry a "real" American wife. Readers of Noonan's *Power to Dissolve* will remember, too, the odd case of Luis Barberini who married Joanna only after she had signed a promise to enter a convent

---

46   *Coram* Huber, 15 December 2000, *RRTDecisiones* 92 (2007) 732.
47   *Coram* Defilippi, 9 February 2000, *RRTDecisiones* 92 (2007) 152.
48   Ibid., 152-153.
49   Ibid., 153.
50   *Coram* Caberletti, 12 June 2003, *RRTDecisiones* 95 (2012) 366, emphasis added.
51   *Coram* Stankiewicz, 25 October 2001, *RRTDecisiones* 93 (2009) 698.

"within fifteen days" of the wedding and to "profess the state of a religious" within a year.[52] By her professing religious vows the unconsummated marriage would be "dissolved in accordance with decretal law established by Alexander III."[53] Hence, Senior Barberini was entering a marriage that not only *could* be dissolved but that *would* be dissolved within a year—not a quasi-marital relationship that he *could* dissolve if something happened or failed to happen, but a quasi-marital relationship that *would* be dissolved, period. But the fictional Lieutenant Pinkerton was a cad, and events showed that Senior Barberini was a fool. As a general rule people do not by means of the same act of the will shoulder obligations and determine to jettison them.

Far more common than the absolute exclusion of indissolubility is its *hypothetical* exclusion. Defilippi writes, "he excludes this essential property [of indissolubility] if he intends ... to break off the bond in a 'hypothetical' way, or if some dreaded circumstance (e.g., if love or harmony is lacking, if the conjugal relationship becomes unhappy, etc.) should occur."[54] Caberletti agrees that "he excludes indissolubility hypothetically who wants to say good-bye to his marriage, if something defined by him should happen."[55] Huber explains that in this situation

> The contractant makes [the] stability [of the marriage] depend on the positive or negative outcome of the experiment of the common life.... He makes the stability [of the marriage] depend on the judgment of a human being and prevents the arising "by irrevocable consent" of a sacred bond independent of the intention of the contractant.[56]

In cases involving the hypothetical exclusion of the *bonum sacramenti* the future verification or falsification of the circumstance is hypothetical, not the reservation of the right to dissolve the marriage. Defilippi writes that in such a case "'one is not dealing with a hypothetical act of the will, which, to the contrary, should be absolute, as a positive act, but with a hypothetical future event, upon the verification of which the contractant intends—and indeed absolutely—to dissolve the bond' (coram Colagiovanni, 9 April 1991...); in other words, 'hypothetical is only the rupture of the marriage not the denial of the perpetuity of the bond' (coram Giannecchini, 10 April 1992...)."[57] Pena observes that "the hypothetical exclusion does not indicate a certain hypothetical—in other words, inter-

---

52   John T. Noonan, Jr., *Power to Dissolve: Lawyers and Marriages in the Courts of the Roman Curia* (Cambridge, MA: The Belknap Press, 1972) 89.
53   Ibid., 95.
54   *Coram* Defilippi, 9 February 2000, *RRTDecisiones* 92 (2007) 143.
55   *Coram* Caberletti, 12 June 2001, *RRTDecisiones* 93 (2009) 366.
56   *Coram* Huber, 23 July 2003, *RRTDecisiones* 95 (2012) 527.
57   *Coram* Defilippi, 9 February 2000, *RRTDecisiones* 92 (2007) 143.

pretative—act of the will; the act of the will… is real and… absolute, while only the circumstance to which the breaking of the bond is attached is hypothetical."[58] Huber likewise holds,

> Even if someone makes it depend on some circumstance, whether or not to rescind the bond, by that very fact he really excludes indissolubility from [his] consent, and this exclusion is actual and absolute, not truly hypothetical. The object of the exclusion of indissolubility is not the intention to procure a divorce civilly, but the reservation of the right or faculty of somehow dissolving every bond.[59]

"What is required," Huber elsewhere writes, "is a connection between the intention of parting ways and a future circumstance, on which the breaking of the bond depends, in such a way that the disruption is intentionally effective already at the moment of giving consent."[60] Although the hypothetical circumstance lies in the future, the effect of its occurrence is very much in the present. Sciacca, too, holds this opinion:

> …an exclusion [of indissolubility]… can be either absolute, when the contractant excludes the indissoluble bond entirely and in every way whatsoever, or hypothetical, when, e.g., the contractant, because of excessive anxiety about the eventual outcome of his marriage, rejects the perpetuity of the marriage at the very moment of forming consent if the situation should occur, namely, if things turn out badly, always keeping for himself an open door: in this regard, however, it is very important to note that the exclusion which is clearly present at the origin of the consent and renders it invalid is not hypothetical; the only thing that is hypothetical is the concrete event of the breakup of the invalidly entered pseudo-marriage.[61]

Recent Rotal cases highlight a variety of circumstances on which one of the spouses allegedly made the perpetuity of a marriage depend. Probably the most convoluted set of circumstance was the nub of a case decided *coram* Stankiewicz on 13 December 2001. Ubaldus contended that Urania had married him on condition that he would provide her with a comfortable home in which to rear their children.[62] Before the marriage he had promised that he would do so, but he had never intended to keep that promise.[63] Conscious of his own insincerity,

---

58 *Coram* Pena, 17 October 2003, *RRTDecisiones* 95 (2012) 589-590.
59 *Coram* Huber, 28 September 1995, cited in *coram* Turnaturi, 10 April 2003, *RRTDecisiones* 95 (2012) 199.
60 *Coram* Huber, 30 April 2003, *RRTDecisiones* 95 (2012) 241.
61 *Coram* Sciacca, 1 June 2007, *RJ*, 232-233.
62 *Coram* Stankiewicz, 13 December 2001, *RRTDecisiones* 93 (2009) 794-795.
63 Ibid., 795.

Ubaldus foresaw a certain amount of marital unpleasantness when she should discover—as she inevitably would discover—his deceit. He therefore prudently (if despicably) determined that he would obtain a civil divorce in the event that her reaction to his refusal to fulfill his promise was too irksome.[64] The Rotal turnus was not impressed by this tortuous argument. Stankiewicz drily points out, "The insincerity—indeed, *mendacity*—of the Plaintiff, gently termed 'his little honesty,'... constitutes an ambiguous argument, because it could be the cause not only of simulating consent in entering marriage, but also of simulating simulation itself in the canonical process for the obtaining of a declaration of the nullity of his marriage."[65]

Only slightly less unusual was a case decided *coram* Turnaturi on 10 April 2003. A perusal of the Auditor's initial sketch of the facts does not reveal the strangeness of the couple's relationship. Turnaturi blandly reports that Rosalinus married Rosamund on 24 October 1988 after a three-year-long courtship. Their pre-marital quarrels had occasionally led to breakups. Their marital squabbles led to a final separation about seven months after the wedding.[66] Not until halfway through the sentence does the reader discover the cause of the parties' disagreements: Rosalinus was a chauvinist. The Auditor accepts the argument Rosalinus' own advocate advanced: "the Plaintiff intended to enter marriage 'as a hypostatic society in which [there] was left to the woman a merely subordinate position, and [the Plaintiff] conditioned the indissolubility [of the marriage] only on this fact, that is that the woman would be prepared to accept and to bring about in practice this abnormal type of conjugal society.'"[67] Even before the marriage

> the man really feared the conflictual relationship of the parties because of their different mindsets—the Plaintiff's, which demanded the entire subjection of the woman, and the woman's, which scarcely tolerated this mindset of the man. This was... the cause of the rejection (although conditional) of the perpetuity [of the marriage] on the part of the man, not directly because of fear of the unhappy outcome of the marriage but indirectly related to the woman's obedience throughout the time of the conjugal relationship.[68]

Rosalinus was willing to establish a stable relationship with Rosamund, but only on condition that she subject herself entirely to his bidding. If she failed to do so, he would regard himself as justified in dissolving the bond. "As is evident,"

---

64 Ibid, 806, 807.
65 Ibid., 812.
66 *Coram* Turnaturi, 10 April 2003, *RRTDecisiones* 95 (2012) 194-195.
67 Ibid., 205.
68 Ibid., 207.

concludes Turnaturi, "it is a case of hypothetical recourse to divorce determined by the Plaintiff with firm intention before the marriage because of the bride's behavior."[69]

Premarital concerns about the future fidelity of one's intended spouse can inspire a hypothetical exclusion of indissolubility. Thus, in a case decided *coram* Pena on 15 December 2000 Leo claimed to have had doubts about his impending marriage to Eleanora because of incidents which gave rise to questions about her faithfulness. The Rotal turnus, however, was skeptical: "…the episodes which are recounted are not 'diverse' but only two and also equivocal, because they in no way prove the infidelity of the spouse or her corrupt morals; at most, in the Fathers' judgment, they show the Plaintiff's jealousy."[70] In a case decided *coram* Funghini on 19 January 2001 a certain Demetrius alleged that he made a premarital decision "to take recourse to divorce not because of a lack of love for his bride but because of fear of observing conjugal fidelity on both sides, more accurately because of fear his wife would not change her prenuptial pattern of behavior."[71] It was the groom's contention that "Although nobody insisted on [their] celebrating the marriage, nevertheless fear lest the woman might break conjugal fidelity led the Plaintiff to simulation of consent through exclusion of the indissolubility of the bond."[72] The Rota handed down a negative decision, however, in part because there was no evidence of a remote motivation for his simulating,[73] and in part because no witness could verify a connection between the groom's premarital concerns about the bride's fidelity and his supposed reservation of the right to dissolve the marriage.[74]

In a case decided *coram* Sciacca Orville's similar petition for the annulment of his marriage to Pauline was more successful.[75] He had entertained doubts about her future fidelity because during his premarital absences for naval duty she was intermittently involved with another man.[76] The Rotal panel "determined that from the acts in the case it was clear that the Plaintiff invalidated or annulled the consent by deciding to separate from his partner by means of the law if and

---

69   Ibid., 209.

70   *Coram* Pena, 15 December 2000, *RRTDecisiones* 92 (2007) 727.

71   *Coram* Funghini, 19 January 2001, *RRTDecisiones* 93 (2009) 65.

72   Ibid., 66.

73   Ibid., 67.

74   Ibid., 69.

75   *Coram* Sciacca, 9 May 2003, *RRTDecisiones* 95 (2003) 284-296—in the Latin text the Plaintiff bears the name Zephyrinus. His not-exactly-blushing bride is improbably called Zenaida. The English text is in *RJ*, 169-190.

76   *Coram* Sciacca, 9 May 2003, *RJ*, 170.

inasmuch as the conjugal life should have become intolerable because of the unpropitious moral behavior of his wife."[77]

A contractant's fear that his/her impending marriage may prove unhappy also deserves mention as a circumstance on which the hypothetical exclusion of indissolubility might depend. One might think of the "trial" marriage in a more or less strict sense of the term, in which "The contractant... makes [the] stability [of the marriage] depend on the positive or negative outcome of the experiment of the common life."[78] The simulator will remain in the marriage if and only if the marriage proves "happy."[79] In a case decided *coram* Pinto, for example, a certain Sophia was herded into marriage by her parents and her fiancé.[80] She consistently and credibly maintained that she entered the marriage firmly intending to obtain a civil divorce if the marriage proved unhappy.[81] A turnus *coram* Bottone was convinced that Luciano and Daniela had the "intention to seek a divorce if matters turned out badly...."[82] The couple had argued violently even before marrying, but their parents had insisted that marrying was the only proper response to Daniela's pregnancy.[83] Given these circumstances, it was not surprising that the parties thought of taking recourse to divorce if their marriage turned out badly.[84] In a case heard *coram* Huber a certain Telephorus noticed during a seven-year-long courtship that he and his fiancée were very different in temperament. He was therefore doubtful about the outcome of the marriage.[85] Huber writes, "Having attended to founded reasons for suspecting that the marriage about to be entered would turn out unhappily, the Plaintiff determined himself to act in accordance with his feelings and therefore posited a positive act of the will against the indissolubility of the bond."[86]

---

77   Ibid., 178.

78   *Coram* Huber, 23 July 2003, *RRTDecisiones* 95 (2012) 527.

79   One recalls here the young people about whom Wrenn wrote: "If they actually planned or intended to divorce after five years if their values were not being met, that of course would constitute an intention against the substance of marriage, namely against the perpetuity of marriage." Wrenn, 312. Such a young person would be entering marriage with the mindset: "If in five years I discover that my spouse is not providing me with the friendship and assistance that I need, or if I discover that we are not experiencing mutual love in our relationship, I will end the marriage." His/her obligation to persist in the relationship would depend on his/her assessment that the marriage was providing what he/she needed.

80   *Coram* Pinto, 14 January 2000, *RRTDecisiones* 92 (2007) 12.

81   Ibid., 15.

82   *Coram* Bottone, 8 June 2000, *RRTDecisiones* 92 (2007) 457.

83   Ibid., 452.

84   Ibid., 457.

85   *Coram* Huber, 30 April 2003, *RRTDecisiones* 95 (2012) 239.

86   Ibid., 246.

A reprise of the always-incisive Huber provides a suitable conclusion to this section of the presentation:

> According to the constant and unanimous jurisprudence of [the Roman Rota] the exclusion of indissolubility occurs whether someone decides to dissolve the bond absolutely or whether he proposes to himself to do this only hypothetically. In both cases the exclusion is absolute. Even if someone makes it depend on some circumstance, whether or not to rescind the bond, by that very fact he really excludes indissolubility from [his consent], and this exclusion is actual and absolute, not truly hypothetical.[87]

On the "Positivity" of the Act of the Will

In order to simulate, the spouse must reserve the right to dissolve the bond "by a positive act of the will." "It is not an easy thing to say, [however,] what a positive act of the will is," Civili admits.

> There are persons who energetically argue that every act of the will is positive. For in the dynamic life of the will they distinguish between an absence of willing and willing. If an act of the will is lacking, a positive act of the will is also lacking. If an act of the will is present, because it is an act, it always is "positive." And so the positive act is placed in opposition to an absence of an act, and therefore also an absence of the adjective "positive." If one understands the matter in this way, the word "positive" is nothing other than a quibble, which can easily lead to confusion. However, both canon 1086, §2 [of the 1917 Code of Canon Law] and canon 1101, §2 [of the 1983 Code] require that the simulator in contracting marriage *positively does not want* to give and receive perpetually.[88]

The Auditor appears to be defending the legislator against a charge of pleonasm: the word *positive* must mean something; it is not in the text as a mere place holder. It must specify some essential qualification of the kind of will act necessary for simulation. Civili continues,

> For the transition from inertia into choosing simulation Rotal sentences demand an act of the will posited "firmly," "absolutely," "seriously," "truly," "expressly," "categorically," "explicitly," "really." All these adverbs point out that simulation is something positive, which proceeds from the will, and does not consist in a mere lack

---

87 *Coram* Huber, 28 September 1995, as cited in *coram* Turnaturi, 10 April 2003, *RRT-Decisiones* 95 (2012) 199.

88 *Coram* Civili, 14 December 2000, *RRTDecisiones* 92 (2007) 716.

of consent or absence of an act of the will. But in different adverbs different meanings lie hidden. All [these] expressions seem to depend greatly on the manifestation of the positive act of the will. An act of the will begins within the human being and frequently [*haud raro* = hardly rarely] ends there. Therefore the internal act of consent "which is presumed in conformity with the words and signs used in celebrating marriage" (canon 1101, §1) must be investigated. In order to invalidate the consent it is sufficient and required that the contractant internally does not want to enter marriage. It is not necessary that this act be published, indeed the act generally is hiding in the heart and will therefore be difficult to prove.[89]

Here the Auditor acknowledges that the qualifications of the *positive* act of the will on which Rotal sentences tend to focus do not modify the act of the will as such. They modify the way in which that act of the will becomes manifest. Civili continues:

A positive act is not conceived "apart from a previous consideration of the object on the part of the intellect" (*coram* Bejan, 6 July 1964)...). In the same line it is asserted that: "The act of the will, of which simulation consists, should be 'positive' that is to say really posited, elicited and perfectly human, which namely proceeds from a consideration of the object towards which the will is directed" (*coram* Boccafola, 15 February 1988...). An act of the will does not become positive by means of simple *volition*, but by *intention*, through which the will is effectively borne towards an object. Such is the jurisprudence of Our Forum: "Such simulation cannot consist in the mere inertia of the will, or as is said *passim* by Our Sacred Tribunal, 'in not willing,' but in 'willing not': hence the canon requires a positive act rejecting the marriage itself'"(*coram* Colagiovanni, 15 December 1982...). Thus we learn that the adjective "positive" does not indicate an opposition to a negative act of the will, but an opposition to mental inertia, which does not move the will to action. A positive act of the will proceeds directly from the agent.[90]

According to Civili, before positing a *positive* act of the will, the simulator will engage on "a previous consideration" of the nature of the marriage he/she is about to enter. "A positive act of the will is the fruit of a dialogue between the intellect and the will," he writes. In the case Civili is discussing, for example, "... before the marriage, because of the woman's unexpected pregnancy, the Plaintiff reflected on the marriage and its consequences."[91] Because the existence of this

---

89 Ibid., 716-717.
90 Ibid., 717.
91 Ibid., 719.

prior process of reflection was clearly proven, the Rotal turnus was more easily able to conclude that the Plaintiff's exclusion of indissolubility was indeed the product of a positive act of the will.

In a decision dated 27 January 2000 Huber, too, carefully analyzes the *positive act of the will*. He begins by clearing some underbrush:

> The text of the law says that not sufficient for contracting marriage invalidly are the mere foreseeing of divorce, a false notion concerning the possibility of divorce, an habitual intention, a mere disposition of mind, an abstract error or desire, generic statements about seeking divorce or about the usefulness of divorce, etc.; but a positive act of the will is required, whereby some essential property of marriage is excluded. The reason why dispositions of mind and [the other factors] listed here do not contain exclusion in themselves is found in this, that they remain in the ambit of the intellect and do not enter into consent. It must be noted besides that the contractants in marrying do not fix eyes on the theoretical institute but on their own [relationship] defined singularly and individually.[92]

Because invalidating exclusions, whether of marriage itself or of some essential element or of some essential property of marriage, are accomplished *positivo voluntatis actu*, what remains in the intellect cannot, in itself, constitute such an exclusion. If erroneous notions or mental dispositions or even well-founded expectations that a contemplated marriage will not succeed do not impinge upon the act of consent, they cannot bring about the positive act of the will which constitutes a legally significant exclusion of anything essential to marriage. Moreover, there is a difference between the abstract theories a person entertains and the concrete choices which shape that person's life. Huber is aware that a person might have some very odd ideas about marriage in general and still marry validly because he/she does not bring those ideas to bear on his/her own marriage.[93]

"It is not easy to say what a positive act of the will is," Huber continues. "Not rarely in Rotal sentences it is taught to be posited 'firmly,' 'absolutely,' seriously,' 'truly,' 'expressly' and the like. These adverbs, however, do not explain everything about the 'positivity' of the will."[94] The Auditor looks closely at a

---

92   *Coram* Huber, 27 January 2000, *RRTDecisiones* 92 (2007) 117.

93   This he says explicitly in a later decision: "Often divorce is defended in favor of the freedom of others: someone, although Catholic educated, because of a false concept of freedom can struggle in favor of divorce, because he/she holds that the law of indissolubility should not be imposed on those who do not freely accept it. The person who acts in this way often does not think of acquiring freedom from the bond of his/her own marriage." *Coram* Huber, 15 December 2000, *RRTDecisiones* 92 (2007) 732.

94   *Coram* Huber, 27 January 2000, *RRTDecisiones* 92 (2007) 117.

first instance sentence lying before the Rota for review. It contains the passage, "Under the positive act of the will one understands the determined [or resolute], fundamental [or principled] and unequivocal commitment of the will." The Auditor is not impressed:

> And so from adverbs adjectives are made.[95] From the way in which the will must be posited, in order to be accomplished positively, the determination of the will should come about. It is a real pity that the sentence does not inspect the matter more deeply.[96]

Huber recalls some Rotal findings that the aforesaid act of the will is "the fruit of a dialogue between the intellect and the will." Giannecchini had defined the word *positive* as referring to "'an intention which effectively is directed towards the object of consent and specifies it.'" Huber also notes in passing Pinto's position that the "positivity" of the act of the will should be "considered within the whole intellective-estimative-elective process whereby a human being categorically decides for himself that something must be done."[97] But in the end Huber's reflections in this particular sentence, however conducive to further thought, do not create in the reader a clear and distinct idea of the elusive meaning of the *positive act of the will*.[98]

---

95 Less literally, "And so adverbs are transmuted into adjectives."

96 Ibid., 117.

97 Ibid., 117-118.

98 This reader speculates that the facts of the case under discussion did not require Huber to pursue his reflections. The couple had married when Herrmann was twenty-nine, and Anna, twenty-six. They had met two years earlier when Anna was engaged to another man. That relationship ended, and Herrmann and Anna began living together. They decided to marry when she became pregnant. Their decade-long common life began happily. It soured (at least from Anna's viewpoint) when Herrmann completed his medical degree and began to look down on his less-educated wife. She left him for another man (Ibid., 115). Huber considered it indisputable that the couple had loved each other before the marriage (Ibid., 119-120). "Even if it is true that the woman's pregnancy induced the parties to wed, nevertheless it is likewise true that the proposal to marry proceeded from a deliberate will and from rational deliberation" (Ibid., 123). Herrmann claimed that his "conscience" led him to marry. "But right moral conscience advocates for the giving of true consent—that is, for the desire of mutually and definitively giving oneself for living in a covenant of faithfulness and fruitful love" (Ibid., 123). After they married, "Through many years the spouses diligently fulfilled the matrimonial and familial obligations" (Ibid., 120). When Anna left him, Herrmann tried to bring about a reconciliation. Huber concedes that these attempts do not constitute a decisive argument against Herrmann's having excluded indissolubility. "But it is difficult to understand how he, who intended to make the marriage depend on the woman's fidelity, could salvage the marriage and restore the previous [common] life, after the infidelity of the woman was known" (Ibid., 125). In fine, the evidence that the marriage might have been invalid on any ground was so weak that one is surprised that the Auditor was as thorough as he was in surveying the jurisprudence.

Huber returns to the study in a sentence dated 30 April 2003. "If we take our stand on the text of the law," he writes,

> three [things] are required for perpetrating exclusion or simulation: *an act, the will, and positivity*. A few [words] must be said about these expressions. *Act* denotes some operation, a deliberate motion towards an end. The word *of the will* is equivocal, for it can signify both a potency and an act. A doubt, an error, a foreseeing, an idea, a generic mindset, and an habitual intention and other things of this sort are not an act of the will: they remain in the mind and do not pass over into an active will. *Positivity* is frequently considered as if it were superfluous, because every act really posited is *positive*. This is true, but it is also true that a *positive* act of the will is not opposed to a *negative* will but to an *inert* will. Consequently, the adjective *positive* is necessary to distinguish a positive intention from an inactive intention. This is [our] conclusion: a positive act of the will is an act which passes from potency into act, from inertia into active simulation, from the mind into the will.[99]

In a decision dated 23 July 2003 Huber adds further refinement. "The exclusion of indissolubility, in order to be effective," he writes,

> requires a positive act of the will. An operation of the will, that is, an act of the will—is not enough. "Not to want" is also "to want." "A positive act of the will" is not opposed to an inexistent intention, but to an inert intention, which from passivity does not pass over into active simulation.
>
> [This] positive act of the will must be considered within the whole intellectivo-aestimativo-elective process. Previously intellectually apprehended in a certain circumstance is the dissolution of the bond. This apprehension, however, does not remain in an interior existence as a certain *species*, but it is intended in objective reality. In other words: the object is not only present in spirit as known, but as intentionally ordered to "realization."... A causal connection is therefore demanded between the apprehended object and its "realization" in such a way that the "realization" follows like an effect from the pre-ordered intention.[100]

Huber stresses the dynamic character of every *positive* act of the will. Such an act always reaches out towards its object. Prior to making a decision, the simulator conceives his/her contemplated marriage as a relationship lacking in the es-

---

99   *Coram* Huber, 30 April 2003, *RRTDecisiones* 95 (2012) 241.
100 *Coram* Huber, 23 July 2003, *RRTDecisiones* 95 (2012) 527.

sential property of indissolubility. This corrupted simulacrum of marriage does not remain an idea in the simulator's mind. The simulator concretely, if only implicitly, chooses it rather than marriage as the relationship he/she wants to establish with his/her spouse. Even if any future dissolution of the marriage would depend on a circumstance the simulator considers improbable, the intention to make that dissolution happen is already operative when the simulator expresses his/her consent.

One might hazard a synthesis of these Rotal reflections on *positivity* by suggesting that every *positive* act of the will is *dynamic* inasmuch as the simulator engages in some kind of internal conversation about what he/she is planning to do and *intentional* inasmuch as the simulator reaches out towards a substantially deficient image of marriage as a value he/she wishes to realize. If the alleged simulator engaged in no internal shaping of a defective image of marriage, it would be difficult for a judge to conclude that he/she did not intend to accept marriage as God established it; and if the alleged simulator did not make the defective image the direct object of the consent he/she elicited during the ceremony of marriage, the judge would conclude that he/she remained simply in error.

"No One Acts without Reasons..."

Because exclusion of the *bonum sacramenti* is a *positive act of the will*, involving some kind of interior dialogue, the reasoning process that led to its formation should leave traces which a church court can identify. Hence, Rotal jurisprudence is very interested in the reasons motivating the actions of the alleged simulator. Ragni observes, "...a human being never acts without a suitable motivating cause...."[101] Verginelli agrees that "human actions are always directed toward some end...."[102] In cases involving allegations of simulation, judges look for evidence of three such "motivating causes" or ends: a reason for undergoing the ceremony of marriage (the *causa contrahendi*); a remote reason for excluding the indissolubility of the marriage; and a proximate reason for excluding the indissolubility of the marriage (both of which are termed *causae simulandi*).

Obviously there would be no case pending before the court unless the parties had undergone a ceremony of marriage. Typically, the reason for their celebrating the marriage is love,[103] but a premarital pregnancy can also lead the parties

---

101 This *dictum* from a decision of 19 April 1994 is cited *coram* Pena, 15 December 2000, *RRTDecisiones* 92 (2007) 724.

102 *Coram* Verginelli, 28 April 2000, *RRTDecisiones* 92 (2007) 575.

103 For example, "persistent mutual love," although it was cooling on the young woman's part, led Elizabeth and Fabius to marry. *Coram* Defilippi, 9 February 2000, *RRTDecisiones* 92 (2007) 105. In the case of John and Margaret, "The reason for contracting [their] marriage was vehement love between the parties." *Coram* Civili, 26 October 2000, *RRTDecisiones* 92 (2007) 600. Examples could be multiplied.

to the altar.[104] The case of Paula and Aloysius offered a variation on this theme: Paula found herself pregnant by Roberto, who declined to marry her. Aloysius, on the other hand, was willing to marry her and also to accept the child as his own. Huber writes; "the woman... married the man without love, so that she might conceal the true paternity of her unborn child...."[105] This sort of reason for marrying could easily coexist with simulation. A 9 June 2000 decision *coram* Pinto concerns a young woman who married to gain access to her fiancé's patrimony.[106] A turnus *coram* Boccafola viewed skeptically a young man's claim that he had married only to get his fiancée a visa.[107] A turnus *coram* Stankiewicz was equally unimpressed by a Plaintiff's claim that he had married only to have an heir: if having an heir was so important to him, why was he so uninterested in the child's well-being, and why did he so vigorously resist paying child support?[108] The desire to free themselves from irksome parental control can induce young persons to marry.[109] In a case decided *coram* Sciacca, the *causae contrahendi* were the groom's physical infatuation with the bride and his feelings of guilt arising from an abortion.[110] One of the strangest reasons for contracting the marriage comes to the fore in a case heard *coram* Serrano. Despite his solidly-Catholic upbringing, Dagobert was living rakishly, even to the extent of cohabiting with a divorcee. When she unceremoniously threw him out, he sought solace from Domitilla; but she refused him her favors outside marriage. He therefore proposed marriage. Serrano observes, "...the transition from foul concubinage to sacred covenant [*a foedo contubernio ad sacrum foedus*] was not, as it should

---

104 This appears to have been true for Hermann and Anna: Huber concedes that it might have been "true that the woman's pregnancy induced the parties to wed," although he believes that the couple loved each other, too. *Coram* Huber, 27 January 2000, *RRTDecisiones* 92 (2007) 123; but also 119-120. Luciano and Daniela clearly contracted marriage only because of the premarital pregnancy. *Coram* Bottone, 8 June 2000, *RRTDecisiones* 92 (2007) 452, 456-457. *Coram* Civili, 14 December 2000, *RRTDecisiones* 92 (2007) 714-721, concerns Raymond, whose reaction to the discovery that Rosa was pregnant was the suggestion of a merely civil marriage so that he could get a civil divorce if the marriage did not work out (p. 714): "The cause of contracting was the woman's pregnancy. The man desired a civil marriage as the lesser evil" (p. 719).

105 *Coram* Huber, 15 December 2000, *RRTDecisiones* 92 (2000) 740. The decision of this case puzzled this reader. It appears (p. 730) that before the marriage Paula had demanded absolute secrecy about the paternity of the child, adding "that in the case of violation of the secret she would immediately seek a divorce" (p. 730). The Rota nevertheless concluded that "by no means is it proven that the woman Respondent at the moment of consent excluded the essential property of indissolubility from her matrimonial consent" (p. 736). Instead, the Fathers concluded that she had excluded the *bonum prolis* (p. 740).

106 *Coram* Pinto, 9 June 2000, *RRTDecisiones* 92 (2007) 467.

107 *Coram* Boccafola, 28 June 2001, *RRTDecisiones* 93 (2009) 444-445.

108 *Coram* Stankiewicz, 13 December 2001, *RRTDecisiones* 93 (2009) 811.

109 *Coram* Defilippi, 9 February 2000, *RRTDecisiones* 92 (2007) 150.

110 *Coram* Sciacca, 9 May 2003, *RRTDecisiones* 95 (2012) 293.

have been, an improvement but a further step on the road to perdition.... The plan to marry was a means of enjoying a woman like a mistress...."[111]

Counterbalancing the reason(s) for contracting the marriage are the reasons, remote and proximate, for excluding the *bonum sacramenti*. According to Huber, "Jurisprudence... constantly teaches that simulation cannot be proven unless there sprouts from the acts a clear and coherent reason for simulation."[112] Bottone writes

> Because an act of the will can hardly be elicited without suitable motivation, a serious cause for simulation is required.... When one speaks about a *proportionate* cause for simulating, one should not in the least think of a cause objectively most serious, but of a cause which is serious for the contracting party in view of his nature, his mindset, and his circumstances. Not rarely can it happen that a cause neither grave nor insistent for the majority of human beings for some peculiar individual becomes serious and therefore can induce him to simulate.[113]

The remote reason for simulating is the background against which the simulator makes a decision with respect to entering this particular marriage. According to Pompedda, "a remote cause has in itself no connection with the marriage to be entered here and now, although it can dispose the mind to seek something specifically for celebrating the marriage without some essential element."[114] Remote causes for simulating are as varied as the parties who claim to have simulated. In deciding a Sicilian case Turnaturi identified "The remote cause of simulating [as] the man's personality."[115] The Plaintiff was imbued with "obsolete Sicilian tradition" about a husband's superiority over his wife.[116] The man's erroneous mindset concerning the relationship between men and women made it impossible for him to admit perpetuity into his notion of marriage.[117] In the case in which the bride married in order to gain access to the groom's patrimony, Pinto saw "the depraved and perverse will of the Respondent" as the source of her simulating.[118]

Civili observes, "Anthropology brings into light the fact that a person makes those decisions which are congruent with his personality. One therefore

---

111 *Coram* Serrano, 3 August 2001, *RRTDecisiones* 93 (2009) 602.
112 *Coram* Huber, 27 January 2000, *RRTDecisiones* 92 (2007) 118.
113 *Coram* Bottone, 15 June 2001, *RRTDecisiones* 93 (2009) 387.
114 As cited *coram* Turnaturi, 10 April 2003, *RRTDecisiones* 95 (2012) 200.
115 Ibid., 208.
116 Ibid., 205.
117 Ibid., 207.
118 *Coram* Pinto, 9 June 2000, *RRTDecisiones* 92 (2007) 466.

pays attention to the nature, the education, and the upbringing of the alleged simulator."[119] Hence, a person's overall "mindset" can constitute the remote reason for his/her simulating.[120]

Such a mindset can, but need not be, the result of a person's irreligious or antireligious upbringing. A turnus *coram* Pinto, for example, decided affirmatively a case involving a young woman who was reared under Communist influence, which thought nothing of matrimonial permanence or indissolubility.[121] To the contrary, another turnus ruled that the mere fact of atheism does not entail that a person excluded the *bonum sacramenti*: "it is not lawful to deduce—so to speak, 'automatically'—from a mere allegation of atheism of a party or from a circumstance that he or she grew up in an environment opposed to religion, the rejection on his or her part of the essential property of indissolubility of marriage."[122]

A mindset opposed to marital indissolubility can also arise from a person's idiosyncrasy. Defilippi writes about a young woman who "was endowed with a character by which she really sought freedom in her behavior and in her lifestyle."[123] Being married, especially for life, involves obligations—limitations on the freedom that was the object of her passionate desire. Monier points to a Plaintiff's "libertine and dissolute life before the marriage" as a remote reason for simulating.[124] To marry validly would involve a commitment to abandon ingrained habits.

The strange case of Dagobert, already mentioned, provides a segue into another sort of remote cause for simulation. According to Serrano, the remote cause of Dagobert's simulation was his deliberate opposition to the principles with which his parents had reared him as a child.[125] Prior to the marriage the young man had firmly rejected Christian principles; and his rejection was not mere indifference to them (which might be reconciled with genuine marital consent),

---

119   *Coram* Civili, 14 December 2000, *RRTDecisiones* 92 (2007) 717.

120   Ibid., 720. Sable seems to agree: "For if the contractant's habitual mindset contrary through and through to the perpetuity of matrimony is proven, then a most vehement *presumptio hominis*… arises that having left the intellect it certainly found its place in the will." *Coram* Sable, 13 April 2000, *RRTDecisiones* 92 (2007) 342.

121   *Coram* Pinto, 14 January 2000, *RRTDecisiones* 92 (2007) 14.

122   *Coram* Arokiaraj, 13 March 2008, *Studia canonica* 42 (2008) 529. Boccafola makes a similar point in a case involving error of law: "…it would be extremely rash to insist that by the very fact of membership in a Protestant religion or by being born in a nation under an atheistic regime, someone must necessarily reject the permanence of matrimony." *Coram* Boccafola, 21 November 2002, *RJ*, 79.

123   *Coram* Defilippi, 9 February 2000, *RRTDecisiones* 92 (2007) 146.

124   *Coram* Monier, 26 January 2001, *RRTDecisiones* 93 (2009) 112.

125   *Coram* Serrano, 3 August 2001, *RRTDecisiones* 93 (2009) 605.

but a positive hostility towards the fundamentals of Christian life and morality.[126] His was not the situation of the young Communist, reared with no appreciation of the goods of marriage. He did know what the Catholic Church teaches, and he was therefore in a position to reject it. About young people in his situation Monier writes,

> It should also be remembered that very often in our times there are many who, although they were reared Catholic, depart from Catholic doctrine and the magisterium and for their own convenience assume false ideas commonly admitted today in society about the institution of marriage and the sense of perpetuity; in these cases they accede to a religious marriage only to comply with the desire of their partner or their family, while they really are holding that no perpetual bond arises from the rite.[127]

Similarly, in deciding a case involving a marriage celebrated in May of 1976, Bottone recalls that the 1970's, and especially the first five years of that decade, were a time of youthful rejection of traditional values. In Italy it was also a time of agitation for reform of divorce law. Young people—even from good families—who married at that time might easily have adopted views common among their peers, and such a mentality could be the remote cause of their excluding indissolubility from their attempted marriages.[128] In a case decided *coram* Sciacca the Plaintiff unabashedly reported,

> ...I had a secular outlook and was actively caught up on the propaganda about the law of divorce of which I was a supporter. I did consider and I still consider marriage as a serious institution and I was disposed to commit myself fundamentally to its success.... I was, however, firmly against the absolute indissolubility of the bond.[129]

Sciacca observes, "...especially these days, deeply afflicted by the plague of relativism, it can happen that someone—as we have said, endowed with a Catholic

---

126 Ibid., 606.

127 *Coram* Monier, 16 February 2001, *RRTDecisiones* 93 (2009) 157. Sciacca quotes Wynen making a similar point: "Nor is it an impediment for this case that [it] deals with two Catholics who had an appropriate formation with regard to the indissolubility of Christian marriage; for as rotal auditor Msgr. Wynen taught: '...precisely because they know it, they want to reserve for themselves an open door by adding to the matrimonial contract a special clause and reject both in their mind and with a subsequent act of the will the sanctity of marriage but [not] their own freedom which they refuse to lose forever, especially if they enter marriage not altogether freely.'" *Coram* Sciacca, 9 May 2003, *RJ,* 175-176, also *RRTDecisiones* 95 (2012) 287.

128 *Coram* Bottone, 8 June 2000, *RRTDecisiones* 92 (2007) 455-456.

129 *Coram* Sciacca, 1 June 2007, *RJ,* 238.

education—for his own convenience and to guard by every means his unbridled freedom which he does not know how nor wish to renounce may adhere to erroneous opinions about married life and cause those same opinions, positively, to affect his specific marriage."[130]

Proof of the existence of a *remote* cause for simulating only lays the foundation of establishing that simulation occurred. As was noted above, "a remote cause [for simulating] has in itself no connection with the marriage to be entered here and now."[131] The *proximate* reason for simulating is the trigger for the simulator's determination that this marriage, which he/she is entering here and now, will be dissoluble, at least under certain circumstances. In the absence of proof of the existence of such a proximate reason for simulating, it is very difficult to conclude that a person simulated.

In a case decided *coram* Pinto a certain Sophia underwent a ceremony of marriage with Ivan on 18 August 1984. Even during the engagement Sophia openly told Ivan that she did not love him; but he and her parents corralled her into marrying him, despite her having twice suggested a merely civil marriage.[132] Pinto observed, "From indubitable facts shines forth a proximate cause [for simulating, a cause both] proportionate and serious, namely that Sophia was forced into the marriage without love" for Ivan.[133] Because of her Communist upbringing[134] she had always been imbued with a mindset favoring divorce.[135] Her lack of love for Ivan and her being coerced into marrying him caused her to apply her divorce-favoring principles to the marriage she was contracting then and there.

Somewhat similar was the situation of Raymond and Rosa. The couple met in the fall of 1982, and Raymond became infatuated with her. When she became pregnant in 1988, Raymond wanted to marry only civilly so that he could get a divorce if the marriage did not work out well. Because both sets of parents rejected his suggestion, the couple married in the church on 29 January 1980. The common life became unhappy almost immediately, with both parties indulging in physical abuse. In 1991 Rosa began an affair, and on 8 February 1992 she deserted the conjugal home and began living with her lover.[136] According to the evidence—including testimony from Rosa, who branded her former husband a liar—

---

130   Ibid., 239.
131   Cf. *coram* Turnaturi, 10 April 2003, *RRTDecisiones* 95 (2012) 200.
132   *Coram* Pinto, 14 January 2000, *RRTDecisiones* 92 (2007) 13.
133   Ibid., 16.
134   Ibid., 14.
135   Ibid., 15.
136   *Coram* Civili, 14 December 2000, *RRTDecisiones* 92 (2007) 714-715.

before the marriage, because of the woman's unexpected pregnancy, [Raymond] reflected on the marriage and its consequences. With his family and friends he had discussions about his life condition, and he responded to their warnings that he would take recourse to separation and divorce if the conjugal and familial life turned out badly.[137]

The premarital pregnancy forced Raymond to think concretely about his future. His "doubts about the happy outcome of the marriage" functioned as "the proximate cause of simulation."[138] He therefore applied to his own marriage the general favorable view of divorce he had entertained before the marriage.

A bit more unusual was the case of Elizabeth and Fabius. Elizabeth highly valued her own freedom. She also desired a career in music.[139] She had known Fabius since childhood. They began a romantic relationship about 1981. In 1983, chafing under parental authority and eager to pursue her career, she began talking to him about marriage. Over time, however, her ardor for him waned. Elizabeth was especially apprehensive about Fabius' lack of enthusiasm for her career. In the judgment of the Rotal panel, "as the wedding neared, the woman grew really uncertain about the future happy outcome of the conjugal relationship, whether because her love for the Respondent was cooling, or whether because she was already experiencing that he was endowed with a nature which possibly would hamper the kind of life which she thought to be necessary for the marriage to be happy."[140] For all practical purposes, Elizabeth had written a script for her life; and during the engagement she observed that Fabius was not ideally suited to the part in which she had cast him. The proximate reason for her reserving the right to dissolve the marriage was her serious premarital doubt that he was the sort of husband she needed in order to live the life she had chosen.

Premarital doubts inducing a party to reserve to the right to dissolve the marriage can sprout from many seeds. Narses and Norma either enjoyed or endured a seven-year-long courtship marred by frequent arguments and separations.[141] The parties' disparity of temperament, about which all of the witnesses gave evidence, provided a remote reason for simulation.[142] The proximate reason, which inspired the groom's decision to simulate, consisted in his "certain doubts about the happy outcome of the marital life."[143] The origin of Orville's doubts about

---

137 Ibid., 719.

138 Ibid., 720.

139 *Coram* Defilippi, 9 February 2000, *RRTDecisiones* 92 (2007) 146.

140 Ibid., 149.

141 *Coram* Monier, 12 June 2003, *RRTDecisiones* 95 (2012) 439.

142 Ibid., 445.

143 Ibid., 445. A similar case is discussed in *coram* Huber, 30 April 2003, *RRTDecisiones* 95 (2012) 239-251.

the outcome of his marriage to Pauline was her behavior with other men.[144] Because he knew that she had been sexually involved with her employer before the marriage, and because she dressed and acted suggestively, Orville suffered from doubts about her possible future infidelity. In the Sicilian case mentioned above, Rosalinus had noticed during the courtship Rosamund's reluctance to submit to his complete domination. Therefore "the man really feared the conflictual relationship of the parties because of their different mindsets—the Plaintiff's which demanded the entire subjection of the woman, and the woman's which scarcely tolerated this mindset of the man."[145] In the case of Nathan and Madaleva, years before the marriage the groom had developed a passionate conviction in favor of divorce.[146] As marriage approached, "doubts ... arose in the man's mind because of the woman's depression and because of the pre-nuptial, though inchoate, conflicts regarding the combining of their patrimony."[147] The existence of these doubts constituted the reason for his applying to his own marriage his firm general conviction that "'it would make no sense to ruin the life of two people in order to keep faith with a marriage that was now "empty"....'"[148]

Pena offers a concise summary of typical proximate causes of simulation: "Among reasons for exclusion [the following] are wont to be considered: a love of too much freedom, a fear of the breakup of the marriage on account of a sharp difference in [the parties'] temperaments, weak trust in the other party, not to mention inflicted fear, which sometimes is turned into a motivation for excluding the perpetuity of the bond imposed on the self."[149] Because each human individual is unique, each marriage case will be unique, too: the behavior of some of the parties whose cases we have surveyed was anything but "typical." No list of possible reasons for excluding the *bonum sacramenti* can be exhaustive, but Pena's at least suggests some starting points for a court's investigation.

On the Implications of Circumstances
Just as a simulator does not form a positive act of the will against one of the essentials of marriage without a proportionate reason, so the proportionate reason for forming such an act of the will does not crop up in a vacuum. The circumstances surrounding a person's decision whether and how to marry therefore provide support for his/her claim of simulation, or they render the claim improbable. Similarly, the circumstances surrounding the couple's establishment of their common life can indicate whether either of them entered a marriage he/she intended to be dissoluble.

---

144   *Coram* Sciacca, 9 May 2003, *RJ*, 184-185; also in *RRTDecisiones* 95 (2012) 294-296.
145   *Coram* Turnaturi, 10 April 2003, *RRTDecisiones* 95 (2012) 207.
146   *Coram* Sciacca, 1 June 2007, *RJ*, 238-243.
147   Ibid., 245.
148   Ibid., 239.
149   *Coram* Pena, 17 October 2003, *RRTDecisiones* 95 (2012) 591.

When discussing circumstances that might render a claim of exclusion of the *bonum sacramenti* more or less probable, one could easily imitate Abelard by contrasting a Rotal recognition that this circumstance supported the allegation with a Rotal assertion that the very same circumstance did the opposite. The fact that the couple's common life was very short might suggest that one of them excluded the *bonum sacramenti*,[150] or it might not.[151] The fact that the couple first discussed marrying only after discovering a premarital pregnancy might suggest that one of them excluded the *bonum sacramenti*,[152] or it might not.[153] The fact that the alleged simulator happily conceived a child might undermine the claim that she excluded the *bonum sacramenti*;[154] on the other hand, as Sciacca argues, "The birth of offspring, from a marriage contracted in this way [viz., in fear that it might turn out unhappily], proves nothing against simulation…"[155] A less ambiguous circumstance in the judgment of Civili was the fact that the groom had tried to avoid the marriage altogether and had then suggested a merely civil marriage (so that it could be more easily dissolved): this did seem to point unmistakably to the groom's exclusion of indissolubility.[156] The fact that the couple

---

150 For example, *coram* Caberletti, 10 April 2003, *RRTDecisiones* 95 (2012) 213-238; *coram* Stankiewicz, 27 November 2003, *RRTDecisiones* 95 (2012) 692-708.

151 For example, *coram* Caberletti, 12 June 2003, *RRTDecisiones* 95 (2012) 359-383. The bride left the conjugal home forty days after the wedding. The groom commenced annulment proceedings six and one-half months after the wedding. Ibid., 359. In *coram* Alwan, 21 October 2003, *RRTDecisiones* 95 (2012) 599-608, the fact that the couple separated fourteen months into their marriage because of the wife's adultery did not convince the Rota that she had excluded the *bonum sacramenti*. An especially sad case is *coram* Stankiewicz, 26 January 2001, *RRTDecisiones* 93 (2009) 92-104: the groom abandoned his wife and unborn child forty days after they began their common life and spurned all attempts at reconciliation.

152 For example, *coram* Civili, 14 December 2000, *RRTDecisiones* 92 (2007) 714-721; *coram* Bottone, 8 June 2000, *RRTDecisiones* 92 (2007) 451-459.

153 For example, *coram* Huber, 27 January 2000, *RRTDecisiones* 92 (2007) 115-126; *coram* Verginelli, 28 July 2000, *RRTDecisiones* 92 (2007) 572-580.

154 Cf. *coram* Caberletti, 5 April 2000, *RRTDecisiones* 92 (2007) 304.

155 *Coram* Sciacca, 9 May 2003, *RRTDecisiones* 95 (2012) 287. This translation differs from that appearing in *RJ*, 176. The Latin reads: "Genita soboles, a tali contracto coniugio, nihil probat adversus simulationem, e contra, paternus [the text in *RJ* mistakenly reads *patemus*] amor erga parvulam prolem tantummodo differre, natura, potuerit separationem coniugalem ac praetensae nullitatis accusationem." The subject of the verb *probat* is *soboles* (nominative singular) modified by the perfect passive participle *genita* (which is, in turn, qualified by the phrase, "*a tali contracto coniugio*"—"from a marriage contracted thus"): literally: "The having-been-born (from a so-contracted marriage) offspring… proves nothing…." The *e contra* clause provides an alternative explanation: "fatherly love for the tiny child could, naturally, only postpone the conjugal separation and the accusation of the alleged nullity."

156 *Coram* Civili, 14 December 2000, *RRTDecisiones* 92 (2000) 714-721, especially p. 720: "The man contends that he tried to avoid marriage, then to put it off, and finally

had serious, and occasionally physical, altercations during their "courtship" also made more probable their exclusion of indissolubility.[157] Pena states that "among circumstances [the following] have importance: the prenuptial behavior of the simulating party, possible arguments and discord between the spouses, [and] the beginning of a separation on the part of the other [viz., the non-simulating] party."[158] None of the recent cases I was able to study involved a multiply-married party, so none of the Auditors opined about the possible significance of the fact that the alleged simulator had been divorced once or twice before contracting the impugned marriage.

Whether romantic love argues for or against the probability of partial simulation is a disputed question. There have been recent cases in which the Rota regarded the parties' mutual love during the courtship as proof that neither of them would have simulated.[159] In a case from 2008 a turnus declared, "The love between the parties, as is well known, was the cause for contracting marriage, which gainsays particularly the exclusion of the stability of the bond."[160] But

---

to marry only before a civil magistrate. The woman confirms all of this." Similarly *coram* Monier, 16 February 2001, *RRTDecisiones* 93 (2009) 159. In *coram* Huber, 30 April 2003, *RRTDecisiones* 95 (2012) 239-251: "After seven years of dating the Plaintiff wanted to live with Tarsilla without any civil or religious bond" (p. 248). "The man's desire to establish a 'free relationship' clearly showed his lack of certitude and his fear of imposing upon himself a strong and perpetual bond" (p. 249).

157 In *coram* Bottone, 8 June 2000, *RRTDecisiones* 92 (2007) 452: "...having given attention to the differences in their character and the increasing arguments which even led the young people to violence, by common counsel they decided to take recourse to divorce if matters turned out badly."

158 *Coram* Pena, 17 October 2003, *RRTDecisiones* 95 (2012) 591.

159 For example, *coram* Verginelli, 28 July 2000, *RRTDecisiones* 92 (2007) 579; *coram* Sciacca, 5 October 2000, *RRTDecisiones* 92 (2007) 584: "the person who is enraptured by great love… does not think about the future dissolution of the marriage…."; *coram* Civili, 26 October 2000, *RRTDecisiones* 92 (2007) 600: "The reason for contracting [this] marriage was vehement love between the parties. From the Acts it is evident that the parties fostered their courtship with chaste love. There is no cause for wonder if the man entered marriage so that he could express and complete his love even by means of sexual relations"; *coram* Bottone, 15 June 2001, *RRTDecisiones* 93 (2009) 389; *coram* Stankiewicz, 28 October 2001, *RRTDecisiones* 93 (2009) 710; *coram* Ciani, 21 May 2003, *RRTDecisiones* 95 (2012) 328; *coram* Arokiaraj, 13 March 2008, *Studia canonica* 42 (2008) 538: "The love between the parties, as is well known, was the cause for contracting marriage, which gainsays particularly the exclusion of the stability of the bond; indeed, love, which bears all things and endures all things (I Cor 13: 7), makes the person who loves open to forgive as well as to preserve and restore the bond."

160 *Coram* Arokiaraj, 13 March 2008, *Studia canonica* 42 (2008) 538. The Plaintiff was alleging the nullity of a twenty-year-long marriage on grounds of the Respondent's exclusion of both the *bonum sacramenti* and the *bonum coniugum* (p. 525). The evidence showed, however, not only that the Respondent had entered the marriage out of love, but also that she lovingly and patiently endured the Plaintiff's misbehavior during the long

there have also been cases in which the Rota issued affirmative decisions despite the parties' premarital affection.[161] Turnaturi sees merit on both sides of the argument. "As a general rule," he observes, "love, which is held to be a reason for contracting, contradicts simulation, either because 'love by its nature aspires to perfect union' (coram Massimi, 30 December 1927…) [or because] 'those overcome by great love do not think about the future dissolution of the marriage nor do they spontaneously posit anything, whence a separation will follow in the future' (coram Felici, 14 July 1959…)."[162] At the same time, he recalls Pinto's warning that love is not altogether repugnant to exclusion of the *bonum* sacramenti, but that its presence only renders proving the exclusion more difficult, especially to the degree that love is more vehement.[163] Turnaturi notes that there are different kinds of love: "the love of benevolence is one thing; the love of concupiscence is another."[164] His conclusion is that "only from genuine conjugal love, not from erotic or inconstant love, can the perpetuity of the bond be deduced."[165] Like Turnaturi, Sciacca also distinguishes between "erotic love or… especially strong sexual allurement" which can draw a person into a marriage and even delay his/her dissolving the bond,[166] on the one hand, and, on the other hand, "immense" love, "love [which] in truth is also charity, or a mutual donation which also includes sacrifice,"[167] which "can be reconciled with the absolute will to contract marriage"[168] and which would be incompatible with exclusion of indissolubility.

---

common life. Her behavior was inconsistent with the Plaintiff's claims about her.

161 One might note here Sciacca's dictum, "…very little opposes the simulator who is roused by fervent love and passion for the partner if he truly fears that entering into marriage could lead to an unhappy end and that the spouses and the marital life may be exposed to probable difficulties." *Coram* Sciacca, 9 May 2003, *RJ*, 176, also *RRTDecisiones* 95 (2012) 287. One recalls, too, the case of Nathan and Madaleva. A witness credibly testified, "'When he committed himself to enter marriage, [Nathan] was solidly convinced that Madaleva was the woman of his life.'" *Coram* Sciacca, 1 June 2007, *RJ*, 241. The Rota did not view Nathan's love for Madaleva at the time of the marriage as an obstacle to concluding that he had hypothetically excluded the *bonum sacramenti*. Ibid., 246.

162 *Coram* Turnaturi, 10 April 2003, *RRTDecisiones* 95 (2012) 201.

163 Ibid., 201. He is citing *coram* Pinto, 27 November 1969.

164 Ibid., 201.

165 Ibid., 202. This argument may be circular, though: genuine conjugal love tends towards the establishment of a permanent bond, therefore a person willing to contemplate the possibility of dissolving the bond does not have genuine conjugal love. Because Titius claims to have contemplated the possibility of dissolving the marriage, he must have been animated, not by genuine conjugal love, but by something else.

166 *Coram* Sciacca, 9 May 2003, *RJ*, 186, also *RRTDecisiones* 95 (2012) 294.

167 Ibid., 187.

168 Ibid., 186.

Huber has helpfully provided a catalog of circumstances that Rotal precedents had found to be not altogether incompatible with the exclusion of *the bonum sacramenti*. Although a superficial consideration of the following circumstances might argue against the occurrence of simulation, the Rota has issued an affirmative decision:

1. Even if the simulator "desires a true marriage" (cf. *coram* Palazzini, 28 June 1972);
2. Even if the simulator neither knows nor foresees that the conjugal bond will really be broken later (*coram* Filipiak, 23 March 1956);
3. Even if the simulator is imbued with love for the other party (*coram* Filipiak, 16 October 1984);
4. Even if the simulator wants children (*coram* Faltin, 19 February 1992);
5. Even if the simulator foresees that the marriage will last until death (*coram* De Jorio, 14 December 1966);
6. Even if the simulator does not know that he/she is contracting invalidly (*coram* Felici, 14 July 1959); and
7. Even if the simulator does everything to avoid dissolving the bond by divorce (*coram* Funghini, 11 March 1987).[169]

As a counter-balance to this list, in a more recent decision Huber enumerated circumstances that Rotal precedent identified as negative signs of simulation:

1. "Love between the parties" (*coram* Stankiewicz, 20 December 1988);
2. The desire "of having offspring" (*coram* Colagiovanni, 15 December 1987);
3. [In the case of hypothetical exclusion of indissolubility,] the persistence of the common life after the hypothesis [viz., justifying the dissolution of the marriage] has been verified (*coram* Agustoni, 21 November 1975);
4. A reason for the breakup that is supervening and extrinsic to the will of the contracting party (*coram* Davino, 15 October 1987).[170]

---

169 This list, from *coram* Huber, 28 September 1995, n. 5, is cited in *coram* Monier, 26 January 2001, *RRTDecisiones* 93 (2009) 108, in *coram* Monier, 16 February 2001, *RRTDecisiones* 93 (2009) 156, and in *coram* Turnaturi, 10 April 2003, *RRTDecisiones* 95 (2012) 199.

170 *Coram* Huber, 23 July 2003, *RRTDecisiones* 95 (2012) 528. Huber also lists "ratio sese gerendi […] in vita communi" (*coram* Funghini, 11 March 1987), but this author has no idea what that means. A spouse's pattern of behavior during the common life might undercut any claim that he/she simulated (cf., for example, *coram* Arokiaraj, 13 March 2008, *Studia canonica* 42 [2008] 538: "'The very fact [that] the respondent remained in marriage for a period of twenty years and notwithstanding the repeated instances of infidelity on the part of her husband, constitutes a much stronger argument against the affirmation of the petitioner that, at the moment when the marriage was contracted, she did not feel bound to its indissolubility. If this was true, she would have certainly left long before.'"), or it might make more credible the claim that he/she simulated (cf. *coram* Boccafola, 23 February 2006, *RJ*, 222: "There is no doubt but that the petitioner's reaction to

The attentive reader notices that "love" appears on both lists, as does a willingness to have children in the marriage. It is clear that most circumstances are not univocal. When deciding a case involving an allegation of exclusion of indissolubility, the judge most certainly must examine the circumstances before and after the marriage so as to determine how they affect the Plaintiff's claim; but rarely will the presence of a single circumstance fully prove or disprove that claim.

On the Simulator's Admissions

In Huber's opinion,

> The proof [of simulation] begins with the declaration of the alleged simulator. For he better than anyone else knows with what intention he celebrated the marriage. From the perspective of natural law alone, nothing prevents the achievement of moral certitude concerning the nullity of the marriage solely from the declaration of the parties or someone else.[171]

Church law, not natural law, prescribes that "the force of full proof cannot be attributed to" the parties' declarations.[172] Were it not for canon 1536 §2, a judge might well base an affirmative decision solely on the deposition of a plaintiff.

"Before the declaration [of the alleged simulator] is admitted [as] proof," Huber writes elsewhere, "the credibility of the simulator must be secured." The credibility the deponent enjoys will determine the evidentiary value of the con-

---

the news of the illness with which the respondent was afflicted is completely consonant... with the ground of the exclusion of indissolubility. For the woman, only five months after the marriage celebration, and right after the man's incapacitating illness was detected, denied him sexual relations and opposed his attempts to resume their previous emotional life."). Thus, an alleged simulator's "ratio sese gerendi [...] in vita communi" may or may not be a counter-indication of exclusion of the *bonum sacramenti*.

171 *Coram* Huber, 27 January 2000, *RRTDecisiones* 92 (2007) 118.

172 Canon 1536 §2 "In cases which concern the public good, however, a judicial confession and declarations by the parties which are not confessions, can have a probative value that is to be weighed by the judge in associate with the other circumstances of the case, but the force of full proof cannot be attributed to them unless there are other elements which wholly corroborate them." The translation is from *Code of Canon Law Annotated*. *Dignitas connubii*, Article 180 §1. "Confessions and other judicial declarations of the parties can have probative force, to be evaluated by the judge together with the other circumstances of the cause, but the force of full proof cannot be attributed to them, unless there are present other elements of proof that entirely corroborate them (cf. can. 1536, §2)." Article 181 "In regard to extrajudicial confessions of the parties against the validity of the marriage and other extrajudicial declarations of theirs introduced into the trial, it pertains to the judge, having considered all the circumstances, to evaluate how much to make of them (cf. can. 1537)."

tents of his/her deposition.[173] Monier warns against adopting a "hermeneutic of suspicion" in evaluating the judicial confession of an alleged simulator, even though he/she might be speaking in his/her own best interests, "because such a method would be contrary to justice and human dignity. Between absolute suspicion, without a rational basis, and acceptance without moderation of every affirmation, there really is the virtue of prudence which always seems the law for the judge in weighing and judging a case."[174] Stankiewicz is somewhat more wary:

> Although in cases concerning simulation of consent much [importance] must be attributed to the credibility of the person who confesses his own simulation in court, nevertheless witnesses confirming that credibility are hardly sufficient. For the law requires also other indicia and adminicula, unless by chance the full proofs are already had in other ways.[175]

When the Acts do not contain an alleged simulator's admission that he/she simulated, it is not impossible for a judge to become morally certain that simulation occurred; but it is difficult.[176] That it is not impossible is evident from a case decided in June of 2000 *coram* Pinto. The Auditor wrote, "It is true that the confession of the Respondent is lacking in the acts, but the true intention of the woman of establishing an invalid marriage gushes out with greater evidence from the horde of indicia, of adminicular proofs, of occurrences, of half admissions, and even of silences, related in the trial by persons worthy of belief and immune to all suspicion...."[177] The parties—Christian and Martha—had met in 1970 and had engaged in a long-distance courtship. Not "precious and few," but "Rare and fleeting were their meetings," Pinto reports.[178] As their wedding neared, Christian noticed Martha's increasing coldness. When he reproached her about it, they had unpleasant scenes. Fearing that the marriage would be unhappy, Christian thought about cancelling it. Possibly because he still loved his fiancée, possibly because, having only recently lost his mother, he was hoping that Martha would fill the gap in his emotional life, and possibly because everything was ready for the wedding and he had spent lots of money remodel-

---

173 *Coram* Huber, 23 July 2003, *RRTDecisiones* 95 (2012) 528.

174 *Coram* Monier, 26 January 2001, *RRTDecisiones* (2009) 109.

175 *Coram* Stankiewicz, 13 December 2001, *RRTDecisiones* 93 (2009) 805.

176 Sciacca's citation of Mattioli is very much to the point: "First of all, one must inquire about the judicial confession of the alleged simulator: 'not indeed in the sense'—we read in a case *coram* Mattioli, 8 February 1951—'that such a confession is absolutely necessary, or, if there is one, that it constitutes a peremptory argument; but according to the rule that, if it is missing, and it cannot be supplanted [*sic*; would *substituted for* or *supplied by* not be a better translation of *suppleri*?] by other extra-judicial statements of the simulator, the pivotal evidence falls to pieces.'...." *Coram* Sciacca, 1 June 2007, *RJ*, 237.

177 *Coram* Pinto, 9 June 2000, *RRTDecisiones* 92 (2007) 466.

178 Ibid., 460.

ing his home, he did nothing. The bride was nearly two hours late for the wedding. The ensuing common life was unhappy "on account of Martha's very bad behavior": she resisted consummating the marriage; she did not want to have children; she berated her husband without cause. Four months after the wedding, she left him.[179] From her behavior the Rota was able to infer "the depraved and perverse will of the Respondent against the indissolubility of the bond and the good of the spouses."[180] The absence from the Acts of "an express confession, whether judicial or extrajudicial, by the Respondent of her intention of entering a non-permanent marriage and without the obligation of procuring her and her spouse's good in the communion of life or the partnership of the whole of life"[181] did not prevent the Auditors from concluding that she entered the marriage with precisely that intention.

The affirmative decision about Martha's alleged simulation is the exception, however, not the rule. What Sable observes in a case involving an absent Respondent tends to be the rule: "In the estimation of the Fathers, in the absence of the Respondent's judicial confession, sufficient proof cannot be obtained from the testimony of the Plaintiff and [his] witnesses."[182] Genovefa's case provides a heart-wrenching illustration. Having lost both parents in Auschwitz, she was reared in an orphanage. As a young adult she fell in love with Hyacinth. His father prevented them from marrying because Hyacinth was destined for a career as a bailiff or estate manger whereas she did not want to live in the country. After the breakup with Hyacinth, Genovefa met Gerard. His mother disapproved of the parties' relationship, either because she did not like Genovefa's looks or because Gerard had not completed his military duty. Nevertheless, the couple married civilly. When she became pregnant, Genovefa induced Gerard to marry her in the Catholic Church.[183] Stankiewicz reports,

> ...the common life, which the newlyweds established in the meantime, was quite brief. Having completed his military service, the Respondent remained in the conjugal home with his wife for only forty days. Moreover, he undertook no employment to support his family. After the lapse of time, Gerard abandoned his still pregnant wife and returned to his mother.[184]

The 1 February 1972 birth of their son did not lead to a reconciliation, nor did Gerard ever show any interest in rearing the boy. In 1973,

---

179 Ibid., 461.
180 Ibid., 466.
181 Ibid., 466.
182 *Coram* Sable, 12 June 2003, *RRTDecisiones* 95 (2012) 356.
183 *Coram* Stankiewicz, *RRTDecisiones* 93 (2009) 92.
184 Ibid., 92-93.

the Plaintiff resumed… her romantic relationship with Hyacinth, whom she had never stopped loving; and she bore two children sired by him. After obtaining a civil divorce, on 15 December 1978 Genovefa married Hyacinth in a civil ceremony. [In this civil marriage] she bore two more children. Moreover Hyacinth civilly adopted the boy Joseph born of the marriage between the Plaintiff and the Respondent.[185]

The course Genovefa's procedural history ran no more smoothly than her romances. On 12 January 1984 she petitioned for the annulment of the marriage on grounds of Gerard's exclusion of the *bonum sacramenti*. On 16 November 1992—nearly nine years later—the first instance court handed down a negative decision. On 24 November 1993 the second instance court issued an affirmative decision. The Rota's negative third instance decision bears the date of 26 January 2001: Genovefa's ultimately futile quest to regularize her marital situation consumed seventeen years. While composing a negative sentence, Stankiewicz sympathetically notes the "sad recollection of the Plaintiff's tragic infancy who was atrociously bereaved of [her] parents during World War II." He continues,

> Nor were the Plaintiff's endeavors of establishing a family life and of having her own home, of which she was violently despoiled in infancy, undertaken under happy auspices. For when the Plaintiff desired to marry Hyacinth, his father firmly hindered the marriage, lest his son, remaining in town, abandon his country occupation.[186]

In addition, the Plaintiff's marriage to the Respondent clearly broke up because of the Respondent's behavior, not the Plaintiff's.[187] "More sinned against than sinning" might be a cliché, but it does apply to Genovefa.

Many—perhaps most—Tribunal practitioners would suspect that there must have been something wrong with Gerard's act of consent. People do not elicit valid consent in mid-August, then definitively abandon their spouses and unborn children within six weeks. If Gerard embraced Genovefa with genuine marital affection in August, how could he have become totally estranged from her by the first of February? This kind of reasoning led the second instance judges to the conclusion that the Respondent must have simulated. Stankiewicz objects,

> …in argumentation of this sort the existence of an act excluding indissolubility is only presumed, not in the least is the existence of an act, at least implicit, proven. In [the case of] a presumption the positive existence of the object of the presumption is not proven, but

---

185   Ibid., 93.
186   Ibid., 97.
187   Ibid., 103.

is rendered only probable, in light of the fact that a presumption is 'a probable conjecture about an uncertain matter' (can. 1584). The conviction... or even the moral certitude, dependent on a presumed act cannot change the presumptive nature of the same act. For a presumed act does not contain exclusion, but can only suggest it and render it probable.[188]

In this case, not only did Gerard not admit that he had excluded the *bonum sacramenti*, but he also asserted that "he married the Plaintiff with sincere mind" and that he had wanted to remain with her for life.[189] Stankiewicz insists that Gerard's "postmarital behavior... and the brevity of the common life (broken off by the same man) cannot take the place of the positive act of the will against the *bonum sacramenti* required by the law...."[190] One might reply that, although the Respondent's postmarital behavior cannot *take the place of* a positive act of the will, it might *reveal* its existence. Even so, the Auditor's argument might justify a judge's remaining in doubt about the sufficiency of the evidence when the Acts do not contain the alleged simulator's admission that he/she simulated;[191] and in cases of lingering doubt, the ecclesiastical judge must rule, *non constat*.[192]

Three other cases in which the brevity of the common life and the behavior of the Respondent might give rise to the suspicion that she excluded the *bonum sacramenti* confirm that the Rota's treatment of Genovefa's case was not atypical. (1) A certain Vincent married Angela on 28 September 1985. She had already had a child out of wedlock, but this did not bother him. Despite being pregnant, Angela left their home in April of 1986 and "obstinately" refused reconciliation.[193] Although the couple's courtship had been too brief to provide a foundation for the establishment of a community of life and love, in Sable's opinion this was no proof that either party had simulated.[194] Moreover, Angela maintained that she had celebrated the marriage with the right intention, that

---

188 Ibid., 96.

189 Ibid., 99.

190 Ibid., 103.

191 Readers of *Studia canonica* might recall here a contrasting decision *coram* Monier concerning exclusion of the *bonum coniugum* (*coram* Monier, 27 October 2006, *Studia canonica* 43 [2009] 243-260). The Respondent in that case denied having simulated: "The respondent on his part confesses that he had no intention contrary to marriage" (p. 255). The sentence cites no testimony from any witness reporting an extrajudicial confession by the Respondent. The turnus nonetheless concluded, largely on the basis of what witnesses said about the Respondent's behavior during the marriage, that "there is proof of nullity of marriage in the case due to exclusion of the good of the spouses on the part of the Respondent..." (p. 260).

192 Cf. canon 1608 §§1,4 as well as canon 1060.

193 *Coram* Sable, 13 April 2000, *RRTDecisiones* 92 (2007) 339.

194 Ibid., 342.

neither before nor after the marriage had she wanted a soluble marriage, and that she had never posited an act of the will against the good of the sacrament.[195] Notwithstanding her incomprehensibly rapid desertion of the marriage, the Rota could not conclude that she had excluded its indissolubility. (2) A turnus *coram* Huber decided similarly the case of Aloysius and Paula. Prior to the marriage she had been in love with Roberto; but he broke off their relationship when she became pregnant, and Aloysius was willing to marry her and accept the child as his own. The couple married on 30 April 1988,[196] but she obtained a civil divorce less than two years later.[197] Aloysius alleged that Paula had excluded the *bonum sacramenti*, in part because she had told him before the marriage that if he ever revealed that he was not the father of her child, she would immediately seek a divorce.[198] Although Paula gave no testimony to the Court, she denied in writing that she had excluded any essential property of marriage.[199] The turnus concluded that, from the testimony of Aloysius, they could not discover what the woman had meant when she threatened divorce: "whether she intended to break off the common life or whether she intended to rescind the matrimonial bond with a positive intention…."[200] (3) Gordianus sought the annulment of his former marriage to Glyceria on several grounds, including her exclusion of the *bonum sacramenti*. Their four-year-long courtship had been turbulent: on one occasion the young woman became so angry that she threw away their engagement ring. "According to the man, Glyceria agreed to marry only because of [her] mother's persistent instigation."[201] Only forty days after the wedding Glyceria left the conjugal home. The common life was never resumed. Gordianus commenced divorce proceedings only seven months after the wedding.[202] During the annulment action he was able to prove that Glyceria was hesitant about marrying him[203] and had "felt doubt about the happy outcome of the marriage…."[204] But she strenuously denied that she had excluded the *bonum sacramenti*. At most, she admitted having had a mindset favoring divorce.[205]

One cannot avoid concluding that, in the absence of his/her admission of simulation, Rotal panels tend to respond negatively to allegations of exclusion of

---

195 Ibid., 343.
196 *Coram* Huber, 15 December 2000, *RRTDecisiones* 92 (2007) 730.
197 Ibid., 731.
198 Ibid., 730.
199 Ibid., 735.
200 Ibid., 735.
201 *Coram* Caberletti, 12 June 2003, *RRTDecisiones* 95 (2012) 359.
202 Ibid., 359.
203 Ibid., 377-379.
204 Ibid., 379.
205 Ibid., 379.

the *bonum sacramenti*, even when the alleged simulator's postmarital behavior suggests a cavalier attitude towards maintaining the common life.

A Word or Two About Witnesses

The bulk of the evidence in formally-processed marriage cases generally consists in the statements of witnesses. Because, in cases involving allegations of exclusion of the *bonum sacramenti*, the court is attempting to discover whether the alleged simulator entered marriage reserving the right to dissolve the bond, the strongest and most relevant testimony will come from credible witnesses who heard the alleged simulator say, at a non-suspect time, that he/she was intending to do precisely that. For example, the free-spirited would-be musician told her sister before the marriage that she would regain her freedom if the marriage proved unhappy.[206] She told her mother, too, that nothing lasts forever and that if her marriage was unhappy she would end it.[207] At his bachelor party a Plaintiff told his military buddies that, if his fiancée did not change her behavior after their marriage, there was always divorce.[208] On the other side of the ledger, when witnesses in whom the judge presumes the alleged simulator would have confided know nothing about the alleged simulation, the court might find the allegation doubtful. Thus Huber writes, "…it is astonishing that the man never in the presence of the cited witnesses breathed a word about his simulated consent."[209] The same Auditor elsewhere states, "No witness ever heard notices from the mouth of the Respondent, from which one might educe a positive act of the will against the indissolubility of marriage. Therefore lacking is any kind of extrajudicial confession."[210] Pena is equally emphatic: "…no one before and after the marriage heard the Plaintiff confessing, in explicit words, an exclusion related to indissolubility; consequently, they cannot corroborate the alleged simulation, because they know nothing about" it.[211] Credible witness testimony about the alleged simulator's extrajudicial statements is obviously critically important.

Witnesses might also testify about the reasons the alleged simulator had for

---

206 *Coram* Defilippi, 9 February 2000, *RRTDecisiones* 92 (2007) 151.

207 Ibid., 151.

208 *Coram* Sciacca, 9 May 2003, *RRTDecisiones* 95 (2012) 29; also *RJ*, 181.

209 *Coram* Huber, 23 July 2003, *RRTDecisiones* 95 (2012) 532.

210 *Coram* Huber, 14 December 2000, *RRTDecisiones* 92 (2007) 735. One notes that *the Plaintiff* had reported an extrajudicial confession: when the Respondent became pregnant by a young man who declined to marry her, the Plaintiff proposed and indicated his willingness to accept the unborn child as his own. The Respondent demanded absolute secrecy about the paternity of the child, adding "that in the case of violation of that secret she would immediately seek a divorce" (p. 730). But the turnus concluded that they could not ascertain from the Plaintiff's testimony what the woman meant when she threatened divorce (p. 735). Thus, the absence of any independent corroboration of her words and her meaning left the matter in doubt.

211 *Coram* Pena, 15 December 2000, *RRTDecisiones* 92 (2007) 726.

excluding permanence from the marriage. For example, most of the testimony Sciacca cites in the case of Nathan and Madaleva concerns Nathan's adamant conviction that unhappy spouses should have the right to dissolve their marriages.[212] No witness testified about Nathan's having said, "I will divorce Madaleva if our marriage becomes unhappy"; but several credible witnesses verified his energetic opposition to the indissolubility of marriage.

Witnesses might also provide evidence about the circumstances which made it more likely that the alleged simulator simulated. For example, almost all of the witnesses in the case of Telephorus and Tharsilla testified that Tharsilla insisted on marrying, whereas Telephorus wanted the couple to live together.[213] Moreover, on the day before the wedding a certain Frederica, who knew Telephorus since infancy, heard him say that he was emotionally bound to another young woman.[214] In the case of Narses and Norma,

> ...all the witnesses confirm the difficulties between the young people. Even the Respondent's witnesses clearly show the disagreements—indeed serious disagreements—on account of the man's imperious behavior so that, according to the words of the Respondent's sister, the relationship was carried on "between serenity and storm."[215]

But witness testimony about circumstances can also undermine claims of simulation. For example, a certain Calmerus claimed to have been romantically involved with both his future wife Crescentia and Chlothilda at the same time.[216] Chlothilda admitted having been his friend but denied having been sexually involved with him;[217] and this supposed romantic relationship was the foundation of Calmerus' claim that his marital consent was substantially defective. In another case, the fact that "the witnesses... describe a peaceful and serene courtship" made the Rota doubt that the Plaintiff would have excluded the *bonum sacramenti*.[218]

On the interpretation of witness testimony, Huber offers sage advice:

> With respect to evaluating the depositions of witnesses, the judge should abstain from exaggerated skepticism, but should remember that many are witnesses who depose not so much what is true as

---

212 *Coram* Sciacca, 1 June 2007, *RJ*, 241-244.
213 *Coram* Huber, 30 April 2003, *RRTDecisiones* 95 (2012) 247, 249.
214 Ibid., 246.
215 *Coram* Monier, 27 June 2003, *RRTDecisiones* 95 (2012) 445.
216 *Coram* Ciani, 21 May 2003, *RRTDecisiones* 95 (2012) 318.
217 Ibid., 330, 332.
218 *Coram* Pena, 15 December 2000, *RRTDecisiones* 92 (2007) 727.

what they think is useful to help the Plaintiff achieve freedom from the bond. They do not want to deceive the judge, but they intend rather to do a work of charity.[219]

Occasionally both the Plaintiff and the Respondent will have named witnesses; and in that case, each witness may try, if only subconsciously, to help the party on whose behalf he or she is testifying. Monier laments, "The solution of a case turns out to be more difficult, but not impossible, when grave discrepancies emerge in the depositions of the parties and the witnesses, as happens very often in these cases."[220] He recalls an observation of Giannecchini that, when the witnesses band together with the party who submitted them, the trial assumes the likeness of two armies battling, sometimes bitterly. In such a situation Giannecchini advises paying attention, not only to the credibility of each witness, but also to the source of his/her knowledge. Sometimes they testify about what they presume rather than know, and sometimes all of their knowledge comes directly and exclusively from the party on whose behalf they are testifying.[221] What a witness presumes may be evidence only of the witness' ingenuity, and hearsay from a suspect time may have little evidentiary value.

Monier usefully cites a dictum of Bruno about interpreting what witnesses say. "'The judge should not stop at the surface meaning of the words,'" that Auditor advises, "'nor at their peculiar external signification. It is more proper to inspect, within the context of the entire discussion, the substance of the depositions and the mind of the deponents so as to distinguish the [deponents'] intention and what they really meant to say by means of the words they employed.'"[222] Most witnesses are not canon lawyers or philologists. In testifying, they tend not to use technical language, nor do they use ordinary words with a lexicographer's precision. What they say may not always be exactly what they meant. What Monier says about evaluating the statements of the parties applies equally, *mutatis mutandis*, to the evaluation of testimony from witnesses: "Between absolute suspicion, without rational basis, and acceptance without moderation of every affirmation, there really is the virtue of prudence which always seems to be the law for the judge in weighing and judging a case."[223] Marshaling the evidence in a marriage case is not like listing the givens and theorems in a geometric demonstration. It requires close attention, insight, evaluation.

---

219 *Coram* Huber, 23 July 2003, *RRTDecisiones* 95 (2012) 528.
220 *Coram* Monier, 26 January 2001, *RRTDecisiones* 93 (2009) 109.
221 Ibid., 109.
222 Ibid., 109.
223 Ibid., 109.

Documents in the Case

Although most of the evidence in marriage cases tends to consist in statements by the parties and their witnesses, documents,[224] especially private documents,[225] can be important sources of proof. In none of the cases I was able to study while preparing this presentation was a document conclusive proof of simulation. In other words, in no case was there a letter or a journal entry written by the simulator at a non-suspect time admitting his/her intention to enter a dissoluble marriage;[226] but in three cases private documents provided important corroboration of the Plaintiffs' claims.

In the case of Telephorus and Tharsilla, a letter the Respondent wrote before the marriage undercut her judicial attempts to rebut the Plaintiff's claim that he entered their marriage with the intention of seeking a divorce if the common life turned out badly.[227] The couple had become acquainted some seven years before their marriage. Initially they were friends, but they gradually became romantically involved. Telephorus claimed that during the courtship he noticed how temperamentally different they were. Other people discouraged them from marrying. He accordingly became anxious about the probable outcome of their marriage. He suggested to Tharsilla that they not marry but simply begin living together. Because she rejected his proposal, he proceeded to the altar—but with the intention of taking recourse to divorce if the common life proved unhappy. It did.[228]

The Rota considered the Plaintiff to be a reliable source of information: "In the concrete case the Plaintiff's external credibility is beyond doubt."[229] Throughout the processing of the case Telephorus freely admitted that he had not wanted to

---

224 Cf. canon 1539 "In any sort of trial proof through both public and private documents is admitted."

225 According to canon 1540, private documents are (1) not formally drawn up by an ecclesiastical official in the exercise of his/her official duties and (2) not considered public civil documents by the civil laws in force in a given place. Letters and the like are typical private documents.

226 See, however, *coram* Alwan, 21 October 2003, *RRTDecisiones* 95 (2012) 606; English translation: *coram* Alwan, 21 October 2003, *RJ*, 64: "…letters provided by the petitioner in the process, letters exchanged between the lovers both right before the wedding and immediately thereafter, underscore their mutual love and amorous relationship…" These letters, however, tended to prove, not the Plaintiff's exclusion of the *bonum sacramenti*, but her exclusion of the *bonum fidei*. Moreover, they apparently did not contain a clear admission that the Plaintiff was planning to simulate or that she had simulated; they verified the relationship with her lover that was her reason for simulating.

227 *Coram* Huber, 30 April 2003, *RRTDecisiones* 95 (2012) 239-251.

228 Ibid., 240.

229 Ibid., 243.

marry Tharsilla and had therefore contracted a "trial marriage" with her.[230] The Acts contained ample witness testimony corroborating his admissions:

> Having attended to founded reasons for suspecting that the marriage about to be entered would turn out unhappily, the Plaintiff determined himself to act in accordance with his feelings and therefore posited a positive act of the will against the indissolubility of the bond. The interventions of others and [their] dissuasions forced the man to think about the marriage and about its consequences and to determine means for the case of the shipwreck of the marriage.[231]

The Respondent, however, disputed these conclusions.[232] To deal with her objections the Rota focused attention on a letter she had written a month before the wedding.[233] "If anyone reads through the letter attentively," writes Huber, "he arrives at the conclusion that the groom's mind as the marriage approached was estranged from the bride's."[234] In the course of the letter Tharsilla implicitly admitted that the couple's relationship had changed for the worse. By means of this letter the Respondent in effect provided testimony from a non-suspect time verifying the circumstances in the midst of which the Plaintiff would have acted the way he now claims that he acted. Her letter proved, not so much that the Plaintiff was truthfully confessing his simulation, as that she was being less than candid in combating his claim.

In the case of Orville and Pauline[235] a key piece of evidence was a telegram. On the eve of the wedding[236] Orville's military buddies wired him, "There is divorce. Stop. Congratulations and good wishes."[237] Telegrams, with the exception of George Keenan's, tend to be laconic: the reader needs to know their context in order to understand them. The context of this telegram was Orville's bachelor party. While ostensibly celebrating his impending marriage, some friends confronted him about his "stupidity" in marrying "a woman whose behavior would not change after the wedding." Orville told them, "'I hoped Pauline could change… but in case she had not changed I would have the possibility to have

---

230   Ibid., 244.

231   Ibid., 246.

232   Ibid., 244.

233   Ibid., 243. Huber considered the letter a "hermeneutical key" for interpreting the evidence.

234   Ibid., 245.

235   *Coram* Sciacca, 9 May 2003, *RJ*, 169-190. The original Latin is published as *Coram* Sciacca, 9 May 2003, *RRTDecisiones* 95 (2012) 284-296, in which the parties are "yclept" Zephyrinus and Zanaida. Citations will be from the English translation.

236   Ibid., 181.

237   Ibid., 183.

recourse to divorce.'"²³⁸ Young men—and sometimes not so young men—are capable of boorish antics;²³⁹ and the telegram considered in a vacuum could have been no more than a tasteless attempt at humor; but against the background of the argument during the bachelor party it was portentous. Because he did not write it, the telegram did not prove and could not prove that Orville had entered the marriage with the intention of dissolving it if Pauline's behavior did not become less provocative; but it did imply that he had made comments to the senders about the future applicability of divorce to his own marriage. Unless a judge were to disregard the telegram entirely, the judge would have to conclude that the bachelor party provided an opportunity only a week before the wedding for Orville to think concretely about his own coming marriage and the possibility that he might someday want to dissolve it.

Finally, in the already-mentioned case of Dagobert, before the marriage his parents were so convinced of their son's unsuitability for marriage that they wrote about their concerns to the parish priest. Their letter mentioned his emotional instability, their having urged him to seek psychiatric therapy, and their conviction that his behavior presaged difficulties in the marriage.²⁴⁰ Their letter could not demonstrate what was in their son's mind and heart as he approached marriage, but it did prove that his behavior shortly before the wedding was so outlandish that his loving parents tried to prevent him from doing what he was planning to do. In other words, the letter was evidence from a non-suspect time that Dagobert was acting like a person who would not elicit valid matrimonial consent.

Although not smoking guns in the hands of shooters, the private documents in these cases did verify important circumstances that bolstered the Plaintiffs' claims of simulation. It is true that documents like them might not be available in every case involving allegations of simulation, but it is no waste of time for a judge to consider whether some such document might be available in a given case.

The Interrelationship of Various Grounds

A few remarks on the relationship between exclusion of the *bonum sacramenti* and some other traditional grounds of nullity serve as a postscript to this discussion.

Some Rotal Auditors argue vigorously that total simulation and exclusion of the *bonum sacramenti* are completely incompatible grounds of nullity. For example, Caberletti insists, "[The person] who simulates totally, in no way wants

---

238   Ibid., 181.

239   One should note on the other side of the ledger that young men tend to be diffident about confronting their friends—especially in public—about the foolishness of their marital plans.

240   *Coram* Serrano, 3 August 2001, *RRTDecisiones* 93 (2009) 602-603.

marriage; to the contrary [the person] who excludes something essential, intends to contract marriage, but he subtracts something essential to the object of consent in such a way that one is in no way dealing with the natural object of matrimonial consent."[241] From this it follows, according to this Auditor, that "the grounds of nullity of exclusion of marriage itself and of the exclusion of some essential element or property of marriage must be harmonized subordinately."[242] Funghini likewise recognizes the different subjective orientations of the total simulator and the partial simulator: "...in [the case of] total [simulation] the contractant has the intention of not contracting, i.e. he does not want to establish a partnership of the whole of life with his partner; in [the case of] partial [simulation], however, his intention directs itself towards a sort of marriage, conceived according to his pleasure or accommodated to his ideas or his situation."[243] Boccafola is equally emphatic:

> [The person] who simulates has no intention of contracting marriage; but [the person] who excludes this or that good of marriage desires, to the contrary, to contract marriage, but intends it just as he conceives it, to wit, wills something whose object is something other than the object toward which, by its nature, matrimonial consent is directed. In total simulation, therefore, the contract itself that is to say marriage is rejected; but in partial, the substance of the contract, i.e., this or that of its essential properties, for example the *bonum sacramenti* or the *bonum fidei* or the *bonum prolis*.... Partial [simulation] limits the consent manifested by spouse, while in total simulation no consent is present.[244]

Auditors likewise seem averse to admitting compatibility between force and fear and simulation. Boccafola puts it clearly:

> Fear-inspired consent, which by its nature is true and in its object is perfect, is vitiated, not by a positive act of the will of the contracting party, who excludes the marriage itself or its essential properties, but by an injury inflicted *ab extrinseco* on the contracting party through grave coercion. In celebrating the marriage the contracting party manifests consent; but it is coerced consent, by means of which *by law* a valid marriage cannot be effected.[245]

---

241 *Coram* Caberletti, 5 April 2000, *RRTDecisiones* 92 (2007) 297.
242 Ibid., 297.
243 *Coram* Funghini, 19 January 2001, *RRTDecisiones* 93 (2009) 62-63.
244 *Coram* Boccafola, 28 June 2001, *RRTDecisiones* 93 (2009) 442.
245 Ibid., 442.

Caberletti agrees:

> The same marriage cannot be invalid on grounds of fear and on grounds of the simulation of consent. For consent elicited by fear, although vitiated, is true consent, when the same would not be [true] about simulation; therefore the grounds of the nullity of the marriage from fear and from simulation are not compatible; but nothing prevents the two grounds, namely fear and simulation, from being proposed in the same case subordinately.[246]

The relationship between the exclusion of indissolubility and other forms of partial simulation is less straightforward. Civili's discussion of the interrelationship between exclusion of the *bonum sacramenti* and exclusion of the *bonum fidei* is thought-provoking:

> When the *bonum sacramenti* collapses, the *bonum fidei* falls in ruins, too, because the person who reserves to himself the faculty of divorcing and yoking himself in a new marriage takes away [from the marriage] unity as well as indissolubility.... For this reason, if perpetuity is excluded, faithfulness also, at least implicitly and indirectly, is always excluded, even though explicitly and directly only the former is rejected with an intention directed against this specific good. To the contrary, the intention by which the *bonum fidei* is excluded does not necessarily strike the *bonum sacramenti*, unless in the sense that, if the essence of the contract has been changed by rejecting one good, all the goods collapse with the contract itself.[247]

Because exclusion of the *bonum sacramenti* necessarily involves the intention of recovering one's freedom to marry, it consequently involves the intention of retaining the freedom to give to a person other than one's spouse specifically marital rights; and retaining at least conditionally the freedom to give to a third person the rights one should be giving exclusively to one's spouse is precisely exclusion of the *bonum fidei*. The 21 October 2003 decision *coram* Alwan demonstrates that the contrary is not true. Felicia and Gerald married in 1990 after a lengthy, though sometimes broken-off, courtship. Even before the marriage, however, Felicia was sexually involved with Benjamin. "The relationship with Benjamin ended three days before the marriage and resumed in 1991, when Gerald and [Felicia] had just returned from [their] honeymoon."[248] The Rotal turnus was convinced "that the Plaintiff by a positive act of the will was steadfastly determined to pursue an amorous relationship with her lover despite the reality of the marriage.... Continuous and proven love of this kind, along with an amorous

---

246 *Coram* Caberletti, 12 June 2003, *RRTDecisiones* 95 (2012) 364.

247 *Coram* Civili, 26 October 2000, *RRTDecisiones* 92 (2007) 598.

248 *Coram* Alwan, 21 October 2003, *RJ*, 62.

relationship both before and after the marriage, proves beyond any ambiguity whatever the exclusion of the fidelity on the part of the woman."[249] At the same time, the Auditors found that "Although there is a close connection between the exclusion of the good of fidelity and that of indissolubility, at least as a motive for marrying and for simulating, they are by no means necessarily linked."[250] Felicia's intention to establish a quasi-marital relationship with Gerald while retaining the right to continue her affair with Benjamin did not imply an intention not to remain for life in that quasi-marital relationship with Gerald.

Huber offers interesting observations on the interrelationship between exclusion of the *bonum sacramenti* and exclusion of the *bonum prolis*:

> [At issue in this case are] exclusions of the *bonum sacramenti* and the *bonum prolis* between the same parties. Some contend in this case the exclusions must be treated subordinately.... For if exclusion of indissolubility has been proven, ontologically and psychologically there is no place for proposing exclusion of the *bonum prolis*. For in a community between a man and a woman which is not a true marriage—as is declared by the first *caput*—there cannot be any talk about the *bonum prolis*. The *bonum prolis* presupposes some valid marriage, from which there arises the right to "the conjugal act per se apt for the generation of children, toward which by its nature marriage is ordered, and by which the spouses become one flesh" (canon 1061, §1). If the nullity of a marriage has been proven by reason of exclusion of the *bonum sacramenti*, the *bonum prolis* cannot be excluded by lack of matrimonial communion between the man and the woman. For outside of marriage no right to properly matrimonial acts is given.[251]

This line of reasoning does not reflect Huber's opinion: he agrees with Ferraro that no just judgment is possible in cases such as the one he is considering without a careful and free evaluation of the evidence concerning each ground on its own merits. Nevertheless, the question underlying the argument he sketches is worth considering: if a given relationship between a man and a woman is not truly marital because it lacks from the outset one of the essential properties of marriage, is it coherent to ask whether that non-marital relationship also suffered from the lack of an orientation which really belongs only to marriage?

Caberletti's comment on the relationship between exclusion of the *bonum prolis* and exclusion of the *bonum sacramenti* is less philosophical. "A connection, and sometimes a strict one, can be had between exclusion of the *bonum*

---

249 Ibid., 65.
250 Ibid., 67.
251 *Coram* Huber, 30 April 2003, *RRTDecisiones* 95 (2012) 242.

sacramenti and the refusal of the *bonum prolis*," he writes.[252] The Auditor approvingly cites a 30 October 2002 decision *coram* Ciani:

> When exclusion of children occurs with exclusion of indissolubility, by means of which the spouse reserves to himself the power of breaking the bond, if matters turn out badly, and decides to have no offspring in the meantime, the presumption stands in favor of the exclusion of the right to conjugal acts per se apt for the generation of children, or the *bonum prolis*. To be sure, the exclusion of children could in some way be considered under the appearance of temporality for pursuing a test of the happy marriage, still the same exclusion turns out to be perpetual because of the prevailing intention of dissolving the marriage, because really the perpetual obligation itself of conjugal acts per se apt for the generation of children is excluded, since the inclusion of the indissolubility of the marriage excludes the object itself of the matrimonial contract, which much be handed over wholly, which object is the perpetual and exclusive right over the body to acts per se apt for the generation of children...[253]

The argument here appears to be, not that exclusion of indissolubility entails exclusion of the *bonum prolis*, but that proof of exclusion of indissolubility might transform what looks like a temporary restriction of the exercise of the right to potentially fruitful acts of intercourse into an invalidating restriction of the very right to those acts.

An especially interesting case decided *coram* Caberletti on 10 April 2003 casts light on the relationship between exclusion of the *bonum sacramenti* and error concerning a quality of the person of one's spouse. The parties—called Symphorosa and Spyridion in the definitive sentence[254] and Alicia and Bernard in the decree of equivalent conformity—[255]appear to have enjoyed a serene four-year-long courtship.[256] "The common life, however, proceeded along happily only for the first five months; the marriage broke down four months later when the local hospital diagnosed the respondent-husband as suffering from epilepsy."[257] Alicia originally petitioned for the annulment of the marriage "on the grounds of deceit about a personal quality of the husband which seriously disturbed the *consortium vitae*."[258] Against an affirmative decision on grounds of both *dolus* and error of

---

252 *Coram* Caberletti, 12 June 2003, *RRTDecisiones* 95 (2012) 366.
253 Ibid., 366-367.
254 *Coram* Caberletti, 10 April 2003, *RRTDecisiones* 95 (2012) 213-238.
255 *Coram* Boccafola, 23 February 2006, *RJ,* 213-225.
256 *Coram* Caberletti, 10 April 2003, *RRTDecisiones* 95 (2012) 213.
257 *Coram* Boccafola, 23 February 2006, *RJ,* 213.
258 Ibid., 214.

quality directly and principally intended, the Respondent appealed directly to the Rota.[259] He was able to demonstrate that prior to the marriage neither he nor any member of his family had any reason to suspect that he was suffering from epilepsy. Caberletti concluded, "Therefore, since in the man and in his relatives before the marriage not even a suspicion arose about the... illness from which Spyridion suffered, by means of their 'silence' they perpetrated no fraud towards the Plaintiff, especially not in order to induce her into celebrating the marriage. Any foundation of the question of *dolus* is therefore lacking."[260]

Still, the turnus was certain that there was something essentially wrong with the young woman's act of consent. She enjoyed an unusually strong relationship with her father. This relationship manifested itself in her fixation on working with her father in the family business. She therefore demanded in her future spouse the capacity to work in the family business.[261] According to Caberletti,

> The woman's constancy and pertinacity in proposing to the man both before and after the marriage [his] employment in her father's business and her never-abandoned expectation that Spyridion would be her partner in business show the mind and intention of the woman with respect to the marriage... for her marriage should subsist together with the economic activity of her family, and consequently if this sort of connection should be broken, the partnership of life itself should be dissolved; therefore her positive act of the will against the perpetuity of the future marriage is considered proven, and it is a case indeed of the hypothetical exclusion of the *bonum sacramenti*.[262]

The Rotal turnus *coram* Boccafola which reviewed the case in third instance concluded that the appellate decision on grounds of the Plaintiff's hypothetical exclusion of the *bonum sacramenti* was formally equivalent to the first instance decision on grounds of the Plaintiff's error of quality. "Without doubt," writes Boccafola, "the acts of the case... demonstrate that the woman petitioner above all intended to contract marriage with a healthy and responsible man who could be true 'partner' with her and would help her and work together with her in her father's business."[263] True, "the sentence of first instance directed excessive attention to the other ground in the case which also received an affirmative re-

---

259 *Coram* Caberletti, 10 April 2003, *RRTDecisiones* 95 (2012) 214.

260 Ibid., 229.

261 Ibid., 234-234.

262 Ibid., 236; also 237: "because Symphorosa was so firmly rooted in the necessity of her husband's working in the family business, she herself implicitly intended to say goodbye to the wedding in the case of the non-fulfillment of her wishes..."

263 *Coram* Boccafola, 23 February 2006, *RJ*, 220.

sponse, that is, the ground of deceit."[264] As was noted above, neither the Respondent nor any member of his family could have deceived the Plaintiff about his epilepsy because he did not know that he had the disease. Nevertheless, the evidence did show that the Plaintiff had directly and principally intended a specific quality: "The quality sought was the natural character of the man as a healthy person, capable of responsibly working together with the woman as a partner in economic affairs...."[265] In the view of the first instance judges, the marriage was invalid because the quality that was the principal and direct object of the Plaintiff's consent did not exist. In the view of the appellate judges, the marriage was invalid because the Plaintiff had implicitly reserved the right to dissolve the bond if the Respondent proved not to be endowed with the quality she desired. "In conclusion," writes Boccafola, "the undersigned Prelate Auditors think that the two sentences are based on the same juridic facts which lead to nullity...."[266] This conclusion implies that exclusion of the *bonum sacramenti* and error of quality directly and principally intended are compatible grounds of nullity. Indeed, sometimes they provide alternative jurisprudential routes converging on the same conclusion.[267]

---

264 Ibid., 223.

265 Ibid., 224.

266 Ibid., 224.

267 A decision *coram* Monier (27 April 2001, *RRTDecisiones* 93 [2009] 294-306) confirms this negatively. This odd case involved a widowed Plaintiff (Anthimus) who met his second wife (Adreilla) by means of a magazine ad. They courted briefly and married in May of 1990. He claimed that during 1992 he discovered "that the woman was altogether different—i.e., not at all religious, nor moral, nor dedicated to the care of children, but a practitioner of magic (*adhaerentem ad artes magicas*)" (p. 294). Anthimus attacked the validity of this marriage on grounds of exclusion of indissolubility on his part and also on grounds of error. Because Anthimus had entertained no premarital doubts about Andreilla's endowment with the qualities he desired, the Rota decided he had had no reason for excluding indissolubility (pp. 301-302). During the marriage, when he discovered that she lacked these qualities (the turnus considered them "genericae"—p. 303), he did nothing, ostensibly at the advice of his attorney (p. 304). But if the qualities had been the direct and principal object of his consent, he would have withdrawn from the relationship. The reader can infer that, if Anthimus had proven that some specific quality which Adreilla lacked had been the object of his consent, he would have proven the marriage invalid on grounds of error of quality and would have also laid the foundation of proving the marriage invalid on grounds of implicit exclusion of the *bonum sacramenti*.

SEMINAR

THE QUEST FOR TRUTH IN CONSENSUAL INCAPACITY CAUSES: *DIGNITAS CONNUBII* AND THE USE OF PSYCHOLOGICAL EXPERTS
Deacon Gerald T. Jorgensen

Introduction

In many ways there is nothing radically new about the topic of this presentation. What we are about in this presentation builds on presentations by John Beal and myself at the annual meeting of this society in 2004, then another presentation I gave at the annual meeting of this society in 2008, and John Foster's presentation at last year's annual meeting, in 2011.[1] Simply stated, I will put two premises before you today. First, if there was any doubt before *Dignitas connubii*, there is no doubt now that it is a rare exception that the judge in a canon 1095 cause can decide not to use an expert to assist him in his search for the truth. Second, as a consequence of the first premise, ecclesiastical judges need to be aware of what to look for in an expert and in the opinion of the expert.

In establishing the relevance and importance of the premises I just put before you, I begin with the imperative that the judge has to search for the truth in his work as judge in a cause before him. On 1 October 1942, Pope Pius XII, in the middle of World War II, gave what only can be described as a prophetic address not just to the prelate auditors of the Roman Rota but to everyone involved in their various capacities in tribunals throughout the Church. As you no doubt recall, Pope Pius XII in his 1942 address to the Roman Rota spoke about the moral certitude necessary for judgment and warned, "truth is the law of justice. The world has need of that truth which is justice, and of that justice, which is truth."[2]

Then, in his 28 January 1994 address to the Roman Rota, Pope John Paul II explicitly referenced and expanded upon Pope Pius XII's very fundamental

---

1   John Beal, "Finding Method in the Madness: Writing Sentences in Lack of Due Discretion Cases," *CLSA Proceedings* 66 (2004) 57-79; Gerald Jorgensen, "The Role of the Expert in Tribunal Proceedings," *CLSA Proceedings* 66 (2004) 137-151; Gerald Jorgensen, "Navigating the Minefield of the Psychological Evaluation," *CLSA Proceedings* 70 (2008) 177-192; and John Foster, "Tips for Building Better Law Sections," *CLSA Proceedings* 73 (2011) 75-107.

2   Pope Pius XII, Allocution to the Roman Rota, 1 October 1942, in William Woestman (ed.), *Papal Allocutions to the Roman Rota 1939-2011* (Ottawa: Saint Paul University, 2011) 21.

issue of truth as the basis of justice. Pope John Paul II exhorted the prelate auditors, "*Love for truth* must be expressed in *love for justice* and in the resulting commitment to establishing truth in relations within human society; nor can its subjects be lacking in love for the law and the judicial system, which represent the human attempt to provide concrete norms for resolving practical cases. ... *Truth, however, is not always easy*; its affirmation is sometimes quite demanding. Nevertheless, it must always be respected in human communication and human relations. *The same applies for justice and the law*: they do not always appear easy together. ... It is indeed true that resolving practical cases is not always easy. But charity or mercy – as I mentioned on the same occasion – 'cannot put aside the demands of truth'."[3]

Early in his pontificate, Pope John Paul II began to articulate this fundamental issue of truth as the basis of justice in ecclesiastical judicial processes. In his 1980 address to the prelate auditors of the Roman Rota, John Paul II stated, "In all ecclesiastical trials truth must always be, from the beginning to the judgment, the foundation, mother, and law of justice. ... The immediate purpose of these trials is to ascertain whether or not the facts exist that by natural, divine or ecclesiastical law invalidate marriage, in order to issue *a true and just sentence* (emphasis added) concerning the alleged non-existence of the marriage bond."[4]

Pope Benedict XVI continues to echo, amplify, and develop the relationship between justice and the search for truth. In his very first address to the prelate auditors and officials of the Roman Rota and thus to everyone involved in their various capacities in tribunals throughout the church, Pope Benedict XVI stated, "The *canonical procedures* for the nullity of marriage are essentially *a means of ascertaining the truth* about the conjugal bond (emphases added). Thus, their constitutive aim is not to complicate the life of the faithful uselessly, nor far less to exacerbate their litigation, but rather to render a service to the truth."[5] The very next year on 27 January 2007, Pope Benedict XVI continued his explication of this fundamental theme of truth as the basis for justice. "Last year, at my first meeting with you, I sought to explore ways to overcome the apparent antithesis between the institute of causes of the nullity of marriage and genuine pastoral concern. In this perspective, *the love of truth* (emphasis added) emerges as a point of convergence between procedural research and the pastoral service for people. We must not forget, however, that in causes of nullity of marriage, the procedural truth presupposes the 'truth of the marriage' itself."[6] Finally, at least

---

3   Pope John Paul II, Allocution to the Roman Rota, 28 January 1994, Woestman (ed.), *Papal Allocutions*, passim 228-230.

4   Pope John Paul II, Allocution to the Roman Rota, 4 February 1980, Woestman (ed.), *Papal Allocutions*, 159-160.

5   Pope Benedict XVI, Allocution to the Roman Rota, 28 January 2006, Woestman (ed.), *Papal Allocutions*, 290.

6   Pope Benedict XVI, Allocution to the Roman Rota, 27 January 2007, Woestman

for now, in his 29 January 2010 allocution to the Roman Rota, Pope Benedict XVI followed up on this theme of justice and truth that he addressed in his 2006 and 2007 allocutions to that Apostolic Tribunal. "Today I wish to emphasize that both justice and charity postulate love for truth and essentially entail searching for truth. In particular, charity makes the reference to truth even more exacting. 'To defend the truth, to articulate it with humility and conviction, and to bear witness to it in life are therefore exacting and indispensable forms of charity. Charity, in fact, 'rejoices in the truth'.'"[7]

Perhaps in no other instance is the ecclesiastical judge's task to search for the truth in order to render justice more difficult than in dealing with what is referred to as consensual incapacity for marriage causes. Indeed, John Paul II in his 1987 allocution to the Roman Rota described it as an "arduous task" and "a ministry of truth and charity in the Church and for the Church."[8]

With the promulgation of the Instruction *Dignitas connubii* on 25 January 2005, it appeared that the Apostolic See further recognized that the judge's search for truth in an ecclesiastical matrimonial trial was difficult. In fact in the Preface to the Instruction we read that *Dignitas connubii* was promulgated, "With the intention that it be a help to judges and other ministers of the tribunals of the Church, to whom the sacred ministry of hearing the causes of the nullity of marriage has been entrusted."[9] Moreover, as an indicator of just how arduous a task the judge has in searching for the truth in consequential incapacity causes, this Instruction, aimed at how tribunals are to handle causes of nullity of marriage, devotes a level of attention to the grounds of nullity outlined in canon 1095 (consensual incapacity) that is not evident in relation to any other ground of nullity.[10] Indeed, there are eleven articles that specifically address the use of the grounds of nullity outlined in canon 1095, with eight of the articles comprising more than one paragraph (see *Dignitas connubii*, articles 203-213). However, in this presentation, I will prescind from the academic debate about the nature and juridical force of *Dignitas connubii* as well as from an analysis as to perhaps why this Instruction devotes such great attention to canon 1095 and refer you to the

---

(ed.), *Papal Allocutions*, 293.

7   Pope Benedict XVI, Allocution to the Roman Rota, 29 January 2010, Woestman (ed.), *Papal Allocutions*, 308-309.

8   Pope John Paul II, Allocution to the Roman Rota, 5 February 1987, Woestman (ed.), *Papal Allocution*, 195.

9   Pontifical Council for Legislative Texts, Instruction *Dignitas connubii*, Instruction to be Observed by Diocesan and Interdiocesan Tribunals in Handling Causes of the Nullity of Marriage (Vatican: Libreria Editrice Vaticana 2005) Preface, 17.

10   Aidan McGrath, "Assisting Judges in Their Arduous Task: *Dignitas connubii* and the Assistance It Offers in Cases Based on Canon 1095," *Studies in Church Law* 4 (2008) 114.

2008 article by Aidan McGrath in *Studies in Church Law*.[11] Nevertheless, in my opinion *Dignitas connubii* is an excellent synthesis of the common, mainstream rotal jurisprudence.

McGrath in concluding his introduction in his 2008 article states, "It is not very surprising that *Dignitas connubii* should devote significant attention to canon 1095. It has been observed that the grounds of nullity contained in this canon occupy the time and energy of the judges in ecclesiastical tribunals to an overwhelming degree, if not exclusively. Even at the Roman Rota itself, the number of cases based on these grounds has grown steadily from 38 out of 199 in 1983 ... 93 out of 155 in 1999. In some parts of the world, the fact is that the vast majority of matrimonial causes – whether rightly or wrongly – are judged on the basis of a ground based in canon 1095."[12]

Dignitas connubii and Assistance Concerning the Role of Experts (Articles 203-213)

McGrath asserts that there are four principal areas in which the Instruction offers assistance – explicitly and implicitly – to judges in relation to cases based on canon 1095.[13] However in my presentation today I am only going to address one of the areas that McGrath asserts, namely, the role of experts as addressed in the Instruction. After addressing the contribution of *Dignitas connubii* concerning the use of an expert in relation to canon 1095, I will proceed to analyze three rotal decisions to see whether an expert was used and if an expert was used, how the specific rotal turnus evaluated and used the opinion of the expert.

The need for experts

It seems to me that the most significant contribution of *Dignitas connubii* in relation to canon 1095 has to do with the norms it provides for experts. According to Article 203 §1: "In causes concerning the impotence or a defect of consent because of a *mentis morbum* or because of the incapacities described in canon 1095, the judge is to employ the assistance of one or more experts, unless from the circumstances this would appear evidently useless." Although in my presentation at this meeting in 2004 I allowed for the possibility, slim though I thought it was, that the use of an expert might be optional, I think the norm of law now is quite unambiguous.[14] The intervention of experts in cases of the nul-

---

11   See Aidan McGrath, "Assisting Judges in Their Arduous Task: *Dignitas connubii* and the Assistance It Offers in Cases Based on Canon 1095," 109-142, for several references addressing the academic debate about the nature and juridical force of this document and for his analysis as to why canon 1095 receives so much attention in the document.

12   McGrath, 115.

13   McGrath, 120.

14   See Jorgensen, "The Role of the Expert in Tribunal Proceedings," 141-143.

lity of marriage being considered under canon 1095 is mandatory, not optional. Indeed, John Foster in his presentation last year, following his analysis of canons 1095 and 1680 of the Code and article 203 of *Dignitas connubii*, concluded: "In other words, because canon 1095 cases require some psychic anomaly, article 203 mandates the normative use of an expert."[15]

Yes, article 203 §1 still does indicate the possibility of an exception to the norm but an exception cannot become an alternative norm. Nevertheless, in my limited review of rotal decisions since the promulgation of *Dignitas connubii*, I could not find one rotal decision where an expert did not intervene. Unfortunately, even if a person would be allowed to review every rotal decision issued since the promulgation of *Dignitas connubii* or even going back farther to Pope John Paul II's landmark allocutions to the Roman Rota of 1987 and 1988, in which he first focused so directly on the task of judges when dealing with what is now referred to as psychic incapacity for marriage, the decisions are not indexed in a way that would allow for the easy accumulation of such statistical information. However, from background conversations with knowledgeable sources with first hand acquaintance and experience at the Rota, no one could remember a case considered under canon 1095 in which there was not the intervention of an expert. Indeed, the parties noted that almost the first task when a prelate auditor of the Rota is appointed as the presiding judge/*ponens* on a case being opened to an ordinary examination under canon 1095 is to appoint a psychological expert.

That exceptions exist to what the law and jurisprudence mandate is clear, but, as John Foster noted in his presentation, the Apostolic Signatura has identified in jurisprudence only two exceptions and a third exception has been identified by commentators.[16] The two exceptions that the Apostolic Signatura has identified are as follows:

> An expert report about the psychic state of a party can be seen to be "evidently useless" in order to prove the nullity of a marriage: a) when, even if the matter in hand is not "an expert report" in the technical sense, in the acts there exists a document or testimonial, which is so qualified, that it provides sufficient relevant proof to the judge; b) when from proven facts and circumstances, without any doubt, there appears either a lack of sufficient use of reason or a serious lack of discretion of judgment or an incapacity to assume the essential obligations of marriage. The reason is that in this case the nullity of marriage can be declared on account of an evident lack of consent, without the need of a carefully drawn up diagnosis of the psychic cause due to which there exists that defect. However, in such

---

15   See Foster, "Tips for Building Better Law Sections," 96-97.
16   See Foster, 97-98.

cases the judge can ask the expert to explain some document of fact, which exists or is alleged in the acts.[17]

However, I find it difficult to consider the first exception listed above to be a true "exception." It is an exception only in the strict sense that an expert is not appointed to conduct a direct examination of the party in question and/or to conduct a review of the acts and then offer his/her opinion. Even under this so-called first exception there is still expert data available to assist the judge in coming to a decision. In essence this first "exception" is stating that direct examination and review of the acts by an expert are not absolutely necessary.

As stated above, a third exception is recognized among commentators. For example, Lüdicke and Jenkins write, "The use of an expert is not required:

> negatively speaking, when the proofs are so conclusive that a report from an expert becomes superfluous. This applies above all in causes of impotence in which, for example, the instruction of the cause has already established that the condition was merely one of sterility and not impotence; or for a petition based on c. 1095, 1°, but for which insufficient facts have been adduced to indicate a basis for the ground;

> positively speaking, when prior reports of experts are available which the judge can use in accord with Art. 204, §1, and which clearly respond to the questions that are raised in an ecclesiastical trial."[18]

Nevertheless, I reiterate what I stated back in 2004 that the exception must not become the norm![19] Recall what I stated just a few paragraphs above, albeit in background conversations with knowledgeable sources, no one could remember a single rotal definitive sentence issued since 1988 in which a psychological expert was not used. This is true even though the Roman Rota strictly speaking is not bound by *Dignitas connubii* because the Rota operates under its own norms. But, as I mentioned above, *Dignitas connubii* is an excellent synthesis of the common jurisprudence of the Rota and therefore frequently is cited by the prelate auditors of the Rota in their decisions.

However, given the Signatura's private response of 1998, again quoted above, there must be some rotal jurisprudence upon which the Signatura based its response about what were examples of the exception that the law allowed. Of

---

17 Supreme Tribunal of the Apostolic Signatura, response, 16 June 1998, n. 5: Prot. N. 28252/97 VT, in *Forum* 9/2 (1998) 54.

18 Klaus Lüdicke and Ronny Jenkins, *Dignitas connubii*: Norms and Commentary (Alexandria, VA: Canon Law Society of America, 2006) 346, n. 7, at Article 203 §1.

19 See Jorgensen, "The Role of the Expert in Tribunal Proceedings," 142.

course, the Signatura may be making a fine distinction regarding the use of an expert. In its response, the Signatura may be implying that the true use or formal use of an expert means that the expert, in addition to reviewing what is in the acts, conducts a direct examination with the party in question, including even the possibility of psychological testing of the party. In my background communications with knowledgeable sources with first hand acquaintance and experience at Rota I did not make the distinction with them that I just made here.

Finally, as I indicated back in 2004, the expert is part of the overall evidence of a case – not the whole of it, thus the expert does not replace the judge but assists the judge and it is expected that the judge engages in a dialogue with the expert so that the expert's findings assist the judge in reaching a definitive decision.[20] The just indicated conclusion is an important point not only for judges at the local tribunal level but also is an important point for the prelate auditors of the Rota to remember as well.

The qualification of experts

Article 205 §1 of *Dignitas connubii* requires that the judge chooses experts who are suitable and who "are outstanding for their knowledge and experience of their art, and commended for their religiosity and honesty." Although the use of experts in the field of psychology or psychiatry reflects what the church sees as legitimate progress in the human sciences, the Preface of *Dignitas connubii* indicates that such progress is not without its dangers.[21]

Thus, it is not surprising to find that article 205 §2 of *Dignitas connubii* states: "In order that the assistance of experts in causes concerning the incapacities mentioned in canon 1095 may be truly useful, special care is to be taken that experts are chosen who adhere to the principles of Christian anthropology." Such a reference to Christian anthropology echoes Pope John Paul II's landmark allocutions to the Roman Rota of 1987 and 1988. It is clear that the judge, whenever he considers the opinion of the expert and the weight to attribute to the expert's

---

20 See Jorgensen, "The Role of the Expert in Tribunal Proceedings," 143.

21 *Dignitas connubii*, Preface, 9, 11: "To this doctrinal progress in the understanding of the institution of marriage there is added in our day a progress in the human sciences, especially the psychological and psychiatric ones which, since they offer a deeper understanding of the human person, can offer much help for a fuller understanding of those things which are required in the human person in order that he or she be capable of entering the conjugal covenant. The Roman Pontiffs, since Pius XII, while they called attention to the dangers to be encountered if in this area mere hypotheses, not scientifically proved, were to be taken for scientifically acquired data, always encouraged and exhorted scholars of matrimonial canonical law and ecclesiastical judges not to hesitate to transfer for the advantage of their own science certain conclusions, founded in a sound philosophy and Christian anthropology, which those sciences ha offered in the course of time."

report, must make sure that the expert is providing his opinion out of a mindset that is at least consistent with the Christian understanding of human nature.[22]

Moreover, in my 2004 presentation to this society, I provided some criteria for assessing what article 205 §1 of *Dignitas connubii* states are the first requirements for the experts the judge chooses: "are outstanding for their knowledge and experience of their art."[23] Again, I will prescind from repeating what I said at that time but refer you to that presentation. In 2004 I observed, "Judges must consider the competence and technical skill of the expert" and went on to provide numerous criteria that the judge might use, as well as suggesting other persons the judge might appoint as an assessor to assist him in his evaluation of the expertise of the expert.[24] From an anecdotal perspective, it has been my observation that the Roman Rota only appoints a psychiatrist as an expert; although it is my understanding that many of the psychiatric experts that the Rota uses also have training in psychology. I have not seen any rotal decision, published or unpublished, in which the rotal turnus appointed an expert who called himself or was licensed as a "mental health counselor," a "marriage and family therapist," a "psychiatric social worker," or a "licensed social worker" – professionals who in hospital settings here in the United States are called "Allied Health Professionals." As I observed in my 2004 presentation, "The expert may be licensed in a behavioral science area but the professional licensure law in that specific civil jurisdiction may not permit the licensee to diagnose mental disorders or to perform psychological or psychiatric evaluations of persons because the professional licensure law of the jurisdiction presumes that persons seeking that specific behavioral science license do not have the training and expertise to carry out certain diagnostic and assessment functions."[25] In my 2008 presentation to this society, I addressed the distinction between a properly qualified expert who is fact witness and not a true expert or an expert who is providing a mental health assessment or evaluation as opposed to a forensic assessment or evaluation, which also relate to the weight a judge ought to attribute to the expert's opinion.[26]

---

22 Aidan McGrath in his article, "Assisting Judges in Their Arduous Task," 122, provides as follows his summary of what he sees as the essential elements of Christian anthropology from the teaching of Vatican II, *Gaudium et spes*, nn. 12; 13; 17: "- every person is created in the image of God; - every person is created for God, i.e., is called to be with God for ever; - every person is created free, endowed with free will; - every person is capable of knowing and loving God and neighbour; - every person shows signs of the effects of original sin; - every person remains capable of sinful behaviour; - every person has been redeemed by Christ; - every person remains fundamentally free and redeemed, and retains the possibility of seeking and achieving union with God."

23 See Jorgensen, "The Role of the Expert in Tribunal Proceedings," 145-146.

24 See Jorgensen, "The Role of the Expert in Tribunal Proceedings," 145-146, including footnote 26 on 146.

25 Jorgensen, "The Role of the Expert in Tribunal Proceedings," 146.

26 See Jorgensen, "Navigating the Minefield of the Psychological Evaluation," 180-183.

What to Look for in an Expert and in the Opinion of the Expert

In my presentation today, I am not going to repeat for you the explicit norms regulating the interaction of tribunal officials and experts. *Dignitas connubii*, article 209, goes into some detail about the fundamental task of the judge in his dialogue with the expert and article 54 provides assistance to the Defender of the Bond and his role in relation to the expert and the judge. Both Aidan McGrath and John Foster in their journal articles provide a good analysis of the norms and the task of the judge and defender in relation to the expert.[27]

However, to illustrate what we can learn from the Rota about this fundamental task of the judge in his dialogue with an expert in search of the truth in consensual incapacity causes, I propose to examine three relatively recent rotal decisions in canon 1095 cases: a decision *coram* Sciacca issued on 16 June 2005,[28] a decision *coram* Sciacca issued on 1 February 2008,[29] and a decision *coram* Erlebach issued on 7 April 2011. The two decisions, *coram* Sciacca, are published in the CLSA publication, *Rotal Jurisprudence: Selected Translations*. The third decision, *coram* Erlebach, is an unpublished decision but is quite recent and involves a case that arose in the English-speaking world and the testimonies of the parties and witnesses, including expert witnesses, except for the expert witness that the rotal turnus used, are in English. Furthermore, the two decisions, *coram* Sciacca, are affirmative decisions and the decision, *coram* Erlebach, is a negative decision.

None of these three decisions involve cases with bizarre or unusual fact situations. The stories related in these definitive sentences are scenarios familiar to tribunals in the United States and Canada. The law sections of the decisions present the updated, mainstream jurisprudence in consensual incapacity cases and integrate not only the guiding allocutions of John Paul II to the Roman Rota in this area but also the norms of *Dignitas connubii*.[30]

---

27   See McGrath, 123-131; see Foster, 98-101.

28   Victoria Vondenberger, ed., "Rotal Jurisprudence: Selected Translations," (Washington, DC: Canon Law Society of America, 2011) 191-212.

29   Vondenberger, "Rotal Jurisprudence: Selected Translations," 247-278.

30   For example, see law section of *coram* Sciacca, 1 February 2012 (Prot. N. 18.631), n. 22: "Wherefore it must be strictly noted – as previously pointed out in the teachings of the pontifical *magisterium* already referred to – that there is an irreducible difference between incapacity, which invalidates consent because of the connection between the disorder and consent (which must indeed be verified) – and difficulty, which conversely does not juridically diminish consent. To prove incapacity, insofar as it flows from a real psychic anomaly or severe disorder, judges must have the valid, indeed necessary, assistance of expert reports which are required by the precept of the law itself (canons 1680 and 1574); and are greatly and clearly affirmed most recently in the instruction *Dignitas connubii*, articles 203-213, excerpts of which are quoted here as a fitting conclusion." In Vondenberger, "Rotal Jurisprudence: Selected Translations," 201-202.

Coram Sciacca, 16 June 2005

The Facts

The facts in this case originating in an unnamed tribunal (I suspect an Italian tribunal given that the expert the Rota appointed conducted a direct examination) and decided by the rotal turnus with Sciacca as *ponens* joined by Verginelli and De Angelis are as follows:

> Amelia, 26 and a Catholic, met Blaise, 31 and also a Catholic, in 1985 while both were actively serving in the parish to which they belonged. Amelia had "a doctorate in letters (probably literature), attended to matters easily and efficiently, indeed with respect to church matters, principally in the preparation of marriage couples, but also in fulfilling the office of keeping the daily parish diary."[31] Amelia and Blaise also were serving with two other young men who, while the four of them were serving together, entered religious life. Amelia, upon seeing these two young men enter religious life, decided to become engaged. Thus, very soon after the friendship began between them, Amelia and Blaise got to know each other and soon were at the altar to bind themselves in a conjugal covenant, which occurred in a parish church in 1986. Although the parties had one child, the marriage apparently ended when they failed to produce a second child. The parties were together for more than a decade but grew emotionally disengaged from one another and definitively separated. Amelia introduced a petition for a declaration in nullity in 1996. The formulation of the doubt in the Tribunal of First Instance was whether nullity of the marriage should be upheld on Amelia's grave defect of discretion of judgment or incapacity to assume the obligations of marriage or on Blaise's exclusion of the good of the spouse or on Amelia's exclusion of the good of the spouse. The Tribunal of First Instance in 1998 issued a negative decision on all four grounds. Amelia appealed this negative decision and the appellate tribunal in 2001 issued an affirmative decision on Amelia's grave lack of discretion of judgment and inability to assume the obligations of marriage (canon 1095, 2°-3°), while dismissing the ground of the exclusion of the good of the spouses. Because conformity of decisions was lacking, the case was deferred to the Roman Rota for a third instance decision.

---

31   *Coram* Sciacca, §24; 203. Here and hereinafter the rotal decisions under discussion will be cited by the paragraph and page number in "Rotal Jurisprudence: Selected Translations," when the decision is a published decision.

The Use of an Expert

When the case arrived at the Rota and it was opened to an ordinary examination at third instance, the only new instruction of the case was to supplement the case by a new expert report. The *ponens* sought an expert report at third instance even though there were two expert reports by psychiatrists at first instance and an expert report by a psychologist at second instance, which referenced the psychologist administering psychological testing. Recall that the first instance tribunal, even with two expert reports in which the experts considered the petitioner psychologically impaired or impeded at the time of her exchange of consent, decided in the negative and it was the second instance tribunal, after requesting yet a third expert, that decided in the affirmative. The expert at third instance (the Roman Rota) apparently was a psychiatrist with psychological training because his report referenced psychological testing that he administered. Also, this was a case in which all four experts conducted a direct examination of the petitioner who was alleged to have suffered from consensual incapacity at the time of the celebration of the marriage in question. Four expert opinions were sought in this case even though I suspect most of our tribunals would have found the scenario so familiar that they might not have sought one expert opinion much less a third or fourth expert opinion in arriving at an affirmative decision. However, it is clear that the rotal turnus struggled with whether consensual incapacity on the part of the petitioner was proven.

In his law section, Sciacca discusses the church's teaching about marriage as a human act and therefore the psychological conditions that are specifically proper to every human act and thus, why the law addresses those who are incapable of such an act due to a psychic anomaly are incapable of giving matrimonial consent. Sciacca then analyzes grave defect of discretion of judgment as well as the incapacity to assume the essential obligations of marriage. In his analysis, Sciacca addresses the fact that the gravity that the law requires does not inhere solely in the anomaly of psychic disturbance but in certain cases in a combination of factors when all are considered together and conjointly. As part of his discussion about grave defect of discretion of judgment and the incapacity to assume the essential obligations of marriage, Sciacca considers a specific psychic disorder, namely, "narcissism." His entire discussion in the law section, leads Sciacca to conclude his law section articulating the necessity of having an expert report and the necessary interaction between the judge and the expert.[32]

An Analysis of the Expert's Opinion

In the opening section of his argument, Sciacca presented what the issue was for the turnus when it came to stating that the woman petitioner was incapable of consenting to marriage due to a grave lack of discretion of judgment about the essential obligations of marriage: "In truth, the woman was awarded a doctorate in letters, attended to matters easily and efficiently, indeed with respect to church

---

32   *Coram* Sciacca, §§5-22; 192-202.

matters, principally in the preparation of marriage couples, but also in fulfilling the office of keeping the daily parish diary."[33] Although the rotal turnus found the first expert's report of some value, they did not appear to find it convincing because it apparently was too general and in the end ambiguous, given how the expert concluded her report: "This does not depict a fatal anomaly, but rather a quite serious interwoven complex of defects that in truth produced a psychic handicap in the woman."[34]

Then when the prelate auditors moved on to consider the report of the second expert at first instance, they found his report to be more complete than the report of the first expert, however, "the prelate auditors cannot entirely accept his conclusions insofar as they do not fully coincide with the woman's personal history, who – as we have seen – completed a strict course of studies and was actively and with mature deliberation involved in the fabric of ecclesial society."[35] In other words, the prelate auditors thought the expert was too excessive or expansive in his conclusions about the petitioner and the severity of the pathology the expert psychiatrist was attributing to the petitioner in view of her academic and professional performance before and after the celebration of the marriage in question. The conclusion of the prelate auditors about the assessment of the second expert was as indicated, even though they obviously knew him and had respect for him as a practicing psychiatrist.

After considering the reports of the two experts used at first instance, the rotal turnus went on to consider the report of the expert used at second instance. Recall that the expert at second instance apparently was a psychologist, or at least a psychiatrist with explicit psychological training, because the results of psychological testing of the petitioner were incorporated in the expert's report. What the turnus valued out of the report of the expert at second instance was her integration in her report of her review of the acts and her examination of the petitioner through the administration of "the psycho-diagnostic Rorschach test."[36] As an aside, I find it interesting that the rotal turnus not only seemed to place substantial weight on the use of psychological testing but also on the use of the Rorschach. From the perspective of someone who does do forensic psychological assessment, there are multiple issues that arise in the use of the Rorschach in forensic settings here in the United States and those issues would have to be well addressed under intense cross examination before the results of the administration of the Rorschach would carry much weight with a judge or before the judge would allow such testimony to be heard by a jury. However, the conclusion of the expert that appeared to have the greatest impact upon the decision of the prelate auditors was, "a personality incapacitated by a fundamental lack of trust in

---

33 *Coram* Sciacca, §24; 203.
34 *Coram* Sciacca, §31; 209.
35 *Coram* Sciacca, §32; 209.
36 *Coram* Sciacca, §33; 210.

her [the petitioner's] own abilities which tends to diminish the possibilities of a healthy reaction to events that occur."[37]

But Sciacca leaves the best for the last, as he moves to his analysis of the opinion provided by the rotal expert appointed at third instance – the fourth and final expert. The *ponens* builds up support for the opinion of this fourth expert by referring to the fact that he relied "on approved science and sound scientific methodology" in his response to the questions the turnus posed to him and by referring to the expert as "this great expert."[38] This expert not only provided his report regarding his review and analysis of the acts as well as his examination of the petitioner but also he appeared in person before the rotal turnus to give "his expert testimony, under solemn oath."[39] In the expert's testimony that Sciacca quotes in his decision, the expert attests, "We are in the context of personality disorders of the intermediate level; the judgment about severity falls in this diagnostic area. Such a degree of seriousness can become concentrated and critical and to a certain measure present itself only later on in light of circumstances and contextual influences regarding which the patient would not have been able to react in an adequate way."[40] It is clear that it is the report of the expert at second instance followed by the report of the expert at third instance that leads the turnus to decide in the affirmative, with Sciacca stating the following: "The undersigned Apostolic Judges have concluded that – all things considered – the woman disturbed by some kind of disorder and beset by various unfortunate circumstances, as set forth above, was not free to choose her marriage; speaking absolutely, if, however, she truly could have done so, which in this case did not happen, she might possibly have been capable of sufficiently fulfilling her marital obligations. For the free choice of a particular marriage is one thing; the capacity to carry out conjugal burdens or obligations is another."[41]

It is worth noting that nowhere in Sciacca's definitive sentence is there any reference to the prelate auditors extrapolating back to the time of the exchange of consent of the marriage in question nor does Sciacca quote any of the experts about how or why they could extrapolate back to the petitioner's exchange of consent. Apparently the prelate auditors assumed that how the experts described the current psychological functioning of the petitioner, with all four experts casting the petitioner's psychological functioning as her personality style, also was characteristic of her functioning twelve or more years earlier. Of course, it seems readily apparent that the fact that the petitioner consulted a psychic (fortune-teller) about her decision to marry a respondent also carried considerable weight with the prelate auditors.

---

37 *Coram* Sciacca, §33; 209.
38 *Coram* Sciacca, §34; 210.
39 *Coram* Sciacca, §34; 211.
40 *Coram* Sciacca, §34; 211.
41 *Coram* Sciacca, §35; 211.

Coram Sciacca, 1 February 2008

The Facts

The facts in this case originating in an unnamed tribunal (again, I suspect it is an Italian tribunal because the expert the Rota used engaged in a direct examination of one of the parties in question, with the other party refusing direct examination) and decided by the rotal turnus with Sciacca as *ponens* joined by Huber and Defilippi are as follows:

> Having duly considered what they were to undertake, having resolved various difficulties in their relationship and after sustaining a ten-year engagement, Jeremiah Jones, 27 years of age, and Karen Kant, 25 years of age, properly celebrated canonical marriage in 1998. Jeremiah was a mechanic and Karen was a coach. The end of the parties' conjugal life was unhappy, beginning with their trip to South America where Jeremiah's uncle was living, a missionary priest, and Karen had a strong desire to return to her own home. Shortly after the parties married, Karen revealed sexual difficulties, which actually had emerged already during the couple's engagement period. Because Karen refused sexual intimacy, the marriage had been consummated only once. The parties' situation did not improve after they returned to their home, as even with disagreements, temporary separations, and passing reunions, the couple's common life scarcely persisted for two and half years, without any children and with very few acts of sexual intercourse between them. In 2000, Karen left the man and returned to her parents. The civil authorities recognized this separation in early 2001. Late in 2001, Jeremiah accused the marriage in question of nullity before the Tribunal of First Instance on the grounds indicated in canon 1095, 2° and 3° on both parties. Once the instruction was completed through the hearing of the parties and witnesses and by obtaining an expert report *ex officio*, the tribunal, in 2003, issued a definitive sentence stating that the nullity of the marriage was not proven. The petitioner was not happy with the decision of the Tribunal of First Instance and appealed directly to the Roman Rota. After the petitioner completed a new deposition and Sciacca was substituted to be part of the turnus adjudicating the petitioner's appeal by a decree in 2006, the doubt to be resolved was agreed upon under the following formula: "Whether there is proof of nullity of the marriage in the case due to a defect of discretion of judgment and/or due to the incapacity to assume the essential obligations of marriage in both or at least in one of the parties, and subordinately, as if in first instance, due to the exclusion of the *bonum prolis* on the part of the woman-respondent."[42]

---

42   *Coram* Sciacca, §4; 248.

The Use of an Expert

When the case arrived at the Rota and after Sciacca was substituted, Sciacca entrusted the preparation of an expert report to a psychiatrist often used by the Rota and the expert presented his report in 2007. Again the rotal *ponens* sought an expert report at second instance even though there was an *ex officio* expert report by a psychiatrist at first instance. Moreover, not only did the first instance court appoint an expert *ex officio* but also two of the witnesses at first instance were psychologists, one was a priest-psychologist who apparently had some clinical contact with both parties and the second psychologist saw both parties for marital counseling. The prelate auditors clearly saw these two experts as fact witnesses and did not attribute the same weight to their testimony as they did to the experts appointed *ex officio*. Also, recall that the first instance tribunal, with the acts including a formal or designated expert report and two experts as fact witnesses, decided in the negative, even though the psychiatrist expert and the two psychologists addressed what they saw as serious problems in the woman's sexuality from a psychological perspective, which had significant impact upon the parties' conjugal life.

This was a case in which the two *ex officio* experts did conduct a direct examination of the man-petitioner but the woman-respondent strenuously refused to meet with either expert. The experts who were fact witnesses did have direct clinical contact with both parties.

Even though the expert reports were somewhat conflicting when it came to the man-petitioner, the rotal turnus did not struggle with whether consensual incapacity on the part of the petitioner was proven – they determined that it was not. The rotal turnus focused its attention on considering the question of consensual incapacity on the part of the woman-respondent and, unlike in the first decision considered above, appeared to have minimal struggle in achieving moral certitude on an affirmative decision.

An Analysis of the Expert's Opinion

In the opening section of his argument, Sciacca first addressed consensual incapacity on the man-petitioner based on canon 1095, 2° and 3°. After addressing consensual incapacity on the part of the man-petitioner, he addressed consensual incapacity on the woman-respondent based on canon 1095, 2° and 3°. When it came to the man-petitioner, it was clear from the citation of Jeremiah's own testimony and then from Sciacca's summary of other facts present in the acts that proving consensual incapacity on the part of Jeremiah was not going to happen. "Thus, he [Jeremiah] speaks openly about himself in the first statements which he made in 2002: 'I consider myself to be a normal person with the capacity for relationships and friendship, open to sharing my inner feelings'."[43] It is easy to see that the prelate auditors might have some difficulty with Jeremiah's self-

---

43 *Coram* Sciacca, §27; 263-264.

assessment, while at the same Jeremiah was asserting that he considered himself incapable of eliciting valid marriage consent because of consensual incapacity on his part. Sciacca then goes on to summarize Jeremiah's developmental background, which seems completely inconsistent with a person who lacks consensual capacity due to a psychic anomaly. "Indeed, he [Jeremiah] received fine instruction, and since his youth he has done his work in a praiseworthy manner, cultivating also his own study of the humanities: 'I have a diploma from the eighth grade. ... I have also been a believing and practicing [Catholic]. I have had and still have a good relationship with my family. ... I have never had a need for admission to a hospital of any kind'."[44]

It is true that the expert the first instance tribunal appointed, after reviewing the acts of the cause at first instance and examining the petitioner (Jeremiah) determined that Jeremiah had a grave, pre-nuptial disturbance. However, the prelate auditors discounted the expert's report for two reasons. First, the expert's judgment went beyond what all the observations to contrary seemed to allow. This rotal turnus, as inferred from Sciacca's statements, seemed to think that the over extension of this expert or his opinion "manifesting itself more broadly than the previous observations seem to allow"[45] was even more egregious than the second expert at first instance that was noted above in *coram* Sciacca, 16 June 2005. Second, the psychiatrist expert at first instance stated that he used the psychoanalytical method in arriving at his opinion. It appears that using the psychoanalytical method, in and of itself, might be enough to discount the expert's report: "We truly know that the psychoanalytical vision is in no way corresponding with the constitutive principals of Christian anthropology, and that, since it is based on determinism, it entirely denies all human freedom, forcing man into necessity."[46] However, it seems that the first reason I listed above was the decisive one for the prelate auditors: "Indeed, the conclusions of the expert report regarding the man-petitioner seem greatly divergent from the elements which are drawn from the acts of the cause, as we elaborately and meticulously recounted above."[47]

Finally, when it came to the man-petitioner, it was clear that the prelate auditors found the expert that they appointed to have provided the weightiest opinion of any of the experts, psychiatrist or psychologists, and nailed the decision for them. "One with more expertise was chosen before the Rota, namely, Prof. Giovanni Francesco Zuanazzi. He did not detect any disturbance in the man whatsoever: 'neither in thought nor in perception. ... He has a good intellectual level: his culture seems higher than the level of scholastic instruction that he received. ... His capacity to judge is effective. ... There are no manifestations of

---

44 *Coram* Sciacca, §27; 264.
45 *Coram* Sciacca, §31; 267.
46 *Coram* Sciacca, §32; 267.
47 *Coram* Sciacca, §32; 267.

free and fluctuating anxiety. His interpersonal relationships are formally correct, and the subject does not lack the capacity to have empathy. His sense of humor is balanced. He clearly affirms his share of traditional ethical and religious values."[48] Sciacca continues to quote even more extensively from the expert chosen by the Rota, all of which speak to Jeremiah's balanced current psychological functioning as well as to his developmental years and to his young adult years. It appears that the prelate auditors found it necessary to have an expert report from an expert that they trusted, given the allegations the man made about himself regarding the grounds to be investigated even though he contradicted himself in his own testimony and given the report of the psychiatrist expert at first instance as well as the statements of the psychologist expert fact witnesses. For the prelate auditors there needed to be a consistency with established facts in the acts and the opinion of the expert or experts.

Next Sciacca turned his attention to the woman-respondent's incapacity based on canon 1095, 2° and 3°. Sciacca begins this subsection of his argument section with the following statement, "Regarding the woman-respondent's grave defect of discretion of judgment, from the pre-nuptial period through the parties' ten year engagement, not a trace of any psychic anomaly is found on account of which her evaluative-critical capacity is hindered with respect to entering marriage or with respect to its rights and obligations."[49] Then Sciacca provides a few examples from the acts to support the prelate auditors' summary judgment and concludes, "Nothing further from almost all the witnesses brought forward – whose depositions we find it useless to cite and repeat here – provide information about anything other than the difficulties arising during the marriage. Moreover, they do not indicate anything about a grave anomaly on account of which the woman's directive and evaluative capacity could have been substantially impaired."[50]

After dismissing the possibility of proving the woman-respondent's incapacity based on canon 1095, 2°, Sciacca then goes to the report of the experts at first and second instance to undertake the woman-respondent's incapacity to fulfill the essential obligations of marriage, that is, based on canon 1095, 3°. To understand how the prelate auditors achieved moral certitude about the woman-respondent based on canon 1095, 3°, it is important to review Sciacca's law section in which he addresses "proper exercise" or "the right exercise of sexuality" as being ordered to obtain the *bonum coniugum*, "that is, to build a conjugal community in which are encompassed the *bonum prolis*, mutual assistance, and sexual donation (the 'remedy for concupiscence')."[51]

---

48   *Coram* Sciacca, §33; 267.
49   *Coram* Sciacca, §36; 270.
50   *Coram* Sciacca, §37; 271.
51   *Coram* Sciacca, §§12-20; 253-261.

Perhaps by now it ought to go without saying, but Sciacca concludes his law section on canon 1095, 3° by addressing the need for the intervention of an expert: "As we already stated above [here Sciacca is referring to the part of his law section that addressed canon 1095, 2°], as far as possible, it is necessary in this (sic) cases (sic) for the judge to be given the assistance of experts (cc. 1680, 1574), both regarding the specifically physical aspect and with respect to the causes of a psychic nature from which the sexual difficulty has arisen. It is the responsibility of the judge only to evaluate and weigh these expert reports and to thoroughly sift them together with the totality of the cause, with careful consideration of everything which occurred before and after the marriage."[52] Although the clause above "as far as possible" that Sciacca inserts is an interesting insertion and causes me to wonder what might be the limits or parameters of that statement, it is only one clause by one rotal auditor and cannot be "captured" and become the citation to provide the justification for a local turnus to avoid using an expert. Certainly this rotal turnus, even with the difficulties it encountered in this case in obtaining the cooperation of the woman-respondent, found it necessary to appoint an expert.

Prescinding from Sciacca's law section and returning to his argument section and the expert opinions, we find that all four experts (the two fact psychologist expert witnesses, the two psychiatrist expert witnesses) are used and cited. Although Sciacca does cite the two fact psychologist expert witnesses who worked with either one or both parties, apparently in a counseling situation, he focused most of his attention on the two psychiatrist expert witnesses, even though the woman-respondent "most strenuously refused to meet with"[53] either one of them. It is noteworthy that even though Sciacca earlier made a specific point of discounting the testimony of the psychiatrist expert summoned by the first instance tribunal because he used the psychoanalytical method, he did not refer to his previous concern at all and placed substantial weight on the psychiatrist's assessment from the acts alone that the woman respondent was "characterized by a lack of sexual desire due to *anorgasmia* and *dyspareunia* … This is a question of a serious psychopathology since it impedes deep contact and a lasting relationship with another."[54]

After extensive quotation of the psychiatrist expert at first instance, Sciacca then considers the report of the rotal expert. Sciacca makes a point of indicating that the rotal expert prefaced his report by saying that the woman refused to allow a clinical interview, which repeated the woman's behavior at first instance, and that the rotal expert explicitly noted that his report is based on the acts alone. In his argument, Sciacca noted that the expert does indicate that in the depositions of the parties and to a certain extent in the testimonies of all the witnesses

---

52 *Coram* Sciacca, §21; 261.
53 *Coram* Sciacca, §40; 272.
54 *Coram* Sciacca, §40; 273.

it is confirmed that the respondent had great difficulties in having sexual relations. Sciacca noted that the expert then continued with his assessment: "There is no doubt that the respondent's sexual conduct is largely situated outside of the common pattern of behavior even if we are not in a position to indicate securely the nature and causes...."[55] As quoted by Sciacca, the rotal expert's speculation about the three theories for the woman-respondent's behavior and the expert's conclusion that all the facts before and after the celebration of the marriage in question are such that "at the time of the marriage, she [Karen] was not in a position to establish a conjugal community in order to the (sic) guarantee the well-being and enrichment of the spouses. This finds justification in the respondent's pathological personality, that is to say a personality characterized by gravely abnormal structural dispositions which cause suffering: ... Her personality rendered the realization of the conjugal community impossible."[56] Again, it is worth noting that the rotal expert in this case was called to appear before the rotal turnus and to repeat his analyses under oath in "a revised expert report," just as what occurred in *coram* Sciacca, 16 June 2005, as indicated above.[57]

When all was said and done, the prelate auditors through the use of the expert reports, especially the experts that were summoned at first instance and at second instance, came to the following conclusion: "From what has been expounded up to this point, it is evident that the woman suffered from grave difficulties in having sexual intercourse with her partner. Although the origin of these difficulties remains somewhat obscure ... it is certain that the woman was incapable of fulfilling her conjugal obligation 'in a human manner' through a healthy sexual life. We especially wish to note that it is not a question only of difficulty but of the woman's true and real repugnance for conjugal intimacy."[58]

In reviewing the expert reports, at least the extensive quotations that appeared in the definitive sentence, it is apparent that the prelate auditors relied on the fact that properly qualified experts named and explained the sexual difficulties the couple were experiencing, especially the woman respondent, that the same experts testified under oath that such difficulties were outside the boundaries of normal limits for a couple and for the woman respondent, indeed were serious abnormalities in and of themselves, and that the woman's impossibility was deep seated in her personality with an explanation of the psychological dynamics involved. Furthermore, what the experts based their reports on was manifested in the behaviors of the parties before and after the celebration of the marriage at bar, as reported by the parties themselves and almost all the other persons who provided testimonies, including two expert fact witnesses. Moreover, it appears the prelate auditors would have preferred that at least one of the summoned experts

---

55   *Coram* Sciacca, §41; 273.
56   *Coram* Sciacca, §41; 274.
57   *Coram* Sciacca, §41; 274.
58   *Coram* Sciacca, §§42-43; 275.

would have been able to conduct a direct examination of the respondent but they accepted an opinion based on a review of the acts, with an indication of what in the acts was precipitating the expert's opinion. Finally, the prelate auditors did not need a formal psychiatric diagnosis to achieve moral certitude, the opinion of the experts that what was being reported was outside of normal limits, was pathologically abnormal, and at least had a psychological basis was sufficient for the prelate auditors.

Coram Erlebach, 7 April 2011[59]

The Facts

The facts in this case originating in an English-speaking first instance tribunal, which I will not name because the decision is unpublished, and decided by the rotal turnus with Erlebach as *ponens* joined by Bottone and Ferreira Pena are as follows:

> Richard, 25 and a baptized Catholic, became acquainted with Catherine, 23 and a baptized Presbyterian, raised Methodist, who, at Richard's suggestion on the occasion of their engagement, was received into the Catholic Church scarcely two weeks before the celebration of the marriage in question. The parties met towards the end 1977 at a branch office of a bank for which both parties worked. After seven months of dating, they became engaged in July 1978. During their courtship, the parties apparently frequently drank to excess, which led to sexual activity, and approximately three or four weeks before the wedding day, Catherine discovered that she was pregnant. The parties came to a mutual decision to terminate the pregnancy through a surgical abortion, which was about the same time that Catherine was received into full communion. The marriage at bar was celebrated at the parties' parish church on 11 November 1978. The marriage produced three children. In the first years of the parties' common life (number of years unspecified), things went well. Later in the couple's conjugal life (apparently 10 years or somewhat more), the woman-respondent experienced multiple difficulties and needed to seek treatment from a psychologist and a psychiatrist. At length and after an unsuccessful eight-month separation for therapeutic purposes, the petitioner initiated a definitive separation on 1 February 2001 and filed for a civil divorce, which was granted on 1

---

59 As indicated above this decision *coram* Erlebach is an unpublished decision and there is no English translation of this decision available. The translation of the decision is my own translation and because it has not been properly verified or the decision released for publication, I will not provide any direct quotations but rather only my own paraphrases. The protocol number that this decision carries is 19.202 and also with the indication, Sent. 66/2011. All the references to this decision that follow simply will indicate the paragraph number of the definitive sentence.

August 2002. Richard, in order to regain his freedom to marry in the Church, introduced a petition for a declaration of nullity of the marriage on 27 January 2003. Although the petitioner sought a declaration of nullity of his marriage for several reasons, the formulation of the doubt in the Tribunal of First Instance was centered on a doubt relative to defect of a grave lack of discretion of judgment on the part of both parties and, subordinately, error on the part of the respondent concerning indissolubility, which error determines the will (c. 1099). Testimony was taken from the petitioner and four witnesses. The respondent opposed the claim of nullity and refused to return the judicial deposition, but "in her writing amply expressed her mind" and "the tribunal found three witnesses on her behalf." Especially the petitioner provided many documents. What stands out among the documents was a statement provided by a psychological expert, which was obtained during the process of the civil divorce in the secular court and was provided by the petitioner to the Tribunal of First Instance. The Tribunal of First Instance also appointed a psychological expert and received his report. On 14 November 2003 the Tribunal of First issued an affirmative decision on the defect of grave lack of discretion of judgment on the part of the respondent. Catherine appealed against this affirmative decision to the Roman Rota. Then after failing to ratify the affirmative decision, the rotal turnus did by decree of 27 January 2005 accept the case for ordinary examination. The matter of the case was stated as follows: Whether the nullity of the marriage in this case is established due to a defect of grave lack of discretion of judgment in both parties and error of the respondent regarding the indissolubility of marriage. A supplemental instruction was given as requested by counsel for the respondent.

The Use of an Expert

When the case was opened to an ordinary examination, Erlebach entrusted the preparation of an expert report to a psychiatrist often used by the Rota and the expert presented his report, although the definitive sentence does not indicate when the expert was appointed or when the prelate auditors received the expert's report. Erlebach sought an expert report even though the first instance tribunal used two expert reports, although one was not an expert report in the technical sense because it was a report entered in the civil dissolution process between the parties. Both experts used at first instance were psychologists, however, the rotal expert was a psychiatrist, Dr. Paul Cianconi. Only one of the experts, the one used in the civil process, had direct contact with and/or a direct examination of either the petitioner or the respondent. It is clear that the question for both the first instance tribunal and the rotal turnus was whether consensual incapacity on the part of the woman respondent was proven. Neither the first instance tribunal nor the rotal turnus struggled with whether consensual incapacity on the part of the man petitioner was proven – both tribunals determined that it was not proven.

In his law section, Erlebach briefly articulates the law at issue in this case and almost as briefly summarizes the common rotal jurisprudence regarding the discretion sufficient to reach a practical judgment regarding marriage. "The heart of discretional judgment concerns the exercise of the critical faculty and choice, which latter presupposes a sufficient internal freedom. Not any old lack of judicial judgment results in the nullity of the marriage. Consensual incapacity in this case can be recognized only according to the meaning of the Supreme Legislator in canon 1095, 2° where he states ...."[60]

In the final paragraphs of his law section, Erlebach, even though he makes no reference to *Dignitas connubii*, emphasizes what must be determined in a canon 1095, 2° case, the necessity of the use of experts, and how the judge ought to consider and weigh the reports of the experts. "Only essential matrimonial rights and duties are the *terminum ad quem* of an incapacitating lack of discretion of judgment. Therefore, for valid consent it is not necessary that 'the one contracting marriage sift and weigh carefully all its ethical, social, religious, public and private consequences' (*coram* Defilippi, sent. 9th day of March 2000, *ibid.*, p. 218, n. 8). Church law does not determine what kind of reasons carry or can carry with them a grave lack of discretion of judgment. Psychological defects can produce such a defect, but each case must be examined on its own, usually with the help of psychological or psychiatric experts to determine whether such a cause was actually present and produced such a result. Proof, in addition to the documents and testimony of the parties and witnesses depends greatly on the use of a skilled (accomplished) psychologist or, if at all possible, a psychiatrist. The judge carefully ought to consider whether all this, namely, the expert testimony can be admitted or not and also other things connected with the case (cf. can. 1579, §1)."[61]

An Analysis of the Expert's Opinion
In the first few paragraphs of his argument section, Erlebach quickly agrees with the first instance tribunal that there was nothing in the acts to support or even lead to a suspicion that there was a flaw of a psychic nature in the petitioner that would cause a grave lack of discretion in the petitioner's judgment. Nevertheless, Erlebach finds it necessary to quote the rotal expert's assessment of the petitioner, "Regarding the petitioner, Richard, does not have an evident psychic flaw which could be found in the DSM-IV TR. The man ... has a personality style that could be described as 'managerial.' ... These are personality traits of an individual but certainly not disturbances or anomalies."[62]

---

60   *Coram* Erlebach, §§3-4; 3-5 (Translation is my own, as in all succeeding quotations from this same decision.)
61   *Coram* Erlebach, §§4-5; 4-5.
62   *Coram* Erlebach, §6; 5-6.

However, in moving on to a consideration of whether there was a grave defect of discretion of judgment on the part of the woman respondent, Erlebach enters into a lengthy analysis of what the parties stated, the witnesses stated, and the reports of the experts. There were several facts about which there was no disagreement: First, the respondent's family background was not the best, as her father abused alcohol and her parents were argumentative at times, with her father physically abusing her mother in front of the children at least once. Second, the respondent did have a surgical abortion just prior to the canonical celebration of the marriage at bar. Third, the respondent struggled with serious episodes of Major Depressive Disorder beginning about ten or eleven years into the marriage. Fourth, the marriage persisted for twenty-three years and three children were born of the union.

In his analysis of whether it was proven that the respondent lacked consensual capacity, Erlebach briefly focuses on the contradictions as to the respondent's consensual capacity at the time of the celebration of marriage in the parties' testimony as well as in the witnesses' testimonies. Erlebach highlighted a statement in which the petitioner appeared directly to contradict what he was alleging about the respondent and to support the respondent's statements as to the adequacy of her psychological functioning at the time of her exchange of consent. Erlebach's analysis of the testimonies of the parties and the witnesses leads him quickly to the reports of the experts and to a dissection of those reports.[63]

Erlebach goes first to the expert testimony in the civil process, which was used by the first instance tribunal. Rightly so, Erlebach noted no matter what the respondent asserted one cannot just disregard what the expert, a psychologist, declared about the family background and lived experience of the respondent and its consequences regarding the psychological functioning of the respondent. At the same time, Erlebach highlighted "the insightful psychological reconstruction of the respondent's family of origin as made by Dr. Cianconi" and went on to provide a lengthy quotation from Dr. Cianconi's report.[64] Erlebach concluded his analysis of what the first expert used by the first instance tribunal and the rotal expert said by noting that the first expert did not address what was relevant to the time of the celebration of the marriage. "But the same therapist (the expert in the civil process) did not speak precisely about the time of the beginning of the marriage, but rather about those things which happened after the death of the respondent's father (1988), when little by little the respondent actually had to seek psychological and then psychiatric help. Furthermore, the woman herself admits: 'I am still making my own peace with it'."[65]

---

63   *Coram* Erlebach, §§7-9; 6-9.

64   *Coram* Erlebach, §8; 6-8.

65   *Coram* Erlebach, §9; 8.

After concluding that the first expert did not really address the questions being raised in the trial whereas the rotal expert did and that the explanations made by the respondent are altogether credible,[66] Erlebach next focused on the report of the designated expert in the first instance. Erlebach begins his analysis in a way that quickly indicates that the report of this designated expert was not convincing for the rotal turnus and that the rotal expert's opinion is going to carry the day in this case. "Strangely, this line of thinking was followed even by the designated expert in first instance, according to whom, 'both factors (which were related above) concurrent with the respondent's basic condition of dysthymia would have seriously impeded her freedom to commit to a marriage much less to this specific marriage'."[67] Erlebach then focused on the two arguments that Dr. Cianconi, the rotal designated expert, brought forth to refute the arguments or conclusions that the first instance designated expert offered. Dr. Cianconi asserted that the fact that Catherine faced up to the troubles in her family of origin and had three pregnancies without having a breakdown pointed to the substantial psychological integrity of Catherine at the time of the marriage and that Catherine not only experienced no immediate consequences of her difficulties but also that a functioning dynamic continued for some time, indeed until the death of her father ten years later, similarly indicated her psychological integrity at the time of the marriage. Erlebach then quoted the rotal expert that the woman respondent's psychic condition at the time of the marriage "is absolutely not to be equated with the period in which she had Major Depression (ten years later). In 1978 the condition of the respondent was decisively reasonable. ... The affective resources if the respondent could be characterized as a moderate immaturity and that the individual tended toward a pessimistic view of life, a sub-clinical trait."[68]

Erlebach concluded his analysis of the expert reports and why the turnus discounted the two expert reports from first instance and relied up its own designated expert, whose report clearly favored validity in this case, by noting the professional skill of Dr. Cianconi because his skill clearly was consonant with the legal processes being used, proceeded according to the necessary methodological processes outlined in *Dignitas connubii*, article 209, and could not be criticized concerning his anthropological presuppositions. Even though in *coram* Sciacca, 16 June 2005, the experts quoted apparently did not extrapolate back to the parties' exchange of consent and thus the turnus appeared to assume that the current psychological functioning of the party in question was characteristic of the party's functioning twelve years earlier, the Erlebach turnus found the lack of what they considered an insufficient extrapolation of psychological functioning back to the exchange of consent to be a major flaw in the expert reports used by the first instance tribunal. From the petitioner's perspective in terms of his desire for an affirmative decision, this was a case where it might have been effective

---

66 *Coram* Erlebach, §9; 9.

67 *Coram* Erlebach, §9; 9.

68 *Coram* Erlebach, §10; 10.

for the petitioner's rotal advocate to have requested supplemental instruction of the designated expert at first instance in which the expert was questioned in greater depth about how the respondent's unquestioned diagnosis of major depressive disorder ten or eleven years into the marriage and the expert's diagnosis of the respondent suffering from dysthymia at the time of her exchange of consent severely impeded either her ability to deliberate critically about specific essential elements of marriage or her freedom to choose this specific marriage. Furthermore, from the petitioner's perspective in terms of his desire for an affirmative decision, this definitely is a case where it would have been good for the designated expert at first instance to have conducted a direct examination of the respondent, assuming that the respondent would have agreed to such an examination, or for the petitioner's rotal advocate to have requested that a direct examination of the respondent be made, with the Rota appointing an expert affiliated with the first instance tribunal to conduct the direct examination. In my background conversations with knowledgeable sources with first hand acquaintance and experience at the Rota, I was informed that indeed there are rotal cases in which the *ponens* has asked a local tribunal for a list of its approved experts and then appointed a "local" expert to conduct a direct examination of a party and to present an opinion to the rotal turnus. Of course, the law does grant a party the right to ask the presiding judge or *ponens* to admit into the acts a private expert opinion commissioned by that party, that is, the report of expert not designated by the tribunal (cf. canon 1575).

Conclusion

The three rotal sentences that have been studied here deal with fact situations that would not give most tribunals in the United States or Canada many sleepless nights. In all three cases under study here, the rotal judges had recourse to the opinions of psychiatric/psychological experts, even though the prior instances of adjudication had had recourse to one or more expert opinions. Indeed, as I noted at the very beginning, I have not been able to find a rotal decision in a case since 1987 in which the grounds are based on canon 1095 and in which one or more psychiatric/psychological experts were not consulted. An expert was used even though the psychic anomaly that causes the grave lack of discretion or the inability to assume the essential obligations of marriage need not be a "mental illness" in the strict clinical sense of the term but may arise as result of factors more circumstantial and transient in nature or from the entire complex of factors and circumstances that are to be subjected to a very diligent inquiry.[69] Thus, given the above analyses, what have we learned:

1. The law and jurisprudence (canons 1095 and 1680, *Dignitas connubii*, article 203) require the use of an expert in canon 1095 cases, with few exceptions.

---

69 *Coram* Sciacca, 16 June 2005, §8; 195. See also *coram* Monier, 21 June 1996, *Romanae Rotae Decisiones seu Sententiae* 88 (1996) 486-493 for an earlier statement of such a practice now being the common or mainstream rotal jurisprudence.

2. There appear to be three possibilities of exception but exceptions are just that, rare events. Indeed apparently the exceptions permitted are such rare events that I have not been able to fine a rotal decision in which one or more experts was not consulted. It appears to be the mindset of the prelate auditors of the Rota that it is almost impossible to encounter an expert report that was generated *in tempore non suspecto* that is "so qualified" as to provide "sufficient relevant proof" to them or that no positive doubts arise "from proven facts and circumstances" that "there appears either a lack of sufficient use of reason or a serious lack of discretion of judgment or an incapacity to assume the essential obligations of marriage."[70] What is envisioned in this scenario is a circumstance in which prior reports of an expert or experts are available that clearly respond to the questions that are raised in the ecclesiastical trial. There is no doubt that *Dignitas connubii*, article 204 §1 permits the *ponens* to admit prior reports of experts into the acts of the case.

3. The "qualified" experts appointed by the Rota are all psychiatrists, although, from background conversations with knowledgeable sources with first hand acquaintance and experience at the Rota, some of the psychiatrists that the Rota uses apparently are psychologists by training and practice as well. Clearly at the Rota the use of a psychiatrist is preferred but the expert designated at least has to be a psychologist. It appears that the reasoning of the rotal prelate auditors is that if one is asking for an expert opinion on physical health, one would consult a physician, not a nurse, nurse practitioner, physician assistant, physical therapist, respiratory therapist, etc., that is, an allied health professional, even though the latter might know and do certain things far better perhaps than a physician. Thus, if one is asking for an expert opinion about psychological health, one would consult the profession that has the most rigorous training in the assessment and treatment of psychological disorders, not a mental health counselor, marriage and family therapist, etc. I suspect that the reason for the Rota's preference for psychiatrists has to do with the disciplines of medicine and psychology in Italian universities and how the treatment of mental disorders is approached in Italy but to go beyond speculation would require a more in-depth study of professional education and the treatment of mental illness in Italy.

4. An expert opinion based on direct examination of the party in question in addition to a review of the acts has the greatest probative value, although determining the weight to be given to an expert opinion is always a matter for the judges in the case. Of course in most cases before the Rota, direct examination of a party is not practical, when the party does not live in Rome or at least in Italy. Nevertheless, rotal jurisprudence indicates that direct examination is more valuable than just a study of the acts of a case. From background conversations with knowledgeable sources with first hand ac-

---

70 Supreme Tribunal of the Apostolic Signatura, response, 16 June 1998, §5.

quaintance and experience at the Rota, the clear presumption of the prelate auditors of the Rota is that in cases in which canon 1095 is a grounds there already will have been at least one expert report from the lower court or courts, most often based on direct examination of the party in question in addition to a study of the acts.

5. There is a definite concern among the prelate auditors of the Rota that for an expert to state that he/she used the "psychoanalytical method" in arriving at his opinion means that the expert in coming to his/her opinion in no way was corresponding with the constitutive principles of Christian anthropology and therefore his/her report has no value.

6. There needs to be a definite consistency between the established facts in the case and the opinion of the expert. The rotal judges were not above taking to task even the experts they designated for going beyond the established facts or making statements about the severity of a psychic anomaly that appeared well beyond behaviors that were reported in the acts.

7. Once the judges receive the report of the expert nothing in the law or jurisprudence prevents the judges from calling the expert to testify in person in order to have him/her spell out precisely what he/she is saying or why there are differences between what he/she is saying and what other experts have stated. Direct testimony in regard to his expert opinion may increase the weight of the expert's report or may cause the judges to discount the expert's opinion.

8. What is crucial in the judge's assessment of the expert's opinion is does the expert make a connection between the presence of a psychic anomaly and the beginning of the marriage. The expert must identify the behaviors before, at the time of, and after the marriage that led to his/her opinion about the presence of a psychic anomaly.

9. Also, the expert's assessment of the level of the severity of the psychic anomaly must be consistent with the behaviors reported in the acts by the parties themselves and/or the witnesses.

10. Furthermore, the longer the duration of the marriage in question the more important the identification of behaviors at the beginning of the marriage becomes and the expert needs to opine as to why the marriage persisted for such a period of time.

11. When there has been serious impairment in marital functioning almost from the beginning of the marriage, the current psychological functioning of the party in question, especially if it is considered a serious psychic anomaly, generally is sufficient for the judge to conclude that the psychic anomaly was present at the time of the marriage.

12. Finally, related to the length of the marriage is the occurrence of a traumatic event in the life of the party in question. If the occurrence of such a traumatic event occurs several to many years into the marriage, it is difficult to almost impossible to prove that the current psychological functioning of the party in question has any relevance in regard to the presence of a psychic anomaly at the beginning of the marriage, unless there has been at least noticeable impairment in marital functioning and the expert can make the relevant connections.

What is clear from mainstream rotal jurisprudence is that neither the judge nor the expert can be sidetracked by or focus on the final difficulties between the parties in a marriage. It is all too easy to become confused about the question before the court and the law and jurisprudence regarding canon 1095, especially when the psychic condition of the party in question is serious at the end of or during the last years of the marriage.

Also, the judge must focus on the essential matrimonial rights and obligations of marriage and his questions for the expert ought to help him to do that. For valid consent it is not required that a party in contracting marriage carefully sift and weigh all its ethical, social, religious, public and private consequences.

Dignitas connubii is of great assistance to the judge because it expressly warns the judge about the type of questions that he needs to ask the expert in canon 1095 cases and thus, the judge can be assured that the expert in responding to such questions is not entering into the canonical field but is remaining in his/her field of expertise. With the promulgation of *Dignitas connubii* and the consistency of rotal jurisprudence for at least twenty years or more, there seems to be little option for the judge when it comes to the use of a psychological expert in canon 1095 cases. Perhaps we as judges have been our own worse enemy when it comes to the use of an expert because we have failed to separate the wheat from the chaff in our cases in the decisions we have written or to explain why some evidence is reliable and some is not. No longer does John Beal's musing toward the end of his presentation to this Society in 2004 seem possible, "one can wonder whether consultation with an expert is necessarily required in all lack of due discretion cases without exception."[71] As indicated above, yes, there remain exceptions but such an exception is rare and the judge ought to express in his decision the reason for an exception. The use of experts, provided they are suitably qualified and their methods meet the necessary anthropological presuppositions, definitely can be of great assistance to judges in their search for the truth and may even lead to greater transparency and logical rigor in the decisions judges write. However, there are many practical consequences regarding the use

---

71 Beal, "Finding Method in the Madness: Writing Sentences in Lack of Due Discretion Cases," 77.

of experts that we as judges, tribunal staff, and the larger church will need to face if we truly are to integrate the use of experts into our practices.

SEMINAR

NEW MODELS OF PARISH SCHOOLS
Reverend Monsignor Patrick R. Lagges
Sister Mary Paul McCaughey, OP

Part I: Canonical Considerations [Rev. Msgr. Patrick R. Lagges]

In the pastoral letter of the bishops of the United States, issued at the conclusion of the Third Plenary Council of Baltimore on 7 December 1884, the "clergy and laity in their charge" were told:

Two objects, therefore, dear brethren, we have in view, to multiply our schools, and to perfect them. We must multiply them, till every Catholic child in the land shall have within his reach the means of education. There is still much to do were this be attained. There are still thousands of Catholic children in the United States deprived of the benefit of a Catholic school. Pastors and parents should not rest till this defect be remedied. No parish is complete till it has schools adequate to the needs of its children, and the pastor and people of such a parish should feel that they have not accomplished their entire duty until the want is supplied.[1]

In an age of expansion, where parishes were few and often far between, this meant that each parish would have its own parish school. This was particularly necessary during the various waves of immigration, where numerous parishes were established for particular ethnic and language groups. Thus, the "one parish one school" model was established. What was probably not envisioned by the bishops gathered in Baltimore in 1884 was the proliferation of parishes in large American cities, with some parishes existing within blocks of the neighboring parish. Certainly not envisioned was the migration of people away from those neighborhoods, or the changing demographics within those areas of the city, which resulted in the original ethnic population being replaced by other national groups.[2]

---

1   Third Plenary Council of Baltimore, "Pastoral Letter" issued 7 December 1884, in *Pastoral Letters of the United States Catholic Bishops* (Washington, DC: USCCB, 1984) I: 225.

2   It would probably also be safe to say that the bishops did not anticipate a multiplication of schools *ad infinitum*. Indeed the pastoral letter maintains that the schools should be multiplied so that "every Catholic child has within his reach the means of education." As will be seen, this is entirely consonant with the canons of the present codes of canon law.

With the church in the United States now reaching an age of contraction, the issue has to be explored anew to see how "every Catholic child in the land shall have within his reach the means of education." Not only must this take into account the changing demographics of the country, but also the changing economics of both our parishes and our parishioners. Therefore, this article will explore some of the various options which are suggested in the documents of the Second Vatican Council and the two codes of canon law which have been promulgated as an outgrowth of the council.

The Teaching Office of the Church

The Declaration on Christian Education (Gravissimum educationis)

In its Preface, the Declaration on Christian Education (*Gravissimum educationis*) makes reference to the Universal Declaration of Human Rights of the United Nations, which states in Article 26:

1. Everyone has the right to education. Education shall be free, at least in the elementary and fundamental stages. Elementary education shall be compulsory. Technical and professional education shall be made generally available and higher education shall be equally accessible to all on the basis of merit.

2. Education shall be directed to the full development of the human personality and to the strengthening of respect for human rights and fundamental freedoms. It shall promote understanding, tolerance and friendship among all nations, racial or religious groups, and shall further the activities of the United Nations for the maintenance of peace.

3. Parents have a prior right to choose the kind of education that shall be given to their children.[3]

Thus education is viewed both by the international community and by the church as a fundamental human right which must be accorded to people everywhere.[4]

---

3 United Nations General Assembly, "Universal Declaration of Human Rights," 10 December 1948, http://www.un.org/en/documents/udhr/index.shtml.

4 See Vatican II, declaration *Gravissimum educationis*, October 28, 1965: *AAS* 58 (1966) 728-739. [hereafter *GE*]; English translation in *Vatican Council II: The Conciliar and Post Conciliar Documents*, ed. Austin Flannery (Collegeville, MN: The Liturgical Press, 1975) [hereafter Flannery]. Footnote #3 of *GE* also cites, among other documents, the encyclical of John XXIII, *Pacem in terris*, as well as the United Nations Declaration on the Rights of a Child of 20 November 1959 (see http://www.unicef.org/lac/spbarbados/Legal/global/General/declaration_child1959.pdf), which states in Principle 7:

"The child is entitled to receive education, which shall be free and compulsory, at least in the elementary stages. He shall be given an education which will promote his general culture and enable him, on a basis of equal opportunity, to develop his abilities, his

This is due to the fact, the council states, that education allows the individual to "take an ever more active role in social life and especially in the economic and political spheres."[5] Its importance lies in both the individual and in the society in which the individual resides. It is for this reason that schools are being multiplied in society and that new forms of schools are emerging.[6]

However, when the church speaks of education, it refers not just to what might be termed "book-learning," or the things which can be acquired outside the context of the human person. For the council states:

> This education should be suitable to the particular destiny of the individuals, adapted to their ability, sex, and national cultural traditions, and should be conducive to fraternal relations with other nations in order to promote true unity and peace in the world. True education is directed towards the formation of the human person in view of his final end and the good of that society to which he belongs and in the duties of which he will, as an adult, have a share.[7]

It also maintains that there is a need for constant updating of education methods, paying particular attention to psychological, pedagogical, and intellectual sciences, so that children and young people can:

> Develop harmoniously their physical, moral and intellectual qualities. They should be trained to acquire gradually a more perfect sense of responsibility in the proper development of their own lives by constant effort and in the pursuit of liberty, overcoming obstacles with unwavering courage and perseverance. As they grow older, they should receive a positive and prudent education in matters relating to sex. Moreover, they should be so prepared to take their part in the life of society that, having been duly trained in the necessary and useful skills, they may be able to participate actively in the life of society in its various aspects. They should be open to dialogue

---

individual judgement, and his sense of moral and social responsibility, and to become a useful member of society. The best interests of the child shall be the guiding principle of those responsible for his education and guidance; that responsibility lies in the first place with his parents." It should be noted here that the language used in previous documents, and in translating documents from other languages, is conditioned upon the historical circumstances of the times. In quoting these, the author has adhered to the translation provided.

5   *GE* Preface.

6   See *GE* Preface: "On every side…schools are being multiplied and perfected and other educational institutions are being established. Techniques of education and training are being refined on the basis of new experimentation."

7   *GE* 1.

with others and should willingly devote themselves to the promotion of the common good.[8]

While the above-cited texts refer to education in general, the council also maintains that the faithful have a right to an education which is specifically Christian.[9] Christian education takes into account what has occurred in the person through baptism, and thus allows those who are baptized to gradually become more aware of the gift of faith which they have received and deepen their awareness of the gift of salvation toward which they strive.[10] It increases their awareness of God's presence in their lives, particularly through the liturgy, and allows them to worship God in spirit and in truth.[11] And it allows Christians to live their lives according to the new person they have become and to continue the task of building up the church.[12] However, the purpose of Christian education is not simply limited to the Christian community. It is for the transformation of the world through the Christian's witness to hope.[13] Thus the council document exhorts pastors of souls "of the acutely serious duty to make every effort to see that all the faithful enjoy a Christian education of this sort, especially young people who are the hope of the Church."[14]

As in other places, the council reminds parents that it is their responsibility to educate their offspring,[15] an obligation which requires the help of society,[16] but the Declaration also places a certain obligation on the church as well, stating that task of education belongs by unique title to the church because the church has the

---

[8] *GE* 1. These words will be echoed in the canons on Catholic education in Book III of the Code of Canon Law and Title XV of the Code of Canons of the Eastern Churches.

[9] See *GE* 2.

[10] Ibid.

[11] Ibid.

[12] Ibid.

[13] Ibid.

[14] Ibid.

[15] *GE* 3: "The family is therefore the principal school of the social virtues which are necessary to every society. It is therefore above all in the Christian family, inspired by the grace and the responsibility of the sacrament of matrimony, that children should be taught to know and worship God and to love their neighbor, in accordance with the faith which they have received in earliest infancy in the sacrament of Baptism. In it, also they will have their first experience of a well-balanced human society and of the Church. Finally it is through the family that they are gradually initiated into association with their fellow-men in civil life and as members of the people of God. Parents should, therefore, appreciate how important a role the truly Christian family plays in the life and progress of the whole people of God."

[16] See *GE* 3.

responsibility to announce the way of salvation, to communicate the life of Christ to believers, and to assist believers in growing into the fullness of that life.[17]

In doing so, however, the church is not just concerned with its own members. Catholic education must exist, the council states, for the betterment of all society and for the transformation of the world. Thus, the church "will offer its assistance to all peoples for the promotion of a well-balanced perfection of the human personality, for the good of society in this world, and for the development of a world more worthy of man."[18] Thus the church's educational mission goes beyond the confines of the Catholic Church. Its purpose, like the purpose of the church itself, is to transform human society and point the way to the Kingdom of God.

The Declaration then goes on to speak specifically of Catholic schools, which it describes as one method among many of imparting Christian education, although it is said to be "of outstanding importance."[19] The Catholic school, the council states,

> develops a capacity for sound judgment and introduces pupils to the cultural heritage bequeathed to them by former generations. It fosters a sense of values and prepares them for professional life. By providing for friendly contacts between pupils of different characters and backgrounds it encourages mutual understanding. Furthermore it constitutes a center in whose activity and growth not only the families and teachers but also the various associations for the promotion of cultural, civil and religious life, civic society, and the entire community should take part.[20]

In further describing the Catholic school, the council maintains that its particular function is to

> develop in the school community an atmosphere animated by a spirit of liberty and charity based on the Gospel. It enables young people, while developing their own personality, to grow at the same time in that new life which has been given them in baptism. Finally, it so orients the whole of human culture to the message of salvation that the knowledge which the pupils acquire of the world, of life, and of men is illumined by faith. Thus, the Catholic school, taking into consideration as it should the conditions of an age of progress, prepares its pupils to contribute effectively to the welfare of the world of men

---

17   Ibid.
18   Ibid.
19   See *GE* 5.
20   Ibid.

and to work for the extension of the kingdom of God, so that by living an exemplary and apostolic life they may be, as it were, a saving leaven in the community.[21]

Thus the function of the Catholic school is very much tied to the circumstances of time and place. It follows from this that not every Catholic school will look exactly the same, either in a particular cultural milieu or at a particular time. A Catholic school that exists in a predominantly Catholic culture may look different from a Catholic school in a more pluralistic culture. Nor can it be assumed that Catholic schools exist for Catholic students only. Different models of schools must be maintained in those areas of the world where there is no public education and where the church remains the only hope for education for a vast populace. In line with this, the council recognized that some schools exist in areas which contain large populations of people who are not members of the Catholic Church. In these situations, "the Church attaches particularly importance to those schools….which include non-Catholics among their pupils."[22]

Finally, the church must also be concerned that "in establishing and conducting Catholic schools one must keep modern developments in mind."[23] To this end, the council urged greater attention to professional and technical schools, institutes for adult education and social work, schools for those with disabilities, and colleges to train teachers of religion and other branches of education.[24]

Thus, the Second Vatican Council, in its Declaration on Christian Education focused on the educational mission of the church, rather than the particular structure of a Catholic school. In doing so, it encouraged the development of various types of schools and various methods of education, adapted to the circumstances of time and place.

The Code of Canon Law and the Code of Canons of the Eastern Churches
The drafters of the two codes of canon law carefully followed the teaching of the council regarding Catholic education, oftentimes taking the wording of the canons directly from conciliar documents. These canons can be found in Book III of the Code of Canon Law (The Teaching Function of the Church), as well as Title XV (The Ecclesiastical Magisterium) in the Code of Canons of the Eastern Churches.

The Teaching Function of the Church
Both canon 747 of the Code of Canon Law and canon 595 of the Code of Canons of the Eastern Churches, state that the church has the responsibility of

---

21 *GE* 8.
22 *GE* 9.
23 Ibid.
24 Ibid.

protecting revealed truth, examining it, proclaiming it, and expounding on it. It has also been entrusted with the responsibility of announcing moral principles, "even about the social order," and to render judgment concerning human affairs that touch upon the fundamental rights of persons or upon the salvation of souls. This gives the church the innate right to preach the gospel to all people. In keeping with Blessed John Paul II's description of the purpose of law in the church, which was "to create such an order in the ecclesial society that, while assigning the primacy to love, grace, charisms, it at the same time renders their organic development easier in the life of both the ecclesial society and the individual persons who belong to it,"[25] the canons which follow try to organize, coordinate, and direct the mission of the church with regard to the word of God.

Thus, canon 756 §2 of the Code of Canon Law describes the diocesan bishop as the "moderator of the entire ministry of the word."[26] Subsequent canons will indicate how the bishop is to carry out this function with regard to the preaching of the word of God,[27] catechetical instruction,[28] the missionary action of the church,[29] Catholic education,[30] and the use of instruments of social communication.[31] For such ministry is not his alone to fulfill. He will do so with the cooperation of his presbyters and deacons,[32] members of those institutes of consecrated life whose charism is concerned with the ministry of the word,[33] and members of the lay faithful.[34] While the bishop must "moderate" the activity of all these

---

25 John Paul II, apostolic constitution *Sacrae disciplinae leges*, 25 January 1983; English translation in *Code of Canon Law, Latin-English Edition* (Washington, DC: CLSA, 1998) xxix-xxx. All citations of canons will be taken from this edition.

26 The term "moderator" is not a well-developed one in the law. It is most often used in conjunction with particular institutions in the church, such as in juridic persons (e.g., c. 115 §3) in seminaries (e.g., cc. 239 §3, 246 §4, 261 §1), in associations of the faithful (e.g., cc. 309, 317, 318, 320, 324 §1, 329), in parishes (e.g., cc. 517 §1, 520 §1, 526 §2, 542, 543, 544), in religious life (e.g., cc. 592 §2, 613, 615, 624-625, 631, 647, 668, 684, 686, 688, 690, 717 §1, 719 §4, 724 §2, 745), and in the diocesan curia (e.g., cc. 473 §3, 474, 487 §1, 488) and in tribunals (e.g., c. 1649 §1). The term "moderation" is also used in conjunction with various directive functions in the church, such as spiritual direction, the direction of liturgy, the direction of morals and ecclesiastical disciple (see c. 445), etc. It is not clear from the canons which of these references also contain the power of governance. Perhaps a further study of the concept would be useful, particularly as it applies to various liability issues in the church.

27 See cc. 762-772.

28 See cc. 773-780.

29 See cc. 781-792.

30 See cc. 793-821.

31 See cc. 822-832.

32 See c. 757.

33 See c. 758.

34 See c. 759. The role of the laity with regard to the mission of the church was de-

various groups, he does not necessarily exercise the power of governance over them, particularly those groups which have their own ministers of governance.

Similarly, the Code of Canons of the Eastern Churches describes the teaching mission of the church as that "of answering the perennial questions concerning the meaning of life and to provide for Christian solutions to the more pressing problems, having examined the signs of the times in light of the gospel, so that the light of Christ might shine more brilliantly everywhere, illuminating all people."[35] This task has been entrusted principally to bishops, but is shared by those who are collaborators of the bishops through sacred orders, or who have been mandated to teach in the name of the church.[36] The Eastern code reminds bishops that they should take into account "not only the principles of sacred sciences, but also the contributions of other sciences are to be recognized and utilized, so that the Christian faithful may be led to a more conscious and reflective life of faith."[37] Moreover, special consideration should be given to literature and the arts, "given their unique power to express and communicate the sense of faith."[38]

Catholic Schools in the Code of Canon Law

In many respects, the canons of the Latin code repeat what is found in *Gravissimum educationis* regarding Catholic schools. Reaffirming that parents are the primary educators of their children[39] and that civil society should assist parents in this task,[40] the code also speaks of the church as having the duty and the right of educating people, "so that they are able to reach the fullness of the Christian life."[41] As the Third Council of Baltimore had stated in the 19th century, pastors

---

scribed in the Dogmatic Constitution on the Church (*Lumen gentium*), which stated in n. 30: "For [pastors] know that they themselves were not established by Christ to undertake alone the whole salvific mission of the Church to the world, but that it is their exalted office so to be shepherds of the faithful and also recognize the latter's contribution and charisms that everyone in his own way will, with one mind, cooperate in the common task."

35   *Codex Canonum Ecclesiarum Orientalium auctoritate Ioannis Pauli PP. II promulgatus* (Vatican City: Libreria Editrice Vaticana, 1990). English translation from *Code of Canons of the Eastern Churches, Latin-English Edition* (Washington, DC: CLSA, 1992). All future quotations in English shall be from this edition.

36   *CCEO* c. 596.

37   *CCEO* c. 602.

38   *CCEO* c. 603.

39   *CIC* c. 793 §1.

40   *CIC* c. 793 §2.

41   *CIC* c. 794 §1. The fullness of this life is described in *CIC* c. 795 as the "complete formation of the human person that looks to his or her final end as well as to the common good of societies," and states that, as because of this, "children and youth are to be nurtured in such a way that they are able to develop their physical, moral and intellectual

are entrusted with the "duty of arranging everything so that all the faithful have a Catholic education."[42] Catholic schools are described as "the principal assistance to parents in fulfilling their function of education;"[43] and parents are enjoined to "entrust their children to those schools which provide a Catholic education."[44]

There are three ways in which the Code of Canon Law states that a school can be considered a Catholic school: (1) a competent ecclesiastical authority directs it; (2) a public ecclesiastical juridic person directs it; or (3) ecclesiastical authority recognizes as a Catholic school through a written document.[45] Furthermore, it directs that "no school is to bear the name *Catholic school* without the consent of competent ecclesiastical authority."[46]

The function of the diocesan bishop as the moderator of the entire ministry of the word can be seen in the canons which give the bishop a supervisory role over the schools within his jurisdiction. Canon 804 states that the religious instruction and education which is imparted through either the school or through other instruments of social communication are "subject to the authority of the Church."[47] Furthermore, the local ordinary seems to have some form of supervisory authority over the schools within his jurisdiction, being "concerned that those who are designated teachers of religious instruction in schools.....are outstanding in correct doctrine, the witness of a Christian life, and teaching skill."[48] Within the confines of his own diocese, the bishop has the right to appoint (if the school is subject to his power of governance) or approve (if the school is subject to the

---

talents harmoniously, acquire a more perfect sense of responsibility and right use of freedom, and are formed to participate actively in social life."

42 *CIC* c. 794 §2.

43 *CIC* c. 796 §1.

44 *CIC* c. 798.

45 *CIC* c. 803 §1.

46 *CIC* c. 803 §3. This creates several possible areas of concern. First, it seems to allow for the possibility that a school which has been established by a public juridic person, which, according to c. 116 §1 acts in the name of the church, might *not* be considered a Catholic school, if the competent ecclesiastical authority has not recognized it as such through a written document. Second, it does not provide for the possibility of a school, having once been designated a Catholic school, losing its designation. If the competent ecclesiastical authority has decided that a school is no longer Catholic, can he remove this designation; and if so, by what procedure?

47 *CIC* c. 804 §1.

48 *CIC* c. 804 §2. It should be noted, however, that the teachers are designated by the schools, not by the local ordinary, so his authority does not appear to extend to matters of governance over the individual teachers themselves. For example, a bishop could not hire or fire teachers who teach in schools that are run by other public juridic persons, such as religious institutes. His concern would most likely take the form of policies regarding the requirements for teaching religion in Catholic schools.

power of governance of another public juridic person) teachers of religion; and he can remove them (if the school is subject to his power of governance) or demand that they be removed (if the school is subject to the power of governance of another public juridic person) "if a reason of religion or morals requires it."[49] But even if he does not have any direct jurisdiction over a school, such as would be the case in those schools founded by or operated by religious institutes, the bishop still has the right to "watch over and visit (*invigilandi et invisendi*)" such schools and to issue "prescripts which pertain to the general regulation of Catholic schools."[50] This right is limited, however, since the same canon reminds the bishop that he does not have this authority regarding the internal direction of schools which are founded or directed by religious institutes.[51]

All of these canons are consistent with the bishop's role as "moderator of the entire ministry of the word," and further spell out the scope of his moderating function. How much "moderating" translates into "liability" would be the subject of another study.

Catholic Schools in the Code of Canons of the Eastern Churches

In many respects, the canons of the Eastern churches are similar to the canons of the Latin church. There are some differences, however. Although the Eastern code describes parents as primarily responsible for the education of their children, it reminds them that education is done "in the context of a Christian family illumined by faith and animated by mutual love, especially in piety toward God and love of neighbor."[52] It also reminds the church that it is to partner with parents in the education of their children "since [the Church] has generated new creatures through baptism."[53] Thus the church's responsibility in baptizing a child also carries through into caring for the children it has baptized.

Catholic schools do not exist as simply the concern of the bishop and the parents of children, but rather is the concern also of the entire ecclesial community.[54] As in the Latin code, parents have an obligation to send their children to

---

49   *CIC* c. 805.

50   *CIC* c. 806 §1.

51   *CIC* c. 806 §1. It is interesting to note that the canon makes a distinction between schools which are "founded" by a religious institute and those which are "directed" by a religious institute. This could be interpreted to include schools which were founded at one time by a religious institute but no longer directed by that institute (for example, having become a separate public juridic person or an apostolate of an association of the Christian faithful), as well as schools which were founded by one religious institute, or even by a diocese, and now directed by another religious institute.

52   *CCEO* c. 627 §1.

53   *CCEO* c. 628 §1.

54   *CCEO* c. 631 §1.

Catholic schools,[55] but the schools themselves also have an obligation: "to create an atmosphere animated by the gospel spirit of freedom and love in the scholastic community, to assist adolescents in the development of their own personality in such a way that at one and the same time they grow in accord with that new creature that they have become through baptism; further, it should so orient the whole of human culture to the message of salvation that the understanding which the students gradually acquire of the world, of life, and of humankind may be illumined by faith."[56] They should fulfill their obligation themselves, but also in cooperation with other schools.[57]

The notion of the Catholic school in service to a pluralistic society is also found in the Eastern canons, which allow the school "to adapt these matters to its particular circumstances…if the majority of its pupils are non-Catholic," and "to pursue cultural goals as well as the human and social formation of the young."[58]

Although Eastern Catholic bishops are not described as "moderators of the entire ministry of the word," the eparchial bishop has similar supervisory authority over the schools within his eparchy: "The eparchial bishop is competent to judge any school whatever and to decide whether it fulfills the requirements of Christian education or not; for a grave cause, he is also competent to forbid the Christian faithful from attending a particular school."[59] He may visit any Catholic school in his eparchy, with the exception of schools reserved for students of institutes of consecrated life.[60]

Catholic Schools

While our experience in the United States has primarily been with parish schools, it should be noted that this is not mentioned explicitly in either the council documents or in the two codes of law. Even the Decree of the Third Plenary Council of Baltimore merely exhorted pastors to make sure that Catholic children in the United States are not deprived of the benefit of a Catholic school.[61] This could be through an individual parish having an individual school, but such a model was not mandated by the Plenary Council. The exact model for how the benefit of a Catholic school should be available to all Catholic children would be left to particular circumstances.

---

55 *CCEO* c. 633 §2.
56 *CCEO* c. 634 §1.
57 *CCEO* c. 639.
58 *CCEO* c. 634 §§2 and 3.
59 *CCEO* c. 633 §1.
60 *CCEO* c. 638 §1.
61 See above.

What is clear from the council documents and the codes which followed upon these documents was that the church has an educational mission. This mission is entrusted to particular individuals in the church, but not given a particular structure. As seen above, it can be carried out either by a competent ecclesiastical authority, by a public ecclesiastical juridic person, or by others, with designation by the competent ecclesiastical authority. The exact structure is left to those individuals who establish the schools. Thus, the concept of Catholic education is mission-driven, rather than structure-driven.

"Competent ecclesiastical authority." Whenever the canons speak of a "competent ecclesiastical authority," most often they will be speaking of a diocesan bishop or his equivalent (a territorial prelate, a territorial abbot, an apostolic vicar, an apostolic prefect, or an apostolic administrator).[62] However, it might be possible for several diocesan bishops to exercise their educational mission cooperatively. Thus, there might be a Catholic school or system of schools established by an ecclesiastical province or region. It would certainly be possible for the Roman Pontiff to establish a Catholic school, since he would obviously be considered a competent ecclesiastical authority. Within the territory or among the people entrusted to him, a parish priest is also a competent ecclesiastical authority, and has been entrusted with the task of providing that "the word of God is proclaimed in its entirety to those living in his parish."[63] He could establish a school for his own parish, or cooperate with neighboring pastors in establishing a Catholic school.

"A public ecclesiastical juridic person." Juridic persons in general are "aggregates of persons or of things ordered for a purpose which is in keeping with the mission of the Church and which transcends the purpose of the individuals."[64] Public juridic person are those aggregates of persons or of things which are constituted by competent ecclesiastical authority, act in the name of the church, and fulfill the function entrusted to them with a view to the public good.[65] Examples of public ecclesiastical juridic persons in the church would be religious institutes, dioceses, parishes, associations of the Christian faithful, and any other aggregate of persons or of things that has been established as a public juridic person in the church.

---

62   See *CIC* cc. 369-371. The Eastern Catholic Churches do not maintain similar distinctions in the common law. Churches which are not patriarchal, major archepiscopal, or metropolitan are governed by *CCEO* cc. 174-176.

63   *CIC* c. 528 §1. See also *CCEO* c. 289, which enjoins the pastor to tend to the catechetical formation of his people with "not only the assistance of members of religious institutes or societies of common life, but also the cooperation of lay persons." It also more clearly delineates that the parish priest is a pastor properly so-called, exercising the functions of teaching, governing, and sanctifying. While these functions are found in the Latin code, they are presented more obliquely.

64   *CIC* c. 114 and *CCEO* cc. 920-921.

65   *CIC* c. 116 and *CCEO* c. 921.

"By designation." A competent ecclesiastical authority designates something through a singular administrative act, which must be put in writing.[66] In the case of a Catholic school, it could be that a group of the laity within a diocese founds a school and asks that it be designated Catholic. It could also happen that a group has formed a private association within the church, which is sponsoring a school as part of its living out of the apostolate.[67] In these cases, there is no need for the group to have been officially constituted in the church, although there is nothing to exclude pious associations or private juridic persons from seeking such designation from the competent ecclesiastical authority.

Forms of Catholic Schools

From church documents and canons, there emerges two requirements for Catholic schools. They must be mission driven; and they must be in the communion of the church. They are mission driven according to the mission that Christ entrusted to the church, and according to the educational mission that is entrusted to a diocesan bishop, a parish priest, a religious institute having the educational charism, another type of public juridic person whose apostolate is Catholic education, or any group of the Christian faithful who are exercising "the mission which God has entrusted to the Church to fulfill in the world"[68] and are directing their efforts "to promote the growth of the Church and its continual sanctification,"[69] so that "the divine message of salvation more and more reaches all people in every age and in every land."[70]

That the schools are also in the communion of the church can be seen from the insistence upon ecclesiastical approval/supervision/vigilance as noted above. It is the intervention of the pastors of the church that ensure the Catholicity of the school and its adherence to Catholic principles with regard to faith, discipline, and morals.

As can be seen from the above, there is nothing to say that a school must be sponsored by a parish. Many are, at least in the United States. But if the school is seen as something that is mission-driven, there is nothing to say that the educational mission of the parish must be accomplished only through a parish school. A number of possibilities exist: a parish school, a multi-parish school, a diocesan school (either as an individual school or a group of schools), a school directed by the apostolate of a religious institute (either as an individual school or a group of schools), a school sponsored by another type of public ecclesiastical juridic person (either as an individual school or a group of schools), a school sponsored

---

66   See *CIC* cc. 35ff and *CCEO* cc. 1510ff.

67   See *CIC* cc. 211, 215, 216, 225, 298, 301 and *CCEO* cc. 14, 18, 19, 401, 406, 573, 574.

68   *CIC* c. 204.

69   *CIC* c. 210.

70   *CIC* c. 211.

by an association of the Christian faithful (either as an individual school or a group of schools), or a school designated as a Catholic school by a competent ecclesiastical authority (either as an individual school or a group of schools).

Canonical Implications of Each Model

Each of the various models presented above has certain canonical implications, both in civil law and in canon law. Some of these implications will depend also upon the form of civil incorporation of each diocese. For example, some dioceses exist as a corporation sole, although the Holy See has discouraged this model since 1911 and has urged dioceses in the United States to move away from it. In other dioceses, individual parishes are civilly incorporated, with various forms of governance of the civil corporation existing. In still other dioceses, parishes exist as religious trusts. Each of these types of civil incorporation would also have implications on the ability of a diocese, a parish, or a group of parishes to structure its Catholic schools. It would go beyond the scope of this paper to go into each of the types of civil incorporation and discuss the canonical implications of each type of school. Before embarking upon a restructuring of the Catholic schools in a diocese, it would be important for discussions to be held with those who handle civil law matters for the diocese and for any canonical restructuring to be done in conjunction with them.

The models which were described above also involve different levels of control and liability on the part of the diocese. In general, the more control a diocese exercises over a Catholic school, the more liability it incurs. The description of the various models will proceed from maximum control to minimal control, and from maximum liability to minimal liability. Within each of these options, however, there are a variety of options.

1. The Diocesan School

This is the first model described in *CIC* c. 803: a school which a competent ecclesiastical authority directs. In this model, the diocesan bishop establishes the school, which is considered part of the educational apostolate of the diocese. The bishop is free to establish such schools and indeed is encouraged to do so.[71] The bishop can also determine how the school is structured and governed. In some cases, the principal of the school relates directly to a diocesan superintendent of schools or to a vicar for Catholic education. There may also be a separate school president who handles functions separate from the day-to-day operations of the school. Both may be assisted by a school board or a board of specified jurisdiction[72] which has been given certain tasks to accomplish in the support of the

---

71 See *CIC* c. 802 and *CCEO* c. 635.

72 The NCEA and other authors often refer to "boards of limited jurisdiction," a term which seems to indicate that the board should have had full jurisdiction over the school, but that the bishop has limited this jurisdiction. The term "board of specified jurisdic-

school.[73]

There are other situations where a diocese may wish to "take over" an existing school which is in danger of failing. This is a more complicated issue, since it may require matters of alienation, depending on the how the diocese is structured. Since a parish is a public juridic person,[74] it is the subject of rights and obligations corresponding to its nature.[75] The pastor is responsible for the administration of the temporal goods of the parish, making sure that they are administered according to the norm of law.[76] If the parish operates a school as part of its educational apostolate, the school and its building would be considered part of the patrimony of the parish. This would need to be taken into account should a diocese wish to "take over" a parish school that is failing, or should a pastor wish to "give up" his school and have the diocese run it. It must first be determined if the school is the pastor's "to give" or if it is the diocese's "to take."

Obviously, in the case of a diocesan school, the diocese exercises maximum control and incurs maximum liability.

II. One Parish – One School

This is the model that we see most frequently in the United States. It is an example of both the first and second model suggested by *CIC* c. 803 §1.[77] Many pastors took seriously the decree of the Third Plenary Council of Baltimore, and established Catholic schools in their parishes. In many cases, because of the great waves of immigration to the United States in the late 1800s and early 1900s, this was done particularly to ensure the children of various immigrant groups were being provided with a Catholic education, and that religion would be taught in the native language of those who came to the U.S. from other countries.

---

tion" seems to describe the reality more precisely, since this allows for certain powers of governance to be reserved to the bishop or his vicar and other powers of governance to be exercised by the board.

73   Some of these tasks could be fund-raising, institutional advancement, public relations, marketing, maintenance, etc. Tasks which would be reserved to the bishop, his vicar, his delegate, or the principal/president would be matters of Catholic identity, mission, etc.

74   See *CIC* c. 515 §3 and *CCEO* c. 280 §3.

75   See *CIC* c. 113 §2 and *CCEO* c. 920.

76   See *CIC* c. 532 and *CCEO* c. 290 §1.

77   A parish priest, who is a pastor according to law, therefore has the authority to teach, govern, and sanctify. If he establishes a Catholic school in his parish, he may do so as the "competent ecclesiastical authority." A parish is also a public juridic person in the church, and therefore it might be considered that the parish is directing the school, under the authority of the pastor. This does not mean that the pastor or the parish directs the school independent of the diocesan bishop, since the bishop is seen as the higher authority of each, and the one who guarantees that they remain in the communion of the church.

In the "one parish-one school" model, the Catholic school is seen as part of the educational apostolate of the parish, and as part of the pastor's obligation to see to it the word of God is proclaimed in its entirety in his parish.[78] The school building and grounds belong to the parish, and the pastor must administer them according to the norm of law. Various models of diocesan governance, particularly civil governance, may suggest various relationships with the diocese. At times, it might be possible that a Catholic school which exists on parish grounds could still be considered a "diocesan school," if, for example, a bishop requests that a given parish "host" a Catholic school, cooperating in a certain manner with the diocese's educational mission. This concept of "hosting," a term which does not appear in either code of canon law, has been used in other situations to explain how one entity assists another entity in its function in the church.[79]

Although the Catholic school in this model is considered part of the parish educational apostolate, nonetheless in most dioceses in the United States, the bishop provides some direction and oversight for the Catholic schools in his diocese through an office of the diocesan curia.[80] In some instances, this involves assisting the parish schools with various administrative tasks, while in other dioceses it is difficult to distinguish between "assistance" and the "power of governance." Oftentimes, this is discussed as whether the Catholic schools in a diocese have formed a "system of diocesan schools" or a "diocesan school system."

Depending on how a diocese is organized civilly, this might be considered a model of somewhat lesser control, but may still incur maximum liability for the diocese, particularly if the diocese has a highly centralized schools office.

III. Many Parishes – One School

In this model, several pastors jointly exercise their educational mission by sponsoring a single school. This would not be seen as an abdication of their obligation, since they would still be exercising their educational mission, but doing so cooperatively with other pastors in the area.

There are many different possibilities for these types of schools: the school might be at a single site or at multiple sites with a single administration. There could also be multiple sites with shared administration for purchasing and services only, with each site retaining its own separate identity and being responsible for its own marketing and development. There could be a formal juridic structure established for the school, or simply a "gentleman's agreement" among

---

78   See *CIC* c. 528 §1 and *CCEO* c. 289.

79   For example, in cases of clerical sexual misconduct, the Congregation for the Doctrine of the Faith has asked individual diocesan bishops to have their tribunals "host" a second instance court of the Congregation.

80   For example, see *CIC* cc. 804-806 and *CCEO* cc. 636, 638, 639.

the pastors, as expressed in a list of "protocols." The pastor of one of the parishes could act as the leader of the school, or the leadership could be exercised on a rotating basis.

However the school is set up, it needs considerable forethought and specification. Matters of organization or governance should not be left to chance. Questions about ownership, upkeep, employment, pastoral leadership, division of authority/responsibility, etc., need to be asked in advance. Expectations of each parish need to be clearly specified, as well as policies regarding tuition, fund-raising, etc. Provisions for change in leadership (e.g., transfer of a pastor) or change in parishes (e.g., one of the parishes closes or several are merged) ought to be made beforehand in order to avoid hasty decisions being made out of necessity. Any new pastor coming into this situation needs to understand clearly what will be expected of him with regard to the educational mission of his parish.

Depending on the amount of oversight provided by the diocese, this model might also be one which expresses maximum control and maximum liability. This is particularly important since these "consortium" schools often need greater assistance in maintaining the model that has been established.

IV. Catholic School Sponsored By a Religious Institute

In this model, a religious institute is the sponsor of a Catholic school that exists in a particular church. There are a number of ways in which religious institutes sponsor a Catholic school. In those cases where a parish had been entrusted *plena iure* to a religious community, or where a parish had been founded by a religious institute even apart from any diocesan intervention,[81] there are certain jurisdictional issues which need to be addressed regarding the parish and its school. In some cases, the parish does not "belong" to the diocese; it belongs to the religious institute which received the money to found the parish. There are other situations in which a diocesan bishop has entrusted the pastoral care of a parish to a religious institute. The parish remains a diocesan parish; it is only the pastoral care that belongs to the religious institute. Finally, there are situations where a diocese or a diocesan parish invites a religious community to establish a Catholic school, as part of the diocese's or the parish's educational mission.[82]

---

81   These sort of situations occurred in an age of expansion where the church was expanding into new, often unsettled territories. In some cases, money was provided to a religious institute by a family or by a foundation to establish a parish in a place where the diocesan church was not well established or organized. These "mission parishes" were oftentimes not established under the auspices of a diocese and sometimes without the knowledge of the diocesan bishop who may have been many miles away from the place where the parish was established.

82   In the case of a diocese inviting a religious community to establish a school within the diocese, it was often the case that the diocese would provide the religious institute with diocesan land on which to build a school. At times, the diocese would also either

This could be as a single school or as individual schools in various parts of a diocese or a group of schools which are joined together in some way.

In each of these cases, there is need for the diocese to clarify issues of ownership, sponsorship, and governance. Specific models for this would go beyond the scope of this paper, but they must be tended to in order to avoid difficulties later on. In general, though, it should be pointed out that the governance of a religious institute and its apostolate is left to the religious institute itself. A diocesan bishop or a parish priest may not interfere in an institute's internal governance. This is not to say that the bishop or the parish priest has nothing to say about schools which are sponsored by religious institutes. The religious instruction and education in such schools is subject to the authority of the diocesan bishop.[83] He must also be solicitous that teachers of religion are outstanding in skill, doctrine, and witness.[84] He can approve teachers of religion within his diocese.[85] And he has the right of visitation and vigilance over all the schools within his diocese, including those directed by members of religious institutes.[86]

If the schools were founded by the religious institutes themselves, the diocesan bishop would have less control and less liability. However, if the diocesan bishop founded the school but entrusted it to a religious community, his liability might increase.

V. A Separate Public Juridic Person

While some schools are joined to a public juridic person, such as a religious institute, and considered part of the institute's apostolate, it is also possible for a school or a grouping of schools to exist as its own separate public juridic person. A bishop could establish a Catholic school as a public juridic person in his diocese, for example, in cases where a new pastor is assigned to a parish who either does not wish to administer a school, is not capable of doing so, or where the diocese wishes to create a "multi-parish school" out of an existing single parish school. A bishop might also wish to establish a group of schools in his diocese as

---

directly fund or act as a guarantor of the funds needed to establish the school. In many cases, these arrangements were made many years ago, with very little documentation. This had led to considerable difficulties when the religious institute can no longer support its school and wishes to sell the buildings and property. Unless there is some indication from the original documents that the building or land would revert to the diocese should it no longer be used for educational purposes, an argument can be made that the diocese had made a grant of land and money to the religious institute for its free use and ultimate disposal.

83   See *CIC* c. 804 §1 and *CCEO* c. 636 §1.
84   See *CIC* c. 804 §2 and *CCEO* c. 639.
85   See *CIC* c. 805 and *CCEO* c. 636 §2.
86   See *CIC* c. 806 and *CCEO* c. 638.

a public juridic person (such as all the Catholic schools in a vicariate or a region of his diocese), or to organize all the Catholic schools in his diocese as a single public juridic person, run by its own board of specified jurisdiction, with certain authority being reserved to the bishop or his vicar or to a superintendent of schools.[87] As above, issues involving alienation of property need to be dealt with if the bishop is removing individual parish schools from the jurisdiction of the pastors of those parishes. The buildings will still belong to the parishes to which they are joined, and will still be considered part of that parish's patrimony. While the parish could join its educational mission to that of its neighboring parishes and include its school buildings in that joint venture, such arrangements need to be made according to both canon law and possibly civil law, depending on the civil status of the parishes of the diocese.

The canons referring to juridic persons are *CIC* cc. 113-123 and *CCEO* cc. 920-930. Juridic persons are distinguished as either private (acting in its own name for a private good) or public (acting in the name of the church for the common good).[88] They can be an aggregate of either persons or things,[89] and can be directed by a single person, a group of persons, or a college of persons.[90] Juridic persons must pursue a useful purpose in the church and also have the means sufficient to achieve that purpose.[91]

A public juridic person, which acts in the name of the church and for the common good, is created either by the law itself or by the decree of the competent ecclesiastical authority.[92] In addition to the decree creating the public juridic person, it must also have statutes, which define the purpose, constitution and methods of operation of the public juridic person and which bind those who direct it.[93] It must also have a finance council or at least two councilors who assist in its administration.[94] By its very nature, a public juridic person is perpetual, although it can be suppressed by the competent ecclesiastical authority or is extinguished if it has ceased to act for one hundred years.[95] Upon suppression or extinction, the allocation of any temporal goods of the public juridic person are governed by the

---

87 These would include such things as Catholic identity, mission, etc.
88 See *CIC* c. 116. The *CCEO* does not contain the concept of private juridic persons.
89 See *CIC* c. 115 and *CCEO* c. 920.
90 See *CIC* cc. 118-119 and *CCEO* cc. 922 and 924.
91 See *CIC* c. 114 §3 and *CCEO* c. 921 §3.
92 See *CIC* c. 116 §2 and *CCEO* c. 921.
93 See *CIC* cc. 94 and 117 and *CCEO* c. 922.
94 See *CIC* c. 1280. There is no corresponding canon in the *CCEO*.
95 See *CIC* c. 120 and *CCEO* c. 927. Issues of suppression of public juridic person can often become contentious, either canonically or emotionally. It is best when drawing up statutes for the public juridic person if the matter of reasons for suppression are also dealt with.

law and the statutes; if there is no indication in either place as to how the goods are to be allocated, they revert to the juridic person immediately superior to the one which is going out of existence.[96]

In this model, there is less control by the diocesan bishop, since the board of specified jurisdiction would be responsible for the tasks entrusted to it. However, there would still be some liability on the part of the diocese, since it still holds some reserved powers and is the immediate superior of the public juridic person. The bishop's relationship with the schools would also be governed by *CIC* cc. 804-806 and *CCEO* cc. 636, 638, 639, as described above.

VI. Association of the Christian Faithful

Another model for Catholic schools would be the establishment of an association of the Christian faithful which would have as its mission the administration of a single Catholic school, a group of schools, or an entire system of schools within a diocese. The difference between the association of the Christian faithful and the public juridic person models would be that in the latter the emphasis is on the structure (the school itself), whereas in the former the emphasis is on the people who operate the school.

In 1988, what was then called the Sacred Congregation for Catholic Education stated, "the declaration *Gravissimum educationis* signifies–in effect–a decisive turn in the history of Catholic schools: a transition from school/institution to school/community."[97] The possibility of establishing associations of the Christian faithful to sponsor and administer schools within a diocese can be seen as an extension of this emphasis on school as community. It also flows from the council document on the Apostolate of Lay People (*Apostolicam actuositatem*).[98] Documents prior to the council spoke primarily of the "apostolate of the hierarchy." Apostolic activity was mostly confined to the successors of the apostles. They laity could participate in that apostolic activity, but the apostolate was not theirs by right. This was reflected in the laws of the church at the time. The laity were seen as those who received from the hierarchy what they needed; but they were not scene as actors in their own right. Thus, the laity had the right of "receiving from the clergy, according to the norm of ecclesiastical discipline,

---

96   See *CIC* c. 123 and *CCEO* c. 930. The allocation of goods can also become a contentious issue. Hence, it is important to spell this out in the statutes.

97   Sacred Congregation for Catholic Education, "The Religious Dimension of Education in the Catholic School: Guidelines for Reflection and Renewal," 7 April 1988, n. 31. English translation can be found at

http://www.vatican.va/roman_curia/congregations/ccatheduc/documents/rc_con_ccatheduc_doc_19880407_catholic-school_en.html.

98   Vatican II, decree *Apostolicam actuositatem*, November 18, 1965: *AAS* 58 (1966) 837-864. See Flannery, 766-798.

spiritual goods and especially that aid necessary for salvation."[99] It was "worthy of praise" if they joined associations established by the pastors of the church, or commended to them by those same pastors.[100] And the laity were allowed to form associations for the promotion of the perfection of Christian life, for the exercise of other pious or charitable works, or for the increase of public cult.[101] The function of the laity, therefore, was limited to supporting to apostolate of the hierarchy.

The Second Vatican Council spoke of an apostolate that belonged to the laity by right. It stated, "As sharers in the role of Christ the Priest, the Prophet, and the King, the laity have an active part to play in the life and activity of the Church."[102] It also referred to the laity as carrying out "their manifold apostolate both in the Church and in the world."[103] This broadened notion of apostolate was reflected in the laws of the church. In referring to associations in the church, as had the prior code, it expanded the scope of those associations in stating

> In the Church there are associations distinct from institutes of consecrated life and societies of apostolic life; in these associations, the Christian faithful, whether clerics, lay persons, or clerics and lay persons together, strive in a common endeavor to foster a more perfect life, to promote public worship or Christian doctrine, or to exercise other works of the apostolate such as initiatives of evangelization, works of piety or charity, and those which animate the temporal order with a Christian spirit.[104]

These associations could either be a private agreement among its members, and which could assume the title *Catholic* if its statutes were reviewed by a competent ecclesiastical authority or if it were designated as such by that same authority;[105] or it could be a public association, if it were established as such by the competent authority.[106] The difference between the two is that a private association is established by private agreement among its members and acts in its own name,[107] whereas a public association is established by a competent author-

---

99 *CIC* 17 c. 682.

100 *CIC* 17 c. 684.

101 *CIC* 17 c. 685.

102 *AA* 10.

103 *AA* 9.

104 *CIC* c. 298 §1. There is no corresponding canon in the *CCEO*.

105 See *CIC* cc. 299-300 and *CCEO* c. 573 §2.

106 See *CIC* c. 301 and *CCEO* c. 573.

107 The activities of a private association of the Christian faithful are limited, according to c. 298, to fostering a more perfect life, promoting worship and doctrine in the church, and exercising initiatives regarding evangelization, piety, charity, and the animation of

ity for the expressed purpose of either handing on Christian doctrine in the name of the church, promoting public worship, or engages in other activities whose pursuit is reserved to the competent authority that established it.[108]

Thus, the diocesan bishop could establish a group of people as a public association of the Christian faithful that had as its apostolate the sponsorship of a single Catholic school, a group of Catholic schools, or even a system of Catholic schools. It would also be possible for such an association to be established by the Holy See or by a conference of bishops.[109] The distinction between the association and its apostolate ought to be maintained, since they are clearly two entities in the church. The establishment of associations of the Christian faithful to sponsor a school would create a situation of minimal control on the part of the bishop, but also minimal liability on the part of the diocese, since the liability for the school would be incurred by the association rather than the diocese.[110] The diocesan bishop would still have his responsibilities under *CIC* cc. 804-806 and *CCEO* cc. 636, 638, 639, however, which may translate into some form of limited liability.

There are certain elements that the public association of the Christian faithful must contain. The association is to have its own statutes, which define the purpose, the seat, the condition for new membership, the manner of acting, and the title of the association.[111] It is also subject to the "vigilance" of the competent ecclesiastical authority and the Holy See, who are to ensure the integrity of faith and morals, prevent the abuse of ecclesiastical discipline, and inspect the association according to the norm of law and the association's statutes.[112] The members of the association must not have publicly rejected the Catholic faith, defected from ecclesiastical communion, or be punished by an imposed or de-

---

the temporal order with a Christian spirit. There seems to be a distinction here between the works of a private association which "promote" Christian doctrine, and the works of a public association which "hand on" Christian doctrine. The former seems to refer to associations which support already existing works, while the latter seems to refer to works that are actually performed by the association "in the name of the Church."

108   See *CIC* c. 301 §1 and *CCEO* c. 574.

109   See *CIC* c. 312 §1 and *CCEO* c. 575.

110   There are certain civil law considerations in this. Since the association and its apostolate are two separate entities, it would probably be necessary to incorporate them separately. The civil "articles of incorporation" and the canonical statutes, while obviously separate documents, can be written in conjunction with one another. Those in charge of writing the canonical statues and those writing the articles of incorporation should collaborate with one another so that there are no areas of conflict between the two documents.

111   See *CIC* c. 304 §1 and *CCEO* c. 576. The Eastern code also states that the statutes are to "determine policies in accordance with the rite of the association's Church *sui iuris* and the needs of time and place or usefulness."

112   See *CIC* c. 305 and *CCEO* c. 577.

clared excommunication.[113] With regard to temporal goods, the association can administer goods according to the norm of law, but it must render an account of its administration to the competent authority.[114] For lay associations of the Christian faithful, their members must have adequate formation,[115] and their leaders are encouraged to cooperate with other associations, especially those in the same territory.[116] Finally, the association can be suppressed by the competent authority, for "grave causes" if the conference of bishops has established the association, and after having heard the moderator and other major officials for all types of associations.[117]

VII. Catholic Schools Designated By an Ecclesiastical Authority

In this model, there is another individual or group within a diocese, separate from the diocesan bishop or from a religious institute, that sponsors and operates a school, and which wants that school to be designated *Catholic*. In a sense, they want to use the "Catholic trademark" on their already existing endeavor. This could be an individual philanthropist or a foundation that has established a school within the territory of a diocese. It could also be another existing group in the diocese that is not part of diocesan structure, for example a personal prelature, a lay ecclesial movement, or even an intentional community associated with a religious institute. In this scenario, they have set up a school which they now want to be called a Catholic school.

In this case, the diocesan bishop would simply issue a decree, declaring the school a "Catholic school." However, it would be helpful if a diocese beforehand had established some criteria for designating a school as *Catholic*, and also indicating how that designation might be removed. It might also want to require that any school which has been designated as a Catholic school in the diocese be subject to the general educational policies of the diocese and participate in diocesan functions, especially those which touch about education and, more importantly, religious education.

For schools which are operated by other entities but designated by the diocesan bishop as *Catholic*, there would be minimal control and minimal liability. The diocesan bishop would still have his responsibilities under *CIC* cc. 804-806

---

113 See *CIC* c. 316 and *CCEO* c. 580. This refers to the members of the association itself, not the apostolate that the association sponsors. Thus, while members of the association would have to be members of the Catholic Church, there would be no such requirement, for example, for the members of the school board which directs the operations of the Catholic school.

114 See *CIC* cc. 319, 325 and *CCEO* 582.

115 See *CIC* c. 329.

116 See *CIC* cc. 328-329.

117 See *CIC* c. 320 and *CCEO* c. 583.

and *CCEO* cc. 636, 638, 639, however, which may translate into some form of limited liability.

Conclusions

When Jesus established the church, he gave her the authority to teach, to govern, and to sanctify. In carrying out her educational mission throughout the centuries, the church praised the establishment of Catholic schools so that the message of the kingdom might reach to the ends of the earth. She has also established various structures, based upon the circumstance of time and place. In the United States, this generally involved a school which was part of the educational mission of a parish or was seen as an apostolate of a religious institute. However, the documents of the Second Vatican Council, as well as the two codes of canon law have given the church a wide range of opportunities in structuring her educational mission. Parish schools or schools sponsored by religious institutes are but two models among many that are possible. Each of these models gives the diocesan bishop various forms of control and incurs various levels of liability. This paper has only been able to sketch in brief form the possibilities for structuring Catholic schools, leaving further development to other endeavors. In order to examine some of these models, though, we will now turn to the second part of this presentation.

Part II: New Models of Parish Schools [Sr. Mary Paul McCaughey, OP]

My thanks go to Monsignor Pat for his rich explication of the theology, governance, and mission of Catholic schools in the canons. For this section of the presentation, I hope to detail some of the challenges around school governance and the way several archdioceses have responded to these challenges.

I. While the concepts of school models and governance are often used interchangeably, they are not the same and call for clarification.

Goldschmidt and Walsh (Sustaining Urban Catholic Schools, www.bc.edu/cce) provide these options from their research:

1. Parish
2. Private/Religious sponsorship
3. Inter-parish
4. Diocesan
5. Private network
6. K-12 system
7. University partnerships
8. Faith-inspired charter schools

Their options, while helpful for stimulating discussion on a national level, overlap governance and school models. The first four parallel some of the governance models detailed by Monsignor Lagges. However, many of the school models above may have a variety of governance; a K-12 system, for example, could have any of the first four as basis governance. The last, strictly speaking, departs from canon law in its strictest sense: A charter school, "faith-inspired" or not, is a public school—completely subject to civil law and not relevant to canonical forms of governance. To see charter listed as an option in the research speaks to the funding issues inherent in providing a full education and begs the question as to whether Catholic schools will soon be the step-children to a growing charter movement, especially in the inner city.

The confusion between models and governance often does not emerge until planning or a crisis. As a matter of practical concern, the average school parent does not care how a school is governed as long as the school is managed well. The lack of canon law acumen is general condition for Catholic schools' stakeholders, and the question of governance emerges most often when things are not working well. From my own experience as witnessed by parental concern, lines of responsibility are unclear during crisis: "Oh, Lord to whom shall we go?" Frequent confusion as to "where the buck stops" at schools leads to the cardinal being contacted about a fourth grade teacher in a parish school before the pastor and the Office of Catholic Schools (oh, the joy to refer the calls for thirty-three of the forty high schools) being first contacted about issues in a school sponsored by a religious congregation. While most "petitioners" are open to an understanding of the governance and lines of authority, the lack of best practice/business model frustrates the most discerning. Frankly, they simply want it "fixed" expediently and fairly, and find the "pass off" of accountability annoying or disingenuous.

II. Some dioceses are responding to lack of sustainability, need for transparency, and accountability to stakeholders and donors in part by creating new models and/or examining governance.

On the local level, with the school budgets often being a part of the parish budget and the growing use of boards, lay persons often challenge the parish business model. As planning progresses, these boards often hit "the governance wall" and want to know what other models are out there which can empower their own leadership. On the (arch)diocesan level, the fiscal crisis is driving structural changes. As resources for the mission shrink, stark realities hit hard. For me, there is a further subtext: Has the fiscal crisis become a mission crisis? (Or is our mission crisis becoming a fiscal one?) My personal view tends toward the latter. Can we re-image our church as the real advocates for children, with strong academics flowing from our very faith as a catholic imperative open to all families?

In trying to answer the questions, many ordinaries have opened up new governance models with far-ranging implications. I gently but firmly suggest that details around these models be sought from these innovators, as the landscape is shifting, even from already announced plans:

1. Bridgeport, Connecticut: Pastors asked to sign over parish operation of schools to the Office of Catholic Schools for principals, finance, best academic and religious identity practice as a "system of schools," not a school system.

2. New York, New York: Ten regions establish their own deliberative local boards with ability to manage their own debt, supported by a sliding tax on parishes. Foundational "take over" of mission sites recently fell apart over facilities/parish patrimonies.

3. Brooklyn, New York: A two-tiered civil model (no corporation sole) with members responsible for appointment of director, Catholic identity. Directors are appointed by the members for each school's board, hire principals, and form key committees. Parishes host these "academies" for $1 per year; $7 million dollars to date from sliding scale assessments, particularly from those renting out former Catholic school buildings.

4. Philadelphia, Pennsylvania: Executive Board chaired by bishop. Four other boards in formation: elementary, secondary, religious education, and special needs. Faith formation in hands of parishes, but September 2012 saw seventeen high schools and four special needs elementary schools in a five year "management agreement" with a lay-led foundation to manage all but curriculum and standards (Catholic Schools Office).

Wichita, Kansas: Remains among the most traditional of stewardship models with tithing across the board allowing Catholic students to attend parish schools with little or no cost. Schools "belong to the whole church."

Like Los Angeles (the largest diocese in the U.S.), Chicago (with the largest Catholic school population) uses a variety of models and governance:

1. Parish: Works well in about one hundred sites, with strong pastor and principal leadership. If that strength changes around leadership, schools become vulnerable. However, current consensus is that, "If it ain't broke, don't fix it."

2. Direct AOC (with and without board): These are primarily high schools "abandoned" by religious communities or schools whose parishes have

closed, most in mission areas. Inherited in the days before strong boards of specified (limited) jurisdiction, these are often the most challenged.

3. Associations of the Christian Faithful (appointed by cardinal) as sponsors: The high school's ACF was formed when the religious community withdrew and is its own corporation; the elementary was opened to deliberately include inner city children of all socio-economic status and faiths and its board (appointed by ACF) rents buildings for $1 from two parishes (including the cathedral!) with responsibility for all operating and capital expenses.

4. AIM (Archdiocesan Initiative Model) hybrid: Begun as a pilot for fifteen schools (now with twenty-two and a waiting list), the pastor signs off all administrative duties and appointments, but remains responsible for spiritual formation. It is voluntary, for three years, with each parish contract custom-designed around parish facilities and support.

5. Religious Congregation sponsored (schools and networks): Most typically, a congregation sponsors each school corporation according to its charism. While termed "private," they are not: they serve at the cardinal's invitation.

6. Inter-parish

    - Single school: Four parishes building one school, rotating pastoral leadership.
    - Multiple system/consortium: Spiritual charter with shared board (all pastors as members) and executive director for three preK-5 schools and the formation of a new high-tech junior high.
    - Historical agreement/consolidations: Reduction of sites with signed agreements of support, often problematic as players and demographics change, especially as site pastor was left with "control."
    - "Virtual mergers": Two schools with one principal and pastor but respecting name and function of the individual parishes and schools with no formal agreement.

7. Other associations (not ACF): Lay governing boards of the interested faithful currently run schools "independently" of their Opus Dei and Legionnaires of Christ clergy, but are authorized as Catholic schools by the cardinal.

III. Governance and leadership are interconnected —and essential.
While new models are often compelled by the need for best practice to sustain the mission, clarity of roles is needed the start and as the models evolve. Great ideas do call for more nimble governance—but often the planning runs ahead,

often to fail because of lack of consensus around "who is in charge" or the facilities/patrimonial arrangements.

No matter what the model, it is clear that the lay board appears to be governance nexus today, both for individual school sites, a diocese, or the nation. The Sacred Heart Network implemented boards in the 1970's and, as one of their leaders recently told me, believe that the schools are now, while in their spirit, "fully owned" by the lay boards. School and regional boards are often mandates, although implementation and capacity varies widely.

Other sponsorship models are emerging: The Holy Childhood Schools have ten schools and co-sponsored schools which evidence a co-existence of a variety of reserved powers in a single "brand" of governance. With a two-tier board, half have seven reserved powers to the member board; the remainder one (mission, philosophy, and Catholicity) because of property ownership.

The Xaverian Brothers model of sponsorship is set up to grow—rather like an "adopt a charism" model, even though the board reserved powers are along traditional lines.

A final thought: No matter what the governance model, no Catholic school survives without strong and distributed leadership. Finding models which support this with power and transparency holds the same challenges as finding the leaders themselves.

Seminar

The Sacramental Life of the Parish: Selected Issues
Reverend Bruce Miller

The convention theme is "The Parish, Parish Life, and Leadership," a theme that touches upon many arenas in canon law. An important dimension of parish life of course is the criteria for admission to the sacraments. This paper is especially concerned with the initiation of infants, youth and young people as they develop. It will begin with a consideration of access to the sacraments in general. Then, it will focus more narrowly on the issues and concerns faced by the pastoral leadership and decision-makers of each parish family who determine who will be included and excluded when candidates are presented for the sacraments of baptism, confirmation, and first Eucharist. It seeks to discuss aspects of the just administration of these sacraments as a keystone of parish life and ministry.

This paper is not about the RCIA, as noteworthy as that development has been. It also does not seek to advocate a specific age for confirmation, the sequence of the initiation sacraments, or other debated topics. Rather, it is an attempt to provide canonists a ready reference in their ministry of forming and guiding pastoral leaders and decision makers in doing justice.

Church leaders do not have an exclusive claim on doing justice, however. "From injury and injustice to abstain"[1] is a phrase also found in the so-called Hippocratic Oath that has fallen out of vogue in modern-day medical schools. However, the call for medical doctors to do justice is still repeated frequently, no less than six (6) times in the "American College of Physicians Ethics Manual, Sixth Edition."[2] Doing justice to others and creating just environments is still the task of all the traditional professions.

From the canonical perspective this paper presents in a practical and proactive way the efforts that ought to be made to do justice rather than merely abstaining from injury in the parish setting. A fundamental contention that runs throughout this presentation is that doing justice is the foundation not merely of avoiding evil but also a positive expression of *caritas*.

---

1 "ἐπὶ δηλήσει δὲ καὶ τἀδικίῃ εἴρξειν"
2 Lois Snyder for the American College of Physicians Ethics, Professionalism, and Human Rights Committee "American College of Physicians Ethics Manual, Sixth Edition" *Annals of Internal Medicine*, 156 / 1 (2) (January 3, 2012) 75-104.

Pope Benedict XVI wrote in his first encyclical letter *Deus caritas est:*

> Love of neighbor ... consists in the very fact that, in God and with God, I love even the person whom I do not like or even know.... Love of neighbor, grounded in the love of God, is first and foremost a responsibility of each individual member of the faithful.... Love thus needs to be organized if it is to be an ordered service to the community. The awareness of this responsibility has had a constitutive relevance in the church from the beginning: 'All who believed were together and had all things in common; and they sold their possessions and goods and distributed them to all, as any had need' (Acts 2:44-45).[3]

Blessed Pope John Paul II, in his apostolic letter *Novo millennio ineunte*, on January 6, 2001, called for the Christian faithful not only to open their hearts to the love of God, but also to the service of all—especially the least, the last, and the lost.

The late Holy Father then reminds the faithful that relationships in the church "must all be clearly characterized by communion."[4] For this reason he said "the structures of participation envisaged by canon law ... must be ever more highly valued."[5] Quite naturally, there must be a "fruitful dialogue between pastors and faithful."[6]

The universal and particular laws of the church provide the means for pastoral actions that are fundamentally just. Beyond the just treatment of all without any arbitrariness, there is room for "promoting a trust and openness wholly in accord with the dignity and responsibility of every member of the People of God"[7] according to Pope John Paul II.

Such attention to justice coupled with a true spirituality of communion supplies the institutional reality of the church "with a soul"[8] as the late Holy Father put it.

The 'great commission' or the context for doing justice was given to the church and each member by Christ himself:

---

[3] Benedict XVI, encyclical *Deus caritas est*, December 25, 2005: *AAS* 98 (2006) 233-234.

[4] Pope John Paul II, apostolic letter *Novo millennio ineunte*, January 6, 2001: *AAS* 93 (2001) 298-299.

[5] Ibid.

[6] Ibid.

[7] Ibid.

[8] Ibid.

> And Jesus came and said to them, "All authority in heaven and on earth has been given to me. Go therefore and make disciples of all nations, baptizing them in the name of the Father and of the Son and of the Holy Spirit, and teaching them to obey everything that I have commanded you. And remember, I am with you always, to the end of the age."[9]

This commission is summed up for the pastor in the following canons from the 1983 Code of Canon Law. From these canons about the pastor, the mission of the parish itself and the responsibilities of all of its pastoral leadership and decision-makers as they encounter those who seek the sacraments in the context of parish life can also be deduced. In other words, while the canons speak specifically about the parish priest and many of his pastoral responsibilities they also provide an outline, *mutatis mutandis*, for the job descriptions of all the pastoral ministers and decision-makers in a parish, while defining its nature.

> Can. 528 §1: A pastor is obliged to make provision so that the word of God is proclaimed in its entirety to those living in the parish; for this reason, he is to take care that the lay members of the Christian faithful are instructed in the truths of faith, especially by means of the homily on Sundays and holy days of obligation and by offering catechetical instruction. He is to foster works through which the spirit of the Gospel is promoted, even in what pertains to social justice. He is to have a particular care for the Catholic education of children and youth. He is to make every effort, even with the collaboration of the Christian faithful, so that the message of the gospel comes also to those who have ceased the practice of their religion or do not profess the true faith.

The breadth, depth and full scope of bringing the word of God to even those who have turned a deaf ear to the gospel is a challenge that would bring any honest pastor to reciting a three-fold *mea culpa* for having fallen short. Even with the collaboration of the other Christian faithful, the creative ministry of hospitality that actively seeks to draw-in those who do not wish to take to heart the gospel is an arduous and sometimes irksome task. Nonetheless, it is necessary for the pastor to embrace hospitality so that his efforts and those of his coworkers are effective in the entirety of the territory of and among everyone within the parish. Therefore, a characteristic of the ambiance of the parish must be inclusivity such that all, not only find welcome should they happen to come, but also all are invited in such a way that the offer of friendship is compelling enough for them to desire to come and remain.

---

9 Matthew 28:18-20.

As a consequence, there should be a growing number of persons joining the church through the parish or returning to the practice of their Catholic faith each year.

> Can. 528 §2: The pastor is to see to it that the Most Holy Eucharist is the center of the parish assembly of the faithful. He is to work so that the Christian faithful are nourished by the devout celebration of the sacraments, and, in a special way, that they frequently approach the sacraments of the Most Holy Eucharist and penance. He is also to endeavor that they are led to practice prayer, including prayer even as families, and to take part consciously and actively in the sacred liturgy which, under the authority of the diocesan bishop, the pastor must direct in his own parish and is bound to watch over so that no abuses creep in.

What already had been said in a general way about the experience of the life of the parish is now specifically applied to the sacraments and foremost to the Holy Eucharist and reconciliation, noting the importance of participation consciously and actively in the sacred liturgy in accord with the liturgical norms. In this iteration it is expected that these efforts are effective so that attendance is notably frequent.

> Can. 529 §1: In order to fulfill his office diligently, a pastor is to strive to know the faithful entrusted to his care. Therefore he is to visit families, sharing especially in their cares, anxieties and, griefs of the faithful, strengthening them in the Lord, and prudently correcting them if they are failing in certain areas. With generous love he is to help the sick, particularly those close to death, by refreshing them solicitously with the sacraments and commending their souls to God; with particular diligence he is to seek out the poor, the afflicted, the lonely, those exiled from their country, and similarly those weighed down by special difficulties. He is to work so that spouses and parents are supported in fulfilling their proper duties and is to foster growth of Christian life in the family.

Empathy should characterize the pastor as he comes to know the people of his parish territory. Striving diligently he is to administer the sacraments to those notably weakened in anyway. Zeal should even bring him to admonish those who fall short. Above all he is to have a special care for the least, the last, and the lost. Finally, he is to cultivate family life and foster Christian values in the home.

The pastor is joined in his entire ministry, depending on the size and nature of the parish family, by a wide variety of volunteer to paid individuals who form a cadre with him. Whether the parish is large or small, a significant percentage of human resources are executing a plan based on carefully analyzed decisions usually in the form of programs. At other times, however, individuals or small groups are acting alone and spontaneously in the moment, usually in an unforeseen set of events that arguably require a solution and some that do not admit delay. In parishes, pastoral leaders and decision-makers vary greatly in organization and the need to be organized depending on the local circumstances.

Regardless, maxims that have guided decision-makers for centuries seem particularly useful, especially when they contribute to the just treatment of the Christian faithful. Their utility will be noted especially when the decision taken will affect the reception of a sacrament. One such set of rules are the *Regulae Iuris* of Boniface VIII. While not all are equally applicable in the parish setting, many can be the source of fruitful reflection and a sure guide to doing justice when contemplating a decision that involves the people of the parish, especially the various elements that come into play in dealing with the administration of the sacraments.

Often, when the parish representatives are called upon to respond, their decisions become binding and set precedents. Thus, reflection on and attempts to employ these principles of judgment and governance will avoid injury and assure justice. They are found in Latin and English in **Appendix A**.

Perhaps it is important to mention a few additional 'thoughts' concerning sacraments that pastoral ministers and decision-makers should know and keep in mind as they exercise their pastoral ministry:

- **First**, those who are to receive the sacraments, their parents and their sponsors are 'called to be saints,' but will not be canonized at the reception of whatever sacrament that is to be received; they will only live in a church of sinners inclusive of the pastoral leadership and decision-makers of the parish.
- **Second**, no one in the hierarchical communion of the church other than the Holy Father and a diocesan bishop can legislate concerning sacraments and any requirement, rule, guideline, or policy to the contrary is not binding.
- **Third**, the laws of the Holy Father and of a diocesan bishop can often be dispensed (disallowed in a particular case for a specific cause) and often are by the limited few who have a special faculty to do so.
- **Fourth**, no one, other than the Holy Father and those limited few he specifically allows by law, may create impediments (prohibitions) to any sacrament as to who may receive it or when it may be received.
- **Fifth**, follow the golden rule.
- **Sixth**, follow the silver rule (do not do unto others what you do not want done to you).
- **Seventh**, because "it" was done to you, you heard that it was done elsewhere or you saw it done, does not mean that it is in accord with the norm of canon or liturgical law or that it can or should be done by you.
- **Eighth**, religion textbooks and associated materials listed on the USCCB's

Conformity Review[10] webpage, the interactive *Catechism of the Catholic Church* and the current revision of the New American Bible, both on the bishops' website, assure the parish-decision makers that the tools employed in handing on the faith will be in conformity with one another and the magisterium.
- **Ninth**, because of their sensitive nature and the damage that may result, the use of psychological tests, psychological exercises, or psychotherapeutic techniques may not be used in classes, retreats, and other programing by those who are not qualified psychologist.[11]
- **Tenth**, no one has a right to require that an individual manifest his or her conscience in the external forum (e.g., you cannot require proof that someone attended Mass) much less use the same information obtained from the internal forum.

Rights to Sacraments and the Strict Interpretation of the Laws Governing Them

> Can. 18: Laws that prescribe a penalty, or restrict the free exercise of rights, or contain an exception to the law, are to be interpreted strictly.

When any law, guideline, policy, etc. by whatever name touches upon the free exercise of rights to obtain access to the sacraments of the church, canon 18 comes into consideration as the norm governing the interpretation of that statement. As is traditionally said, the words employed are to be construed in ways no more, no less, and no differently than their proper meaning, and therefore, not extended to encompass more circumstances or have a broader meaning than a narrow understanding would lend them. Precision is required in interpretation, therefore, so that every circumstance or person is given the benefit of the doubt, and no one is held to a higher standard to meet the requirements of the law or the requisites broadened or lowered so as to make one subject to the law not intentionally covered by the legislator.

The limitation of the rights of the Christian faithful, cleric and lay, are to be interpreted strictly. These rights are outlined in the context of obligations and duties that naturally arise from the nature of the institution of the church and when individuals or groups are recognized as naturally having them or they are granted them by law.

---

10   http://www.usccb.org/about/evangelization-and-catechesis/subcommittee-on-catechism/upload/Current-Conformity-List.pdf

11   Congregation for Catholic Education, *Guidelines for the Use of Psychology in the Admission and Formation of Candidates for the Priesthood*5, June 29, 2008. English translation in *Origins*, 38:23 (2008) 358-363. *Mutatis mutandis* this entire document should inform those who have a bent for mixing psychology and religious education or formation ministry at any level.

The universal law of the church as expressed in canon law or liturgical law cannot be reinterpreted in particular law or policy, guideline or other similar statement contrary to canon 18. Such a limitation may be imposed when explanations are drawn for distribution to candidates and parents or those who take their place by well-meaning pastoral leaders who unintentionally restrict the lawful freedom granted by the universal law.[12]

> Can. 213: The Christian faithful have the right to receive assistance from the sacred pastors out of the spiritual goods of the Church, especially the word of God and the sacraments.

This canon cannot be invoked apart from other canons touching upon the teaching and sanctifying offices. There is no place for canonical fundamentalism that reads one canon out of context or to the exclusion of other canons that more precisely deal with a particular matter. For instance, one could read this canon such that there is no right to baptism, since prior to baptism, one is not a member the Christian faithful. Such an interpretation would be absurd. Equally, one cannot demand that the diocesan bishop himself do all the teaching and administer all the sacraments. Rather, this canon provides the context that is to come later in the code in the book on the Teaching Office and in the book on the Sanctifying Office in canon 843. It is in that canon that primarily the rights of the Christian faithful and correspondingly the obligations of the ministers of the church will be more specifically delineated. Then, within the canons of each individual sacrament, even more specific requirements for their reception will be listed. It is to this final group of canons regarding specific sacraments that the strict interpretation required by canon 18 would more necessarily apply.

> Can. 217: Since they are called by baptism to lead a life in keeping with the teaching of the gospel, the Christian faithful have the right to a Christian education by which they are to be instructed properly to strive for the maturity of the human person and at the same time to know and live the mystery of salvation.

With this canon the language becomes formational and not merely educational as it begins to talk about a right to acquire those things necessary to strive for the maturity of the human person. When hearing the language of this canon, one cannot help but think of the four pillars (human, spiritual, intellectual and pastoral) around which seminarians and deacon candidates are to be formed as they prepare for ordination. To teach as Jesus did requires gifted educators who draw out of their charges their giftedness and inspire them to desire to know and

---

12 An interesting discussion of this principle of strict interpretation is found in Javier Otaduy, "Commentary on Canon 18," in *Exegetical Commentary on the Code of Canon Law*, English language edition ed. Ernesto Caparros et al. (Chicago and Montreal: Midwest Theological Forum and Wilson & Lafleur, 2004) [hereafter *Exegetical Commentary*] 1:338-345.

live a life of grace that brings about the salvation of human persons. This goal is a lofty one that is not easily achieved.

Sacraments in General

> Can. 843 §1: Sacred ministers cannot deny the sacraments to those who seek them at appropriate times, are properly disposed, and are not prohibited by law from receiving them.
>
> §2. Pastors of souls and other members of the Christian faithful, according to their respective ecclesiastical function, have the duty to take care that those who seek the sacraments are prepared to receive them by proper evangelization and catechetical instruction, attentive to the norms issued by competent authority.

It is not uncommon to hear canon 843 quoted out of context, that is, without reference to canon 843 §2. In §1 the burden of proof that one or more of these elements is lacking is, in fact, on the sacred ministers who cannot refuse the sacrament otherwise. Then, in the second paragraph not only are the clergy's duties specifically identified, but also other members of the Christian faithful are named and denoted as having specific responsibilities. These other members of the Christian faithful seem to be the very ones that have been called in this paper pastoral ministers and decision-makers in the parish. In this second paragraph it is clearly stated that there is a duty on the part of the leadership of parishes to receive those who seek the sacraments by proper evangelization and catechetical instruction. Indeed this description is of a proactive welcome and not merely a reactive exclusion to those who come.

This canon emphasizes that those who come seeking the sacraments are not to be simply delayed much less be denied and they are to be received in the spirit of evangelization and afforded catechetical instruction necessary to achieve the fruitful reception of the sacraments. It does not appear that this canon is here as an obstacle to those who approach asking for a sacrament but it is an exhortation to those who have the pastoral responsibility to evangelize and to catechize.

It is important to note, both for the sacraments that are not to be repeated and those that are to be received for the first time, that the candidate receiving the sacrament is not completing anything but commencing a journey in faith by grace. No sacrament is the celebration of the individual's perfection. Every sacrament is a sanctifying moment of grace that begins to operate effectively in the person's life.

It is not within the power of the pastor of souls or the other pastoral leadership and decision-makers in the parish to create impediments to the sacraments of salvation. It is only within their power to evangelize and catechize so that candidates or their parents ask more opportunely, are more rightly disposed and have the opportunity to overcome any impediments imposed by *legitimate* authority. Bearing this responsibility in mind, when questions arise in the parish setting; when devising their own policies or interpreting them; pastoral leaders will be advocates for the rights of the Christian faithful in the reception of the sacraments. This canon ultimately calls for the inclusion of persons and is not a measure for their exclusion in the reception of the sacraments at the beginning of the various phases of their faith journeys.

> Can. 846 §1: In celebrating the sacraments the liturgical books approved by competent authority are to be observed faithfully; accordingly, no one is to add, omit, or alter anything in them on one's own authority.

In many ways this canon is a continuation of canon 838. It is a reaffirmation also that the Christian faithful have a right to the celebration of the sacraments as the church proposes them and protects the Christian faithful from both innovation or anachronism, as creative and good intentioned as they may be.

The Baptism of Infants

> Can. 868 §1: For an infant to be baptized lawfully it is required:
>
> 1° that the parents, or at least one of them, or the person who lawfully holds their place, give their consent;
>
> 2° that there be a realistic hope that the child will be brought up in the Catholic religion. If such hope is truly lacking, the baptism is, in accordance with the provisions of particular law, to be deferred and the parents advised of the reason for this….
>
> Can. 872: In so far as possible, a person being baptized is to be assigned a sponsor. In the case of an adult baptism, the sponsor's role is to assist the person in Christian initiation. In the case of an infant baptism, the role is together with the parents to present the child for baptism, and to help it to live a Christian life befitting the baptized and faithfully to fulfill the duties inherent in baptism.
>
> Can. 873: One godfather or godmother at least, or even a male and female may assume the role.
>
> Can. 874 §1: To be admitted to undertake the office of godparent, a person must:

1° be appointed by the candidate for baptism, or by the parents or whoever stands in their place, or failing these, by the parish priest or the minister; to be appointed the person must be suitable for this role and have the intention of fulfilling it;

2° have completed sixteen years of age, unless a different age has been stipulated by the diocesan Bishop, or unless the parish priest or the minister considers that there is a just reason for an exception to be made;

3° be a catholic who has been confirmed and has received the blessed Eucharist, and who lives a life of faith which befits the role to be undertaken;

4° not labor under a canonical penalty, whether imposed or declared;

5° not be either the father or the mother of the person to be baptized.

§2 A baptized person who belongs to a non-Catholic ecclesial community may be admitted only in company with a catholic sponsor, and then simply as a witness to the baptism.

This present reflection has avoided repeating the fine standard commentaries, preferring to review anew two documents found in the *fontes*[13] of these canons but known to students long before the publication of the sources.

The *Rite of Baptism for Children* already contained many of the requirements similar to the ones that would be codified in 1983. By 1980 the Congregation for the Doctrine of the Faith with Cardinal Seper as Prefect, had become alarmed that there was some danger of the loss of the practice of infant baptism on account of the implementation of these provisions of the ritual following the revisions after the Second Vatican Council. An instruction *Pastoralis actio* was issued that sounds as though it might have been issued quite recently. It begins,

The pace of change in society, however, is making it difficult for the young to be brought up in the Faith and to persevere in it, and the resulting problems encountered by Christian parents and pastors have not been completely eliminated.[14]

---

13 Pontifical Commission for the Authentic Interpretation of the Code of Canon Law, *Codex Iuris Canonici fontium annotatione et indice analytico-alphabetico auctus* (Vatican City: Libreria Editrice Vaticana, 1989).

14 Sacra Congregatio pro Doctrina Fidei, instruction *Pastoralis actio* [*Past. Act.*], October 20, 1980, *AAS* 72 (1980) 1154-1155, #1 [both the Latin and English can be found on the Vatican website at present] (http://www.vatican.va/roman_curia/congregations/cfaith/documents/rc_con_cfaith_doc_19801020_pastoralis_actio_lt.htm); Sacred Congrega-

> Many parents are distressed to see their children abandoning the Faith and no longer receiving the sacraments, in spite of their own efforts to give them a Christian upbringing, and some pastors are asking themselves whether they should not be stricter before admitting infants to Baptism. Some think it better to delay the Baptism of children until the completion of a catechumenate of greater or less duration, while others are asking for a re-examination of the teaching on the necessity of Baptism, at least for infants, and wish the celebration of the sacrament to be put off until such an age when an individual can make a personal commitment, perhaps even until the beginning of adult life.[15]
>
> However, this questioning of traditional sacramental pastoral practice cannot fail to raise in the Church justified fears of jeopardizing so essential a doctrine as that of the necessity of Baptism. In particular, many parents are scandalized at finding Baptism refused or delayed when, with full awareness of their duty, they request it for their children.[16]

The instruction then concludes:

> In addressing the Bishops, the Congregation for the Doctrine of the Faith is fully confident that, as part of the mission that they have received from the Lord, they will take care to recall the Church's teaching on the necessity of infant Baptism, promote an appropriate pastoral practice, and bring back to the traditional practice those who, perhaps under the pressure of comprehensible pastoral concerns, have departed from it. The Congregation also hopes that the teaching and guidelines contained in this Instruction will reach all pastors, Christian parents and the ecclesial community, so that all will become aware of their responsibilities and make their contribution, through the Baptism of children and their Christian education, to the growth of the Church, the Body of Christ.[17]

What are the proper pastoral practices in light of the 1980 instruction and the 1983 code so that the practice of infant baptism would not be jeopardized

---

tion for the Doctrine of the Faith, Instruction on Infant Baptism, October 20, 1980, *CLD* 9:508-527 [The English from the Vatican website is used in the present text.] (http://www.vatican.va/roman_curia/congregations/cfaith/documents/rc_con_cfaith_doc_19801020_pastoralis_actio_en.html).

15 *Past. Act.*, #2.
16 *Past. Act.*, #3.
17 *Past. Act.*, #34.

by overly stringent requirements or that it would become a meaningless cultural ritual? In other words, how might the extremes be avoided?

To understand the view of the Congregation of the Doctrine of the Faith, let us journey to an even earlier response given after some three years of study. On July 13, 1970 in a private communication, Most Reverend Barthélemy-Pierre-Joseph Hanrion, O.F.M., Bishop of Dapango, Togo, was informed of the decision of the Cardinals of the Congregation that had been ratified by the Holy Father.[18] In it a distinction was drawn between the Christian parents, who were "regular" for whom it was said to be "normal" for them to desire to have their infants baptized as soon as possible after birth and parents who were not Christian or were "irregular Christians." The latter were characterized as those who would turn to Islam if baptism were not granted, and if it were, for the most part, the children would not receive a Catholic education. Among these irregular Christians were the polygamists, "concubinaries," lawful spouses who had abandoned all regular practice of their faith or who requested baptism of the infants for the sole reason of social propriety.

For the latter group, it was deemed sufficient that they were conscious of their responsibilities to rear the children as Christians and thus judgment by their proper pastors was to be passed based on the sufficiency of the guarantees made regarding the Catholic education of the infants to be baptized. These guarantees could be given by some member of the family or by the godfather or godmother. Or the sufficiency that could be found even in the support of the community of the faithful, would suffice. The guarantee was concerning the "founded hope of Catholic education." When these conditions were met, in the judgment of the pastors, the infants were to be baptized because "the infants were baptized in the faith of the Church."

Failing any finding of some evidence that would be sufficient to warrant baptism, infants were to be enrolled in a kind of catechumenate with a view to baptism later. Then, action was required of the clergy who were to have continual pastoral contacts with the infants as they matured and with their parents, with a view to eventual preparation and the reception of baptism.

This venture to Africa has not been in vain because very similar elements were mentioned again in the 1980 *Pastoralis actio*. In this document the traditional doctrine on baptism was reviewed as well as the teaching of the magisterium. Then, the church's mission was outlined. In Part Two, in light of the teaching that had been recalled some of the current - day concerns were reviewed.

---

18   It is cited in the *fontes* of c. 868 §1, 2°, but had long been known before its publication. Sacred Congregation for the Doctrine of the Faith, Response [Private], July 13, 1970: *CLD* VII 592-594. It is only referenced on the Vatican website as a CDF document.

Concerning the link between baptism and a personal act of faith the document echoes the 1970 response stating, "Baptism is never administered without faith: in the case of infants, it is the faith of the Church."[19] The document insists on the deposit of Christ in the person of the child who is thereby not deprived of freedom, once consciousness and freedom awake. Lamentably, it noted the possibility that the child may indeed reject the grace given. Against the notion that baptism is only suitable in a homogeneous society and is inappropriate in a pluralistic one, the document astutely notes:

> It is worth adding that all too often pluralism is being invoked in a paradoxical way, in order to impose on the faithful behavior patterns that in reality are an obstacle to the exercise of their Christian freedom.
>
> In a society whose mentality, customs and laws are no longer inspired by the Gospel it is therefore of great importance that in questions connected with infant Baptism the Church's own nature and mission should be taken into consideration before all else…. In particular with regard to infant Baptism… [the Church's] practice must not depend only on criteria borrowed from the human sciences.[20]

Finally, the document answers those who would criticize the baptism of infants on the ground that it is a practice merely serving the numerical proliferation of the church. Here again, it is mentioned that children are baptized into the faith of the church and is for the purpose of gifting them with eternal life, not for statistical gain.

In the third part, the suggestion of the definitive abandonment of infant baptism or even offering a choice between immediate and deferred baptism were all to be rejected. Rather, two principles were enunciated: first, baptism, since it is necessary for salvation and is a blessing to infants, must not be delayed and second, assurances were required that the gift would be nurtured by an authentic education in the faith and Christian life. Not surprisingly, these assurances were allowed from the parents or close relatives and then it was said that "various substitutions are possible within the Christian community." Only if the assurances were not serious or if they were non-existent can the sacrament of baptism be "refused."[21]

Again, the distinction was drawn between believing families and families with little faith or non-Christian families.

---

19 *Past. Act.*, #18.
20 *Past. Act.*, #24.
21 *Past. Act.*, #28.

It noted that all the rules for believing families were given in the introduction to the baptismal ritual, notably at number 8. It stipulated that, unlike the prior ritual, the parents have priority over the godparents who still were to assist in the education of the child. Also, special importance is to be given at the time to prayer, catechesis, and appropriate advice. There was no sense of a need to rush from the birth to the baptism. The document counsels consideration of the welfare of the child and the mother that she may be present, giving time for preparation and actual celebration in keeping with the Paschal character of the sacrament unless there was a danger of death of the child.

While the document spoke of "refusal" of baptism as noted above, in no sense should this statement be interpreted as a summary dismissal. Rather, pastors must have had a dialogue with families with little faith or non-Christian families. The instructions were all rather precise:

> In this case, the pastor will endeavor by means of a clear-sighted and understanding dialogue to arouse the parents' interest in the sacrament they are requesting and make them aware of the responsibility that they are assuming.
>
> In fact, the Church can only accede to the desire of these parents if they give an assurance that, once the child is baptized, it will be given the benefit of the Christian upbringing required by the sacraments. The Church must have a founded [reasonable] hope that the Baptism will bear fruit.
>
> If the assurances given – for example, the choice of godparents will take sincere care of the child or the support of the community of the faithful – are sufficient, the priest cannot refuse to celebrate the Sacrament without delay, as in the case of children of Christian families. If on the other hand, they are insufficient, it will be prudent to delay Baptism. However, the pastors should keep in contact with the parents so as to secure, if possible, the conditions required on their part for the celebration of the sacrament. If even this solution fails, it can be suggested, as a last recourse, that the child be enrolled in a catechumenate to be given when the child reaches school age.[22]

The rules were then clarified since they had already been in force as of the publication of the baptismal ritual. Thus, one could in no way speak of "refusal" as it is generally understood, but rather of a need for a pedagogical delay that looked to the advancement of the family in faith as it became more aware of its responsibility. In no sense was it envisioned that such faith development could transpire in a vacuum or on its own. Otherwise, the action to delay would be

---

22 *Past. Act.*, #30.

tantamount to denial. With regard to the promises made, it was sufficient that there was a reasonable or realistic hope[23] that the children would have a Christian upbringing.

Furthermore, for those for whom baptism was delayed, there was to be no ceremony since it might have been mistaken for baptism. Rather, they were to be presented later in the Rites of Christian Initiation as Children of Catechetical Age. Mention was then made that in no way did the church consider it preferable or typical to delay baptism until such an age.

Finally, if Christian families were to live in areas where there was a proliferation of families of little faith or non-Christian families, special provision was to be made so that they may retain their full right to have their infants baptized shortly after birth as usual.

The role of the family in the parish community had also been highlighted. Notably, the whole spectrum from care for engaged couples, young marrieds without children and families with children should have received special attention and catechetical formation concerning the baptism of infants. This whole undertaking was to be a task for the parish community as it undertook the preparation and celebration of the baptism of infants.

A note on translation: Both the Latin 1980 document and canon 868 §1 use the phrase "*spes fundata.*" A proper translation may be "well-founded hope" as found in some English editions. It may also be rendered "reasonable hope," "realistic hope" or "founded hope." The context sets out the minimum requirements, not the ideal ones. Thus, the optimal translation would seem to be denoted a less stringent option.

Moreover, it should be further considered that the hope required has no specified object for the one in whom it is to be placed. It is possible that the hope could be placed in the godparents. The whole tradition of having godparents springs from their responsibility for the spiritual formation of their godchild. It could be placed in the grandparents who might have the greatest influence both on the parents and the grandchild to be baptized. It might be in the fact that older siblings are attending a Catholic school or the religious education program of the parish. It might even be placed in the excellence and success of the parish's outreach to parents just such as the ones asking for the baptism of their child.

Furthermore, one should recall that only one parent need make the request for the baptism. If this is the requirement, then it cannot be adduced that a child's baptism can be delayed because both parents do not attend Mass. Moreover, it would seem that it cannot be demanded that the parents or godparents manifest

---

23 A further reflection on the translation of *spes fundata* can be found below.

their consciences in order to obtain what by right they request for the child.

In light of these considerations, one wonders if it is appropriate pastoral practice to require extensive training or indeed repeated training by parents who wish to have their children baptized. What is accomplished by a pastor requiring registration in the parish, letters of testimony on behalf of the parents or the godparents, or a record of giving? Does a stricter approach in fact not run the risk, as suggested in 1980, that the baptism of infants will be a thing of the past in the church? Will full initiation in the church later in life become the norm rather than the exception, because infant baptism has become so difficult to achieve? Is there a kind of profiling going on in our parishes as people approach and some have their infants baptized and others are put through rather rigorous ordeals? Are parents actually being turned away from the church without the kind of evangelization *Pastoralis actio* envisions?

If baptism is necessary for salvation, and the gateway to the sacraments, then efforts in the church to promote an appropriate pastoral practice and restore traditional infant baptism might need to be revisited.

Appendix B offers a form letter developed for responding to parishes when proof that godparents, where they are unknown, are qualified to stand in a baptism. These letters of reference can contain all sorts of information, sometimes very personal information that need not be divulged. This form is an attempt to assist parish ministers in responding with 'no more, no less and no different' than what must be said. Whether such a letter should be required is not being scrutinized here, but offers the means of a proper response.

Index A

Here and elsewhere in this paper a species of an annotated index relating specifically to the three sacraments of initiation at their reception at the appropriate developmental ages have been presented from the various editions of *Roman Replies and CLSA Advisory Opinions*. The items shared have been presented chronologically. These summaries do not adequately address the issues canonically and the original opinions alone should be deemed truly reliable and sufficiently nuanced.

Can a member of the Orthodox Church function as a godparent at a Catholic baptism? Yes, provided that the other godparent is a fully qualified Catholic.[24]

---

24   J. James Cuneo and John D. Faris, "Canon 874: Members of Greek Orthodox Church as Sponsors at Catholic Baptism," in *RRAO 1988*, ed. William A. Schumacher and J. James Cuneo (Washington, DC: CLSA, 1988) 83-87.

Can a former Catholic be a godparent or Christian witness at a Catholic baptism? No, in either case; no one is a "former Catholic." Thus by canon 874 §2 the person cannot be a witness since s/he is not a non-Catholic. By canon 874 §1, 3°, since s/he is excommunicated, s/he cannot be a godparent because s/he is also failing to lead a life in harmony with the faith.[25]

Can the sacrament of baptism be denied in accord with canon 843? No, but it can be delayed only if the conditions for delay are being met by the ones who offer this pastoral solution. While the denial of some sacraments cannot always be seen as a penalty and therefore subject to a process, e.g. the refusal of absolution to a non-repentant sinner,[26] the delay of baptism has been foreseen in law.

May a child who has reached the "age of reason" petition of his or her own accord for baptism–and by implication for the other sacraments of initiation? Canon 852 would specifically permit one who has reached the age of reason to petition for his or her own baptism if the requisites of canon 865, in accord with the child's age, have been duly met. Thus, the canons on baptism provide an exception to canon 98 § 2.[27]

When, and under what circumstances, is it permissible to delay baptism in accord with cann. 852, 865 and 868? There must be true freedom and the intention to be "incorporated" into the church after a sufficient period of instruction and testing during the catechumenate corresponding to the local circumstances, especially where many inhabitants have a totally different way of life or even one opposed to Christian life. For infants particular law must be observed and parents have to be informed of the reason that there is a delay. The founded hope in an infant's baptism is based on observable facts in local circumstances.[28]

Can a Catholic unable to receive the Eucharist act as a godparent? No, the role of godparent is truly an ecclesial function (an *officium*; see: *Catechism of the Catholic Church,* #1235 and *Sacrosanctum concilium* #67). As such, both the

---

25 John M. Huels, "Canon 874: Ex-Catholic as Christian Witness at Baptism," in *RRAO 1988*, ed. William A. Schumacher and J. James Cuneo (Washington, DC: CLSA, 1988) 87-88.

26 John M. Huels, "Canon 843: Denial of a Sacrament without Due Process," in *RRAO 1991*, ed. Kevin W. Vann and Lynn Jarrell (Washington, DC: CLSA, 1991) 86-90.

27 J. James Cuneo, "Canons 852 and 865: Right of Adolescent to Baptism," in *RRAO 1995*, ed. Kevin W. Vann and James I. Donlon (Washington, DC: CLSA, 1995) 62-66.

28 Stephanus Wellens, "Canons 852, 865, and 868: The Lawful Reception of Baptism," in *RRAO 1997*, ed. Kevin W. Vann and James I. Donlon (Washington, DC: CLSA, 1997) 65-66.

baptismal ritual and canon 874 §1, 3° require that the godparent live in harmony with the faith of the church.[29]

Does baptism by a Catholic clergyman always incorporate the child of non-Catholic parents into the Catholic Church? Yes, the baptism of anyone by a Catholic clergyman always results in the incorporation of that person into the Catholic Church.[30]

What are the responsibilities of a Christian witness at a baptism? There are essentially none.[31]

May a child be baptized with the consent of only one parent as provided in canon 868 §1, 1°? This is one area addressed in the literature and not resolved. In practice it would seem that the implementation of this provision has many potential pitfalls. Thus, it would not be prudent to summarize here one or several answers. Rather, in each difficult circumstance as it is presented, both canonical and legal counsel should be obtained and an equitable course of action followed.

First Holy Communion of Youth

> Can. 912: Any baptized person not prohibited by law can and must be admitted to Holy Communion.

The requirement enunciated in canon 912 is somewhat stark and startling. It cannot be read out of context, however. First, canon 844 concerning *communicatio in sacris* has established limits to the access to the sacraments by those validly baptized but who are not Roman Catholic. It applies even to those persons, and in the case at hand to youth, making their first Holy Communion. Therefore, "*quilibet baptizatus*" does not really mean "any" validly baptized youth, but those who meet the requirements of canon 844 and any other applicable laws. Then, the following canons outline other considerations.

> Can. 913 §1: The administration of the Most Holy Eucharist to children requires that they have sufficient knowledge and careful prepa-

---

29 William H. Woestman, "Canon 874: Catholic in Invalid Marriage as Godparent," in *RRAO 1998*, ed. F. Stephen Pedone and James I. Donlon (Washington, DC: CLSA, 1998) 65-66.

30 J. Michael Ritty, "Canon 844: Baptism of Child of Non-Catholic Parents by Catholic Priest," in *RRAO 2000*, ed. F. Stephen Pedone and James I. Donlon (Washington, DC: CLSA, 2000) 65-66.

31 Edward N. Peters, "Canon 874, §2: Responsibilities of Christian Witness at Baptism," in *RRAO 2008*, ed. Joseph J. Koury and Siobhan M. Verbeek (Washington, DC: CLSA, 2008) 94-95.

ration so that they understand the mystery of Christ according to their capacity and are able to receive the body of Christ with faith and devotion.

§2. The Most Holy Eucharist, however, can be administered to children in danger of death if they can distinguish the body of Christ from ordinary food and receive communion reverently.

In the first section of this canon, the bar is set to give meaning to the proper preparation and disposition the child must achieve before being admitted to receiving first Holy Communion. Then this next section lowers the requirements so that a child in danger of death may receive the Most Holy Eucharist even though s/he does not achieve this greater level of knowledge or has fully reached the age of reason. Although not mentioned here, it would seem that this section provides an alternative standard as well for the accommodation that is to be made for children who are mentally challenged in accord with canon 777, 4°. As noted in the subsequent canon, it is ultimately for the pastor to make the judgment concerning when those who are in danger of death or those who are not foreseen to be able to acquire the expected knowledge in the typical way can receive Holy Communion.

Can. 914: It is primarily the duty of parents and those who take the place of parents, as well as the duty of pastors, to take care that children who have reached the use of reason are prepared properly and, after they have made sacramental confession, are refreshed with this divine food as soon as possible. It is for the pastor to exercise vigilance so that children who have not attained the use of reason or whom he judges are not sufficiently disposed do not approach Holy Communion.

The age at which a child reaches the use of reason figures not only in the first reception of the Eucharist, but also is the age at which one is capable of receiving the sacraments of penance, confirmation, and anointing of the sick. It should be noted that in accord with canon 97 §2, as of the seventh birthday a minor is presumed to have the use of reason; before that age the presumption is to the contrary. This is a legal presumption that can be overturned by contrary proofs.

The question naturally arises what defines 'children who have reached the age of reason'? Reading the decree *Quam singulari*[32] of the Sacred Congregation of the Sacraments, approved by St. Pius X, is very instructive since it seeks to clarify universal law as of the time of the Lateran Council in 1215 and is the

---

32   Sacred Congregation for the Sacraments, decree *Quam singulari*, August 8, 1910. *AAS* 2 (1910) 577-583. Petri Gasparri, ed, *Codicis Iuris Canonici Fontes* (Vatican: Typis Polyglottis) 5 (1930) 80-85.

touch-point of subsequent legislation and instructions.[33] Most of the decree is devoted to defining the age of reason.[34]

It makes clear that there is but one and the same age at which children of both sexes begin to reach the use of reason, however. Prior to this decree, sometimes a younger age for the use of reason for children relative to confession and an older age for the use of reason relative to the reception of first Holy Communion were employed. At other times both sacraments were delayed to as late as fourteen years of age.

Following St. Thomas Aquinas, the decree emphasizes the **beginning of some kind** of use of reason (*incipiunt aliqualem usum rationis* – emphasis in the original) was denoted as the time when a child might be able to conceive a devotion to the Eucharist. The moral theologian St. Anthony is then quoted in the decree in order to make the definition more precise, leading into the teaching of the Council of Trent. From St. Anthony and the council, comes the notion that the use of discretion is tied or linked to the capacity to sin (mortally; "*dolus*").[35] As a consequence, it is argued, once there is recognized in the child a capacity to sin, the child is compelled to receive the Eucharist in order to restore grace lost by sin. There are two implicit presumptions within the decree: 1) if a child can sin, he or she has sinned; 2) confession always precedes Holy Communion.

The following norms from the decree provide an understanding of its tenor that has influenced current law:

1. The age of discretion, both for Confession and for Holy Communion, is the time when a child begins to reason, that is about the seventh year, more or less. From that time on begins the [annual] obligation of fulfilling the precept of both Confession and Communion.

2. A full and perfect knowledge of Christian doctrine is not necessary either for First Confession or for First Communion. Afterwards, however, the child will be obliged to learn gradually the entire Catechism according to his ability.

3. The knowledge of religion which is required in a child in order to be properly prepared to receive First Communion is such that he will understand according to his capacity those Mysteries of faith which are necessary as a

---

33 For a contemporaneous study see: F. M. De Zulueta, *Early first Communion: a commentary upon the decree "Quam singulari"* (London: R. & T. Washbourne, 1911).

34 It should be noted that the phrases 'the age of reason' or 'the age of discretion' are used synonymously in the document and herein.

35 Arturo Lobo, et al., *Comentarios al Codigo de Derecho Canonico* (Madrid: Biblioteca de Autores Cristianos, 1963) 2:324.

means of salvation (*necessitate medii*) and that he can distinguish between the Bread of the Eucharist and ordinary, material bread, and thus he may receive Holy Communion with a devotion becoming his years.

4. The obligation of the precept of Confession and Communion which binds the child particularly affects those who have him in charge, namely, parents, confessor, teachers and the pastor. It belongs to the father, or the person taking his place, and to the confessor, according to the Roman Catechism, to admit a child to his First Communion.[36]

As one can see in the text cited, the nuances of the current law as well as its forerunner in the 1917 code are evident.

On the other hand, from April 15-17, 1986 the Congregation for the Sacraments addressed the issue of placing first confession before first Holy Communion. It is noted by the congregation that children are to be prepared for first confession, not so much because of the state of sin in which they may be, but with a formative and pastoral aim. Cultivating in children who have reached the age of reason a sense of sin, even venial sin helps them grow in self-knowledge and self-control while encouraging them to seek pardon from God. At the same time they experience the serene joy of having abandoned themselves to the loving mercy of the Father through the absolute forgiveness or absolution of the priest.[37]

The qualifications for first penance and first Holy Communion are no more demanding than the requirements for infant baptism. Rather than restricting the sacraments to the highly qualified, they are open to those who are only beginning minimally to understand the call to holiness, the exercise of their own free will contrary to those who love them, the gift of forgiveness, and the restoration to grace through Eucharist. In light of the correction and restoration initiated under St. Pius X, a just administration by pastoral ministers and decision makers in the parish family, the first experience of penance and Holy Communion require that religious formation for these sacraments carefully take into account the develop-

---

36 http://www.papalencyclicals.net/Pius10/p10quam.htm

37 A circular letter from the Congregation for the Sacraments dated December 20, 1986 and sent to the President of the National Conference of Catholic Bishops destined for the bishops and tribunals of the United States in *RRAO 1987*, ed. William A. Schumacher and J. James Cuneo (Washington, DC: CLSA, 1987) 12-13. See also the address of Blessed John Paul II, Address to the Participants of the Plenary Assembly of the Congregation for Divine Worship and Discipline of the Sacraments (April 17, 1986). Also see a dialogue between a diocesan bishop and the same Congregation, including the notations of the mother of children, in the same volume of *RRAO* pages 13-20 on the issue of whether first penance should precede first Holy Communion.

(http://www.vatican.va/holy_father/john_paul_ii/speeches/1986/april/documents/hf_jp-ii_spe_19860417_congregazione-sacramenti_it.html.)

mental ages of the children as they approach their seventh birthdays.

Pastoral ministers, especially those who lead and teach children approaching seven years of age, from about the age of five, should be on the watch for notably weakened youngsters who have physical or mental conditions. Special efforts should be made so that these precious children in the eyes God are not deprived of the Eucharist and subsequently of the anointing of the sick. Then, after observation, others, who for various reasons may be more mature in relation to their grade-level, should be prepared in order that they may work toward self-mastery aided by the assistance of their parents, teachers and parish priests; in time they should be admitted first to the sacrament of penance and later to the sacrament of the Eucharist.

While there is every reason to admit those who have reached the age of discretion well before their seventh birthdays, it is equally prudent not to admit those who have crossed that mark and yet have not shown any signs of moving beyond the age of innocence.

It should be noted that the child who has reached the use of reason, should actually ask to receive the sacraments of first penance and first Holy Communion. While canon 914 spells out for the parents a roll in preparation, there is no mention of any requirements that they must meet in order to be deemed suitable to present a child for first penance or first Holy Communion. Furthermore, the pastors are to arrange for the appropriate preparation of the child and then to judge whether the child been properly disposed and has reach the age of reason before approaching Holy Communion. Therefore, it cannot be adduced from the law that any extraneous demands can be made of the parents that would qualify their children for the reception of the sacrament. Moreover, it would seem that it cannot be demanded that the child or parents manifest their consciences in order to obtain what by right the child requests.

Some part in the preparation of the child for the reception of these sacraments by the parents or those who take their place can be expected. It can be properly argued, that the parents might be required to prepare for this role of teaching their children about the sacraments of penance and Eucharist. It does not appear to be a possibility for requiring registration in the parish, letters of testimony on behalf of the parents, or a record of giving.

Again it is appropriate to ask whether a stricter approach, in fact, does not run the risk, that the first Holy Communion, preceded by first penance, will be unduly delayed? Will reception of the sacraments later in life become the norm rather than the exception, because they have become so difficult to achieve? Is there a kind of profiling going on in our parishes as people approach and some have access and others are put through rather rigorous ordeals? Are parents actually being turned away from the church contrary to the spirit of the new evangelization?

Index B

Interestingly the issue of first Holy Communion and, with it, first penance is addressed only once in *RRAO* over the years.

Since first confession is required before first Holy Communion, must a child who cannot go to confession, such as one who suffers from autism and is unable to communicate with a priest, be excluded from receiving Holy Communion? No. Canon 913 §2 provides a guide for exceptional circumstances. And Pope Benedict XVI clearly states: "whenever possible, eucharistic communion should be made available to mentally handicapped, if they are baptized and confirmed: they receive the Eucharist in the faith also of the family or the community that accompanies them."[38]

The Confirmation of Young People

In the traditional order of the sacraments of initiation, confirmation precedes the sacrament of Holy Communion. When celebrated apart from baptism, the sacrament of penance would precede confirmation and is normative when it and first Holy Communion are received in the same Mass around the age of discretion.

Sequentially in this paper confirmation is being treated after first Holy Communion since most of what has been said relative to its reception and that of first penance could be repeated *mutatis mutandis* regarding confirmation. The only notable differences in the canons themselves is that in the danger of death, even an infant is able to be confirmed or, in the judgment of the minister some other grave cause suggests that it is appropriate to confirm someone not meeting the qualification of age as determined by the conference of bishops and particular law.

In the United States the options for conferral of confirmation on youth is contained in the following complementary norm that was effective, July 1, 2002:

> The National Conference of Catholic Bishops, in accord with the prescriptions of canon 891, hereby decrees that the Sacrament of Confirmation in the Latin Rite shall be conferred between the age of discretion and about sixteen years of age, within the limits determined by the diocesan bishop and with regard for the legitimate exceptions given in canon 891.

---

38 William H. Woestman, "Canon 914: Admission of Autistic Child to Holy Communion," in *RRAO 2008*, ed. Joseph J. Koury and Siobhan M. Verbeek (Washington, DC: CLSA, 2008) 100-101.

What has been said about the sponsor for baptism can be said about the sponsor required for the celebration of confirmation. Thus, that discussion will also not be repeated.

> Can. 889 §1: Every baptized person not yet confirmed and only such a person is capable of receiving confirmation.
>
> §2. To receive confirmation licitly outside the danger of death requires that a person who has the use of reason be suitably instructed, properly disposed, and able to renew the baptismal promises.
>
> Can. 890: The faithful are obliged to receive this sacrament at the proper time. Parents and pastors of souls, especially pastors of parishes, are to take care that the faithful are properly instructed to receive the sacrament and come to it at the appropriate time.
>
> Can. 891: The sacrament of confirmation is to be conferred on the faithful at about the age of discretion unless the conference of bishops has determined another age, or there is danger of death, or in the judgment of the minister a grave cause suggests otherwise.

When the age of confirmation is set well beyond the age of reason or even at the upper limit, it must be noted that the requirements for the sacrament clearly are not those for graduation from a high school religion program. Regardless of the age, however, at which it is administered,

> Can. 879: The sacrament of confirmation strengthens the baptized and obliges them more firmly to be witnesses of Christ by word and deed and to spread and defend the faith. It imprints a character, enriches by the gift of the Holy Spirit the baptized continuing on the path of Christian initiation, and binds them more perfectly to the Church.

The readiness to receive the sacrament of confirmation at any age is to be measured against this canon beginning at the age of discretion and outside of special circumstances. The age-appropriate and person-appropriate formation process involves developing a fertile and receptive ground for the gift of the Spirit. The sacramental gift will be able to oblige the candidate, *by a comparative degree*, more firmly to be a witness of Christ and that binds him or her, *by a comparative degree*, more completely to adhere to the church.

It is to be noted furthermore, that *the superlative degree* is not used in describing the effect of the sacrament. Thus the task of the formation program and the questions at the time of the judgments that are to be made about readiness concern the betterment of the person and his or her overall formation in the faith as well as willingness to practice it and share it with others. Confirmation is a sacrament of initiation not of accomplishment.

In the Roman Replies section of the *RRAO* of 2006 at canon 891 there is recorded a series of letters between the Congregation for Divine Worship and Discipline of the Sacraments and a diocesan bishop. They are introduced as follows:

> *A diocesan bishop established a policy concerning the age of the reception of the Sacrament of Confirmation for the local diocese. The parents of a youngster in that diocese sought to have their child confirmed at an age below that set by diocesan policy. The bishop denied the parents' request on behalf of their child. He explained that he was not refusing administration of the sacrament but only delaying its reception at a later time, at the age set by diocesan policy. The parents appealed the bishop's decision to the Congregation for Divine Worship and Discipline of the Sacraments.*[39]

There are a total of four letters from the congregation to the diocesan bishop insisting that the young lady be confirmed. The diocesan bishop immediately acknowledged in a response to the first that she was well instructed and explained that he was merely delaying her reception of the sacrament in accord with diocesan policy. Unfortunately, this is the only letter published from the diocesan bishop.

Of particular interest in this study is the third letter from the congregation in which its authoritative decision is pronounced. It should be noted as inferred that the congregation had already twice attempted to have the bishop dispense from his particular law and confirm the young lady. The dispositive part of the "authoritative examination" affirms:

> In reply to this Congregation's decision that appropriate steps be taken to provide for her confirmation in the near future, Your Excellency had proposed essentially two [contrary] arguments:
>
> 1. Though willingly admitting that she is well instructed and that her parents are very good Catholics, you point out that "instruction is not the sole criterion for recognizing the opportune time for confirmation.... The evaluation is a pastoral one which involves much more than just being instructed."
>
> 2. Your Excellency indicated that the Diocesan Policy establishing that conferral of the sacrament is to be no earlier than the sophomore

---

[39] "Canon 891: Age for the Reception of the Sacrament of Confirmation," in *RRAO 2006*, ed. F. Stephen Pedone and Paul D. Counce (Washington, DC: CLSA, 2006) 22.

year of high school is within the right inherent in the law in light of the legislation complementary to can 891 for the United States of America.

With respect to Your Excellency's first point, it is no doubt true that there is a pastoral judgment to be made in such cases, provided that by "pastoral judgment" one is speaking of the obligation of the Sacred Pastors to determine whether those elements required by the revised *Code of Canon Law* are indeed present, namely, that the person be baptized, have the use of reason, be suitably instructed, and be properly disposed and able to renew the baptismal promises (cf. cann. 843 §1; 889 §2). This Dicastery notes from the testimony submitted by the family, as well as that provided by Your Excellency, that it is clear this young girl has satisfied each of the canonical requisites for reception of the sacrament.

In regard to Your Excellency's second point, while it is clear that the Diocesan Policy is within the right inherent in the law in light of the complementary legislation of the United States for can 891, it is also clear that any such complementary legislation must always be interpreted in accord with the general norm of law. As has been stated before, the *Code of Canon Law* legislates that Sacred Ministers may not deny the sacraments to those who opportunely ask for them, are properly disposed and are not prohibited by law from receiving them (cf. can. 843 §1). Since it has been demonstrated that she possesses these requisite qualities, any other considerations, even those contained in the Diocesan Policy, need to be understood in subordination to the general norms governing the reception of sacraments.

The Congregation considers it useful to point out that it is the role of the parents as the primary educators of their children and then of the Sacred Pastors to see that candidates for the reception of the Sacrament of Confirmation are properly instructed to receive the sacraments and come to it at the opportune time (cf. can. 890). Consequently, when a member of the faithful wishes to receive the sacrament, even though not satisfying one or more elements of the local legislation (e.g., being younger than the designated age for ministration of the sacrament), those elements must give way to the fundamental right of the faithful to receive the sacraments. Indeed, the longer the conferral of the sacrament is delayed after the age of reason, the greater will be the number of candidates who are prepared for its reception but are deprived of its grace for a considerable period of time.

In conclusion, this Congregation for Divine Worship must insist ... that the opportunity to receive the Sacrament of Confirmation be extended ... as soon as is conveniently possible.[40]

Apparently, the diocesan bishop responded pleading that he believed to accede to the instructions of the congregation would be perceived by certain local groups as undermining his authority. The fourth letter from the congregation contained an apology for not understanding his uncomfortable situation and asked that the bishop "communicate to me [the Prefect] at your earliest convenience your own suggestions."[41] These "suggestions" clearly were to indicate how the diocesan bishop intended to comply with the instructions of the congregation and confirm the young lady sooner than he wished.

Also denoted in this letter were the motives of the congregation in making its decision that are: protection of access of the faithful to the Holy See when their rights might be unjustly infringed or overlooked; and the application of particular and universal law with *aequitas canonica*. The letter indicated that this latter principle contains within itself "the notion of a dispensation in order to avoid an excessive *rigor iuris*, thus making certain exception[s] which are always intended for the sake of the spiritual good of the faithful, as contrasted with the ordinances of civil law."[42]

Appendix C presents a sample of a diocesan policy that delays confirmation until near the end of high school. It attempts to take into consideration the various circumstances in which young people are being formed and the realities of a scattered, rural diocese. It is also an attempt to respect the right that these young people have to the sacrament so that it is not denied by truly burdensome requirements, stringently enforced.

Index C

Is the conferral of confirmation by a schismatic bishop valid? Yes, the confirmation is valid if the bishop is validly ordained.[43]

When children of catechetical age are initiated in accord with the Rite of Christian Initiation of Adults (RCIA), may the required administration of confirmation be delayed until the time their peer-group is formed and administered the sacrament? No. Only in danger of death, when the person

---

40 Ibid., 27-28.

41 Ibid., 29.

42 Ibid., 29.

43 John M. Huels, "Canons 535 and 882: Confirmation of Baptized Catholics in a Schismatic Church," in *RRAO 1993*, ed. Kevin W. Vann and James I. Donlon (Washington, DC: CLSA, 1993) 43-45.

who baptizes is a lay person or deacon, or when a priest baptizes and does not have the sacred chrism available may the sacrament of confirmation legitimately be omitted.[44]

Is it possible for children around or after the age of discretion to be confirmed before the reception of first Holy Communion even if the diocesan practice is confirmation at a later age? Yes, the diocesan bishop can certainly dispense from his own law. The candidate can be from around seven to sixteen years of age, in conformity with the complementary norm established by the Conference of Bishops with the *recognitio* of the Holy See. If the diocesan bishop does not confer confirmation himself, he can delegate a priest to do so.[45]

May a stepparent who has not legally adopted a child serve as that same person's confirmation sponsor? Yes, so long as the child is not been legally adopted by the stepparent before the confirmation. Since laws are not retroactive in their effect, if a sponsor were to adopt the person who was his or her candidate, the once auxiliary role of sponsor would morph into one of co-responsibility with the natural parent.[46]

For those coming into full communion of the Catholic Church whose baptisms are already recognized as valid and who have also been confirmed, are they merely received into the Catholic Church without the reception of either baptism or confirmation? If the baptisms are valid, there is no "rebaptism," not even conditionally. The answer to the question concerning confirmation is: for confirmation conferred in those churches whose priests and bishops that have valid orders, there is no "reconfirmation" since it has been validly conferred by one having the power to confirm. In those ecclesial communions such as the Anglicans, Episcopalians as well as Lutherans and any others originating with the Reformation of the 16th century that have the practice of confirmation, confirmation is invalid since the validity of their orders are not recognized. Persons being received from these ecclesial communions must be confirmed.[47] If the validity of the orders of the one administering the sacrament of confirmation is

---

44   John M. Huels, "Canons 885: Delay of Confirmation Following the Baptism of Children of Catechetical Age," in *RRAO 1994*, ed. Kevin W. Vann and James I. Donlon (Washington, DC: CLSA, 1994) 126-129.

45   John M. Huels, "Canon 891: Confirmation of seven year old by pastor," in *RRAO 1995*, ed. Kevin W. Vann and James I. Donlon (Washington, DC: CLSA, 1995) 70-72.

46   Barbara Anne Cusack, "Canon 893: Delay of Infant Baptism and Related Issues," *RRAO 1996*, ed. Kevin W. Vann and James I. Donlon (Washington, DC: CLSA, 1996) 91-92.

47   William H. Woestman, "Canons 882: Validity of Confirmation by Protestant Minister," in *RRAO 1997*, ed. Kevin W. Vann and James I. Donlon (Washington, DC: CLSA, 1997) 66-67.

questionable, then confirmation should be administered conditionally.[48]

When a person is delayed in receiving first Holy Communion, may confirmation be administered by a priest? No, merely the admission to Holy Communion does not give by law the faculty to confirm.[49]

Must a pastor give his consent to the confirmation of his parishioner by the diocesan bishop? If the pastor has indicated his decision that confirmation is to be delayed in a particular case, administrative recourse can be taken against it to his hierarchical superior the diocesan bishop. Since the bishop's decision, whether affirmative and negative, is also an administrative act, recourse may be had against it to the Holy See. It should be noted that it is the bishop and not the pastor who is the one to administer the sacrament of confirmation in the case presented.[50]

What is the consequence when a candidate participates in the conferral of confirmation but "in my heart" refused the sacrament? "Neither faith nor probity of life is required for the valid reception of confirmation." Even indifference to the reception of the sacrament does not invalidate. However, "...an intention against the reception of confirmation would undoubtedly prevent its valid conferral."[51]

May a parent of a child act as sponsor at confirmation? No.[52]

Conclusion

May all pastoral leaders and decision makers seek to do justice so that it is the foundation of every action in their parish communities. Thus, by avoiding harm and following an ordered service to the community may each parish family have love as its constitutional element.

---

48   Peter J. Vere, "Canon 845: The Validity of Confirmation Administered Outside of the Church," in *RRAO 2001*, ed. F. Stephen Pedone and James I. Donlon (Washington, DC: CLSA, 2001) 96-98.

49   Bredan Daly, "Canons 882 and 883: Minister of Confirmation," in *RRAO 2001*, ed. F. Stephen Pedone and James I. Donlon (Washington, DC: CLSA, 2001) 103-105. This article is a careful enunciation of the circumstances under which a priest may obtain the faculty to confirm.

50   Thomas J. Paprocki, "Canons 213 and 843: Refusal of Confirmation by Pastor," in *RRAO 2004*, ed. F. Stephen Pedone and James I. Donlon (Washington, DC: CLSA, 2004) 93-94.

51   Edward N. Peters, "Canon 845: Invalid Confirmation Due to Contrary Intention of the Recipient," in *RRAO 2007*, ed. Joseph J. Koury and Siobhan M. Verbeek (Washington, DC: CLSA, 2007) 68-70.

52   Brendan Daly, "Canon 893: Parents as Confirmation Sponsors," in *RRAO 2009*, ed. Sharon A. Euart and Siobhan M. Verbeek (Washington, DC: CLSA, 2009) 91-93.

Appendix A
REGULAE IURIS

The following was a class handout prepared by Father Ladislas Orsy, S.J. and then, with his permission used in the same fashion by Sister Elizabeth McDonough, O.P. She has granted permission for its publication here.

1. Beneficium ecclesiasticum non potest licite sine institutione canonica obtineri.	1. An ecclesiastical benefice cannot be obtained licitly without canonical institution.
2. Possessor malae fidei ullo tempore non praescribit.	2. No prescription for a possessor of bad faith.
3. Sine possessione praescriptio non procedit.	3. No prescription without possession.
4. Peccatum non dimittitur nisi restituatur ablatum.	4. No forgiveness of sin unless there is restitution.
5. Peccati venia non datur nisi correcto.	5. There is no forgiveness, unless the sinner has mended his ways.
6. Nemo potest ad impossibile obligari.	6. No one is bound to do the impossible.
7. Privilegium personale personam sequitur et extinguitur cum persona.	7. A personal privilege follows the person; it comes to an end when the person dies.
8. Semel malum semper praesumitur esse malum.	8. Who does wrong once is presumed to be a wrongdoer always. (Who does wrong out of malice once, is presumed to be a malicious person).
9. Ratum quis habere non potest quod eius nomine non est gestum.	9. No one can ratify what was not done in his name and through his mandate. (No one can ratify what he did not mandate to do).
10. Ratihabitionem retrotrahi et mandato non est dubium comparari.	10. Ratification can be retroactive; it can be equivalent to a mandate.
11. Cum sunt partium iura obscura reo fovendum est potius quam actori.	11. When the rights of the parties are obscure the accused should be favored over the accuser.
12. In iudicii non est acceptio personarum habenda.	12. In judicial procedure no special favor is given to any person. (All are equal before a court).

13. Ignorantia facti non iurii excusat.	13. Ignorance of a fact constitutes an excuse; ignorance of law does not.
14. Cum quis in ius alterius succedit iustam ignorantiae causam habere censetur.	16. When someone succeeds into the rights of another, he is assumed to have a good reason to plead ignorance.
15. Odia restringi et favores convenit ampliari.	15. Whatever is odious ought to be restricted; whatever is favorable ought to be extended.
16. Decet beneficium concessum a Principe esse mansurum.	16. It is fitting that a benefice given by a prince should stay. (A favor once granted by the superior should have stability).
17. Indultum a iure beneficium non est alicui auferendum.	17. When the law grants a benefice, no one should take it away. (A favor granted by a law should not be taken away by anyone).
18. Non firmatur tractu temporis quoad ab initio non subsistit.	18. The passage of time will not remedy a situation that had no legal foundation. (What was illegal in the beginning will not become legal with the passage of time)
19. Non est sine culpa qui rei quae ad se non pertinet se immiscet.	19. If someone interferes in a business that is not his own, he is not without fault. (To interfere with the business of a third party is to accept liability).
20. Nullus pluribus uti defensionibus prohibetur.	20. No one is forbidden to use several defenses.
21. Quod semel placuit amplius displicere non potest.	21. What was approved once cannot be disapproved later.
22. Non debet aliquis alterius odio praegravari.	22. No one must be judged unfavorably because someone hates him. (In judicial procedure emotional prejudice must be excluded.)
23. Sine culpa, nisi subsit causa non est aliquis puniendus.	23. Who is not culpable, should not be punished; but disadvantages may be imposed on him if there is a permanent cause.

24. Quod quis mandato facit iudicis, dolo facere non videtur, cum habeat parere necesse.	24. When someone does something by the order of a judge; he cannot act out of malice since he must obey the judge.
25. Mora sua cuilibet nociva est.	25. Who delays harms himself.
26. Ea quae fiunt a iudice si ad eius non spectant officium non subsistunt.	26. Whatever a judge does outside the scope of his office has no legal force.
27. Scienti et consentienti non fit iniuria neque dolus.	27. Who knows and agrees has no cause to complain of injury or malice.
28. Quae a iure communi exorbitant nequaquam ad consequentiam sunt tradenda.	28. Whatever is beyond the scope of common law must not be further extended.
29. Quod omnes tangit debet ab omnibus probari.	29. What concerns all must be approved by all.
30. In obscuris minimum est sequendum.	30. When the meaning is obscure, the obligation is reduced to the minimum significance
31. Eum qui certus est certiorari ulterius non oportet.	31. If someone knows with certainty, there is no need to inform him further.
32. Non licet actori quod reo licitum non exsistit.	32. The accuser is not permitted to do what is not permitted to the accused.
33. Mutare quis consilium non potest in alterius detrimentum.	33. No one can change his mind (intention) at the expense of another.
34. Generi per speciem derogatur.	34. The particular takes precedence over the general. (The diocesan laws, unless it is contrary, take precedence over universal laws.)
35. Plus semper in se continet quod est minus.	35. The more includes the less. (If one can do a greater thing, the lesser can certainly be done.)
36. Pro possessore habetur qui dolo desiit possidere.	36. If someone abandoned possessions maliciously, he is held as the possessor. (No one can free himself from the duties or liabilities of the possessor by abandoning maliciously the state of possession).
37. Utile per inutile non debet vitiari.	37. The useful must not be vitiated by the useless.

38. Ex eo non debet quis fructum consequi quod nisus extitit impugnare.	38, No one should profit from something (law, document, fact), that he himself contested previously.
39. Cum quid prohibetur, prohibentur omnia quae sequuntur ex illo.	39. When something is forbidden, everything is forbidden that follows from it.
40. Pluralis locutio duorum numero est contenta.	40. Any speech in plural refers to two (at least).
41. Imputari ei non debet per quem non stat si non fiat quod per eum fuerat faciendum.	41. No one should be blamed for not having done what he had to do, when the possibility of doing it did not depend on him.
42. Accessorium naturam sequi congruit principalis.	42. The accessory follows the nature of the principal.
43. Qui tacit consentire videtur.	43. Who keeps silent seems to (is deemed to) consent.
44. Is qui tacit non fatetur, sed nec utique negare videtur.	44. Who keeps silent does not confess anything, but he does not deny anything either.
45. Inspicimus in obscuris quod est verisimilius, vel quod plerumque fieri consuevit.	45. In obscure things we should hold to what is more likely or what is more customary.
46. Is qui in ius succedit alterius, eo iure quo ille uti debebit.	46. When someone succeeds into the rights of another, he has the same rights as the other one did.
47. Praesumitur ignorantia ubi scientia non probatur.	47. Ignorance is presumed when knowledge is not proved.
48. Locupletari non debet aliquis cum alterius iniuria vel iactura.	48. No one should profit from the injury or failure of another one.
49. In poenis benignior est interpretatio facienda.	49. In matters of penalty a more benign interpretation is the right one.
50. Actus legitimi conditionem non recipiunt neque diem.	50. Certain legal acts cannot be restricted by the imposition of a condition or of a time limit.
51. Semel Deo dicatum non est ad usus humanos ulterius transferendum.	51. Once given to God it should not be transferred to the use of man.
52. Non praestat impedimentum quod de iure non sortitur effectum.	52. An act when null and void in the beginning cannot be a legal obstacle later.

53. Cui licet quod est plus licet utique quod est minus.	53. Who can do more, can do less.
54. Qui prior est tempore potior est iure.	54. The one first in time has a stronger right.
55. Qui sentit onus sentire debet commodum et contra.	55. Who feels the burden should feel the comfort as well. (Burden and relief, advantages and disadvantages originating in the same law or legal situation must go together).
56. In re communi potior est conditio prohibentis.	56. When rights are held in common, the negative vote outweighs all others. (I.e. for a decision unanimity is necessary).
57. Contra eum qui legem dicere potuit apertius est interpretatio facienda.	57. In case of doubt all interpretation should go against the one who should have spoken clearly.
58. Non est obligatorium contra bonos mores praestitum iuramentum.	58. An oath against good morals does not bind.
59. Dolo facit qui petit quod restituere oportet eumdem.	59. To ask immediately for what must be restituted is to reveal malicious intention.
60. Non est in mora qui potest exceptione legitima se tueri.	60. Someone who can defend himself with a legitimate exception should not be faulted for delay. (I.e. he would be excused anyway).
61. Quod ob gratiam alicuius conceditur non est in eius dispendium retorquendum.	61. Whatever is given to the benefit of another should not be turned to his disadvantage.
62. Nullus est consilio, dummodo fraudolentum non fuerit obligatur.	62. No liability arises from advice given provided it was not fraudulent.
63. Exceptionem obiiciens non videtur de intentione adversarii confiteri.	63. To move an exception is not the admission of the accusation. (The accused may use even contradictory exceptions).
64. Quae contra ius fiunt, debent utique pro infectis haberi.	64. Whatever is done against the law should be held null and void (should be held as not done, vitiated).
65. In pari delicto et causa potior est conditio possidentis.	65. All things being equal, the possessor has the stronger right.

66. Cum non stat per eum ad quem pertinet quominus conditio impleatur, haberi debet perinde ac si impleta fuisset.	66. When a person is bound to fulfill a condition, but the possibility of doing so does not depend on him, the condition should be deemed fulfilled.
67. Quod alicui suo non licet nomine nec alieno licebit.	67. When someone is forbidden to do something, he cannot escape the prohibition by doing it for someone else.
68. Potest quis per alium quod potest facere per seipsum.	68. Whatever someone can do by himself, he can do it by another (unless the power to act cannot be delegated).
69. In malis promissis fides non expedit observari.	69. A promise to do wrong does not generate a duty to be faithful.
70. In alternativis debitoris est electio et sufficit alterum adimpleri.	70. In case of alternative duties the debtor is entitled to choose one of them; by doing one he can satisfy all obligations.
71. Qui ad agendum admittitur est ad excipiendum multo magis admittendus.	71. Whoever is entitled to sue is even more entitled to raise an exception.
72. Qui facit per alium est perinde ac si faciat per seipsum.	72. When someone acts through another (a representative, a deputy, an agent) he is as much responsible as if he did it himself.
73. Factum legitimum retrotrahi non debet, licet casus postea eveniat a quo non potuit inchoari.	73. A valid legal transaction cannot be annulled because of an invalidating factor that came into being afterwards.
74. Quod alicui gratiose conceditur trahi non debet ab aliis in exemplum.	74. A gracious concession to someone should not be quoted by another as a precedent.
75. Frustra sibi fidem quis postulat ab eo servari, cui fidem a se praestitam servare recusat.	75. No one should ask for faithful compliance by another when he is not faithful in his duty towards the other. (He who breeches faith toward his partner, is not entitled to ask him to be faithful).

76. Delictum personae non debet in detrimentum Ecclesiae redundare.	76. The crime of a person should not be harm (cause damage) to the Church. (The Church should not: suffer because of personal wrong doing.)
77. Rationi congruit ut succedat in onere qui substituitur in honore.	77. It is fair that when someone succeeds another one in an honorable position, he should take the burden that goes with.
78. In argumentum trahi nequeunt quae propter necessitatem aliquando sunt concessa.	78. When a concession is made out of necessity it cannot serve as a legitimate precedent.
79. Nemo potest plus iuris transferre in alium quam sibi ipsi competere diagnoscatur.	79. No one gives more right to another than what he has.
80. In toto partem non est dubium contineri.	80. No doubt, the part is contained in the whole.
81. In generali concessione veniunt ea quae quis esset verisimiliter in specie concessurus.	81. A general grant does not contain those particular concessions that the superior was never likely to give.
82. Qui contra ius mercatur bonam fidem praesumitur non habere.	82. Those who bargain against the law are presumed to lack good faith.
83. Bona fides non patitur ut semel exactum iterum exigatur.	83. To try to exact the same duty twice is against good faith.
84. Cum quid una vita proibetur alicui ad id alia non debet admitti.	84. Once forbidden, it is forbidden in every way.
85. Contractus ex conventione legem accipere diagnoscuntur.	85. Contracts make law for themselves.
86. Damnum quod quis sua culpa sentit sibi debet non aliis imputare.	86. If someone does wrong, he should blame himself for the harm that he suffers.
87. Infamibus portae non pateant dignitatum.	87. Dignities are closed to persons of bad reputation.
88. Certum est quod is committit in lege, qui legis verbum complectens, contra legis nititur voluntatem.	88. Those who comply with the letter of the law but against the intention of the law, are really against the law.

Given in Rome by St. Peter's on the Fifth Day of the Nones of March in the Fourth year of our Pontificate

Boniface VIII

These 88 legal dicta known as the "*Regulae Iuris*" were published in 1298. The "*Regulae Iuris*" appear at the end of the so-called *Liber Sextus (in VI°)*, promulgated by Boniface VIII and now published as one of the five *Decretals* in the *Corpus Iuris Canonici*.

Appendix B
Sample Letter from a Pastor in Support of Godparents

Dear Pastor Requiring Affidavit:

I am happy to provide the following as the formal testimony you require:

Andrew "Drew" Luke N is the son of Britton and Leslie (Maiden) N. Drew's Baptism at St. X is tentatively set for M D, 20YY. The godparents chosen by and who represent the parents are Brad and Eva (Maiden) N.

There is a realistic hope that Drew will be brought up in the Catholic religion (Canon 868 §1, 2°).

Eva and Brad understand that their role is, together with the parents, to present Drew for baptism, and to help him to live a Christian life befitting the baptized and faithfully to fulfill the duties inherent in baptism (Canon 872).

Brad wishes to serve as Drew's godfather and Eva as his godmother; they fulfill the qualifications and limitations of Canon 873.

In accord with Canon 874 §1, in light of Canon 18 and in my judgment, Eva and Brad should be admitted to the office of godparent because they:

1° have been appointed by the parents of Drew, are suitable for this role and have the intention of fulfilling it;
2° have completed sixteen years of age;
3° are both Catholics who have been confirmed, have received the blessed Eucharist and who live lives of faith that befit the role to be undertaken;
4° do not labor under any canonical penalty, whether imposed or declared;
5° are neither the mother nor the father of Drew.

I so swear from the knowledge gained as Eva and Brad's pastor until their recent move to your city and church parish.

Sincerely,

Pastor Sending Affidavit

Appendix C
Diocesan Confirmation Policy

§8. PREPARATION FOR THE SACRAMENT OF CONFIRMATION OF JUNIORS AND SENIORS TO BE CONFIRMED BY THE DIOCESAN BISHOP

1° Parish Policy – RCIA Model: Since those who ask have a right to all sacraments when properly prepared and rightly disposed, parish practice cannot unduly or arbitrarily abridge this right. Parish policy, if any, and practice must be in accordance with diocesan policy and universal law and absolutely cannot be more stringent or require more of the candidates or their sponsors and parents. There shall be great latitude in practice exercised at the discretion of the pastor so that no candidate is excluded from the sacrament of confirmation who cannot legitimately be included for presentation to the bishop. There must be a yearly confirmation program in each parish and mission if there is even one candidate.

The preparation should follow the Rite of Christian Initiation for Adults as a model. This approach emphasizes: (1) the relationship to baptism and the Eucharist; and (2) initiation into the Catholic Christian community that truly welcomes the candidates and wishes them to embrace their faith that embraces them now and in the future.

2° General Norms: Those desiring to be prepared, their parents, and their sponsors shall be made fully aware of what is required to celebrate the sacrament of confirmation.

3° Freely Chosen and Personally Requested: The decision to celebrate confirmation shall be a free choice on the part of each candidate. Candidates must personally request confirmation. Requirements for confirmation should never be presented as something to "earn" or as "a completion of one's religious education."

4° Requirements: Remote preparation for this sacrament begins with baptism and continues through years of catechesis and involvement in a faith community. The candidates for confirmation should attend Mass on Sundays and days of obligation but no manifestation of conscience can be demanded in this matter.

5° Elements of the Process: Proximate and immediate catechesis must take place in the faith community into whose life of prayer and worship a candidate will be more fully initiated. At the candidate's discretion, there should be some participation in [1] a parish service or other project, [2] some retreat or day of reflection. The catechetical process shall enable the candidate to: (a) articulate some understanding of the role of the Holy Spirit in his/her life; (b) demonstrate some understanding of the sacraments of initiation: baptism, confirmation and Eucharist; (c) participate in, according to the candidate's interests, the Catholic community and its mission; and (d) approach the sacrament freely. Several ritual celebrations may mark the movement through the stages of the preparation process using the RCIA as a model.

6° Collaboration: Those coming together from distinct confirmation programs such as those in the parish/mission, the Catholic high school and the home school association, ought to come together in some common experiences before a joint celebration if this option has been elected. The bishop, however, will be happy to confirm, in a place approved by him, those who are prepared in groupings such as Catholic high schools or home school associations. Nonetheless a single candidate can be confirmed by the bishop in a mission church, for instance.

7° Baptismal Name: The candidate's baptismal name or given name, even if it is not a saint's name, may be used as the confirmation name. A new name may also be chosen if the candidate has a special devotion to a saint. Each confirmand is free to choose any one of these possible alternatives.

8° Sponsors: A sponsor must be a fully initiated, practicing Catholic. The sponsor may fittingly be one of the baptismal godparent(s). Parents absolutely *cannot* be sponsors for the sacraments of baptism or confirmation. Sponsors may be of either sex and may have, according to their interests, some participation in the preparation and discernment process.

9° Discernment: Candidates, parents and sponsors, along with catechetical leaders and parish priests, shall together discern the readiness of a candidate for the celebration of this sacrament. Interviews with candidates, parents and sponsors (if practically available) at particular points throughout the preparation process facilitate such discernment.

10° Confirmation is ordinarily administered to candidates in their *junior or senior* year of high school only.

11° Additional information including models for preparation, celebration and assistance are available through the Diocesan Office of Religious Education.

SEMINAR

MODERN FAMILY LIFE AND THE EXCLUSION OF OPENNESS TO CHILDREN
Doctor Lynda Robitaille

Introduction

Exclusion of the *bonum prolis*, or openness to children,[1] is a ground of invalidity well known to us all. We are all familiar with those cases where a couple marries but chooses never to be open to having children. If one or both parties decide never to be open to having children, that person excludes the *bonum prolis*. The absolute, perpetual exclusion of openness to children is straightforward. Exclusion must be absolute to invalidate consent. This absolute exclusion can be temporary or perpetual: "Absolute exclusion is the denial of the right to procreation, entirely independent from any other internal or external factor of time, place, occurrence or conditions."[2] A temporary exclusion can be for a specific period of time or until a specific event (determinate), or it can be for a time that is not specified or determined (indeterminate).

When evaluating temporary exclusion of the *bonum prolis*, the distinction between the exchange of the right (*ius*) or the exchange of the exercise of the right (*exercitium iuris*) continues to be important. The right to the *bonum prolis* includes the right to those acts apt for the procreation of children. This right encompasses natural, physical acts, thus, it is encompasses consummation *humano modo*. When two people marry, they consent to being open to having children together by means of natural acts. Both parties have the right to request such acts from the other. In other words, both parties have the right to try to have a child with the other. This right is spoken of in the literature as 'absolute,' and 'without limitation.' What does that mean? Recent literature on the exclusion of the *bonum prolis* speaks of marriage as a relationship ordered both to the good of the spouses, and to the procreation and education of children. The unitive and procreative aspects of marriage are necessarily linked. Thus, procreation is not a single goal of marriage; it must be seen in conjunction with the unitive, the good of the spouses and the partnership of life. How to evaluate the decision of whether or not to be open to having children when spouses believe that for the good of their marriage and family, they should not have children? What role does

---

1 Although exclusion of the education (rearing) of children also forms part of the exclusion of the *bonum prolis*, it will not be part of this paper.
2 *Coram* Alwan, 12 April 2002, in *Rotal Jurisprudence: Selected Translations*, ed. Victoria Vondenberger, RSM (Washington, DC: Canon Law Society of America, 2011) [hereafter *Rotal Jurisprudence*] 114, #8.

responsible parenthood (responsible procreation) have in forming consent with regard to openness to children?

In cases of exclusion of openness to children, personnel in marriage tribunals are accustomed to a disconnect between morally correct behaviors and behaviors with legal consequences. Thus, a person might choose to exclude openness to children by either moral (natural family planning, or making use of infertile periods) or immoral means (contraception or abortion). What is evaluated is the person's choice: did he/she exclude the *bonum prolis*? The only consequence of the 'how' of the exclusion might be a *vetitum* on the party, as an attempt to prevent such behavior in future. However, we will see recent literature evaluating decisions based on responsible parenthood made by morally licit decisions. If for the good of the family, a couple makes a decision to avoid openness to children, is that an exclusion of the *bonum prolis*? Does it make a difference if they fulfill that choice by morally licit or illicit means? As we will see, the 'how' of the exclusion, the moral choice, is having an impact on assessing consent.

Modern life and scientific development have given couples the ability to choose whether or not, or even how, to be open to having children. An understanding of the biology of fertilization, gestation, and birth have opened choices to couples with regard to the timing of their families, the number of children they wish to have, help with infertility, and help with genetically inherited diseases, or infectious diseases. In addition, divorce and remarriage have changed dynamics of family structure. Thus, in tribunals we now see some of the following cases: a) one or both parties to the marriage in question had had children prior to meeting this spouse and because of the needs of the family, they decide not to have children of their marriage; b) one of the parties has a serious infectious or hereditary illness that can be passed on to an unborn child, and so they choose not to have a child of their own, or they choose to make use of artificial reproduction (whether a surrogate mother, or using the sperm or egg of a donor) in order to have their own child; c) the parties choose not to have children in order to work for the good of humankind, or to adopt a child that has already been born, etc. How doctrine understands these choices affects how canon law understands them. For both, the understanding is still in a state of flux and growth.

We will examine some of the newness later in the presentation. Before that, we will examine the state of flux of something not so new: the temporary exclusion of openness to children.

Temporary Exclusion of the bonum prolis
 There are different ways that temporary exclusion of the *bonum prolis* can occur. One or both parties can decide to postpone having children until they have accomplished a specific goal (waited five years, completed education, bought a home, traveled). One or both parties can agree to postpone having children

until a more general time (until they feel ready, until they are financially stable, until they are sure the marriage will last). One or both parties can say that he/she wishes to revisit the issue sometime after the wedding (in other words, not decide at the time of consent). Some are invalidating; others are not. How to tell the difference?

One of the primary ways to distinguish between what is invalidating and what is not is with the distinction between the exchange of the right and the denial of the use of the right (distinction between *ius* and *iusum (exercitium) iuris*).[3] If the right is not exchanged (denied), consent is invalid; this is often clearest in cases of absolute perpetual denial of the right. However, things become less clear when the right is exchanged, but the use of the right is denied (responsible parenthood, for instance). If the right is exchanged, consent is valid, even if the use is denied. Thus, cases of temporary exclusion of openness to children often seem to be explained in this way: 'yes, we wanted children, but not right away.' At first this seems like a valid exchange of consent because the right to openness to children seems to have been exchanged. However, sometimes on closer inspection it *seemed* the right was being exchanged, but in fact it was not. It is the role of the tribunal to discover the person's true intent. Alwan explains:

> Temporary exclusion does not lead to absolute or perpetual denial of the right of procreation: rather the one simulating indeed accepts the right, however he closes off its exercise within limits either specified or unspecified of a time to elapse or of a future event, for example, within a type of condition from which would depend both the right and its exercise. What is involved is 'an abuse and not a denial of the right' (*C.* Funghini, 7 July 1993 ...). It should be noted that 'exclusion for a time, on the other hand, according to the constant jurisprudence of the Roman Rota, makes one presume that the spouses, by the procrastination of procreation, only intended for the duration to decline to grant the exercise of the right, which even as is patent from the doctrine of responsible parenthood, cannot infect matrimonial consent (*c.* Bruno, 1 February 1991 ...). However, a presump-

---

[3] H. Franceschi, "L'esclusione della prole," in *La giurisprudenza della Rota Romana sul consenso matrimoniale (1908-2008)*, in series *Studi giuridici* 83 (Vatican City: Libreria Editrice Vaticana, 2009) 191, explains that this distinction is no longer universally considered applicable by Rotal judges because it seems incongruous to have a will not to oblige oneself at the same time as the will to assume the right. Franceschi agrees. On pp. 191-192 Franceschi gives examples of sentences that continue to use this distinction, namely: *c.* Giannecchini, 28 March 1995, *c.* De Lanversin, 5 April 1995, *c.* Ragni, 4 July 1995, *c.* Boccafola, 22 January 1998, *c.* Faltin, 17 November 1998, and *c.* Pinto, 4 June 1999. At pp. 193-197, Franceschi considers those sentences that deny that the distinction between the *ius* and the *iusum iuris* is important, namely, *c.* Civili, 20 November 1996, *c.* Bruno, 19 December 1995, *c.* Civili, 18 December 1995, *c.* Huber, 6 May 1997, and *c.* Civili, 25 June 1997.

tion of this sort does not hold when, in a temporary exclusion, the contracting party binds the exercise of the right to some future condition, uncertain [in nature] or without limitation of time. In such a case, procrastination acquires the same effects of absolute exclusion of the right. Indeed, the simulator suspends the act or the effect of the very object of his consent and makes it depend on an uncertain event, in the deficiency of which the contracting party holds himself free of the burden assumed in the consent given. Thus the temporary denial turns into an absolute one. For this reason, a temporary exclusion voids matrimonial consent if the delay is hypothetical and bound to some future condition that is uncertain, or indeterminate, or unforeseeable, or dependent on the will of one or other of the spouses. The aforesaid exclusion, even though temporary, voids consent insofar as it suspends it and puts it off just as if it were placing a condition on or even excluding indissolubility and so it destroys the consent ...

Indeed, in rotal jurisprudence, determinate temporary exclusion, whether mutual or without agreement of the parties, is not regarded as voiding consent as, for example, a delay for some determinate number of years while both or one or the other party reaches a certain age, or completes studies, or saves an amount of money for raising and educating children. A delay of this sort is not at all a denial of the right, while a delay conditioned on a good outcome of the marriage or the stability of conjugal life is an indeterminate temporary exclusion and similar to a future condition that voids the marital union for it is contrary to the very essence and nature of matrimony ...[4]

Thus:

- If one or both parties decide that there will never be children, this is an absolute, perpetual denial and invalidating.
- If both parties plan to have children and either agree[5] or one decides to wait for a determined period (until we graduate, after five years, etc.), jurisprudence usually sees this as a valid exchange of consent (the right was exchanged, the use was denied for a time).[6]

---

4   *C.* Alwan, 12 April 2002, in *Rotal Jurisprudence*, 115-116, #8.

5   Some argue that this decision occurs only by mutual agreement, and not by a unilateral decision, see, for example, *c.* Burke, 15 December 1994, in *Simulation of Marriage Consent. Doctrine. Jurisprudence. Questionnaires*, ed. W. Woestman (Ottawa: Saint Paul University, 2000) [hereafter *Simulation of Marriage Consent*] 335, #11; see also *c.* Burke, 19 October 1995, in ibid., 352, #10.

6   *C.* Alwan, 12 April 2002, in *Rotal Jurisprudence*, 115, #8, where he cites *c.* Bruno, 1 February 1991, #5; see also p. 116, #8 where he speaks of a "determinate temporary exclusion, whether mutual or without agreement of the parties ..."

- If, however, one or both parties wish to delay openness to children for an undetermined period (which reads like a future condition: 'if we are happy, we will have children then'), this is more likely an absolute temporary exclusion (the exchange of the right was denied because "even though temporary, [it] voids consent insofar as it suspends it and puts it off just as if it were placing a condition," even though the right seems to have been exchanged).[7]
- If one party reserved to him or herself alone the decision whether or not to have children, that is invalidating.[8] Another way of looking at this: "this unilateral qualification, if intended to limit the rights of the other party, certainly constitutes invalidating simulation ..."[9]

Burke highlights another scenario: "It does not appear easy to give a general rule for the moral or the juridic evaluation of the case where, marriage having been entered with a bilateral agreement to postpone having children for a number of years, one of the spouses changes his or her mind and begins to press for procreation before the full time has elapsed."[10] Does that person have the right to openness before the agreed time? If so, how to evaluate the other party's refusal to be open before the agreed-upon time?

Responsible Parenthood (procreation)

The decision of the number and timing of births is to be taken by the spouses together. Citing *Gaudium et spes* 50, Zuanazzi recalls that the decision is to be

---

7   Burke explains: "if there is a *unilateral* exclusion of offspring for an indefinite time (which may become absolute if certain conditions are not verified), then consent is inadequate" (*C.* Burke, 15 December 1994, in *Simulation of Marriage Consent*, 335, #11).

8   In the case *c.* Boccfola, 11 June 1992, there was a negative decision in first instance and an affirmative in second, followed by this affirmative decision at the Rota. The judge explains the reason for the first negative: "the first instance judges found: '... that the respondent had not clarified his own mind on the matter of children at the time of the wedding ... it was only after the marriage that his views became clarified ... We do not see any evidence that, at the time of the marriage, the respondent had made a specific act of the will not to have children, or that the conception of children would be at his discretion or at a time when he decided ... We take the view that, at the time of the marriage, he had an unclear mind on these matters; and only after the marriage did he come to a conclusion: that there would be no children.'

The second instance judges, however, decided that: 'The burden of proof indicates that at each and every moment of this marriage ... the respondent reserved to himself (... to himself alone) the right to allow to take place that conjugal act generative of children.' The undersigned Fathers fully agree ... that the respondent, because of his formation and family background, and because of his temperament and character ... reserved to himself and to himself alone the right to decide if and whether offspring were to be born of the union ... Oscar ... never ... *gave to his spouse* the right to the good of offspring (*bonum prolis*)." (W. Woestman, ed., *Simulation of Marriage Consent*, 329, ##8-9).

9   *C.* Burke, 19 October 1995, in *Simulation of Marriage Consent*, 353, #12.

10 *C.* Burke, 19 October 1995, in *Simulation of Marriage Consent*, 352-353, #11.

made with a rightly formed conscience, for grave reasons, taking into consideration all involved, including those already born and those to be born.[11] Such a decision is only licit when actualized by methods that retain the link between the unitive and procreative aspects of sexuality. The choice not to procreate can affect 'the whole duration of the marriage' and still be licit.[12] Yet Zuanazzi notes: "the prevailing understanding of Rotal jurisprudence holds that the faculty recognized with regard to responsible parenthood concerns the moral life, not the law. For the Rota, such decisions to restrict births concern the marriage itself (*matrimonium in facto esse*), and not consent (*matrimonium in fieri*). Thus, if the decision not to have children goes back to the act of consent, the fact that the choice was made according to responsible parenthood does not justify it, and the rules for evaluating partial simulation, exclusion of the *bonum prolis* would apply."[13] Zuanazzi reflects that it seems contradictory to recognize the competence of the spouses to regulate the births of their children, and yet not to attribute any value to their decision taken conscientiously. Thus, more study and reflection needs to happen, especially with regard to: *what* reasons could justify the choice not to have children, and *how* can this decision be reconciled with the essential ordering of marriage to procreation.[14] We will return to this later in the paper.

Consummation and the bonum prolis

Consent to marriage is ordered to the good of the spouses and to the procreation and education of children (c. 1055 §1). Consummation is part of marriage. It occurs after consent, as canon 1061 §1 makes clear:

> A valid marriage between the baptized is called *ratum tantum* if it has not been consummated; it is called *ratum et consummatum* if the spouses have performed between themselves in a human fashion a conjugal act which is suitable in itself for the procreation of offspring, to which marriage is ordered by its nature and by which the spouses become one flesh.[15]

John Beal reminds us: "The sequence of ratification and consummation is critical. No matter how frequently a couple has had sexual relations prior to marriage, during an invalid marriage, or before it has become sacramental through

---

11   I. Zuanazzi, "Valori fondamentali del matrimonio nella società di oggi: la filiazione," in *Matromonio canonico e realtà contemporanea*, in series *Studi giuridici* 68 (Vatican City: Libreria Editrice Vaticana, 2005) 198.

12   Ibid., 198-199, where she cites Pius XII, 29 October 1951, and Paul VI, *Humanae vitae*, n. 10.

13   I. Zuanazzi, 199.

14   Ibid.

15   *Code of Canon Law, Latin-English Edition: New English Translation* (Washington, DC: CLSA, 1998).

the baptism of both spouses, this sexual activity does not constitute the consummation of a ratified marriage, because one cannot consummate or 'complete' what does not yet exist."[16]

At the time of consent, what is important is whether the person had the will to be open or not to the procreative dimension of the conjugal act. As Franceschi writes: the *bonum prolis* concerns the acceptance of the procreative dimension of matrimonial acts, and it is through these acts that the mutual self-giving in marriage is manifested.[17] Stawniak adds to this: the conjugal act is the only act that expresses a particular relationship of self-giving. That act must be suitable for the generation of children.[18] This understanding will be important when considering artificial reproduction and its impact on consent.

A Growing Understanding of Consummation and Consent
One way of avoiding the conception of children which is morally licit is non-consummation. Hector Franceschi imagines situations in which a couple might decide not to consummate a union: a couple who have lived together, had children together, and then come to be married (or they married first in a civil ceremony, and after the birth of their children married in a Catholic ceremony), or someone who has a grave infectious illness who does not wish to consummate a marriage for the health of the other party. These limited examples can serve to recall that it is necessary to pay attention to concrete cases.[19]

Moneta speaks more realistically, not asking parties not to consummate their union but asking them to make responsible decisions. He struggles with the traditional understanding of when consent is valid or not. He recalls that people marrying in our century face a different reality from people marrying hundreds of years, or even decades ago. For centuries, reproduction was seen as something outside of one's control. In the present day, people marrying are able to control their fertility, to decide when and how to have a child, to exercise dominion over

---

16   J. Beal, commentary on canon 1061, in *New Commentary on the Code of Canon Law*, ed. J. Beal et al. (New York/Mahwah, NJ: Paulist Press, 2000) 1257.

17   H. Franceschi, "La giurisprudenza di merito sull'esclusione della prole nel recente volume delle decisioni rotali dell'anno 1995," in *Quaderni dello Studio Rotale* 11 (2001)107.

18   H. Stawniak, "*Procreatio, impotentia generandi et coeundi*. Problemi e prospettive," in «*Iustitia et iudicium*». *Studi di diritto matrimoniale e processuale canonico in onore di Antoni Stankiewicz*, Vol. I, eds. J. Kowal and J. Llobell (Vatican City: Libreria Editrice Vaticana, 2010) 214.

19   H. Franceschi, "L'esclusione della prole," in *La giurisprudenza della Rota Romana sul consenso matrimoniale (1908-2008)*, in series *Studi giuridici* 83 (Vatican City: Libreria Editrice Vaticana, 2009) 184, reflecting on the decision c. Huber, 24 November 1995. See also H. Franceschi, "L'esclusione della prole nella giurisprudenza rotale recente," in *Ius Ecclesiae* 11 (1999) 153.

that which had seemed a mysterious force of nature.[20] Much has been written in recent years trying to reconcile the new choices people have when marrying with the traditional understandings of the *bonum prolis*. Moneta highlights one distinction that seems no longer relevant, namely the distinction between the exchange of the *ius* and the *exercitium iuris*, noting that it was elaborated in a time when canonists were trying to reconcile a particular type of union, namely that of Joseph and Mary, where they exchanged the right to acts open to procreation, but chose not to exercise that right. As Moneta states, this is completely foreign to the mentality and experience of people today.[21] Even though it is a solution to modern difficulties advocated by some, it is not a realistic solution. In addition, Moneta states that although under the 1917 Code, this distinction might still have been relevant when speaking of rights and obligations of marriage, under the 1983 Code's understanding of marriage as a *totius vitae consortium*, and speaking of the giving and receiving of the parties one to the other, the distinction does not seem as relevant. Thus, Moneta argues that it is time to seek out a new approach to address the reality of marriage today.[22] In what does the spousal self-gift consist, and how can it be lacking?[23]

Lüdicke also tries to address these situations when he highlights those cases where parties have looked at the situation in the world, whether the economic crisis, the ecological crisis, or the fear of a nuclear disaster, and have chosen to enter a marriage with no children. He sees the invalidity of consent only in those cases where one spouse denies the other spouse an equal say in the choice (cf. c. 1135). Evaluating consent to marriage in this way, we can integrate responsible parenthood into the understanding of *ordinatio ad prolis generationem et educationem* without problems that arise from traditional arguments.[24] Lüdicke's argument is based on canon 1135 which highlights: "Each spouse has an equal duty and right to those things which belong to the partnership of conjugal life."

Responsible Parenthood (reproduction) Revisited

Ricciardi studied responsible procreation in 1990. He speaks of responsible procreation, rather than parenthood. He states that there are three important points: that responsible procreation takes place by licit means; that according *Gaudium et spes* 50, it is a decision made within marriage, not before; and that *Gaudium et spes* speaks of it positively, as a way to space out the children a cou-

---

20 P. Moneta, "Il *bonum prolis* e la sua esclusione," in *Prole e matrimonio canonico*, in series *Studi giuridici* 62 (Vatican City: Libreria Editrice Vaticana, 2003) 88.

21 Ibid., 91.

22 P. Moneta, "Il *bonum prolis* e la sua esclusione," 92.

23 Ibid., 93.

24 K. Lüdicke, "Fondamenti dell'efficacia invalidante dell'esclusione della prole sul matrimonio," in *«Iustitia et iudicium». Studi di diritto matrimoniale e processuale canonico in onore di Antoni Stankiewicz*, Vol. II, eds. J. Kowal and J. Llobell (Vatican City: Libreria Editrice Vaticana, 2010) 817-818.

ple will have, not as a way to avoid having children. He concludes: responsible procreation cannot be contrary to the nature of marriage. Thus, the general presumption is that when a couple chooses to have a specific number of children and to exclude others, that is a valid exchange of consent (because they exchanged the right (*ius*) but denied the exercise of the right (*exercitium iuris*)). However, if they positively excluded the right, then consent is not valid.[25]

In 2003, Serrano Ruiz revisited this article and spoke also of responsible procreation, saying that it is more than just a decision taken in marriage (*matrimonium in facto esse*), but it could also be a decision taken prior to marriage, and thus affecting consent. He cites John Paul II's, *Familiaris consortio*, #41 of 1981, where he speaks of the *bonum familiae*, and that this good of the family must form part of the decision of whether and when to have children. He notes that the couple is responsible—illuminated by the church's magisterium—to make a choice. But, what if they make an irresponsible choice? If the reason for the exclusion is "egoistical or immoral or lacking in moral value" then the exclusion is invalidating.[26] Thus, he is adding the morality of the choice to the evaluation of whether or not it is an appropriate choice. He concludes that in the juridic world we do not yet have the parameters of validity or invalidity of marriage with regard to responsible procreation, so there is not yet certainty or unanimity in this regard.[27] The issues revolve around: whether the couple, as equal partners, is making a decision for the good of their family. In addition, the question of whether the decision is being executed by morally licit means is important. Thus, couples are marrying and making choices about whether having children is right for their families. Those choices may or may not be in accordance with responsible procreation. How do those choices affect the parties' consents, especially in relation to blended families, adoption, and artificial reproduction?

Yet, Lüdicke asks: "On what criteria should one judge whether the pre-matrimonial deliberation of partners concerning the number of children they will have was legitimately based on the call of the council in *Gaudium et spes*, 50, 2 for parents to be responsible for the number and timing of their children? In such cases, the marriage cannot be invalid due to a defect in the will if ecclesial marriage law is to be congruent with the conciliar teaching on marriage."[28]

---

25 G. Ricciardi, "Procreazione responsabile ed esclusione del *bonum prolis*," in *La simulazione del consenso matrimoniale canonico*, in series *Studi giuridici* 22 (Vatican City: Libreria Editrice Vaticana, 1990) 175-182.

26 J.M. Serrano Ruiz, "L'esclusione della prole e la sua assolutezza: il problema della paternità responsabile," in *Prole e matrimonio canonico*, in series *Studi giuridici* 62 (Vatican City: Libreria Editrice Vaticana, 2003) 160.

27 Ibid., 166.

28 K. Lüdicke, "Some Sentences on *Exclusio Boni Prolis*," in *The Jurist* 69 (2009) 562. After reviewing articles by Franceschi and Moneta, he summarizes their arguments at p. 578: "If both persons to be married mutually give themselves to each other in a conjugal

Blended Families
Reviewing a decision *coram* Civili of December 18, 1995, Franceschi argues: it is not sufficient that there is a clear will not to have more children—especially in cases where there already are children. It is important to go beyond these facts and analyze the true will of the parties at the moment of consent. It is possible that there is a true matrimonial will in which the parties decided—in respect for the truth of marriage and of sexual relations—to not have more children for justified reasons. The central question should be whether at the moment of consent there was a concrete giving and receiving of one another.[29] Is a true matrimonial will compatible with a decision not to have children?

The difficulty is to understand in what this concrete giving and receiving of one another consists: can the parties decide in a truly matrimonial mutual decision not to be open to having children in their union? Can that choice be valid? Or is the very fact of that choice a decision to exclude the *bonum prolis*? Zuanazzi made clear above that in the traditional understanding that choice made prior to consent would render consent invalid; that choice made after consent, would be a valid choice because the intrinsic openness existed at the time of consent.

If a couple marry with the intent to take care of children who already exist, but not to have more children, is that a valid consent? Can the spouses choose for the good of the family to exclude openness to further children, while caring for children they already have natural obligations to? In a strict understanding of the exclusion of the *bonum prolis*, such a choice would be an exclusion because the couple are not open at the time of consent to the *bonum prolis*. Yet, is that just? Can we evaluate that choice in light of Moneta and Lüdicke's arguments that the couple, as equal spouses, mutually decides what is best for their family?

Responses to Infertility: Adoption and Artificial Reproduction
Burke recalls: "the absence of offspring in no way invalidates marriage (cf. c. 1084, §3), so long as the *intentio prolis* ... was not excluded from consent."[30] The

---

manner, the mutual decision against having additional children can also be made. It is not the readiness of the couple for children that is determinative, but the readiness of the partners to accept one another and give themselves to one another as spouses." Lüdicke reflects, p. 578: "it is clear that the respect for the other partner is mentioned as a new criterion for the judgment of the validity of a marriage." He finds the source of this new criterion in canon 1135, and explains how the mutual decision can work, pp. 579-580: "the will does not destroy the essence of conjugal consent if it intends to avoid children; rather, it is the denial of the right to the other party to have equal weight in the decision regarding sexual relations and parenthood that does so. It is no longer consent. It becomes a dissent that can allow no *consortium totius vitae* to arise, no valid marriage."

29 H. Franceschi, "L'esclusione della prole nella giurisprudenza rotale recente," in *Ius Ecclesiae* 11 (1999) 157.

30 C. Burke, 15 December 1994, in *Simulation of Marriage Consent. Doctrine. Jurisprudence. Questionnaires*, ed. W. Woestman (Ottawa: Saint Paul University, 2000) 333, #3.

Congregation for the Doctrine of the Faith noted in the instruction *Donum vitae* of February 1987 that the 'right to a child' does not exist; rather, it is a right of the spouses to those natural acts which are ordered to procreation.[31] The parties give to one another the procreative capacity and not the right to have children. It is a right to accomplish those natural acts which give rise the possibility to have children.[32] Citing John Paul II's *Familiaris consortio*, #14, *Donum vitae*, #8, reminds us: "'…Physical sterility in fact can be for spouses the occasion for other important services to the life of the human person, for example, adoption, various forms of educational work, and assistance to other families and to poor or handicapped children.'" As long as parties do not choose adoption over nature acts open to procreation, there is no problem with consent. As *donum vitae* explains:

> Only respect for the link between the meanings of the conjugal act and respect for the unity of the human being make possible procreation in conformity with the dignity of the person. In his unique and irrepeatable origin, the child must be respected and recognized as equal in personal dignity to those who give him life. The human person must be accepted in his parents' act of union and love; the generation of a child must therefore be the fruit of that mutual giving which is realized in the conjugal act wherein the spouses cooperate as servants and not as masters in the work of the Creator who is Love. In reality, the origin of a human person is the result of an act of giving. The one conceived must be the fruit of his parents' love. He cannot be desired or conceived as the product of an intervention of medical or biological techniques; that would be equivalent to reducing him to an object of scientific technology. No one may subject the coming of a child into the world to conditions of technical efficiency which are to be evaluated according to standards of control and dominion. *The moral relevance of the link between the meanings of the conjugal act and between the goods of marriage, as well as the unity of the human being and the dignity of his origin, demand that the procreation of a human person be brought about as the fruit of the conjugal act specific to the love between spouses.*[33]

---

31 "Relazione sull'attività della Rota Romana nell'anno giudiziario 2005," in *Quaderni dello Studio Rotale* 16 (2006) 56, as expressed in *Donum vitae*, B.8.

32 H. Stawniak, "*Procreatio, impotentia generandi et coeundi*. Problemi e prospettive," in *«Iustitia et iudicium». Studi di diritto matrimoniale e processuale canonico in onore di Antoni Stankiewicz*, Vol. I, eds. J. Kowal and J. Llobell (Vatican City: Libreria Editrice Vaticana, 2010) 221.

33 Congregation for the Doctrine of the Faith, Instruction, *Donum vitae*, February 22, 1987, B.4.c, at: http://www.vatican.va/roman_curia/congregations/cfaith/documents/rc_con_cfaith_doc_19870222_respect-for-human-life_en.html.

More recently *Dignitas personae* confirmed: "The Church ... holds that it is ethically unacceptable to *dissociate procreation from the integrally personal context of the conjugal act*: human procreation is a personal act of a husband and wife, which is not capable of substitution."[34]

How could artificial reproduction enter a couple's consent? If a couple does not know if they are fertile and marries accepting to see what will happen, then their consent is valid. If, however, the couple is aware of problems with fertility, and because of those problems they wish to avoid the natural consequences of sexual intercourse and have recourse to artificial reproduction, then one or both could be excluding the *bonum prolis* from their consent.

What if one spouse refuses to have recourse to artificial reproduction, would that be an exclusion of the *bonum prolis*? No, because the birth of children is not an obligation/right for the spouses but rather a gift from God. Thus, the spouses have a *ius ad procreationem*, not a *ius ad prolem*.[35]

What if a couple decides not to have children naturally, but to use methods of artificial reproduction? Because this is contrary to the truly human way of transmitting life through acts of conjugal love, it is, in fact, an exclusion of the *bonum prolis*.[36]

Artificial Reproduction
Addressing artificial reproduction, Hector Franceschi speaks of couples "wanting to beget children while making use of artificial methods of procreation. Such methods, in so far as they do not respect the truth of the conjugal man-woman relationship—the centre of the conjugal complementary reality—do not show a true will of accepting the other in the truth of his or her sexual condition within the framework of marriage, that necessarily implies the potential paternity-maternity, resulting from the personal and inalienable mutual donation of the body."[37] He speaks of "generation without communion between the spouses, that exists in artificial insemination,"[38] and of "fecundity without conjugality."[39] Franceschi considers artificial reproduction: "today the generation of offspring is

---

34 Congregation for the Doctrine of the Faith, Instruction, *Dignitas personae*, September 8, 2008, n. 16, at: http://www.vatican.va/roman_curia/congregations/cfaith/documents/rc_con_cfaith_doc_20081208_dignitas-personae_en.html

35 I. Zuanazzi, "Valori fondamentali del matrimonio nella società di oggi: la filiazione," in *Matromonio canonico e realtà contemporanea*, in series *Studi giuridici* 68 (Vatican City: Libreria Editrice Vaticana, 2005) 208.

36 Ibid.

37 H. Franceschi, "'Bonum prolis' in the Married State of Life and the Canonical Consequences in Case of Separation or Nullity of Marriage," in *Forum* 17 (2006) 392.

38 Ibid., 406.

39 Ibid., 416.

possible without the conjugal act and through the intervention of persons foreign to the couple, without however their taking any part in the sexual conjugal donation in a strict and physical sense."[40] It would be invalidating to choose only artificial reproduction; it would not be invalidating to try naturally to have children first, and if that fails, then to make recourse to artificial reproduction.

The judgment *coram* de Lanversin, of June 15, 1994[41] brings up interesting questions about artificial reproduction and its effects on consent. De Lanversin's judgment is an affirmative judgment in third instance. Renato obtained a vasectomy, but before doing so, he deposited some of his sperm in a sperm bank, in case he would change his mind and want to have a child someday. He married Beata in 1979. She knew about the sperm bank donation and wanted to have a child with him someday. He consistently refused. One day he was asked by the sperm bank if he wanted to save or destroy the sperm. He chose to destroy it. Beata learned of this and left the union in about 1985. The affirmative decision was based on the man's firm and perpetual intention to avoid children, as his vasectomy demonstrated. However, also involved is the question of artificial reproduction. Did his choice to preserve the semen affect his consent? If he entered the union saying: when I am sure of how we are doing we will attempt to have a baby, there is a temporary conditioned choice which is invalidating. What if he said: we will attempt to have a child in two years with the semen? Is his consent valid?

Proving Exclusion of the bonum prolis
This is partial simulation, thus the usual proofs required in simulation cases are required, namely:

- What was the motive for marrying (the *causa contrahendi*)?
- What was the motive for simulating (the *causa simulandi*), i.e. what are the specific circumstances that establish the party's unwillingness to commit to marriage?
- Was there a positive act of the will (choice/motive) made prior to the wedding expressed explicitly or implicitly?
- Is there a confession (judicial or extra-judicial) from the party?
- What are any facts/circumstances/behaviors/actions that help demonstrate the simulation?

An act of the will can be explicit or implicit, actual or virtual. It is commonly accepted that an act once posited is presumed to continue (to not be revoked). For example, canon 1092 of the 1917 Code spoke of "a condition once imposed and not revoked."

---

40   Ibid., 417.
41   See *Romanae Rotae Decisiones* 86 (1994) 313-323.

Boccafola reminds us: "it is of the utmost importance to distinguish between mere hesitation or reluctance or doubt about the opportunity of procreating children and a true will to the contrary. Inactivity of the will, moreover, produces nothing."[42] After reviewing Rotal decisions, Franceschi summarizes helpful points to evaluate when proving an exclusion of the *bonum prolis*:

- What is the person's education, moral and religious convictions, which might have led to this exclusion of the *bonum prolis*?
- What was the courtship/engagement like (interruptions, fights, difficulties)? If there were doubts, fears, preoccupations that were not resolved prior to the wedding, these might have caused the simulation.
- Why would the person have chosen to marry (*causa contrahendi*) if he/she did not wish to have children?
- What were the person's 'matrimonial convictions' (thoughts/opinions) about marriage (were there any contrary to the nature of marriage?)?
- What was the person's personality/character and his/her psychological state?
- What kind of love was involved, erotic attraction, affection, etc.? The presence of a truly self-giving love would make it difficult to prove this exclusion.
- What were the postnuptial circumstances? In other words, how did the person behave during the common life, was there use of contraception, refusal of acts open to conception, recourse to abortion, etc.?[43]

The Rota often notes that the exclusion of the *bonum prolis* often goes hand in hand with the exclusion of the *bonum sacramenti* (indissolubility): someone who does not wish a lifelong union also does not wish to have children who will bind him/her to the spouse for life.[44]

Reflecting on the Newer Understanding of the bonum prolis *and Its Proof*

Many authors highlight John Paul II's teaching that the unitive and procreative aspects of marriage constitute one self gift of the spouses to one another. From this, we need to examine not just the parties' openness to acts that will generate offspring, but their openness to being spouses, caring for the good of one another, as well as the good of their family. Moneta argues that this teaching means that we need to understand the *bonum prolis* and the *bonum coniugum* together, not as separate and distinct ends.[45]

---

42 C. Boccafola, 1 June 1995, in *Simulation of Marriage Consent,* 343, #8.

43 H. Franceschi, "L'esclusione della prole," in *La giurisprudenza della Rota Romana sul consenso matrimoniale (1908-2008)*, in series *Studi giuridici* 83 (Vatican City: Libreria Editrice Vaticana, 2009) 205-206.

44 See, for example, "Relazione sull'attività della Rota Romana nell'anno giudiziario 2004," in *Quaderni dello Studio Rotale* 15 (2005) 39.

45 P. Moneta, "Il *bonum prolis* e la sua esclusione," in *Prole e matrimonio canonico*, in series *Studi giuridici* 62 (Vatican City: Libreria Editrice Vaticana, 2003) 92-93, where he cites John Paul II's reflections on the family of January 11, 1992 and December 17, 1994.

Franceschi sees it differently: "The conjugal act has a double dimension: unitive and procreative. Each conjugal act, and not simply for external exigencies, but because of its own nature, must remain open to potential paternity and maternity. This does not mean that each act will actually realize itself in paternity and maternity, because this depends on other facts, but that the conjugal act should remain open to that fruitful dimension."[46] Franceschi concludes: it is the work of the judge to determine the true will of the parties, analyzing the concrete case in order to know what the person's real choice was at the moment of consent. A will apparently open to children, but which radically reserves the future decision on 'how,' or 'if,' or 'when' to have children is not a truly matrimonial choice because it does not recognize nor accept the dimension of the mutual self-gift of a conjugality open to fertility, which is an essential element of the conjugal pact.[47]

After considering many different possibilities of exclusion of the *bonum prolis*, Zuanazzi reminds us that in every case it is necessary to examine the concrete facts, to evaluate the different decisions (to have a number of children, or to have only one child, to exercise fruitful conjugal relations from the beginning of the common life, or from a certain time, or never, to conceive only by natural means or with the help of medical techniques) to see if at their root we can find the will of the spouses to give themselves to one another reciprocally in their respective dimensions of potential paternity or maternity and to live out their generative capacities responsibly.[48]

Returning to the Lüdicke's suggestion that the equal decision of the spouses is an important key to evaluating whether or not the parties were open to the *bonum prolis*, we turn to the limitation of the number of children of a marriage.

Limitation of Number of Children
The general presumption is that if the number of children is limited, it is presumed that the use of the right to the *bonum prolis* is restricted, but not the right itself. In other words, limiting the number of children one will have is usually seen as a valid exchange of consent.[49] Boccafola suggests that it is not possible to limit the number of children, at least not unilaterally: "since by a true matrimonial consent the parties must give to one another and accept a perpetual

---

46   H. Franceschi, "'Bonum prolis' in the Married State of Life and the Canonical Consequences in Case of Separation or Nullity of Marriage," in *Forum* 17 (2006) 402.

47   H. Franceschi, "L'esclusione della prole," in *La giurisprudenza della Rota Romana sul consenso matrimoniale (1908-2008)*, in series *Studi giuridici* 83 (Vatican City: Libreria Editrice Vaticana, 2009) 200.

48   I. Zuanazzi, "Valori fondamentali del matrimonio nella società di oggi: la filiazione," in *Matromonio canonico e realtà contemporanea*, in series *Studi giuridici* 68 (Vatican City: Libreria Editrice Vaticana, 2005) 211.

49   See, for example, "Relazione sull'attività della Rota Romana nell'anno giudiziario 2004," in *Quaderni dello Studio Rotale* 15 (2005) 38.

and exclusive right to their bodies in relation to actions which of themselves are ordained to the generation of offspring. And this concerns a right which does not admit interruptions or limitations."[50] Thus, if one party limits the right to only one child or two children—and the other party does not agree—is that limitation invalidating?

Lüdicke gives an example of where his theory leads: "Let us imagine a case where both of the persons to be married have discussed and come to a decision based on responsible parenthood not to have more than two children. But the woman ... intends to disregard the thoughts of her husband. She decides she will become pregnant more often. ... In this case, the bride intends to reject the equal right of her future spouse to mutual involvement in the decision making process for having children. Such a marriage would be invalid due to the violation of the necessary consent."[51]

What of returning to the distinction between the exchange of the right and the non-use or abuse of the right: "If the right is excluded either permanently or temporarily, then marital consent is invalid. Even a temporary exclusion of a right invalidates matrimonial consent because the terms *ius* and *perpetuum* do not admit of any limitation. As an object of consent, the right must be one and indivisible ... A temporary exclusion of the right is against the principle of perpetuity of the right to conjugal acts *per se* apt for the generation of offspring. This perpetuity of the right pertains to the very essence of the conjugal covenant and it does not admit any limitation."[52] This is interesting because it is the limitation of the right *which is perpetual* which is invalidating.

Naron gives another example: "a selfish or hedonistic approach to children in which the couple enters marriage with the concept of children pushed far into the background. Their main goal is to obtain the good things of a materialistic life and to satisfy themselves prior to even considering children ... Contraceptives have been used throughout the marriage. This use of contraceptives is not the result of a deliberate decision to permanently exclude children but of a hedonistic approach to marriage that is just as incompatible with a truly Christian marriage. Thus, a couple who has actually used contraceptives throughout the marriage merely on the principle of continued postponement until they have enough material goods and de facto this point is never reached before the rupture of the marriage, the marriage is still invalid on the basis of the exclusion of children."[53]

---

50 C. Boccafola, 1 June 1995, in *Simulation of Marriage Consent,* 343, #7.

51 K. Lüdicke, "Some Sentences on *Exclusio Boni Prolis*," in *The Jurist* 69 (2009) 580.

52 M.A. Naron, "Rotal Jurisprudence on *Bonum Prolis*: A Critical Review," in *Philippine Canonical Forum* 4 (2002) 130-131.

53 Ibid., 131-132.

Conclusion

What is clear from this review of the literature is that there is much ferment in the understanding of the exclusion of the *bonum prolis*: the equality of the spouses in decision making, the decision for responsible procreation, even the moral liceity of the means for avoiding procreation are all factors that need to be assessed. We can expect to see much discussion in the coming years of the meaning of the *bonum prolis*, and the right of the parties to determine how to live their openness to children.

Seminar

Lay Volunteers as Field Advocates in Tribunal Ministry[1]
Sister Marilyn R. Vassallo, CSJ

Blessed John Paul II, in his apostolic exhortation *Christifideles laici*, reemphasized the church's teaching in this regard saying, "The voice of the Lord clearly resounds in the depths of each of Christ's followers who, through faith and the sacraments of Christian initiation is made like to Jesus Christ, is incorporated as a living member in the Church and has an active part in her mission of salvation" (*Christifideles laici*, Chapter 1, No. 3).

Though the call to build up the Body is baptismal (canon 204) it appears that much of the current motivation to involve laity more substantially in the ministries and mission of the church has to do with the changing church and society. No longer are lay ministers to be viewed as second class citizens in this once tightly knit clerical structure.

> A new state of affairs today both in the Church and in social, economic, political, and cultural life, calls with a particular urgency for the action of the lay faithful. If lack of commitment is always unacceptable, the present time renders it even more so. It is not permissible for anyone to remain idle (*Christifideles laici*, Chapter 1, No. 8).

Therefore, as members of the Mystical Body through baptism, members of the laity are called to be collaborators in building up the Body. One area of the church in which such collaboration is clearly evident is seen in lay involvement assisting marriage tribunals serving local parishes.

Many Are Called, Only Some Are Chosen

To ensure adequate staffing to do the work of a tribunal and in view of very limited financial resources to pay personnel, and with the approval of the local Ordinary, tribunals are turning to lay volunteers called "field advocates" for help. (It is important to note here that there is a growing interest in offering some recompense for the service provided by field advocates, but this thrust has not as yet taken hold in most dioceses utilizing the talents of these individuals.)

---

[1] For additional thoughts on lay advocates, see Marilyn R. Vassallo, CSJ, "Lay Advocates: Collaborative Bridge Between Tribunals and Parishes" in *CLSA Proceedings* 68 (2006) 189-196.

In the beginning of a process of recruitment, and working with pastors, there is a clarion call to the laity to get involved in tribunal work. A wide net is cast with the hope that many will indicate an interest in helping out. Frequently, at least one or two individuals from each parish voice an interest in becoming field advocates. However, not everyone recruited is suited to do the work of a field advocate in a tribunal.

Since the role of an advocate is to plead another's cause, selecting the "right" people becomes challenging and is as important as hiring paid personnel. A bad choice can have significant negative implications for a tribunal. One of the most obvious problems that can arise from a poor choice is that paid staff is forced to take time from their own schedules to unravel messy situations created by unqualified field advocates.

Personal Qualities of Field Advocates

There are certain qualities that are necessary in order to carry out the ministry well. Since this is a position that has no formal identification in the Code of Canon Law, it has been helpful in my diocese to parallel canon 1483 in stressing the various qualities helpful in calling forth individuals to assist in the ministry of the tribunal.

A field advocate must be a Catholic of good reputation, having attained the age of majority. Though helpful, it is not necessary for an advocate to hold a doctorate or licentiate in canon law (canon 1483). A field advocate is a person approved by ecclesiastical authority who safeguards the rights of a party in a canonical process by providing advice and technical assistance in preparing evidence for annulment cases.

Other important qualities that are solid foundation blocks needed by lay men and women chosen for this important service to the church are:

Integrity is so necessary for the building up of the Body of Christ through ministry. Maintaining confidences, telling the truth, and following through on promises are but a few aspects of what it means to act with integrity. There should always be correspondence among what we think and say and do. The *Catechism of the Catholic Church* states that, "Christians contribute to the building up of the Church by the constancy of their convictions and their moral lives. The Church increases, grows and develops through the holiness of her faithful..." (#2045).

Intelligence normally provides the gift of understanding the tribunal process and its many nuances. It enables the advocate to ask appropriate questions and to comprehend responses. It helps the advocate to deal with new and/or trying situations, while at the same time safeguarding the integrity of the process and avoiding distortion. There is an expectation that a field advocate be well versed in the specifics of the canons surrounding the processing of a case, as well as familiarity with the various grounds of nullity.

Compassion is the heart of the ministry. Advocates should be able to relate well to others. Their interpersonal encounters must be marked by what they have learned through their own encounters with Christ, in prayer and Scripture, and carried out with humility, gentleness and love, even as they stand boldly for the truth. Saint Paul, in his Letter to the Ephesians (4:15), urges the followers of Christ "to speak the truth with love." Truth without love can deteriorate into tyranny; love without truth can betray the message and those to whom the message is directed.

Formation

In addition to looking for personal qualities, an excellent formation program is necessary prior to a definitive selection of a field advocate. Training provides time to assess the qualities of those recruited before a final selection is made. It also provides the aspiring advocate an opportunity to evaluate whether or not this ministry is a right fit. It is well worth the time and effort to design and execute an excellent formation program. The benefits of such training will reap good dividends in the end. To have field volunteers who know what their role is and how to carry it out helps to ease the considerable burden of tribunal work for pastors and the tribunal staff.

When setting up a formation program it is crucial that approval be given by the bishop of the diocese and those pastors be encouraged to cooperate in the process by recommending possible field advocates from their parishes. A letter to the pastors and an invitation in the parish bulletin are ways of getting the message out.

Diocese of Shreveport, Louisiana: An Example

Over the years, the Diocese of Shreveport has tried many approaches to training of Field Advocates. The process described below worked best for us.

The Process

Field Advocate Formation
Once individuals are identified as possible advocates they are asked to participate in two, six-hour information sessions, a retreat, and a commissioning event.

What is covered in the information sessions?

Session One focuses on an explanation of the advocate's role, goals of the ministry, and relationships. Manuals are distributed. A well-written manual is a helpful tool that a potential advocate can make reference to throughout the program and beyond. Since the annulment process can be very complicated, a clear explanation of the annulment procedures, grounds to be considered when determining the validity of a marriage, and the importance of adhering to a strict timeframe in resolving marriage cases, are but a few of the topics described in the manual and further developed by the formation instructor during the first session. Some dioceses also provide a reputable textbook explaining the annulment process.

Session Two involves the presentation of a formal case using tribunal forms, as well as, the presentation of documentary cases using these forms. Filling out forms accurately and completely helps to move a process along in an expeditious manner. During this session, participants learn how to conduct an interview. How to ask questions and get the responses needed to evaluate a case are explained. The participants are provided case studies to assist in developing interviewing skills. Critical evaluations of interviewing styles are made. (It is realized that interviewing is a skill that takes time to develop and most advocates become better at it the more involved they become in the process, but there are a few who cannot master the skill.)

At the end of the information sessions each field advocate is interviewed in order to point out his or her strengths and weaknesses. A decision is made as to whether or not an individual is suited for the ministry of field advocate. The names of recommended candidates are forwarded to the bishop who accepts or rejects the recommendations.

Why a retreat for newly selected field advocates?

The church, down through the centuries, enjoins us to put one's gifts at the service of others. Saint Peter, in his first letter (4:10-11), reminds us that, "As each one has received a gift, use it to serve one another as good stewards of God's varied grace. Whoever preaches, let it be with the words of God; whoever serves, let it be with the strength that God supplies, so that in all things God may be glorified through Christ Jesus, to who belong glory and dominion forever."

A retreat reminds an advocate of the faith basis of the tribunal ministry to which he or she is called and encourages a deeper union with Christ so that in all encounters with others God's love and justice are evinced.

What does the Commissioning look like?

Soon after the successful completion of the formation program, a commissioning ceremony takes place. Those who have met the requirements of the program receive a letter of appointment from the bishop, a diocesan identification card, and an advocate pin. Acceptance into the ministry of field advocate ends with a reception for the families of the advocates and the clergy of the diocese.

On-going Formation
On-going education is imperative for service excellence. Field advocates are urged to attend diocesan and adult courses on such topics as sacraments, ethics, church history, Vatican II, and canon law. Continuing education helps the advocates to grow in knowledge of the underlying theological principles that are the foundation of marriage law in the Catholic Church.

Field advocates meet as a group as least two times a year to share experiences and to raise questions regarding their ministry. At these meetings, tribunal staff uses these occasions to update the advocates on recent developments in marriage law.

Continuing growth in the spiritual life is necessary for quality ministry (canon 210). Gathering occasionally for afternoons of shared prayer and community, helps the advocates deepen their understanding of their specialized role in church ministry and experience the support of one another both spiritually and personally.

Evaluation
Any program, if it is to continue to be successful, must evaluate the field advocates' effectiveness regarding such areas as quality of work, timeliness, knowledge of canon law, and attitudes. Every three years a questionnaire is sent to both clergy and field advocates in an effort to determine the quality and effectiveness of the ministry. The information provided helps the tribunal staff to improve and direct the field advocate program. Part of the questionnaire is dedicated to the evaluation of each advocate. An advocate is evaluated individually to determine whether or not he or she should remain in the ministry.

A quality field advocates program depends on the advocate's commitment to a responsible canonical understanding of all aspects of the annulment process and a pastoral approach to each situation. Such commitment has potential to enhance service to those seeking an annulment in the church while helping the field advocates to assume a rightful place in church ministry rooted in their baptismal call (canon 204). As a bridge between the tribunal and local parishes, the field advocates insure a more pastoral journey toward reconciliation and full participation in the sacramental life of the church.

Seminar

A Diocese, a Parish, a Religious Institute, a Member: An Exploration of Canon and Civil Law
Reverend Daniel J. Ward, OSB

Background

In the 1917 Code of Canon Law, the law governing parishes was under the section on pastors and benefices. The parish was defined by who the pastor was and by the income that it produced as a benefice. As a benefice, a parish could be united to another moral person such as a religious institute or religious house either *ad temporalis* or *pleno iure* (c. 1425/1917) with the approval of the Sacred Congregation for the Council. If *ad temporalis*, the religious institute had the right to the revenues from the parish but the religious superior had to propose to the bishop a diocesan priest to be the pastor. If the parish were united *pleno iure*, the religious institute or house was itself the pastor. The institute or the house not only had the right to the revenues and the superior had the right to propose to the diocesan bishop for appointment as vicar a member of the religious institute or house to be the vicar (c. 471/1917). With the permission of the religious superior, a diocesan bishop could appoint a religious priest as pastor of a "diocesan parish" (c. 630/1917).

In the 1983 Code of Canon Law, a parish is not defined by the person of the pastor and as a benefice, but rather as "a certain community of the Christian faithful stably constituted in a particular church whose pastoral care is entrusted to a pastor as its proper pastor under the authority of the diocesan bishop" (canon 515 §1). Canon 520 states that a juridic person cannot be a pastor. A diocesan bishop can entrust a parish to a religious institute by a written agreement defining the work to be accomplished, the persons to be assigned to the parish, and the financial arrangements.

In 2000, the Pontifical Council for Legislative Texts ruled against a religious institute in Spain regarding the imposition of a tax on public juridic persons subject to the diocesan bishop. The religious institute argued that since the parish had been entrusted to it *pleno iure*, the parish was not subject to the tax. Among other things, the decree stated that a parish is a distinct public juridic person and that a diocesan bishop has authority to separate a parish that is *pleno iure* from a religious institute.

Again in 2009, the Pontifical Council for Legislative Texts, in a decision regarding a parish united *pleno iure* to a religious institute in the United States, responded by providing a canonical analysis "Concerning parishes united *pleno iure* to a religious house pursuant to Canon 144.2 CIC of 1917" (October 3, 2009). The conclusion of the analysis states:

> With regard to parishes united *pleno iure* to existing institutes of consecrated life, there is no explicit legal provision, but the prohibition to appoint a pastor as a juridical person must be respected: the office of a pastor shall be provided in accordance with the Code in any case in favor of a physical person. A bishop can rescind a parish from a house of a religious institute, but he must always respect any acquired rights: the parish must be entrusted to the same religious institute through a revision of the agreement. Any change achieved with this intervention requires the opinion of the council of priests.

1983 Code of Canon Law: Parishes and Religious Institutes

Before moving to some case studies, it is necessary to recall briefly some present provisions of canon law regarding parishes and religious institutes.

As stated above "a parish is a certain community of the Christian faithful stably constituted in a particular church, whose pastoral care is entrusted to a pastor as its proper pastor under the authority of the diocesan bishop" (c. 515 §1). A key phrase in this canon regarding the governance of a parish is that the pastoral care of the parish is under the authority of the diocesan bishop. He establishes and suppresses parishes according to the norms of law. He alone appoints pastors, parochial vicars. He is responsible to determine if the priest is qualified for the office (c. 524).

It is no longer necessary to receive approval from Rome for a diocesan bishop to entrust a parish to a religious institute. Rather, he enters in to a contract with the religious institute for the staffing of the parish. The contract spells out the terms of the agreement, but the diocesan bishop always retains the right to judge the qualification of a member who is being proposed by the religious superior for the office of pastor or parochial vicar. The diocesan bishop alone appoints the member to the office and can remove him at any time. The religious superior has the right to propose a member for the office and can withdraw his permission for the member to continue in office.

Case Study One: A Parish Staffed by a Clerical Religious Institute

St. Francis Church is known as the "Franciscan parish" because it has been staffed by the Franciscans for over one hundred years. The parish was given to the Franciscans *pleno jure*. Prior to Vatican II, the provincial made a visitation of the parish every three years to examine the records, the buildings, and to ensure that the liturgical norms were being observed. The real property of the parish was purchased by the Franciscans and is civilly titled in the name of the province. The church is used by both the friars and by the parish. The friars live in the house next to the church.

The diocesan bishop proposes to rescind the parish *pleno iure*. The provincial is in agreement because he has heard about disputes between dioceses and religious institutes about liability.

In preparation for the meeting with the diocesan bishop, the provincial seeks canonical advice about the issues involved.

Analysis
Because of the decisions of the Pontifical Council for Legislative Texts, the diocesan bishop can decree that the Franciscans no longer have the parish *pleno iure*. However, he must entrust the parish to the Franciscans and respect their required rights which include the property rights of the Franciscans.

While the written agreement is a canonical requirement, it should be drafted similar to a civil law contract. However, the agreement probably is not enforceable by courts in the United States because of the doctrine of separation of church and state. Therefore, even before considering the other terms of the agreement, the parties need to agree on dispute resolution in case of future disagreements or violation of the terms of the agreement. Such an agreement should be designed to facilitate a resolution of the disagreement in a cost-effective and timely manner.

Specific provisions to be included would be some or all of the following:

1. The term of the agreement, such as, five years.

2. The number of priests the religious institute will provide for the parish.

3. The process and information that is to be included when the provincial proposes a priest to serve in the parish.

4. The compensation to be paid for the services of the priests.

5. The benefits provided the priests or a comparable amount of compensation to be paid to the religious institute in lieu of benefits.

6. The party that will bear liability and associated costs if a lawsuit is brought against a priest appointed to the parish.

7. The right of the provincial and the bishop to unilaterally remove a priest from the parish.

8. The right to terminate the agreement based on cause after providing notice to the other party.

9. The applicability of diocesan policies except as stated in this agreement.

10. The assignment of other friars to live in the house but not appointed to be pastor or parochial vicars.

11. Provisions for dispute resolution.

The diocesan bishop and religious superior also need to discuss real property issues since the real property is civilly titled to the Franciscans. A lease needs to be drafted regarding the use and responsibility for the real property, especially the church. If the parish is a separate corporation apart from the diocese, the agreement should be between the parish corporation and the corporation of the religious institute holding title to the real property. The terms of the lease should include:

1. The term of the lease and renewal provision.
2. A description of the real property to be leased.
3. The permitted uses of the real property by the parish.
4. Any limitations on the use and subleasing the real property.
5. Maintenance.
6. The ownership of personal property.
7. Provisions for dispute resolution.
8. Conditions for termination of the lease by either party.
9. Provisions on what happens to the real property if the diocese terminates the lease.
10. The parish's "right of first refusal" if the Franciscans decide to sell the real property.

Case Study Two: A Women Religious Serving as DRE

A pastor hires a woman religious to be the DRE of the parish. A few years later a new pastor is appointed. After a month, he terminates the woman religious. Their views of church seemed to differ.

Analysis

There are a number of issues to consider in this short scenario. The first is to look at the hiring and employment status of the woman religious when she initially was hired.

First, the person is being hired for a position within the parish. Canon 682 on the appointment of a religious by a diocesan bishop to an ecclesiastical office is not applicable in this case. Therefore, the hiring of the women religious should follow the regular procedures of hiring for any other person to work in the parish. Normally this is done by entering into a contract between the parish and the person. Not only should the terms of the contract clearly set out the job description, salary and benefits, hours, but also the grounds for discipline and reasons for termination of the person. Termination for either disciplinary reasons or for non-renewal of the contract generally requires a notice requirement.

There has been a misunderstanding of the employment status of a religious working within the church. In 1977, the Internal Revenue Service issued Revenue Ruling 77-290 which governs the taxability of wages earned by religious. The Revenue Ruling states that for *the purposes of taxation* a religious will be deemed an agent of his or her religious order under the following conditions: (1) the religious order is listed in the Official Catholic Directory; (2) the religious has the vow of poverty; (3) the religious works for an entity listed in the Official Catholic Directory; and (4) the entire amount of compensation is remitted to the religious order either directly by the employing entity or by the religious him/herself. If all of these conditions are met, the religious *for the purposes of taxation only* is deemed an agent of the order and no withholding is taken and no W-2 form is issued. Therefore, the compensation paid to the religious is not taxable because the compensation is paid to the religious order which is a non-taxable 501(c)(3) entity under federal law.

The misunderstanding of the Revenue Ruling is that many begin to believe that the deemed agency status for tax purposes also determined the employment status of the religious. This is not true. If the religious were truly an agent of his/her religious order, Revenue Ruling 77-290 would not have been necessary since the religious would actually be an agent. The office of the general counsel of the USCCB and the Resource Center for Religious Institutes, along with the Committee on Budget and Finance of the USCCB, concur on this issue.[1]

Therefore, in the above scenario, the woman religious has the rights of an employee according to the terms of her contract. In offering the position, the parish needs to present a clear contract to the religious. On the other hand, before accepting of the contract, the women religious needs to ensure that terms meet her expectations of employment.

The role of the superior of a religious in this case is a canonical role not a civil law role. The superior gives *canonical permission* to the religious to accept the position. This could be done by the superior giving a letter directly to the religious or to the parish. The superior should not sign the contract of the religious.

---

[1] "Diocesan Financial Issues" (Revised January 2009) developed by the Committee on Budget and Finance of the United States Catholic Conference of Catholic Bishops, Chapter V. Compensation of Religious.

However, in lieu of a letter of permission, the superior could sign an addendum to the contract stating that the superior gives canonical permission.

Since the religious superior is not a party to the employment agreement, the superior cannot terminate the contract. Her authority is only canonical, that is, to withdraw permission for the woman religious to continue in the position. This withdrawal of canonical permission has no effect on the employment situation unless a provision is included in the contract that requires the woman religious to have the permission of her religious superior to continue in the position. If the canonical permission is withdrawn, the parish has grounds to terminate the employment contract.

Case Study Three: A Religious Pastor Accused of Violation of the Sacramental Seal

A Catholic contacts the diocese and accuses the pastor of his parish of violating the sacramental seal. The pastor is a member of a religious institute. The chancellor contacts the provincial and informs him of the accusation. The priest is removed as pastor by the bishop. Some months later the provincial contacts the chancellor about the case. The chancellor says nothing has been done since it is the responsibility of the provincial to proceed with the case.

Analysis

Cases of the allegations of violation of the sacramental seal or solicitation within the context of the sacrament of penance seem to be more frequent. Article 16 of *Sacramentorum sanctitatis tutela*[2] requires that

> [W]henever the Ordinary or Hierarch receives a report of a more grave delict, which has at least the semblance of truth, once the preliminary investigation has been completed, he is to communicate the matter to the Congregation for the Doctrine of the Faith which, unless it calls the case to itself due to particular circumstance, will direct the Ordinary or Hierarch how to proceed further, with due, regard, however, for the right of appeal, if the case warrants, against a sentence of the first instance only to the Supreme Tribunal of the same Congregation.

When a priest of a religious institute is a pastor, associate pastor, or assisting the diocese in some other pastoral care of souls and is accused of a delict regarding the sacrament of penance, there does not seem to be a standard practice about who has the responsibility under Article 16 above to investigate and submit the matter to the Congregation for the Doctrine of the Faith (CDF). In some cases,

---

[2] *Sacramentorum sanctitatis tutela*, Congregation for the Doctrine of the Faith, revision 21 May 2010. Printed in *Roman Replies and CLSA Advisory Opinions 2010*, S. Euart, ed., et al., (Washington, DC: Canon Law Society of America, 2010) 88.

the diocesan bishop has conducted the preliminary investigation and submitted the case to CDF. In other cases, the diocesan bishop has conducted the preliminary investigation, turned the investigation material over to the religious superior and informed him that he is to submit the case. Still in other cases, the diocesan bishop has given the allegation to the religious superior to conduct the investigation and submit the matter to CDF. When the allegation has come to the religious superior, the religious superior generally reports the matter to the diocesan bishop and believes that the diocesan bishop will conduct the investigation and submit the report to CDF since it happened in a parish.

A diocesan bishop may not wish to take responsibility for such a case because of time, money, and potential liability. In addition, if the priest is found to have violated the sacramental seal how could the diocesan bishop enforce any penalties imposed since the priest is not subject to the diocesan bishop?

On the other hand, the religious superior may look at the allegation and believe that since this occurred within the priest's role as pastor, the responsibility for conducting the preliminary investigation and submitting the case to CDF belongs to the diocesan bishop. It was the diocesan bishop who appointed the priest to the office of pastor. It is under the authority of the diocesan bishop that the priest serves as pastor. The religious superior realizes that he does not have the expertise to conduct the investigation since religious institutes usually do not use the penal process of canon law. The religious superior also does not wish to give indication that the religious order is assuming liability for the incident.

The attempt to shift responsibility for the canonical process in cases of allegations concerning the sacrament of penance results in injustice for both the accuser and the priest. The penitent desires that some action be taken against the priest so that he is punished for his action and does not violate the seal again. The priest is left in limbo because he is suspended from ministry. He also has no clear indication of the nature and circumstances of the allegation. He has no forum in which to defend himself.

In the scenario given, who should proceed? Different arguments can be made to put the obligation on either the diocesan bishop or the religious superior. The words, "when the Ordinary or Hierarch receives a report..." seem to indicate that the Ordinary or Hierarch who receives the report proceeds with the matter. The canons on parishes seem clear that the pastoral ministry of souls is under the authority of the diocesan bishop. These would argue for the diocesan bishop to proceed.

On the other hand, the practical matter of the life of the priest while the matter is being resolved and the ability to carry out the imposition of a penalty seem to be within the authority of the religious superior.

It seems clear that there needs to be developed some guidance either on the national level or the Roman level on how to proceed in these matters of the allegations involving the sacrament of penance. To argue about the responsibility does not help the cause of healing and justice, and certainly gives the impression that the church is only concerned about legal issues rather than pastoral care of people.

Case Study Four: Religious Priest in the Process of Incardinating to a Diocese

A priest of a religious institute requests incardination into to a diocese. The diocesan bishop is willing to accept him and wishes to appoint him as a parochial vicar in a parish. The question arises about the procedure to be used for the probationary period and the responsibility for the priest during the probationary period.

Analysis

The normal procedure in this case is that the priest receives the consent of both the diocesan bishop and his religious superior. If both consent, he writes a petition addressed to the Congregation for Institutes of Consecrated Life and Societies of Apostolic Life requesting an indult of exclaustration for the purposes of incardination (canon 693). The petition along with the letters of the diocesan bishop and the religious superior are sent to the congregation by either the diocesan bishop or the religious superior. If the indult is granted, it states that the priest will be incardinated by law at the end of a five year period unless he, the diocesan bishop, or his religious superior objects prior to that point. The indult also includes the faculty for the diocesan bishop to incardinate the priest before the conclusion of the five year period. By the act of incardination, the priest is dispensed of his religious vows.

While the priest is in the probationary period and is assigned to a parish, the question arises under whose authority is he. The indult of exclaustration suspends the priest's obligations and rights within the religious institute. He is received into the diocesan ministry on a probationary basis and comes under the authority of the diocesan bishop. The difference is that this situation is temporary and may be terminated by the priest or the diocesan bishop. Therefore, responsibility for the priest lies with the diocesan bishop unless there had been an agreement between the diocesan bishop and the religious superior about various matters such as health care, living expenses, etc. If the priest does something that causes a liability issue, the diocese would be responsible since he is under the authority of the diocesan bishop and appointed as parochial vicar by him. However, if the religious superior held back knowledge about the priest that should have been given to the diocesan bishop prior to seeking the indult or, for that matter, received information later and did not inform the diocesan bishop, liability could shift to the religious institute.

If the priest had been serving in the diocese for several years, the diocesan bishop may decide that a probationary period is not necessary. In such a case, the priest writes a petition to incardinate, the religious superior gives his consent, and the bishop writes a petition requesting the priest to be incardinate the priest. The diocesan bishop sends the materials to the Congregation for Institutes of Consecrated Life and Societies of Apostolic Life. The congregation grants the indult of incardination.

Conclusion

Both canon law and civil law require that formal agreements be entered into between dioceses and religious institutes. While the agreements are usually drafted at a time when things are positive, the provisions of the agreements look to times when the situation has become muddied or the parties are not in agreement. The terms of agreements are to help avoid disputes in the future and to provide means of resolution. Therefore, agreements need to be drafted carefully and with an eye to the long term future.

Issues continue to arise between dioceses and religious institutes such as in the case of violation of the sacramental seal. It seems advisable that the Canon Law Society of America and individual canonists not only be aware of the issues but offer resolutions and processes. This will assist the church in not finding itself in a situation as happened with sexual abuse of minors.

Officer's Report

Report of the President
Rita F. Joyce

This year has been a remarkable year full of graced times in serving as the President of our Society. There were many occasions through the year when I had the opportunity to reflect on the "gift" that the Canon Law Society of America is because of the gifts so freely given by the members of our Society. Saint Paul reminds us in his Letter to the Ephesians: "but grace was given to each of us according to the measure of Christ's gift.... And he gave some as apostles, others as prophets, others as evangelists, others as pastors and teachers, to equip the holy ones for the work of ministry, for building up the body of Christ. ..."

We are a diverse membership of more than 1400 persons from 35 countries, made up of 1046 priests, deacons, and bishops; 98 vowed religious women and men; 95 lay men and 126 lay women; young and some not so young; some students soon to graduate and some working in a vast array of canonical ministry. Yet we all use our many gifts, freely given for the betterment of our Church, our own professional Society and the more global wider society, to help build up the body of Christ.

I am grateful to be a member of the Canon Law Society of America and to be a partner with you in this work. It has been an honor and a privilege to serve in the capacity of Vice-President and now President of the Society. I thank you sincerely for this unique opportunity and experience.

What is Done Throughout the Year

As soon as the annual convention draws to a close, the Board of Governors begins the work of implementing tasks as directed by the convention body, and this year it was no different. When the final address was given in Jacksonville, concluding our 73rd annual convention, the Board began the discussion of the best way to handle the resolution overwhelmingly passed. Specifically, the resolution was to offer to the United States Conference of Catholic Bishops the assistance of the Society in formulating appropriate procedures for the conduct of investigations into the work of theologians in the United States. We then communicated with the President of the Conference telling him of our resolution and offer to assist. We received a gracious acknowledgment from Cardinal Dolan. The Cardinal indicated that he would forward the letter to the USCCB Committee on Doctrine. In April of this year, Cardinal Wuerl wrote to say that the Committee on Doctrine was not engaged in a revision of *Doctrinal Responsibilities* and had no plans to propose such a revision. He said he would consult with the committee on Canonical Affairs and Church Governance regarding further contact with the Society on the canonical aspects of the communion of bishops and theologians, and that he would contact us again sometime in late summer with ways that we could be of assistance.

The largest post-convention task that the Board of Governors handled was examining the committees of the Society and determining where new appointments needed to be made and vacancies filled. In some cases this happens automatically as the senior member of the committee moves into the chair position as the former chair rotates off the committee. In other situations new chairpersons and members need to be appointed. Our membership is likely aware that the Society has a leaner committee structure in place as a result of our reorganization under the Future Initiatives Project (FIP). Nevertheless even with a leaner structure there are still twelve (12) committees with a chairperson and four (4) members. That is sixty (60) members of our Society who are called to perform extra service throughout the year as members of a committee.

There were a number of vacancies that needed to be filled and they were filled on an ongoing basis throughout the year. Special thanks are extended to all members who serve on committees especially those who have assumed the role of chairs of the committees. I wish particularly to thank Dr. Diane Barr, Nominations Committee; Rev. Greg Luyet, Resolutions Committee; Rev. Greg Bittner, Treasurer of the CLSA who serves as Chair of the Resource Asset Management Committee; Ms. Meg Romano Hogan, Board of Governors member and Professional Responsibility Chair; Rev. Msgr. Daniel Hoye, Chair of Church Governance; Rev. Msgr. Ricardo Bass, Clergy Committee Chair; Rev. Patrick Cogan, Convention Planning Chair; Sister Mary Catherine Wenstrup, Chair Institutes of Consecrated and Apostolic Life; Ms. Zabrina Decker, who also serves as Secretary of the CLSA, Chair of the Laity Committee; Rev. Msgr. John Alesandro, Chair of the Publications Advisory Board; Chorbishop John Faris, Chair Research and Development; Sister Victoria Vondenberger, Sacramental Law Committee Chair; Rev. Msgr. Victor Finelli, General Convention Chair; and Sister Ann Rehrauer and Rev. Msgr. Jace Eskind, Co-Chairs Convention Liturgy Committee. Also, gratitude is expressed to a special workgroup chaired by Dr. Lynda Robitaille that, as a result of the Society being awarded a grant of $5,000 from the 2011 Lay Ecclesial Ministry Symposium in Collegeville, Minnesota, is conducting a study on the authorization process for lay ecclesial ministers in twenty to twenty-five dioceses.

I commend those members of committees whose terms of office have concluded for your service. Members who were newly appointed this year graciously accepted the request to serve, and whether you said an immediate "yes" and are currently serving or your schedules and job changes precluded your acceptance, I thank you for the courtesy and generosity of spirit you showed in wanting to help the CLSA. The good work of the Society could not easily go on without you.

I urge you to take the time to read about our committees' progress in this reports booklet. You will see that our Society is doing well both fiscally and in terms of providing service to the Church. Please also know that if you have submitted your name to serve on a committee and you had a specific request, there may not have been any openings on that particular committee at this time, but there may be in the future. Additionally, certain committees have an automatic membership. So, for example, there are no openings on the Committee for Professional Responsibility because that is a committee composed of senior consultors. Also, certain committees have automatic *ex officio* members, so there may not be an open slot. However, your willingness to volunteer is appreciated and your services may be needed in the near future.

With new technology available to us, the CLSA has been considering webinars. This is a wonderful opportunity for continuing education on a particular topic without the need to travel, pay housing expenses, and be away from your office. Hopefully, some programming will be available in the fall of this year. Sister Sharon has been hard at work on this new venture.

Travel to Meetings

There is travel associated with the job of a Board member or officer of the CLSA. This year, both our winter and spring meetings were held at hotels convenient to the Baltimore airport. This saved significantly on expenses as we were able to book hotels that would provide the Society with a discounted rate for multiple stays, plus there was an added advantage in that Baltimore is an airline sale destination from many markets, resulting in another cost savings. The Board works very hard for two days attending to the business of the CLSA, reviewing committee reports, reviewing the work of the convention planning committee, and developing plans for future conventions with the assistance of the Research and Development Committee. A significant responsibility of the Board at their meeting is choosing the Role of Law award recipient.

Additionally, the Board of Governors has assumed travel to the various Regional Meetings hosted throughout the country. As much as possible, when a member of the Board is from a particular region, they represent the CLSA at that meeting. All meetings but one, the Western Regional Meeting, had someone attend from the Board; in one instance, Sister Sharon, as the Executive Coordinator, attended the Eastern Regional. Increasingly, attendance at the meetings becomes a factor of travel time, being able to be away from the office for extended periods of time, and costs. It is a priority to attend each meeting, and this is done as much as is possible. In prior years, the President or the Vice-President attended all of the meetings, being gone for weeks at a time, but this is virtually impossible today with the commitments that we all have in our own dioceses or in our work, and since most of us have multiple jobs to perform.

The President ordinarily attends the annual meetings of our sister societies and this year I had the honor of representing our Society at the Canadian Canon Law Society Convention (CCLS) held at the NAV Centre in Ontario, two weeks following our convention. Rev. Msgr. Wayne Kirkpatrick, President of the CCLS, and now Auxiliary Bishop Kirkpatrick, was a welcoming host. Then, in early May, I travelled to the Canon Law Society of Great Britain and Ireland (CLSGB&I) annual meeting in Edinburgh, Scotland. There were opportunities for spending time with our members who regularly attend there as well as enjoying the hospitality of the CLSGB&I and Rev. Msgr. David Hogan, JCD. The opportunity to interact with our sister societies and their membership is a true highlight. For several good reasons, including the *ad limina* visits of the U.S. bishops continuing until late spring of this year, it was determined that the biennial trip to Rome be postponed until 2013. Therefore, I will take the opportunity to travel to the Canon Law Society of Australia and New Zealand (CLSANZ) meeting in Auckland, New Zealand in September.

As CLSA Presidents before me have been, I was invited by Dean Anne Asselin, JCD to address the students and faculty of Canon Law at St. Paul University in Ottawa. The topic was "Consultative Bodies in the Catholic Church." The trip is usually scheduled for February so it was delightful to see the Rideau Canal frozen over and people skating or pushing baby carriages over the ice. This proved to be a great occasion to come to appreciate St. Paul University Canon Law Faculty and to spend time with Dean Asselin and the faculty, many of whom are members of our Society. I had the opportunity to meet our two scholarship recipients attending St. Paul, Annette Wellman and Paul Matenaer. Speaking of scholarship awards, the CLSA has also awarded scholarships for the upcoming academic year, in various amounts to three lay persons; one recipient is studying at Katholieke Universiteit Leuven, one is studying at the Universidad de Navarra, and one is completing studies at CUA. In many cases, without the assistance of the CLSA, lay persons who have no diocesan sponsorships would be precluded from canonical studies because of the expense. It is a wonderful work of the CLSA to fund these scholarships. For those who have donated, your generosity in making gifts to the scholarship fund is greatly appreciated. I humbly challenge the rest of our membership to assist in this responsibility in whatever amount is possible for you. It is in many respects our legacy to the Church and to our profession. By educating men and women in our discipline we insure that canonists will be available after we are gone to offer their gifts in building up the body of Christ.

Conclusion and Special Thanks

I began this report reflecting upon the diversity of the Society and the many gifts that you bring to the practice of canon law in service to our Church. I must now take the opportunity to briefly commend to you the men and woman in leadership roles who have served the Society for the past year by generously sharing their gifts. Reverend John Vaughan has tirelessly served as Vice-President and has shepherded the committees in their work this past year. He has been a tremendous personal support and a vital member of the leadership team. I pledge to him my prayers and my help in this next year as he begins his service to you in another way, as President.

Reverend Michael P. Joyce, CM has been a mentor and friend in both years I had the opportunity to work with him. His dedicated leadership of the Society never wavered and he was always quick to provide assistance, advice, and good-natured teasing about "our" names. Sister Sharon Euart, RSM, our Executive Coordinator, has made the job so much easier because of her competence and her professionalism and her knowledge about everything canonical. Sister Sharon has served the CLSA with the many gifts that she brings, both formerly as President of the Society and as our professional Executive Coordinator. Sister Sharon is known by the wider Church as the canonical expert and we have all benefitted from her talents. Obviously noted elsewhere in these reports, I wish to add that it was always a delight to work with Katie Richards, our office administrator. She will be missed as she goes on to other opportunities closer to her home and her family.

The Board of Governors, Reverend Gregory Bittner, Ms. Zabrina Decker, Ms. Meg Romano-Hogan, Very Reverend Mark O'Connell, Dr. Margaret Poll Chalmers, Reverend Thomas Cronkleton, Ms. Catherine Gilligan, and Deacon Jerry Jorgensen all bringing their diversity of gifts have served you well. They did tasks that were asked, took on special projects, and were kind and good to work with. As Meg Romano-Hogan and Mark O'Connell leave the Board they are thanked for their generosity of spirit, their contributions to the discussion, and their service to the Church and to all of us.

Of course I have only been able to do this job, this year and last year, because the director of my department is one of our past Presidents, Very Reverend Lawrence A. DiNardo. He is an understanding "boss" and one who has taught me what service to the Society is all about. Father Larry, I am very grateful for the flexibility and kindness you have shared when I needed to fulfill my responsibilities.

Also, I could not have assumed this role without the permission and support of my Bishop, Most Reverend David A. Zubik. He is a staunch supporter of his staff as they take on roles in the wider Church. Bishop Zubik is convinced of the importance of canonists for the wider Church and he shows this support both personally and financially thorough our scholarship fund.

Lastly, you, our members, are truly gifts to the Church. I prayed and marveled in gratitude that you placed your trust in our hands as the officers and the Board of Governors to be wise and responsible stewards. I offer to each of you a blessing paraphrased from the writings of St. Paul, as I conclude this year:

May the grace of the Lord Jesus hold you near and keep you safe
May the power of the Lord Jesus strengthen you in service to his Church
May the love and joy of the Lord Jesus fill your hearts;
And may the blessing of our God
The Father, the Son and the Holy Spirit
Be with you and remain with you always.

Officer's Report

Report of the Treasurer
Reverend Gregory T. Bittner

This is my second year in the position of Treasurer. I have spent the last year gaining greater familiarity with the budgets and financial operation of the four business units which comprise the CLSA. I continue to recognize and am humbled by the trust you have placed in me to oversee the financial operations of the Society. With the help of the Holy Spirit, the Resource and Asset Management (RAM) committee, and the Executive Coordinator and her office, we work to protect your hard earned and placed assets.

This report begins with last fiscal year's (2011-2012) results. If you look at the Part II: 2012-2013 Budget and its **accompanying schedules** which follow this report and concentrate on fiscal year 2011-2012 Budget and Actual's columns you will be able to understand where the following summary and highlights originate. The General Operations unit came in under budget and continued to reduce expenses. While the General Operations unit budgeted a deficit for the fiscal year 2011-2012; nevertheless, as in past years, it has actually made a profit. Income exceeded expenses by more than $25,000. Included in that gain, was almost $18,000 more in income than budgeted for new member dues. Committee expenses were more than $8,000 under budget. Service charges (which include credit card processing fees) were almost $3,000 under budget. The Office of the Executive Coordinator expenses was almost $2000 under budget. The BOG expenses were almost $7500 under budget. Member Services were almost $1800 under budget. The unaudited Balance sheet for the Operations unit appears very favorable standing at $638,000 on June 30, 2012.

The Publications unit posted a significant loss of almost $28,000 with gross profit of $64,000 and expenses of $92,000. Part of this loss is due to timing in the expenses incurred for books in one budget year and the corresponding income not received until the following budget year. An example of this is the *CIC* Reprint, which cost almost $30,000. Book production costs for *CLD XIV* was a little over $4,000. Also, one of our publications has not generated the income that was anticipated. Income received was from sale of inventory of prior publications and royalties. We continue to pay Bright Key Inc. for its services covering inventory, maintenance, and storage. The unaudited Balance sheet continues to be favorable, at $138,000, despite the loss. This is because we keep cash balance in our publications checking account and have inventory of newly printed publications.

Post-Convention Addendum: *After examining the auditor's "Review" for fiscal year 2011-2012, which was received after the report in the Convention Booklet, I have determined that the loss reported in the Convention Booklet of $28,000, while correct in terms of the revenue and expenditures actually incurred in fiscal year 2011-2012, does not reflect the "Review" figures which the auditor reported. The auditor made an adjustment to certain Publication unit expenses for fiscal year 2011-2012. The auditor properly recommended deferring the expenses incurred which related to the publication of the CIC Reprint and CLD XIV which were not available for sale until the 2012-2013 fiscal year. Consequently, the auditor recommended the deferral of expenses for these publications to the 2012-2013 fiscal year. As a result, with the deferrals we get a more precise snapshot of the financial results for the Publications unit in the 2011-2012 fiscal year.*

The Conventions unit had another very successful year as the Jacksonville convention, much like the prior convention in Buffalo, netted a substantial profit. Income exceeded expenses by $27,000. The unaudited Balance sheet, at almost $103,000, appears very favorable. The favorable financial position of the Convention unit allowed the 2011-2012 Budget to end in the black.

The Scholarship unit again took most of my time and that of the RAM Committee to try to understand how scholarships are accounted for and what number of scholarships we can financially budget. During fiscal year 2011-2012 three students received scholarships of $7000 each. The Resource and Asset Management (RAM), which I chair, again recommended additional changes in the accounting procedures for scholarships to the Board of Governors (BOG) which I hope will set the Scholarship unit on a sound financial course now and for the future. The unaudited Balance sheet, at $514,970, appears very favorable.

In addition to the everyday business operations, I have reviewed the Investments of the Society. The Society's Investments continue, since 2008, in Christian Brothers Investment Services (CBIS). CBIS provides a number of investment vehicles. The Society maintains two separate investment accounts, one for the General Operations unit and one for the Scholarship unit. Both investment accounts are with Catholic United Investment Trust (CUIT) Balanced Fund and have the same investment mix and objectives. The investment mix is generally 60% stocks and 40% fixed income. The fund return on our investments has underperformed relative to its benchmark and similar balanced funds over the last fiscal year, July 1, 2011 to June 30, 2012. This underperformance relative to benchmark was noted by our investment consultant with CBIS and is now being carefully monitored as we enter our new fiscal year. This does not mean we have lost money, only that our return was less than the benchmark by which it is compared. The fund return year to date relative to its benchmark has improved significantly. The Balances for both funds are shown below.

CLSA Business unit	Balance June 30, 2012	Balance June 30, 2011	Balance June 30, 2010
General Operation unit	$585,252.27	$553,793.99	$426,381.80
Scholarship unit	$466,500.09	$400,470.62	$334,334.22

Our investments have done very well, and provide the Society with a solid financial cushion for the future.

The Executive Coordinator continues to work with our new Accountant/Auditor, Mr. Joseph McCathran, a principal of Linton, Shafer, Warfield and Garrett, PA, CPA. The engagement began in April 2011. Their first audit was published in *Proceedings* for last year. I had the opportunity to talk with Mr. McCathran by phone after the audit was completed and I am comfortable with the direction in which we are heading. The current audit for fiscal year 2011-2012 should be in your Convention Booklet. The audit was not available at the time of the completion of this report, but I hope to review it at the Convention. The Accountant/Auditor will be recommending updated accounting procedures and possibly new software, which the Office of the Executive Coordinator (OEC) hopes to put in place in this fiscal year.

Last year, I reported that I had recommended to the BOG that it seriously consider a dues increase for the membership. The current dues are $200 per member. The last dues increase was in 2003. The BOG has discussed this and at the present time has deferred any action on this item. The reason being is that the RAM along with the Accountant/Auditor has determined that we can list the Audited Prior Year Net Assets under the General Operations Income column in our Budget to assist in the Balancing of our Budget. You will see that figure ($24,012) in the General Operations Budget Summary for the current fiscal year 2012-2013. This is real money that we have accrued in that prior fiscal year. This allows us to utilize and to account for the Excess from the Difference between Income and Expenses which we have realized in the past few years and hopefully will continue in the future. Additionally, the financial guidelines for the Society found in the BOG Handbook state that the General Operations unit CUIT Balanced Investment Fund could be utilized to offset General Operations Expenses. This is just one other financial option we have in our arsenal to finance expenses and run a favorable budget.

The OEC spent more time marketing the scholarship that we are able to offer to canon law students. Their efforts are reflected in the increased number of applicants as well as the increased number of donations to the scholarship fund. See the Executive Coordinator's Report for more detail on this matter.

The 2012-2013 Budget along with prior year's budget and actual income and expenses follow this report.

I will provide a report highlighting the 2012-2013 fiscal year Budget in the RAM Committee report.

Independent Auditor Report
Linton Shafer Warfield & Garret, P.A.
Certified Public Accountants

Board of Governors
Canon Law Society of America

We have reviewed the accompanying statement of financial position of Canon Law Society of America (a nonprofit organization) as of June 30, 2012 and the related statements of activities and changes in net assets, and cash flows for the year then ended. A review includes primarily applying analytical procedures to management's financial data and making inquiries of the organization's management. A review is substantially less in scope than an audit, the objective of which is the expression of an opinion regarding the financial statements as a whole. Accordingly, we do not express such an opinion.

Management is responsible for the preparation and fair presentation of the financial statements in accordance with accounting principles generally accepted in the United States of America and for designing, implementing, and maintaining internal control relevant to the preparation and fair presentation of the financial statements.

Our responsibility is to conduct the review in accordance with Statements on Standards for Accounting and Review Services issued by the American Institute of Certified Public Accountants. Those standards require us to perform procedures to obtain limited assurance that there are no material modifications that should be made to the financial statements. We believe that the results of our procedures provide a reasonable basis for our report. Based on our review, we are not aware of any material modifications that should be made to the accompanying financial statements in order for them to be in conformity with accounting principles generally accepted in the United States of America.

Our review was made primarily for the purpose of expressing a conclusion that there are no material modifications that should be made to the financial statements in order for them to be in conformity with accounting principles generally accepted in the United States of America. The Schedules of Program Services and Supporting Services for the year ended June 30, 2012 included as supplementary information are presented for purposes of additional analysis and are not a required part of the basic financial statements. Such information has been subjected to the inquiry and analytical procedures applied in the review of the basic financial statements, and we did not become aware of any material modification that should be made to such information.

The financial statements for the year ended June 30, 2011, were audited by us and we express an unqualified opinion on them in our report dated November 21, 2011. In addition, the supplementary information for the year ended June 30, 2011, contained in the Schedules of Program Services and Supporting Services, was subjected to the auditing procedures applied in the audit of the financial statements and certain additional procedures, including comparing and reconciling such information directly to the underlying accounting and other records used to prepare the financial statements or to the financial statements themselves, and other additional procedures in accordance with auditing standards generally accepted in the United States of America. Our report stated that the information was fairly stated in all material respects in relation to the financial statements taken as a whole. We have not performed any auditing procedures on either the financial statements or on the supplementary information since November 21, 2011.

Linton Shafer Warfield & Garret, P.A.
August 22, 2012

STATEMENT OF FINANCIAL POSITION
June 30, 2012 and 2011

	2012	2011
Assets		
Current Assets		
Cash	192,421	215,129
Cash - scholarship fund	48,470	52,210
Accounts receivable	-	2,084
Inventory	100,704	88,082
Prepaid expenses	14,196	21,816
Total Current Assets	355,791	379,321
Furniture and Equipment - at cost		
Furniture and equipment	16,546	15,383
Less: accumulated depreciation	(10,393)	(7,973)
Furniture and Equipment, Net	6,153	7,410
Other Assets		
Investments	585,252	553,794
Investment - scholarship fund	466,500	400,471
Total Other Assets	1,051,752	954,265
Total Assets	**1,413,696**	**1,340,996**
Liabilities and Net Assets		
Current Liabilities		
Accounts payable	$ 30	$ 1,598
Royalties payable	410	256
Deferred revenue	27,300	23,775
Total Current Liabilities	27,740	25,629
Total Liabilities	27,740	25,629
Net Assets		
Unrestricted		
Undesignated	813,735,	746,217
Board designated - reserve fund	-	55,412
Board designated - special projects/publications	55,266	56,102
Total Unrestricted	869,001	857,731
Temporarily restricted	516,955	457,636
Total Net Assets	1,385,956	1,315,367
Total Liabilities and Net Assets	**$1,413,696**	**$1,340,996**

See Accountant's Review Report and accompanying notes.

STATEMENT OF ACTIVITIES AND CHANGES IN NET ASSETS
For the Year Ended June 30, 2012
(With comparative totals for year 2011)

	Undesignated	Publications	Reserve Fund	Total	Temporarily Restricted	2012 Total (Unaudited)	2011 Total (Audited)
Revenue							
Membership dues	$241,907	$ -	$ -	$241,907	$ -	$241,907	$245,300
Convention, workshops	143,761	-	-	143,761	-	143,761	132,737
Sale of publications	-	74,259	-	74,259	-	74,259	69,302
Contributions	-	-	-	-	11,935	11,935	56,540
Interest and dividends	8,439	-	-	8,439	6,996	15,435	13,647
Royalties	-	3,693	-	3,693	-	3,693	7,067
Reprint permissions	-	1,800	-	1,800	-	1,800	700
Lay Ecclesial Ministry Grant	-	-	-	-	5,000	5,000	
Appreciation on fair value of investments	18,434	-	-	18,434	9,170	27,604	139,953
Net assets released from restrictions	29,194	-	-	29,194	(29,194)	-	-
Total Revenue	441,735	79,752	-	521,487	3,907	525,394	665,246
Expenses							
Program Services							
Publications	-	80,588	-	80,588	-	80,588	69,053
Convention, workshops	116,670	-	-	116,670	-	116,670	95,267
Membership services	7,902	-	-	7,902	-	7,902	13,222
Committees	2,017	-	-	2,017	-	2,017	8,266
Holy See and Austrialia	5,226	-	-	5,226	-	5,226	-
Lay Ecclesial Work Group	2,986	-	-	2,986	-	2,986	1,974
Scholarship fund	26,208	-	-	26,208	-	26,208	19,036
Total Program Services	161,009	80,588	-	241,597	-	241,597	206,818
Supporting Services	213,208	-	-	213,208	-	213,208	198,868
Total Expenses	374,217	80,588	-	454,805	-	454,805	405,686
Changes in Net Assets	67,518	(836)	-	66,682	3,907	70,589	259,560
Net Assets - Beginning	746,217	56,102	55,412	857,731	457,636	1,315,367	1,055,807
Equity transfer	-	-	(55,412)	(55,412)	55,412	-	-
Net Assets - Ending	$813,735	$55,266	$ -	$869,001	$516,955	$1,385,956	$1,315,367

STATEMENTS OF CASH FLOWS
For the Year Ended June 30, 2012

	2012	2011
Increase (Decrease) in Cash	Unaudited	Audited
Cash Flows From Operating Activities		
Changes in Net Assets	$70,589	$259,560
Adjustments to reconcile changes in net assets to net cash provided by operating activities:		
Depreciation	2,419	1,756
Unrealized (gain) loss on investments	(27,604)	(139,953)
Change in assets and liabilities:		
(Increase) Decrease in accounts receivable	2,084	516
(Increase) Decrease in prepaid expenses	7,620	(6,055)
(Increase) Decrease in inventory	(12,622)	11,696
Increase (Decrease) in accounts payable	(1,568)	(4,432)
Increase (Decrease) in royalties payable	154	98
Increase (Decrease) in deferred revenue	3,525	2,950
Net Cash Provided by Operating Activities	44,597	126,136
Cash Flows From Investing Activities		
Proceeds from sale of investments	5,412	-
Purchase of investments	(75,294)	(53,596)
Purchases of fixed assets	(1,163)	(1,415)
Net Cash Used in Investing Activities	(71,045)	(55,011)
Increase in Cash and Cash Equivalents	(26,448)	71,125
Cash Balance - Beginning of Year	267,339	196,214
Cash Balance - End of Year	$240,891	$267,339
Supplemental Disclosures		
Income taxes paid	$ -	$ -
Interest paid	$ -	$ -

See Accountant's Review Report and accompanying notes.

NOTES TO FINANCIAL STATEMENTS
For the Year Ended June 30, 2012 and 2011

1. Nature of Activities

The Canon Law Society of America (CLSA) is a national, not-for-profit corporation, established in November 1939 in Washington DC to promote canonical and pastoral approaches to significant issues within the Roman Catholic Church. In addition to a publication service, CLSA conducts an annual convention and other symposia to promote a better understanding of church law and its pastoral applications. Major sources of gross income are from membership dues, sales of publications and books and annual convention.

2. Basis of Financial Statement Presentation

According to Financial Accounting Standards Board (FASB) Codification Standards, CLSA is required to report information regarding its financial position and activities according to three classes of net assets:

(1) *Unrestricted Net Assets* - represents resources that are currently avail able for support of CLSA's operations.

(2) *Temporarily Restricted Net Assets* - represents resources that may be utilized only in accordance with the restricted purposes established by CLSA's bylaws. When a restriction expires, temporarily restricted net assets are reclassified to unrestricted net assets and reported in the statement of activities and net assets as funds are released from temporary restrictions.

(3) *Permanently Restricted Net Assets* - represents resources for which the principal is to be maintained intact and the income, may only be spent in accordance with the intent of the donor. CLSA currently does not have any permanently restricted net assets.

The financial statements are prepared on the accrual basis of accounting, whereby, revenue is recognized when earned and expenses are recognized when incurred.

3. Summary of Significant Accounting Policies

Cash and cash equivalents – For purposes of the statement of cash flows, CLSA considers all cash accounts and all highly liquid debt instruments purchased with an initial maturity of three months or less to be cash equivalents.

Investments - Investments in marketable securities with readily determinable fair values are reported at their fair values in the statement of financial position. Investment income or loss (including gains and losses on investments, interest and dividends) is included in the statement of activities as an increase or decrease in unrestricted net assets unless the income or loss is restricted by donor or law.

Investments consist principally of two mutual funds. Fair value of investments in securities is based on the latest reported sales price at June 30, 2012 and 2011.

Accounts receivable - Accounts receivable are stated at the amount management expects to collect from outstanding balances. The provision for uncollectible accounts is based on management's evaluation of the collectability of accounts receivable. CLSA considers accounts receivable to be fully collectible; accordingly, no provision for doubtful accounts is required. Books and publication receivables are considered uncollectible if not collected within 90 days after the sale.

Inventory – The inventory of books and publications is valued at cost, on the first-in, first-out method.

Property and Equipment - Purchases of furniture and equipment are recorded at cost. CLSA's policy is to capitalize expenditures for equipment purchased in the amount of $1,000 or more. Depreciation is calculated over an estimated useful life of five to ten years using the straight-line method. Depreciation and amortization for the years ended June 30, 2012 and 2011 totaled $2,419 and $1,756.

Fair Value – Financial Accounting Standards Board (FASB) Codification Standards defines fair value, establishes a framework for measuring fair value, and expands disclosures about fair value measurements and establishes a hierarchy for valuation inputs.

Fair value is the price that would be received to sell an asset or paid to transfer a liability in an orderly transaction between market participants at the measurement date. A fair value measurement assumes that the transaction to sell the asset or transfer the liability occurs in the principal market for the asset or liability or, in the absence of a principal market, the most advantageous market. Valuation techniques that are consistent with the market, income or cost approach are used to measure fair value.

The fair value hierarchy prioritizes the inputs to valuation techniques used to measure fair value into three broad levels:

- Level 1 - inputs are based upon unadjusted quoted prices for identical instruments traded in active markets.

- Level 2 - inputs are based upon quoted prices for similar instruments in active markets, quoted prices for identical or similar instruments in markets that are not active, and model-based valuation techniques for which all significant assumptions are observable in the market or can be corroborated by observable market data for substantially the full term of the assets or liabilities.

- Level 3 - inputs are generally unobservable and typically reflect management's estimates of assumptions that market participants would use in pricing the asset or liability. The fair values are therefore determined using model-based techniques that include option pricing models, discounted cash flow models, and similar techniques.

Revenue Recognition - CLSA bills membership dues annually on a basis which conforms to CLSA's fiscal year-end. Dues, workshop and convention registrations received in advance of the next fiscal year are deferred and recognized as revenue in the subsequent year.

Contributions are recognized when the donor makes a promise to give to the Society that is, in substance, unconditional. Contributions received are recorded as unrestricted, temporarily restricted, or permanently restricted support depending on the absence or existence and nature of any donor restrictions. Contributions restricted by the donor are reported as increases in unrestricted net assets if the restrictions are met or expire in the fiscal year in which the contributions are recognized. When a restriction expires, temporarily restricted net assets are reclassified as unrestricted net assets. Revenue from convention and workshop registration fees are recognized when the events take place.

Tax Status - CLSA is exempt from federal income tax under Section 501(c)(3) of the Internal Revenue Code. CLSA has not been classified by the Internal Revenue Service as a private foundation. Income which is not related to the exempt purpose, less applicable deductions, is subject to Federal and state corporate income tax. For tax purposes the organizations open audit years are 2008 to 2011.

Expense Allocations - Directly identifiable expenses are charged to programs and supporting services. Overhead and expenses related to more than one function are not allocated but are included in supporting services.

Estimates - In preparing financial statements in conformity with generally accepted accounting principles, management is required to make estimates and assumptions that affect the reported amounts of assets and liabilities, the disclosure of contingent assets and liabilities at the date of the financial statements, and the reported amounts of revenues and expenses during the reporting period. Actual results could differ from those estimates.

Financial Instruments – CLSA's financial instruments consist of investments, accounts receivable, accounts payable and accrued expenses. It is management's opinion the CLSA is not exposed to significant interest rate or credit risk arising from these instruments. Unless otherwise noted, the fair values of these financial instruments are market values of these financial instruments, and approximate their carrying values.

8

4. Investments

Investments at June 30, 2012 and 2011, which are all considered level 1, consist of the following:

	Cost	Market
Balanced funds	$983,277	$1,051,752
Total Investments 6/30/2012	$983,277	$1,051,752
Total Investments 6/30/2011	$909,418	$954,265

By fund type at June 30, 2012 and 2011:

	2012 Cost	2012 Market	2011 Cost	2011 Market
Unrestricted	$536,311	$585,252	$519,439	$553,794
Restricted	446,966	466,500	389,979	400,471
Total Investments	**$983,277**	**$1,051,752**	**$909,418**	**$954,265**

CLSA invests in a professionally managed portfolio that contains balanced funds. Such investments are exposed to various risks such as interest rates, market and credit. Due to the level of risk associated with such investments and the level of uncertainty related to changes in the value of such investments, it is at least reasonably possible that changes in risks in the near term would materially affect investment balances and the amounts reported in the financial statements.

Investment income, which is included in the Statement of Activities for the years ended June 30, 2012 and 2011 is comprised of the following:

	2012 Unrestricted	2012 Temporarily Restricted	2011 Unrestricted	2011 Temporarily Restricted
Net Unrealized gains (losses)	$18,434	$9,170	$79,603	$60,350
Interest and dividends	8,439	6,996	7,816	5,831
Net Investment Income	**$26,873**	**$16,166**	**$87,419**	**$66,181**

5. Concentration of Credit Risk

CLSA maintains its cash in bank deposit accounts, which at times, may exceed federally insured limits. CLSA has not experienced any losses in such accounts and believes it is not exposed to any significant financial risk on cash.

6. Commitments

Office Lease - CLSA leased office space in Washington DC for a 10 year period ending December 31, 2017. Monthly rent payments for the first through the fifth year of the lease are $1,564. Monthly rent payments for the sixth through the tenth year was scheduled to increase by the CPI each July 1st. This increase has not yet occurred. Rent expense for the years ended June 30, 2012 and 2011 was $18,768 and $18,768, respectively. Minimum future rental obligations are: 2013 - $18,766; 2014 - $18,766; 2015 - $18,766; 2016 – 18,766; 2017 - $18,766.

Copier Lease - CLSA entered into a four year lease for a copier beginning August 2008. The lease payment is $230 per month. Minimum future lease obligations are $460 for the year 2013.

Postage Lease - CLSA entered into a fifty-four month lease for a postage machine ending November 1, 2010. The lease payment is $127 per quarter.

7. Board Designated Funds

The Board has designated that net income from the sales of publications and books be set aside for special purposes known as the special projects fund.

			2012	**2011**
Balance - Beginning of Year			$56,102	$48,086
	Add	Publication income	74,259	69,302
		Royalty income	3,693	7,067
		Reprint permissions	1,800	700
	Less	Publication expenses	(80,588)	(69,053)
Balance - End of Year			$55,266	$56,102

The Board had designated $55,412 as a reserve account at June 30, 2011 to be set aside for future purposes. This account was transferred to the temporarily restricted scholarship fund during the year ended June 30, 2012.

8. Temporarily Restricted Net Assets

The activity in the temporarily restricted net assets for years 2012 and 2011 is as follows:

	Scholarship Fund	Ministry Grant	Total
Balance June 30, 2010	$353,951	-	$353,951
Income	122,721	-	$122,721
Expenses	(19,036)	-	(19,036)
Balance June 30, 2011	$457,636	-	$457,636
Income	28,101	5,000	33,101
Expenses	(26,208)	(2,986)	(29,194)
Transfer from reserve account	55,412	-	55,412
Balance June 30, 2012	$514,941	$2,014	$516,955

9. Annual Meeting Site Reservation Agreements

CLSA has reserved hotel space for future annual meetings. The terms of these reservation agreements provide that a few will be assessed to CSLA if the reservation is canceled due to site change, within a specified period prior to the meeting dates.

10. Executive Coordinator's Contract

CLSA has contracted with Sisters of Mercy of the Americas South Central Community and Sister Sharon Euart to serve as their Executive Coordinator beginning August 1, 2008 and ending July 31, 2011. The agreement has been renewed extending the contract date to December 31, 2013.

11. Subsequent Events

Management has evaluated subsequent events through August 22, 2012, the date that the financial statements were available to be issued. There were no significant events to report.

SUPPLEMENTARY INFORMATION
Schedule of Program Services
For the Year Ended June 30, 2012

	2012	2011
Publications		
Cost of publications sold	$22,920	$ 14,641
Executive coordinator office	15,540	10,615
Royalty expense	1,781	1,786
Advertising	6	-
BrightKey	40,341	42,011
Total Publication Expenses	80,588	69,053
Convention and Pre-convention Workshop		
Coordination	76,029	49,494
Translation services	-	14,072
Pre-convention expenses		-
Food service	1,888	1,050
Honoraria	8,000	6,560
Speakers' travel	1,892	4,307
Printing	3,127	2,610
Freight	592	334
Other	11,062	3,269
Postage	1,134	1,133
Convention chair	1,338	1,002
Liturgy	1,309	1,797
Supplies	6,7999	6,682
Convention planning	2,840	2,067
Convention company	660	330
Liturgy chair	-	560
Total Convention and Pre-Convention Workshop	116,670	95,267
Membership Services		
Postage	4,248	5,050
Printing	3,587	3,082
Newsletter	67	5,090
Total Membership Services	7,902	13,222

Schedule of Program Services continued

	2012	2011
Visit to Holy See and Australia Trip	5,226	1,974
Committees		
Church governance	$144	$ 67
Resource & asset management	143	198
Publications advisory board	-	3,930
Nominations	1,240	2,050
Clergy		703
Laity	202	959
Other	288	295
Sacramental law	-	64
Total Committees	2,017	8,266
Lay Ecclesial Ministry Work Group	2,986	-
Scholarship Fund		
Scholarships paid	25,120	18,250
Scholarships expenses	1,088	786
Total Scholarship Fund	26,208	19,036
Total Program Services	$241,597	$ 206,818

See Accountants' Review Report and accompanying notes.

SUPPLEMENTARY INFORMATION
Schedule of Supporting Services
For the Year Ended June 30, 2012

	2012 (unaudited)	2011 (audited)
Board of Governors		
Rental housing	$11,821	$ 11,311
Travel	7,348	6,029
Food service	4,401	4,305
Other expenses	1,226	896
President	3,808	3,164
Vice President	-	853
Treasurer	2	-
Executive Coordinator Office	163,375	151,786
Depreciation expense	2,419	1,756
Rent expense	18,768	18,768
Total Supporting Services	$213,208	$198,868

Annual Budget
Fiscal Year 2012-2013

GENERAL OPERATIONS		
Income	$	252,012
Expenses	$	260,283
Excess/(Deficit)	**$**	**(8,271)**
PUBLICATIONS		
Income	$	105,000
Expenses	$	87,975
Excess/(Deficit)	**$**	**17,025**
CONVENTIONS		
Income	$	137,700
Expenses	$	135,950
Excess/(Deficit)	**$**	**1,750**
Subtotal Gen. Ops., Pub. & Conv.*	**$**	**10,504**
SCHOLARSHIP FUND		
Income	$	34,600
Expenses	$	22,600
Excess/(Deficit)	**$**	**12,000**
Grand Total*	**$**	**22,504**

*Note: Since Scholarship income by definition belongs to the Scholarship Fund, it cannot be used to balance the overall budget. Hence, the first three "companies" as a whole need to achieve a balance independently, and the number labeled as "Grand Total" is not a simple "operational" profit. An "excess" in the Scholarship Fund represents an increase in the fund, which is needed for the fund to grow.

GENERAL OPERATIONS

	Budget FY 12-13	Actual FY 11-12	Budget FY 11-12	Actual FY 10-11	Budget FY 10-11
INCOME					
Investment Income/ CBIS	$6,000	$8436	$5,000	$7,809	$6,000
Interest Income/RCT	-	$3	-	$7	$50
Dues Income (Note 1)	$221,000	$241,907	$225,000	$245,300	$240,000
Use of Prior Year Net Assets (Note 2)	$24,012	-	-	-	-
Web Seminar Income	$1,000	-	-	-	-
TOTAL INCOME	**$252,012**	**$250,346**	**$230,000**	**$253,116**	**$246,050**
EXPENSES					
Staff Compensations and Benefits (Note 3)	$138,499	$131,743	$131,772	$118,559	$117,430
Service Charges					
Bank Service Charges/Wachovia	$100	$40	$50	$93	$50
Flex Fund/RCT	$100	$82	$100	$90	$100
Credit Card Fees	$4,000	$3,118	$6,000	$2,867	$6,500
Sub-total	$4,200	$3,240	$6,150	$3,050	$6,650
OEC Expenses (by account number)					
Postage Meter Lease and Supplies	$1,100	$679	$1,100	$1,110	$900
Insurance & Workers Compensation	$2,200	$3,109	$2,500	$1,984	$2,500
Hospitality	$600	$396	$500	$526	$500
Postage/UPS/FedEx	$800	$607	$800	$766	$1,000
Office Supplies	$2,500	$2,732	$2,500	$2,784	$2,800
Telephone/ISP/DSL	$3,000	$3,222	$3,000	$3,191	$3,500
Travel	$2,500	$2,282	$2,500	$1,680	$3,000
Continuing Education, OEC	$1,000	$25			
Taxes	$100	-	$100	-	$100
Furniture and Equipment	$1,500	$311	$1,000	$933	$1,000
Books and Periodicals	$500	$792	$400	206	$400
Prof. Collaboration w/ National Orgs.	$500	-	$500	$2,345	$500
Rent	$19,144	$18,768	$18,768	$18,768	$18,768

GENERAL OPERATIONS continued

	Budget FY 12-13	Actual FY 11-12	Budget FY 11-12	Actual FY 10-11	Budget FY 10-11
Copier Lease and Maintenance	$4,300	$4,366	$4,300	$3,508	$3,700
Sub-total	$39,744	$37,289	$37,968	$37,800	$38,668
Professional Services					
Accountant/Auditor (Note 4)	$4,500	$4,350	$6,000	$6,000	$6,000
Web Design & Maintenance	$5,940	$5,500	$5,500	$ 5,940	$6,500
Legal Services	$500	-	$500	-	$500
Sub-total	$10,940	$9,850	$12,000	$11,940	$13,000
Member Services					
General Printing	-	-	-	-	$100
General Postage	$1,500	$1,314	$1,000	$1,038	$1,500
Newsletter Printing (Note 5)	-	-	$500	$2,463	$5,500
Newsletter Postage (Note 5)	$100	$67	$ 500	$2,627	$4,000
Proceedings Printing	$5000	$4,901	$5,000	$4,574	$6,500
Proceedings Postage	$4,500	$2,934	$4,000	$4,012	$5,500
Sub-total	$11,100	$9,216	$11,000	$14,714	$23,100
Board of Governors, Meetings					
Food	$5,900	$4,401	$5,400	$4,305	$5,500
Lodging	$13,000	$11,821	$12,000	$11,311	$11,000
Meeting Space	$1,400	$1,174	$500	$664	$500
Postage/UPS	$50	-	$100	$11	$100
Supplies	$50	-	$50	$125	$100
Telephone	$100	$93	$100	$96	-
Travel	$9,500	$7,348	$9,500	$6,029	$8,500
Rome or Australia Trip	$10,000	$5,226	$10,000	$1,974	$10,000
Sub-total	$40,000	$30,063	$37,650	$24,515	$35,700
Board of Governors, Officers					
President	$6,000	$3,487	$6,000	$3,164	$7,000
Vice President/Past President	$500	-	$700	$853	$1,000
Treasurer/Secretary (Note 6)	$500	$2	$500	-	$600
Sub-total	$7,000	$3,489	$7,200	$4,017	$8,600

GENERAL OPERATIONS continued

	Budget FY 12-13	Actual FY 11-12	Budget FY 11-12	Actual FY 10-11	Budget FY 10-11
Seminars & Meetings					
Special Faculties Seminar (Note 7)	-	-	-	$(4,567)	-
Sub-total	-	-	-	$(4,567)	-
Committees					
Constitutional Committees *(order of Const.)*					
Nominations Committee	$1,800	$1,240	$1,800	$2,050	$1,500
Resolutions Committee	$100	-	$100	-	$100
Resource & Asset Management	$500	$143	$1,500	$198	$1,500
Professional Responsibilities Committee	-	-	-	-	$200
Standing Committees *(alphabetical)*					
Church Governance Committee	$500	$144	$250	$67	$2,000
Clergy Committee	$1,500	-	$1,500	$703	$500
Institutes of Consecrated Life Cmte.	$150	$13	$150	-	$400
Laity Committee	$250	$202	$2,500	$959	$2,500
Research & Development	$1,500	$144	$250	-	$100
Sacramental Law Committee	$1,000	-	$1,200	$64	$1,200
Approved Cmte. Work Contingency	$1,000	$288	$1,000	$296	$1,000
Sub-total	$8,300	$2,174	$10,250	$4,337	$11,000
Miscellaneous					
General Operations Contingencies	$500	-	$500	-	$500
Sub-total	$500	-	$500	-	$500
Additional Transactions - Previous FY					
Secretary (Note 6)	-	-	-	-	$100

GENERAL OPERATIONS continued

	Budget FY 12-13	Actual FY 11-12	Budget FY 11-12	Actual FY 10-11	Budget FY 10-11
Publications Advisory Board (Note 8)	-	-	-	$2,362	$2,400
Canon Law Digest Committee (Note 8)	-	-	-	-	$500
Former Committees			-		
Advisory Opinions Committee	-	-	-	-	$100
Diocesan Synods Task Force	-	-	-	-	-
Professional Responsibility Rev. Task Force	-	-	-	-	-
Reg. Workshops for Adv. In Penal Cases	-	-	-	-	-
Roman Replies Committee	-	-	-	-	-
Sub-total	-	-	-	$2,362	$3,100
TOTAL EXPENSES	**$260,283**	**$227,055**	**$ 254,490**	**$ 216,726**	**$257,748**
EXCESS/DEFICIT	**$ (8,271)**	**$23,291**	**$ (24,490)**	**$ 36,389**	**$ (11,698)**

Note 1: This line includes all income from dues (past dues, current dues and new member dues).

Note 2: This line item represents the policy to use the Society's net assets to keep membership dues from increasing. The figure for FY 2012-2013 is the audited net asset amount from FY 2010-2011.

Note 3: This line includes the Executive Coordinator & Executive Assistant salaries, compensation for one Part-Time Assistant, all medical benefits, payroll taxes, and a minimal cost for outsourcing the payroll for one employee.

Note 4: This item is apportioned between General Ops and Publications, at a distribution rate of 75% and 25% respectively.

Note 5: These line items are based on four newsletters distributed electronically.

Note 6: The Secretary and Treasurer now share one budget line, whereas in the past they each had a separate budget.

Note 7: This negative number represents a profit of $4,567 from the seminar.

Note 8: These committees' expenses are now included in the Publications Budget.

PUBLICATIONS

	Budget FY 12-13	Actual FY 11-12	Budget FY 11-12	Actual FY 10-11	Budget FY 10-11
INCOME					
Publication Sales	$80,000	$57,960	$100,000	$56,621	$90,000
Reprint Permissions	$1,000	$1,800	$600	$700	$400
Royalty Income	$4,000	$5,777	$5,000	$7,382	$5,000
Shipping/Restocking - BrightKey	$20,000	$14,152	$40,000	$11,983	$20,000
Resolution Implementation (Note 1)	-	$5,000	$5,000	-	-
TOTAL INCOME	**$105,000**	**$84,689**	**$150,600**	**$76,686**	**$115,400**
EXPENSES					
Staff & Professional Services					
Staff Salary (Note 2)	$4,800	$4,237	$4,237	$3,509	$3,509
Accountant	$2,000	$2,000	$2,000	$2,000	$2,000
Publications Advisory Board (Note 3)	$2,200	$246	$2,150	-	-
Canon Law Digest Committee (Note 3)	-	-	$500	-	-
Sub-total	$9,000	$6,483	$8,887	$5,509	$5,509
Royalties Paid					
Royalties/*CCEO*	$200	$153	$250	$181	$400
Royalties/*CIC*	$1,600	$1,241	$1,500	$1,106	$1,200
Royalties/*Dignitas Connubii*	$400	$334	$450	$423	$500
Royalties/*Selected Issues*	$50	$17	$100	$58	$100
Royalties/*Reception and Communion*	$25	$36	$50	$18	$100
Sub-total	$2,275	$1,781	$2,350	$1,786	$2,300
Publication Expenses					
Advertising - Printing	$500	$6	$500	-	$1,500
Advertising - Electronic	$100	-	$500	-	$500
Book Production	$20,000	$40,746	$40,000	$4,067	$40,000
Storage of Negatives	$100	$87	$100	$88	$100
Copyright Applications	$150	$70	$150	$70	$150
Outsourcing - BrightKey	$50,000	$40,585	$50,000	$42,011	$47,000
Sub-total	$70,850	$81,494	$91,250	$46,236	$89,250

PUBLICATIONS continued

	Budget FY 12-13	Actual FY 11-12	Budget FY 11-12	Actual FY 10-11	Budget FY 10-11
Office of the Executive Coordinator					
Postage	$100	$109	$200	$80	$200
Supplies	$150	$42	$100	$154	$100
Sub-total	$250	$151	$300	$234	$300
Special Projects Resolution Implementation (Note 1)	-	$38	$5,000	-	-
Sub-total	-	$38	$5,000	-	-
Service Charges Bank Service Charges - Wachovia	$100	-	$50	-	$50
Credit Card Fees	$5,000	$2,231	$5,000	$ 2,099	$5,000
Sub-total	$5,100	$2,231	$5,050	$ 2,099	$5,050
Miscellaneous Publications Contingencies	$500	-	$500	-	$500
Sub-total	$500	-	$500	-	$500
TOTAL EXPENSES	**$87,975**	**$92,178**	**$113,337**	**$55,865**	**$106,309**
EXCESS/DEFICIT	**$17,025**	**$ (7,489)**	**$37,263**	**$20,822**	**$9,091**

Note 1: These lines are for the Resolution approved by the membership at the 2009 convention. Since it includes designated funds and could stretch across many fiscal years, it is not included in the annual budget.

Note 2: Publications is currently responsible for 10% of staff salary only.

Note 3: The Committees associated with Publications were previously in the General Operations budget.

CONVENTIONS

	Budget FY 12-13	Actual FY 11-12	Budget FY 11-12	Actual FY 10-11	Budget FY 10-11
INCOME					
Convention Fees (Note 1)	$108,500	$108,048	$97,500	$103,750	$105,625
Pre-Conv. Fees (Note 2)	$15,000	$18,805	$13,750	$19,800	$15,000
Exhibitors' Fees	$1,800	$2,205	$2,700	$3,470	$3,600
Sponsors' Donations	-	$500	-	$300	-
Additional Banquet Fees	$200	$300	$100	$300	-
Guest Registrations	$200	$200	$200	$550	-
Hotel Commission (Note 3)	$12,000	$13,703	-	-	-
Contribution from Gen Ops. (Note 4)	-	-	-	$ (24,950)	-
TOTAL INCOME	**$137,700**	**$151,761**	**$114,250**	**$103,220**	**$124,225**
EXPENSES					
Professional Services					
General Conv. Chair	$1,800	$1,292	$1,800	$1,022	$1,800
Conv. Liturgy Chair	$600	-	$600	$560	$600
Conv. Planning Cmte	$2,000	$1,444	$2,000	$2,067	$2,000
Office of the Executive Coordinator	$1,500	$554	$1,000	$998	-
Convention Company	$600	$437	$500	$330	$700
Sub-total	$6,500	$3,727	$5,900	$4,957	$5,100
Pre-Convention					
Honoraria	$3,000	$3,000	$3,000	$3,000	$3,000
Liturgy	$500	$400	$400	$400	$400
Printing	$150	$55	$200	-	$500
Shipping	$50	$40	$50	-	$50
Speaker's Travel	$2,500	$1,365	$1,500	$1,256	$300
Supplies	$150	$69	$200	$13	$200
Sub-total	$6,350	$4,929	$5,350	$4,669	$4,450
Convention					
Convention Company Nix (Note 5)	$40,000	$39,284	$39,000	$32,296	$76,000
Convention Hotel Hyatt (Note 5)	$45,750	$36,745	$27,000	$11,237	-
Audio Visual (Note 6)	$8,500	$7,630	$8,000	$5,960	-
Food	$2,000	$1,888	$2,000	$1,050	$1,200
Honoraria (Note 7)	$5,500	$5,000	$5,500	$3,560	$3,900
Liturgy	$2,000	$909	$2,000	$1,397	$1,500
Postage	$2,000	$1,134	$2,200	$1,133	$ 2,200
Printing	$4,000	$3,072	$4,000	$2,610	$6,000
Shipping	$650	$553	$500	$334	$500
Speaker's Travel	$2,000	$527	$1,200	$3,050	$2,500

CONVENTIONS continued

	Budget FY 12-13	Actual FY 11-12	Budget FY 11-12	Actual FY 10-11	Budget FY 10-11
Supplies	$7,000	$6,730	$7,000	$6,669	$4,000
Telephone/Internet	$100	-	$100	-	$150
Sub-total	$119,500	$103,472	$98,500	$69,296	$97,950
Service Charges					
Bank Service Charges					
Wachovia	$100	-	$50	-	$50
Credit Card Fees	$3,000	-	$3,000	$2,271	$1,000
Sub-total	$3,100	-	$3,050	$2,271	$1,050
Miscellaneous					
Conventions					
Contingencies	$500	-	$500	-	$500
Sub-total	$500	-	$500	-	$500
Additional Transactions - Previous FY					
Pre-Convention					
Postage	-	-	-	-	$50
Translation Services (Note 8)	-	-	-	$14,072	$10,400
Sub-total	-	-	-	$14,072	$10,400
TOTAL EXPENSES	**$135,950**	**$114,618**	**$113,300**	**$95,265**	**$119,450**
EXCESS/DEFICIT	**$1,750**	**$37,143**	**$950**	**$7,955**	**$4,775**

Note 1: FY 2012-2013 budget assumes 310 attendees at $350 each.

Note 2: FY 2012-2013 budget assumes 60 attendees (25 and 35 respectively) @ $250 each.

Note 3: This line represents the hotel room commission we receive as a result of the work of Nix and Associates; this commission was previously included in the hotel bill.

Note 4: This contribution from Gen Ops was made to cover the hotel bill in 2010.

Note 5: These two lines were previously consolidated (to include all hotel and Nix fees); we are now splitting these expenses into two separate accounts.

Note 6: This line used to be included in the Convention Company line. With the increase in AV fees, it is important to categorize this expense separately.

Note 7: This line reflects an increase in honoraria payments to speakers; the last increase was in 1992.

Note 8: The CLSA did not pay the Translation Service Company for the translation of the Keynote Speaker (Bishop Arrieta) during the 2010 convention; however, we were obligated to pay the equipment rental fees (a separate company).

SCHOLARSHIP FUND

	Budget FY 12-13	Actual FY 11-12	Budget FY 11-12	Actual FY 10-11	Budget FY 10-11
INCOME					
Investment Income					
Interest Income/Wells Fargo	$100	$136	$100	$44	$150
CUIT dividends	$5,000	$6,860	-	$5,786	$6,000
Sub-Total	$5,100	$6,996	$100	$5,830	$6,150
Designated Funds (Note 1)					
Previously Designated Funds	$14,000				
This Year's Designated Funds	$7,000				
Sub-Total	$21,000				
Transferred Funds Income					
Board Des. Res. Reserve Fund (Note 2)	-	$55.412	$55,412	-	-
Sub-Total	-	$55,412	$55,412	-	-
Returned Scholarship Award (Note 3)	-	-	-	$6000	-
Scholarship Donations Income					
Donations Accompanying Dues	$1,500	$2,255	$1,200	$1,475	$1,500
Donations from Appeal	$6,000	$6,955	$6,000	$7,295	$6,000
Donations from Convention	-	$725	-	$200	-
Donations from Regional Meetings (Note 4)	$1,000	$2,000	$1,000	$1,570	$1,000
Donation from Bequest	-	-	-	$40,000	-
Sub-Total	$8,500	$11,935	$8,200	$50,540	$8,500
TOTAL INCOME	**$34,600**	**$74,343**	**$63,712**	**$62,370**	**$14,650**
EXPENSES					
Service Charges					
Money Market Fees Wells Fargo	$500	$154	$50	$20	$50
Sub-total	$500	$154	$50	$20	$50
Postage					
General Postage	$50	$3	$50	$7	$50
Appeal Postage	$700	$617	$800	$615	$800
Sub-total	$750	$620	$850	$622	$850

SCHOLARSHIP FUND continued

	Budget FY 12-13	Actual FY 11-12	Budget FY 11-12	Actual FY 10-11	Budget FY 10-11
Printing					
General Printing	$150	-	$200	-	$200
Appeal Printing	$200	$313	$200	$144	$200
Sub-total	$350	$313	$400	$144	$400
Scholarships					
Current Awards (Note 5)	$21,000	$25,120	$28,000	$18,250	$21,000
Sub-total	$21,000	$25,120	$28,000	$18,250	$21,000
Additional Designated Funds (Note 1)					
Approved Future Scholarship Awards					
Set aside funds per 2011 Board Resolution (excess from FY 11-12)			$21,000		
5% of CUIT Investment as of Dec. 31, 2011	$21,725				
Approved Future Awards (Note 6)	$ (21,000)		$ (21,000)		
Sub-Total	$725				
TOTAL EXPENSES	**$22,600**	**$26,208**	**$29,300**	**$19,036**	**$22,300**
EXCESS/DEFICIT	**$12,000**	**$48,135**	**$34,412**	**$43,334**	**$ (7,650)**

Note 1: These are future funds to give out and transfers within scholarship accounts; as such, they are not included in the annual Scholarship budget. Income and expenses in FY 11-12 become income and expenses for FY 12-13.

Note 2: This transfer is to close, as recommended by the auditor during the FY 2009-2010 audit, the 'Board Designated Restricted Reserve Fund'. This transfer was approved by resolution of the Board in June 2011.

Note 3: Income for an award granted in FY 09-10 which was returned from the awardee in FY 10-11.

Note 4: FY 2010-11 was the first year to designate these donations as a separate line item.

Note 5: This budget line assumes three awards at $7,000 each.

Note 6: This line represents the awards approved to current scholarship recipients, to be awarded in future fiscal years (e.g., $14,000 for FY 13-14 and $7,000 for FY 14-15).

Officer's Report

Report of the Executive Coordinator
Sister Sharon A. Euart, RSM

This past year brought a combination of accomplishments, challenges, and transitions to the Office of the Executive Coordinator (OEC). In so many ways I am grateful to you, the members of the Society, for your assistance and support in addressing the needs of the Society and how best to carry out the Society's mission. In this report, as in past years, I will offer observations on the activities and future initiatives of the Society in the four areas of service: general operations, conventions, publications, and scholarship. I will also offer a few personal reflections on future trends for the Society.

General Operations

OEC Staff

At the beginning of July, Katie Richards, OEC Executive Assistant, left the CLSA for a job closer to her home in West Virginia. Katie had been with us for almost four years. We are grateful for her service, her kind manner and her generous assistance in implementing the new functions and technologies in the office. In early August, Colleen Crawford joined our staff as the new Executive Assistant. Colleen who comes from Hershey, PA is a 2011 *magna cum laude* graduate of The Catholic University of America with a BA in English and minors in Philosophy, Medieval Studies, and Theology. Prior to coming to the CLSA, Colleen worked as an editor in the CUA Office of Campus Ministry and as an office assistant in the Center for Academic Success at The Catholic University of America. We are delighted to have Colleen with us and as she continues to learn the functions and procedures of the OEC, I am confident she will serve you well. In addition to Colleen, Amy Tadlock continues to work with us on a part-time basis. Amy completed her JCL in December 2011 and is working with us before taking a new position. Amy has been most helpful with special projects such as compiling the new Advisory Opinions Index for online access. We are grateful for the excellent staff we have and most appreciative of their service to the Society and its members.

Website Management and Development

The CLSA website continues to be a valuable resource for members and non-members alike. An increasing number of members are using the website for dues payment and event registration. With development of the download availability of resources, the website has become an important resource for research by canonists throughout the world. There remain even greater uses we can make of the website for web-conferencing, committee interaction, and surveys, to name a few.

Early this summer Amy Tadlock completed the compilation of a data-based index of CLSA Advisory Opinions from 1984 to the present. The database lists each canon mentioned in the opinion, author, and volume wherein the opinion lies. It will be a valuable tool for members who are looking for an article on a specific canon within the printed volumes and for those who are looking for articles to download. The database/index also has a link to the CLSA compilation volumes and individual volumes of Advisory Opinions for purchase and downloading. Many downloads are free for members. This has been a time consuming project, and we are very grateful to Amy for her work on the Index.

Membership and Dues

Dues collection for 2011-2012 went way beyond expectations. We received 107.51% of the total income budgeted for dues for the fiscal year. This is a very positive response due in large part to the overwhelming number of new members since the beginning of the fiscal year. We had budgeted $7,000 for new member dues; we received $24,700. For the fiscal year we accepted seventy-seven (77) new members representing both U.S. and international active, associate, and student members. Many of our new members find the CLSA through access to the website and apply for membership online.

Increasing student membership is an initiative we have worked to increase in recent years. At the April Spring Open House we hosted for the canon law students from the School of Canon Law at The Catholic University of America, we described the benefits of membership, offered discounts on publications, and provided the students with free bags, pens, mouse pads, and some older publications. Similarly, the CLSA presidents meet with the students from the Faculty of Canon Law at St. Paul's University each February and, during the biennial visits of the president, vice-president, and executive coordinator to Rome, a meeting with the Rome students is a highlight of the schedule. Currently, we have seventy-six (76) student members: forty-seven (47) from The Catholic University of America, twelve (12) from St. Paul's, and seventeen (17) from other schools throughout the world. This is a wonderful experience for the Society and a hopeful sign for the future. We continue to look for opportunities to assist students of canon law in their studies and in their early experience of canonical ministry. It is our often student members, as well as our newer canonists, who invite us to look at new technologies and electronic resources for canonical research. They come to us with a knowledge and experience of electronic technology that will influence the range services that the CLSA will develop and provide in the near future. I believe it is important that we encourage our new members to participate in the activities of the Society in which some day they will be leaders.

Many of our members serve as mentors to new canonists, a relationship that often benefits both the new canonist and the experienced one!

Operational Costs

I am pleased to report that, despite a projected shortfall in General Operations, we ended the year with a healthy surplus. There are several factors that made this possible:

- A significant increase in the number of new members exceeding the budget projection for 2011-2012 by $14,000
- Overall savings on office operations
- Decrease in auditor expenses
- Decrease in member services expenses for printing and mailing
- Decrease in Board of Governors expenses due primarily to deferring the Rome visit to 2013 and reduced costs for the President's trip to the meeting of the Canon Law Society of Australia and New Zealand
- Significantly lower expenses than projected for CLSA committees. Some of this decrease was due to the use of web-conferencing and conference calls; in other cases it was the result of less activity during the year.

We continue to monitor the level of spending in the OEC and believe we have been responsible in reducing expenses. It will be important for the future to maintain at least minimally the current level of income to maintain or increase the level of service to the membership.

Collaboration with Other Groups

Our collaboration with the various national Catholic organizations based in the Washington, DC area continues to develop. Sharing of ideas, resource opportunities, notices of position openings, and social gatherings help to make the Society and its work known to others in the Washington, DC area.

In February, I had the opportunity to participate in the Rome symposium, *Toward Healing and Renewal,* organized by the Pontifical Gregorian University and co-sponsored by several Vatican dicasteries for bishops and major superiors on sexual abuse of minors. It was an excellent meeting as well as an extraordinary experience of the universal Church providing a global, cross-cultural perspective on the crisis. Bishop Daniel Conlon, Bishop of Joliet and chair of the USCCB's Committee on Child and Youth Protection, represented the USCCB at the symposium. Bishop Conlon will be giving a seminar at the 2012 convention on his perspectives on the symposium.

Following the Rome symposium on sexual abuse of minors, opportunities for collaboration with other groups has increased. For example, the Director of the newly established Centre for Child Protection in Munich came to Washington to meet with the Executive Director of CARA and me. He is interested in further collaboration with the CLSA and the new Centre.

Also, CARA is assisting us in the study of the authorization process for lay Ecclesial ministers following the grant of $5,000 from the 2011 Symposium in Collegeville for a study of twenty to twenty-five arch/dioceses. CARA staff is providing consulting services for the survey design and layout, data input and analysis. The LEM Work Group held a conference call on April 3 and a face-to-face meeting in late May at the Hecker Center. The timeline for the study was set and an initial report of the findings will be presented during a seminar at the 2013 convention.

Webinars

We continue to move forward with planning for CLSA webinars in consultation with other local groups who have experience with this type of web-based meeting. We have identified potential topics for which we often receive requests for materials: for example, Book Six revisions, parish closings, marriage/Tribunal topics which would enable entire Tribunal staffs to view the webinar as a continuing education opportunity, and various clergy issues. The financial arrangements depend on the type of service used–annual fee or fee per computer used. The CLSA webinars will not be completely free. We will likely charge a nominal fee per site so as to generate some revenue. We hope to have the program initiated later in the fall. At least initially, we plan to have the presenter(s) with us in the OEC for the broadcast. Our timeline for having the project in place has been delayed due to the staff transition in the OEC this summer.

CONVENTIONS

The 73rd convention in Jacksonville was a very successful convention. It was well attended, received well by the attendees, and the evaluations were overwhelmingly positive especially with regard to the hotel, program, and speakers. The larger than expected number of attendees was attributed to the high level of interest in the theme and the Florida venue.

Financially, the convention was also a success. Despite an increase in speakers' *honoraria*, there was a sizable surplus of $29,348 after all bills were paid. Some of the factors contributing to the financial success included:

Increased Income:
- Higher overall attendance than anticipated (approximately 50 more than budgeted)
- Excellent attendance for pre-convention workshops, larger than budgeted (30 more attendees)
- More hotel rooms, therefore, a higher rebate from NIX commission ($13,700)
- Hyatt additional rebate of 5%

Lower Expenses:
- Savings on some pre-convention and convention expenses
- Few non-member speakers, therefore, lower travel costs
- Lower committee expenses
- Printing of the Liturgy Booklets was a donation of Diocese of Youngstown

As was the case in 2010 in Buffalo, an attractive program generates more attendees. The in-kind contributions of the Diocese of Youngstown and others helped defray some of the cost for the 2011 convention. This is a factor that we cannot budget for each year but for which we are most grateful.

PUBLICATIONS

New Publications

During the 2011-2012 fiscal year, we completed publication of the *2012 Roman Replies and CLSA Advisory Opinions*, *2012 CLSA Proceedings*, *Rotal Jurisprudence*, and the second printing of the *Code of Canon Law: Latin-English Edition*. Two additional publications are in process for printing, *Canon Law Digest XIV*, edited by Rev. Patrick Cogan, SA and *Latin Pastors, Eastern Catholics* (English translation) by Chorbishop John Faris, and should be available in 2012.

Earlier this year we received a request from LOGOS Research Systems, a digital library system, to include the CLSA *Code of Canon Law: Latin-English Edition* on its site. The request came via the USCCB which uses LOGOS for its bibles, *Catechism of the Catholic Church*, and *Adult Catechism*. The website is http://www/logos.com/catholic. After consultation with the USCCB and PAB, we proceeded to discuss the opportunities with LOGOS, which had already obtained permission to use the Latin translation from the Libreria Editrice Vaticana in Rome. Following review of the contract, we moved forward with making the *Code of Canon Law: Latin-English Edition* and the *Code of Canons for the Eastern Churches: Latin-English Edition* texts available to LOGOS. The texts will be included in LOGOS' electronic library and can be accessed via smart phones, iPads, Kindles, computers, etc. The two codes will be available together, always with the Latin, as stand-alone products or as part of the larger Catholic packages available from LOGOS. The price is determined by LOGOS following its marketing research and we will receive 10% royalty on each sale. The marketing research indicated that there is a broad interest in the books and they are being prepared for sale in November 2012. Pre-orders are being taken for $39.95 at http://www.logos.com/products/search?q=Code+of+Canon+Law.

The CLD electronic data base project, follow up to the 2009 convention resolution, is nearing completion. There is a detailed description of the project, referred to as the CLSA Research Database, in the report of the Publications Advisory Board. Members of the PAB will also be demonstrating a version of the database at the CLSA exhibitor's table during the convention. This is an exciting initiative on the part of the Society and one that will prove to be invaluable for anyone doing research in the field of canon law. We are most grateful to Msgr. John Alesandro for his leadership in moving this project forward.

More detail on other publication issues can be found in the report of the Publications Advisory Board. The PAB continues to be a valuable resource for the Executive Coordinator and the OEC. Collaboration with the PAB has been a most fruitful experience for the OEC. Its expertise, research, and advice with the preparation and publication of CLSA publications are greatly appreciated. Its service in coordinating the publication efforts of the CLSA has enabled the Society to move forward in an organized and responsible way, including the CLSA's entry into electronic publishing.

We continue to make several CLSA publications available on Amazon.com and hope to expand our service in this arena in the future. This move, however, depends on the availability of OEC staff to fill the orders within two days as required by Amazon.

Scholarships

We are very pleased with the returns from the 2012 Scholarship Appeal. The average per person donation this year is over $100. Letters were mailed at the beginning of Lent and we continue to receive contributions with several being made in conjunction with annual dues payments. We are especially grateful to the Regional Conferences who have contributed to the fund: the New Orleans/Mobile Regional, Midwest Regional, and the Eastern Regional meetings. We are pleased to announce that three scholarships have been awarded for 2012: Ms. Sarah Lauhead, beginning her canon law studies at the Universidad de Navarra; Mr. Travis Rankin, for the remaining year needed to complete his JCL at Katholieke Universiteit Leuven; and Mr. Carlos Sacasa, for completion of his JCL in the summer semester of 2012 at The Catholic University of America. The three recipients are lay persons pursuing licentiates in canon law for service in the United States following graduation.

We will continue to include features about our scholarship recipients in the CLSA *Newsletters* to familiarize our members with the awardees. Thank you for your generous support of the scholarship fund. No donation is too small. To donate online, visit www.clsa.org/scholarship.

Goals for the Office of the Executive Coordinator

I continue to address, with periodic modification, the following goals identified at the beginning of my term as Executive Coordinator in 2008:

1. To hire the staff necessary to carry out administrative and financial responsibilities, including, but not limited to, computer proficiency, data entry/management, means of communication such as website and newsletter development, and bookkeeping procedures;
2. To initiate contact with Catholic organizations and groups whose mission and agendas include canonical matters or issues having canonical implications;
3. To seek opportunities to collaborate and cooperate with other groups whose educational goals might benefit from the CLSA's canonical input and expertise;
4. To be present to groups and/or activities with and in which the CLSA might have an interest and through which the Society's service to the broader Church might be enhanced;
5. To assist in implementation of the recommendations of the *Futures Initiative Project* as approved by the Board of Governors.

With the assistance of dedicated and competent staff, I believe we have accomplished a great deal; yet there is more to do as we transition with new staff and with new skills to make the Society a vibrant and valuable resource for the canonical community and the Church. I will continue to focus on how the OEC can better serve the mission of the Society by bringing together the gifts of wisdom and knowledge of our more experienced members with the fresh ideas and technological knowledge and skills of our newer members in service to the membership while, at the same time, introducing procedures and services that will help us assess how we can use our technology for mission and move the Society forward for the years to come.

I continue to be grateful for your service, your support and welcome your comments on how the Office of the Executive Coordinator might better serve you and the canonical needs of our Church.

Committee Reports

Constitutional Committees

Committee: Nominations
Constituted: Constitution, Article X
Charge: The mandate of the Committee is:
1. To submit to the active members, at least one month prior to the date of election, the names of nominees as provided for in Article IX of the Constitution; (and)
2. To formulate and recommend to the Board of Governors plans for maintaining and increasing the membership of the Society.
Members: Dr. Diane L. Barr, *Chair*
    Ms. Patricia M. Dugan, *Member*
    Rev. Lawrence Jurcak, *Member*
    Rev. Michael Joyce, *Past President*

Annual Report

The committee met March 20-21, 2012 in Baltimore, Maryland and will present the following slate for nomination at the October 2012 Convention in Chicago, Illinois. All members were present for the meeting. Members actively contacted potential candidates for office and will offer the following slate to the membership at the 2012 annual meeting.

For the Office of Vice-President:
- Rev. Patrick Cogan, SA, Garrison, NY
- Rev. Phillip Brown, SS, Washington, DC

For the Office of Consultor:
- Rev. Patrick Cooney, OSB, St. Meinrad, IN
- Rev. John Foster, Washington, DC
- Rev. Gregory T. Luyet, Fort Smith, AR
- Mrs. Donna Miller (Sauer), Silver Spring, MD

The Nominees' Curricula Vitae and photographs were compiled by the Executive Coordinator's Office, which later published the booklet regarding this information to the membership as part of the materials for the 74th annual convention.

Membership Recommendations

The group had an extensive discussion about how to increase membership in the coming years. Several suggestions were made including:

1. Extending the canon law student discount for an additional 12 months to those same persons after their reception of the JCL;
2. Providing a discount for convention fees for those who are attending their first national meeting;
3. Providing a membership fee discount to those persons who can prove membership in another canonical society;
4. Providing a membership fee discount for those members over the age of 70 so they can still remain active; and
5. Permit absentee voting of members.

The committee submitted these recommendations to the Board of Governors for consideration at their March meeting.

Dr. Diane L. Barr

****

Committee: Resolutions
Constituted: Constitution, Article X
Mandate: *1. To solicit, develop and draft proposed resolutions which will express the concerns of the Canon Law Society of America;*
2. To consult with the membership at large and, in particular with the Board of Governors, the standing and ad hoc committees of the Society, and the organizers of the convention
3. To formulate resolutions on given points in response to requests of the members of the Society;
4. To compose differences in the formulation of similar proposals and to revise all proposals so that the meaning of each is clear; (and)
5. To encourage resolutions which authentically express in a positive way the activities and concerns of the Society.

Members: Rev. Gregory Luyet, *Chair*
Rev. Michael Clark
Mrs. Susan Mulheron

Annual Report

Since the majority of the work of the Resolutions Committee occurs at the annual convention, our committee does not have anything new to report.

Rev. Gregory T. Luyet

****

Committee: Resource and Asset Management
Constituted: Constitution, Article X, as last amended in 2008
Mandate: *1. To develop a comprehensive budget for all the activities of the Society and report on the funding available for projects;*
2. To submit the proposed budget for the coming fiscal year to the Board of Governors for approval at its spring meeting;
3. To conserve, invest and disburse the monies of the Scholarship Fund in accord with the criteria established by the Society;
4. To select recipients for the CLSA scholarships based on criteria approved by the Board of Governors; (and)
5. To advise the Treasurer on all matters pertaining to the Society's investments.

Members: Rev. Gregory T. Bittner, *Chair*
Rev. Thomas E. Cronkleton
Rev. John Vaughan, *ex officio*
Rev. Joseph R. Binzer, *Investment Consultor*
Sr. Margaret A. Stallmeyer, CDP, *Investment Consultor*

Annual Report

The Resource and Asset Management (RAM) Budget Committee met by web conference on Thursday, February 26, 2012. Members included the Treasurer, Rev. Gregory T. Bittner; Rev. John Vaughan, V.P. *ex officio*; and Rev. Thomas Cronkleton, Jr., Senior Consultor. The Executive Coordinator, Sr. Sharon Euart, RSM, and her Executive Assistant, Katie Richards, were present. The committee arrived at a budget to present to the Board of Governors (BOG).

The RAM committee presented its budget for fiscal year 2012-2013 to the BOG at the April 2012 meeting. The BOG received the budget and after much discussion approved the budget with amendments to include an increase in compensation for the Executive Coordinator.

At that same time, a subcommittee of the BOG, consisting of Mark O'Connell and Gerald Jorgensen, was requested to review applications for scholarship awards that had been received. The subcommittee enthusiastically endorsed two candidates for varying awards totaling $21,000 and the BOG approved the scholarship awards. When one of the awardees declined the full amount of the award due to a change in circumstance, the BOG reviewed the applicants who were not originally awarded a scholarship. The BOG then awarded the remaining amount of scholarship money to a third qualified candidate, bringing the total amount awarded for fiscal year 2012-2013 to $21,000.

Highlights of the fiscal 2012-2013 Budget include the following. The budget is balanced and projects an overall modest profit for the Society. The Publications unit is expected to cover the projected deficit in the General Operations unit. The Convention and Scholarship budgets are forecast in the black.

In the General Operations unit we again budget a deficit, although much smaller than in previous years. This is due to the inclusion of Audited Prior Year Net Assets in General Operations unit Income as referred to in the Treasurer Report. Again, this is arrived at by using the Excess from the Difference between Income and Expenses in the General Operations unit from the 2010-2011 audited fiscal years. This accounting procedure is suggested and approved by the Accountant/Auditor.

Historically, while we have budgeted deficits for the General Operations unit, the deficits have not been realized because expenses have been less than budgeted and income has been greater than budgeted. This has been a very positive outcome.

Continuing to highlight the General Operations unit we note that Salary and Compensation for the OEC and staff have been increased by about $8,500 in the Budget. Part of the increase is due to merit increases recommended and approved by the BOG for the Executive Coordinator and the Executive Assistant. Additionally, the BOG also felt it was appropriate to fund a part-time assistant to the office because of increased office demands from the membership and the level of services provided the membership and the BOG. There is also a modest increase in expenses of the BOG. The budgeted amount for Service Charges, Professional Services and Committees has been reduced by a total of almost $5,000.

The Publications unit expects to make a modest profit this year as new publications expensed and put into the pipeline at the end of the last fiscal year (2011-2012) begin to provide income in the 2012-2013 fiscal year.

The Convention unit is running another very tight budget. The BOG is not unmindful that the Convention unit has done extraordinarily well in the past three years and that the Society has received significant monetary gains over projections. It must be remembered that those gains have assisted in balancing the overall budget when the General Operations unit or the Publications unit has not met budget or incurred deficits. Additionally, Chicago will be a much more expensive convention site and we may not achieve an excess as in the past. Yet, the BOG and OEC believe that the program will attract enough participants to meet the budget numbers.

The Scholarship unit has budgeted for five scholarships (three new and two continuing) of varying amounts for a total of $21,000 for fiscal year 2012-2013. Significant changes to scholarship accounting and funding will again take place during the new fiscal year. The RAM proposed a Resolution to the BOG in reference to the method of accounting for the amount of money available for scholarship awards, administration, and fund raising activities in any given year. The amount will be determined by taking up to 5% of the total market value of the Scholarship Investment Fund computed on the basis of a three (3) year rolling quarterly average, as of the December 31st immediately preceding the January BOG meeting. There is a caveat that the Fund's total value not be harmed by the size of the distribution in a given year. The BOG also approved the RAM calculation relative to the sum of all contributions to the Scholarship Fund since its inception in 1985 to be $368,978.71 as of December 31, 2011. Contributions and donations to the Fund are to be updated annually. Additionally, all contributions and donations to the Scholarship Fund are to be deposited in the Scholarship Investment Fund within 30 days of receipt and all interest and dividends are to be reinvested into the Scholarship Investment Fund so as to correspond with a total return investing policy. The RAM continues to work on Scholarship accounting policies and procedures.

I want to thank the members of the RAM and the Executive Coordinator's Office for their assistance and input into the financial affairs of the Society. All of us recognize the significant responsibilities we have toward the BOG and the Society. It is our objective and purpose to do our best to utilize the resources you have entrusted us with. This report was generated as of August 20, 2012.

Rev. Gregory T. Bittner

****

Committee:	Professional Responsibility
Constituted:	Constitution, Article X, as last amended in 1995, and the Code of Professional Responsibilities, canon 9c(1), d(1)
Mandate:	1. *Regarding complaints:*
	a) To receive complaints of any party aggrieved with respect to provisions of the Code of Professional Responsibility originally adopted by the CLSA in October 1983, and its can. 9d(1);
	b) To make an initial finding that the complaint is not frivolous but is serious in character; (and)
	c) By majority vote to refer the matter to the hearing officers;
	2. *To issue advisory opinions and decisions on the application of the Code of Professional Responsibility; (and)*
	3. *To advise on all other questions concerning the professional responsibility of canonists.*
Members:	Mrs. Meg Romano-Hogan, *Chair*

Rev. Mark O'Connell, *ex officio*
Rev. Thomas Cronkleton, *ex officio*
Sr. Lynn M. McKenzie, OSB, *Hearing Officer*
Rev. Paul Hartmann, *Hearing Officer*

Annual Report

In late 2011, the committee received a complaint from a person regarding a canonist who had acted as an advocate for the person. The matter was discussed in committee in January 2012. It was determined at that time that while the complaint was not frivolous and would, in the ordinary course of things, merit an investigation, the accused canonist was not a member of the CLSA, and therefore could not be sanctioned by the Committee on Professional Responsibility. There was some discussion about attaching a warning to the canonist's name, such that a future request by this canonist to join the Society might be scrutinized more closely, but this course was determined to be ultra vires of the Committee.

Meg Romano-Hogan

****

ON-GOING COMMITTEES

Committee: Church Governance
Constituted: 2009
Mandate: *1. To initiate as needed any projects pertinent to the study of canon law pertaining to Church structures and governance or the implementation thereof, including but not limited to the following:*
 a) diocesan and parish temporalities;
 b) consultative bodies;
 c) diocesan and parish structures;
 d) power of governance;
 e) comparative law issues;
 f) inter-ritual matters;
 g) Eastern canon law and institutions
2. To oversee projects referred to the committee by the Board of Governors;
3. To oversee its subcommittees working on projects concerning Church governance; (and)
4. To collaborate with national organizations and other groups dealing with issues of Church governance.

Members: Rev. Msgr. Daniel F. Hoye, *Chair*
Ms. Patricia M. Dugan
Chorbishop John D. Faris
Msgr. Charles Antonicelli
(vacancy)

Annual Report

The Committee received the agreement of PAB to prepare an English translation of *Latin Pastor and Oriental Faithful* by Lorenzo Larusso, OP.

Chorbishop John Faris reports that the translation is expected to be sent to the Office of the Executive Coordinator by the end of July and then on to PAB for a peer review. The Office of the Executive Coordinator has previously obtained the necessary copyrights.

With the completion of the term of Sr. Ann Rehrauer, the drafting of a "pamphlet" on closing parishes was suspended. It was the intention of the Committee to post this document on the CLSA web site. The Committee will reconsider this at a later date.

Ms. Dugan and Msgr. Antonicelli have decided to suspend the proposal to have a quick signpost to the most recent cases in U.S. civil law that involves religious issues or matters that might impact the Catholic Church in the U.S.. It is thought that the process was getting too complicated to use the CLSA website. Tish will explore using the list-serve for this project.

I want to thank Tish Dugan, John Faris (and Ann Rehrauer) for their service to the committee. Their terms, along with my own, expire at the end of this convention. I also thank Charles Antonicelli as well; his membership on the committee continues through 2014.

Rev. Msgr. Daniel F. Hoye

****

Committee: Clergy
Constituted: 2008
Mandate: *1. To initiate as needed any projects pertinent to the study of canon law pertaining to the life and ministry of bishops, priests and deacons or the implementation thereof, including, but not limited to, the following:*
a) canonical issues related to the sexual abuse of minors,
b) clergy personnel issues and resources,
c) advocacy for clergy in penal cases,

2. *To oversee projects referred to the committee by the Board of Governors;*
3. *To oversee its subcommittees working on projects concerning clergy; (and)*
4. *To collaborate with national organizations and other groups dealing with clergy issues.*

Members: Rev. Msgr. Ricardo E. Bass, *Chair*
Rev. James I. Donlon
Rev. Msgr. Tomas Marin
Rev. Daniel J. Ward, OSB
Rev. Gary D. Yanus

Annual Report

The members of the Committee had a very interesting and informative conference call on April 2. Msgr. Tomas Marin was officially welcomed onto the Committee and, although not present for the call, Rev. Gregory Bittner was thanked for his many contributions to the work of the Committee.

The Committee unanimously endorsed recommending to the Board of Governors that they propose the name of Rev. James Coriden for honorary membership at the Business Meeting of the members of the CLSA at its annual meeting in 2012 to be held in Rosemont, Illinois. The Board of Governors approved of this recommendation. The Committee will develop the "Wherefore" clauses and the Board of Governors will develop the "Be It Resolved" clause.

The Committee, at the suggestion of Rev. Daniel J. Ward, OSB, had a lengthy discussion concerning the possibility of offering webinars as a member service. The Committee found it to be a very worthwhile idea and, in the minutes of that meeting, passed along to Sr. Sharon Euart, RSM, a few of the ideas about possible webinar topics.

The Committee intends to have another conference call before this year's annual meeting.

Rev. Msgr. Ricardo E. Bass

****

Committee: Convention Planning
Constituted: 2008
Mandate: *1. To receive from the Board of Governors the approved general theme of the next convention as well as any suggestions, from the Committee on Research & Development for the development of the theme;*

2. To recommend to the Board of Governors, in accord with the general theme, topics for major addresses, seminars, or other presentations at a future convention, as well as a list of potential speakers and the honoraria for such speakers;
3. Following the Board of Governors' approval, to arrange for the speakers, addresses, and seminars for the annual convention;
4. To plan all convention liturgies and prayer services; (and)
5. To review the evaluations of the most recent Convention and asisst the Convention Chairperson in planning future arrangements, as needed.

Members: Rev. Patrick J. Cogan, SA, *Chair*
Sr. Sharon A. Euart, RSM, *ex officio*
Very Rev. Paul J. Hachey, SM
Rev. John J.M. Foster
Rev. Michael Joyce, *ex officio*
Rev. Msgr. Victor Finelli, *Convention Chairperson*
Sr. Ann Rehrauer, OSF, *Convention Liturgies*
Rev. Msgr. Jace Eskind, *Convention Liturgies*

Annual Report

The Convention Planning Committee convened at the CLSA office in Washington, DC, in January 2012 to project the program for the 2013 convention that will meet in Sacramento, California. The 2013 program theme "Celebrating 75 Years: Honoring the Past, Building the Future" offers a particularly inviting opportunity to identify a program that testifies both to the CLSA's legacy and future involvements.

The Committee wishes to thank the Office of the Executive Coordinator and the Board of Governors for their generous assistance and advice, and the membership for their various suggestions.

The following is the program for the 2013 convention:

Celebrating 75 Years: Honoring the Past, Building the Future

Keynote Address
Archbishop John Myers, Archdiocese of Newark—*75th Anniversary of the CLSA: Honoring the Past and Building the Future*

Major Addresses
1. Msgr. Charles Scicluna, Promoter of Justice, Congregation for the Doctrine of the Faith—*Response to and Prevention of Clerical Misconduct: Current Praxis* (tentative)

2. Bishop Brian Dunn, Diocese of Antigonish, Nova Scotia—*30 Years of the CIC: A Bishop's Perspective*

Seminars
1. Msgr. Michael Padazinski – *Privilege of the Faith/Favor of the Faith*
2. Sr. Victoria Vondenberger, RSM – *The Defender of the Bond*
3. Mr. Timothy Cavanaugh – *Conditioned Consent*
4. Rev. John Beal – *Publication Issues in Stages of the Nullity Process*
5. Rev. Robert Oliver – *International Priests in Dioceses*
6. Rev. Daniel Smilanic and Deacon Daniel Welter – *The Special Faculties of the Congregation for Clergy*
7. Rev. Robert Kaslyn, SJ – *Irregularities for the Exercise of Orders: Canon 1044*
8. Dr. Chad Glendinning – *Current Issues in Sacramental Law on the Eucharist*
9. Msgr. William King – *Canon 1284: Good Steward for Temporal Goods*
10. Mr. Jay Conezimus – *Sacramental Record-Keeping*
11. Dr. Lynda Robitaille and members of the Lay Ecclesial Ministry Work Group – *Findings from the Project on Authorization for Lay Ecclesial Ministry*
12. Sr. Catherine Darcy, RSM – *Associates and the Canonical Relationship to Religious Institutes*
13. Rev. Mario Balam (Mexico City) – *Cultural Perspectives in Tribunal Cases*

Rev. Patrick A. Cogan, SA

****

National Convention Chair Report

2012: Chicago, Illinois

As we travel to the windy city for this year's CLSA National Convention I need to thank, in a special way, Rev. Daniel Smilanic and his team of archdiocesan employees and volunteers. What a great group of people they were to work with! Thank you to all of you for making us feel so welcomed and working so diligently to make our 74th Annual Convention a wonderful moment of learning and sharing for all. Additionally, I would like to thank Kathy Best of Nix Associates who has helped me tremendously in planning for our convention. Finally, thank you to those in the Office of the Executive Coordinator who assisted greatly in the planning. I am, and I know all the members of the CLSA are, most appreciative.

2013: Sacramento, California

Plans are well under way to travel to the pacific coast in 2013. The dates for this convention are October 13-17, 2013 (including pre-convention). We will be staying at the Hyatt Regency at the rate of $149/night for single or double occupancy. The CLSA will be the major occupant in the hotel during our stay. Within walking distance of the hotel there are many eateries and places to shop. The area certainly is quite picturesque with the state capital directly across the street from the hotel. We look forward to our visit to Sacramento; undoubtedly, it will be a great convention.

2014: St. Louis, Missouri

Further planning moves us to St. Louis for the 76th Annual Convention. We will be staying at the Millennium Hotel at the rate of $135/night for single and double occupancy during October 13-16, 2014. The North Tower where we will be staying recently has undergone a renovation. Be sure to visit the restaurant on the 28th floor of our tower for some spectacular views. Free wireless internet is provided for all who attend. The Basilica of St. Louis, King, is just a four to five minute walk from the hotel and many restaurants are within a ten minute walk. Of course, a real must see is the Arch of St. Louis in Jefferson Memorial Park. Do not forget to ride to the top of the arch—you will not want to miss it!

2015: Pittsburgh, Pennsylvania

Planning is under way for the 77th Annual Convention at the Westin Convention Center. To date, I have not personally visited this site, but it has been visited by Rita Joyce and Rev. Lawrence DiNardo. More details will follow. The dates for this convention will be October 10-16, 2015 (dates include the pre-convention).

2016: Houston, Texas

In August, I traveled to Houston to begin the planning for the 78th Annual Convention which will be held October 8-14, 2016 (dates include the pre-convention). I visited two hotels both of which have wonderful potential. At the time of printing this booklet, no decision has definitively been made as to which hotel we will use. One hotel is somewhat better appointed, while the other is in the downtown area and conveniently located to many places to both visit and dine. Speaking of food, Houston is a wonderful town of fine eateries ranging from Tex-Mex, wonderful steakhouses, and of course many barbeque establishments. Houston will be yet another great location for us to visit.

We have much to look forward to in the coming years, that's for sure!

Rev. Msgr. Victor Finelli

Convention Liturgies

On February 8, 2012 Sister Ann Rehrauer and the planning team visited the Convention Hotel in Rosemont, Illinois. Rev. Daniel Smilanic and Mrs. Alice Zimmerman (from his parish), Deacon Dan Welter, and Todd Williamson from the Archdiocese of Chicago, as well as Katie Richards, Msgr. Victor Finelli, and Kathy Best from Nix Associates were also present to discuss arrangements, schedules, and assistance the Archdiocese would provide.

This year, because of distance, transportation, and traffic, the Convention Liturgy on the evening of October 10 will be celebrated by Bishop Thomas Paprocki in the Convention hotel rather than at a nearby church. This will require use of an additional, larger meeting room (other than the banquet room).

Sister Ann toured the facility with the other members and has a sense of the smaller liturgy room for the weekend and daily morning liturgies. The space is adequate for our needs but we will need to find a musical keyboard or some other form of accompaniment because the hotel will not move the piano from the main floor. The piano will be available for the major convention liturgy on Wednesday.

Audiovisual equipment and microphones have been ordered through Kathy Best as part of the convention package.

On August 7, Sister Ann and Msgr. Jace Eskind met by conference call regarding more specifics on the liturgies for the week. They decided that the opening prayer for Monday afternoon, October 8, will be a celebration of Evening Prayer.

Mass texts and readings, celebrants and ministerial personnel, and music options were also discussed. Msgr. Eskind will contact Bishop Paprocki regarding his preferences for texts for the Liturgy.

Sister Ann and Msgr. Eskind met again on August 28 by phone to review all decisions and finalize details. Following that meeting, ministerial invitations were issued based on registration of participants.

Sister Ann is working with Todd Williamson of the Archdiocese of Chicago to secure needed vessels, vestments, musicians and cantors, some liturgical environment assets, the specific planning of music, and the liturgical booklets.

The Archdiocese of Chicago has been extremely helpful in the planning of and preparations for the liturgies at our convention.

Sr. Ann Rehrauer and Rev. Msgr. Jace Eskind, Co-chairs

****

Committee: Institutes of Consecrated and Apostolic Life
Constituted: 2009
Mandate: *1. To initiate as needed any projects pertinent to the study of canon law pertaining to the life and ministry of Institutes of Consecrated and Apostolic Life of the implementation thereof, including, but not limited to, the following:*
    a) sponsorship;
    b) mergers and restructuring of institutes;
    c) governance;
    d) membership;
    e) new forms of consecrated life.
2. To oversee projects referred to the committee by the Board of Governors;
3. To oversee its subcommittees working on projects concerning Consecrated and Apostolic Life; (and)
4. To collaborate with national organizations and other groups dealing with issues of Consecrated and Apostolic Life.

Members: Sr. Mary Catherine Wenstrup, OSB, *Chair*
Sr. M. Dominica Brennan, OP
Br. Patrick T. Shea, OFM
Sr. Sharon L. Holland, IHM
Rev. Kevin W. Niehoff, OP

Annual Report

As I wrote in our last report, the committee is grateful to the Board for accepting our recommendation for a seminar on new and emerging communities to be given at the convention this coming October. We hope to continue this practice.

Since our last report, I have exchanged several emails and had one conversation with Sr. Amy Hereford, CSJ regarding possible collaboration. Currently, Sr. Amy is developing a project to provide comprehensive services to religious institutes that have decided not to merge or reconfigure. The emails and conversation points have been shared with the committee. I, and possibly Sr. Sharon Holland, will meet with Sr. Amy during the LCWR Assembly in August 2012.

The committee's next face-to-face meeting will be during the Annual Convention in October of this year.

Sr. Mary Catherine Wenstrup, OSB

****

Committee: Laity
Constituted: 2009
Mandate: 1. To initiate, as needed, any projects pertinent to the study of canon law pertaining to the life and ministry of lay persons or the implementation thereof, including but not limited to the following:
      a. Lay Ecclesial Ministry
      b. collaboration with clergy
      c. rights of the lay faithful
2. To oversee projects referred to the committee by the BOG
3. To oversee its subcommittees working on projects concerning the laity
4. To collaborate with national organizations and other groups dealing with the role of laity in the Church.

Members: Zabrina Decker, Chair
Jay Conzemius
Lynda Robitaille
Anna Marie Chamblee
Msgr. Steven Callahan

Annual Report

The committee has been asked by the Research and Development Committee and the BOG to focus our energies on collaboration with the Collegeville Lay Ecclesial Ministry Symposium and the question of authorization for ministry. With that in mind, Lynda Robitaille, as chair, and Zabrina Decker are serving on the CLSA workgroup, developing a survey with CARA of 20-25 (arch)dioceses on their process of authorization. A repost is due back to Collegeville in January.

Jay Conzemius is also working with the Sacramental Law Committee on the Sacramental records project developed by the Laity Committee.

The Laity Committee will have a conference call on August 29 and will meet at convention.

Thank you for your support.

Zabrina R. Decker

****

Committee: Publications Advisory Board
Constituted: 2007
Mandate: *1. To advise the Board of Governors about all aspects of current, periodic, and proposed Canon Law Society of America publication projects, including financial, literary, educational and marketing issues;*
2. To monitor the progress of all Society publication projects;
3. To implement the procedures for peer review of Society publications;
4. To review the coordination and management of the Society's publications activity on the part of the Office of the Executive Coordinator; (and)
5. To provide a written report to the Society's membership at the annual convention.

Members: Rev. Msgr. John A. Alesandro, *Chair*
Rev. Msgr. Kevin E. McKenna
Very Rev. Lawrence A. DiNardo
Rev. Patrick M. Cooney, OSB
Rev. Msgr. Thomas J. Green
Chorbishop John D. Faris, *ex officio*
Rev. Patrick J. Cogan, SA, *Canon Law Digest*
Sr. Sharon Euart, RSM, *Roman Replies*

Annual Report

Meetings

During the past year, the members met in person at the October 2011 convention in Jacksonville, Florida, and at the CLSA office in Washington, DC, on July 2-3, 2012. The chair also participated by conference call in the Board of Governors (BOG) meetings in January and April 2012, to offer progress reports on publications.

Electronic Publishing

Much progress has been made by the Publications Advisory Board (PAB) this past year to address the need for more effective electronic methods to access canonical materials. The design started with the implementation of the 2009 resolution sponsored by Jim Coriden "to expedite its investigation of providing the *Canon Law Digest* online, and, if the project seems feasible and affordable, proceed with all deliberate speed to set in motion the process of on-line conversion, indexing documents by canons, chronology, source, and subject matter, maintaining permanent access, constant updating, and easy download-ability."

1. It soon became apparent that the CLSA, while not re-inventing the wheel, should not limit itself to the *Canon Law Digest* (*CLD*), but should provide a wide array of materials for canonical research. PAB had already decided to make the latest volume of *CLD* its last in printed form and to convert the series into an electronic database, in effect transforming future volumes into a subscription service, with a reduced price for members. With the recommendation and support of PAB, the Office of the Executive Coordinator has also continued systematically to make more and more publications accessible on the CLSA website, particularly when they go out of print (e.g., *Proceedings*, *Roman Replies and Advisory Opinions*). These will continue to be accessible electronically through the "Online Bookstore" tab on the website.
2. One of the first questions addressed by PAB was whether the CLSA should contract with a commercial research database service or, alternatively, create and host its own electronic database. After researching the possibility, it was decided to go with a combination: creating its own electronic research tool, hosting it on a professional database hosting service (which provides constant backup and is rather inexpensive), and making it accessible through the CLSA website.
3. This approach was made possible through the expertise and generosity of Reverend Mark Barr, of the Archdiocese of Boston, who has had a great deal of experience in precisely this design and implementation. He has worked closely with PAB to move this project forward. PAB has also been assisted by the chair's brother, Michael Alesandro, who is a computer expert. At its July meeting, PAB was afforded a preliminary demonstration of the database, which was accessible both by computer and iPad, and an opportunity to offer suggestions for improvement of its design.
4. The initial texts for the database will include the Latin and Eastern Codes (in both Latin and English), all past volumes of *CLD*, and all past volumes of *Roman Replies and Advisory Opinions*. As things develop, other materials can be added to the database, provided that copyright permission is available.
5. Translating the past volumes of *CLD* into the database's electronic format has been facilitated to a great degree by the contribution of Rev. Bill Woestman in working up the CD (which remains available through the CLSA Bookstore) in PDF format. Some conversion is still needed, but much less than would have been necessary if only the printed text were available.
6. As the Research Database becomes available, a process for maintaining and magnifying its content should be in the hands of a "*Documents Research Coordinator,*" assisted by a support committee of canonists. Such a figure will report directly to the Executive Coordinator and also work closely with PAB.
7. The first task of the Documents Research Coordinator will be to follow up on *CLD 14* (which includes documents up to the year 2000) so that the latest materials are added to the database to bring it up-to-date. After that, new documents can be added to the database as they appear and older documents

that never appeared in *CLD* to begin with can be added to make the database even more valuable.
8. As of July, PAB was of the opinion that the research tool would be sufficiently developed by October to permit demonstrations at the Chicago convention.

Canon Law Digest, Volume 14

CLD 14 has been completed, thanks to the hard work of its editor, Rev. Pat Cogan, SA. It should be available for sale around the time of the Chicago convention.

Rotal Jurisprudence

Rotal Jurisprudence went to print during the past year. By the summer of 2012, close to 300 copies had been sold. It is hoped that sales will continue at the same rate in the near future. Translations of Rotal decisions (several of which have already been made available by Rev. Gus Mendonça) will also be regularly added to the CLSA's website and its electronic database.

Latin Pastors and Oriental Faithful

Chorbishop John Faris, chair of the Research & Development Committee, completed the process of translating and updating this work, which should prove helpful for Latin-rite pastors and pastoral ministers in dealing with inter-ecclesial pastoral questions. The new text should be available before the end of the calendar year.

Publications Budget
1. This past year saw a shortfall in the area of publications in comparison to budget. Some of the assumptions made in preparing last year's budget did not materialize. All the expenses for *Rotal Jurisprudence* and the reprint of the Latin Code came due during the year whereas sales of these works did not begin until the second half of the fiscal year. In addition, the anticipated completion of *CLD 14* did not materialize until the fiscal year ended.
2. Although the bottom line for publications in 2012 fell well short of the *budgeted* numbers, the *actual* deficit for publications was just about the cost of the production of the Latin code's reprint, something that will correct itself as the code continues to sell without production cost for the next couple of years at about 1,500 copies per year (4,000 copies were printed).
3. A positive development this last year is the fact that royalty income has started to increase with the licensing of the codes to *Logos* and such income should continue.
4. Because of the experience of the past fiscal year, the figures used to project publications income and expenses for FY 2013 (which were calculated in February) were re-examined in detail by the members of PAB at their July meeting, namely:

a. *Projected Publications Income*: Budgeted at $105,000 of which $80,000 is projected as publication sales. This compares to publications sales this past year so far of $50,716, only half of that which had been budgeted.
b. *Projected Publications Expense*: Budgeted at $87,135, of which $20,000 is projected for actual book production. This compares to this past year's book production so far of $40,746, almost precisely what had been budgeted.
c. Given the continued sale of *Rotal Jurisprudence* and the imminent completion of *Canon Law Digest 14*, PAB was confident that the assumptions used for publications and the projected figures for FY 2013 continue to be justified. It does not seem likely that last year's shortfall of bottom-line actuals in comparison to budget will be repeated this year.

Pastoral Resources

PAB continues to urge the publication of a series of "pastoral resources" that would bring canonical expertise into the wider audience of the Church, particularly: parish priests, lay ecclesial ministers, pastoral staffs, and parish volunteers. These publications should offer concise summations of the law with good interpretations that apply the norms to everyday life in the church. Various committees of the CLSA continue to pursue such projects; in particular, the Governance Committee and the Clergy Committee (see the individual committee reports). The idea is to develop brief publications, perhaps fifty pages or less, that could be printed in paperback and could be widely marketed, to CLSA members and many others.

Some topics under consideration:
1. *Foreign/International priests/seminarians*
2. *Departure and Sustenance from a Diocese or Religious Institute*
3. *Permanent Deacons*
4. *The Vacant See*
5. *Parish Consultative Bodies*

Resources in Spanish
1. At the suggestion of the BOG, PAB took up the idea of whether canonical resources might be made available in Spanish. Would it be desirable, for example, to obtain a license to market Spanish materials under the CLSA umbrella? Would translation into Spanish of already-published canonical works be feasible?
2. One immediate possibility might be to translate the diaconate pamphlet. The members of PAB consider this a good idea although the diaconate pamphlet is not yet completed by the Clergy Committee.
3. To translate into Spanish an already-published work requires that we identi-

fy the right publication, one that will have a Spanish-speaking market. Such a project can involve considerable fees.
4. This matter is an ongoing topic for PAB, the Executive Coordinator and the BOG.

Remuneration

The Board of Governors also requested that PAB take up the question of whether authors should receive some remuneration, of a modest sort, perhaps an honorarium or a small portion of royalties. Without such payment we may be losing some publications. The following are some of the points raised by PAB in discussing this idea:

1. Such a change in policy would not seriously jeopardize our tax-exempt status insofar as we are accustomed to offer similar honoraria to those who give major addresses or conduct workshops or seminars: major addresses at $500, seminars at $300, and pre-convention workshops at $1,500.
2. Commissioning authors and offering remuneration for occasional publications might assist in producing works at a faster pace.
3. Not every professional publication offers remuneration. For example, no one is paid for the articles they submit to *The Jurist*. On the other hand, a grant from CARA is funding a study of the authorization of lay ecclesial ministers, which report will be published by the CLSA.
4. Perhaps the CLSA could try a pilot project for *Pastoral Resources*, commissioning a single work and, at the same time, reaching out to CLSA members to come up with ideas for publications. PAB decided to proceed in this limited way for the moment.

Inventory

PAB continues to monitor and manage the inventory, reducing it where there is little likelihood of additional sales of any significance, in order to consolidate the volumes into fewer pallets and thereby reduce monthly storage expenses.

Reprint of the CLSA Translation of the Latin Code
1. The first month after its completion, seventy (70) copies of the reprinted Latin code were sold. It is estimated that the usual sale of 1,500 copies per year will materialize in the coming year.
2. *Logos* has completed its market testing and is satisfied that it should proceed with the production of the electronic version of both codes. The Latin and English will appear exactly as they do in the printed works. See the Executive Coordinator's Report for more detail on the *Logos* partnership.
3. Both codes will also be available for research in the CLSA electronic database when it is offered to the public.

Roman Replies and Advisory Opinions
1. As recommended by PAB, the titles of individual Advisory Opinions have

been entered as an Index on the CLSA website by the Office of the Executive Coordinator. Now that the CLSA is caught up, it will continue to place the titles of new advisory opinions on the website.
2. This method refers the reader to both the original volume of *RR&AO* and to the printed *Collections*, both of which contain the entire article. In the future, there will be a reference only to the individual volumes insofar as there will be no further compilations printed. At the same time, however, the entire text of such advisory opinions will eventually appear in the *CLSA Research Database* for all those who hold a subscription. The work done so far will make this transition much easier.
3. *Roman Replies and Advisory Opinions* was published again this year in time for the Chicago convention. Seventeen Roman documents have been included along with fourteen advisory opinions.

Essential Norms

One of the issues raised at PAB's July meeting was the perceived need for a commentary on *Essential Norms*. The discussion centered on the need for practical guidance on process.

1. Such a commentary could be combined with guidance for Review Boards and the CDF letter of May 2011. One area that is important is the nature of clerical sustenance in such cases. Another area is the need to obtain some helpful facts prior to referring cases to the CDF. One resource is Morrissey's article in the *Journal of the Canon Law Society of Australia and New Zealand*, Vol. 2, 2, pp. 184-198.
2. Perhaps the CLSA could do an updated version of the earlier CLSA commentary, perhaps twenty-five (25) pages in length. This could assist in guiding officials regarding the preliminary investigation process, which, unfortunately, is sometimes unduly truncated, with unverified information packaged and sent off to the CDF. At times, there may be no real decision about whether there is a case or not, whether it truly meets the threshold for referral to the CDF.
3. Another problem is the fact that there is no national auditing of the diocesan preliminary investigation process. The USCCB team is interested mainly in statistics (accusations, priests on leave, dismissals, etc.) and safe environment practices, not in the nature of the preliminary investigation process followed insofar as it varies considerably, depending on the circumstances.
4. This kind of commentary and guidance might be a publication of *Pastoral Resources* and include an explanation about the appropriate work of Diocesan Review Boards.
5. Members of PAB will continue to work on this idea to see whether a viable outline can be developed for such a publication.
6. CLSA has also received a request to translate and publish *Formulario commentato del processo penale canonico* by Prof. Claudio Papale, a staff person at the CDF, and published by *Urbaniana University Press* (2012), which

seems to be a worthwhile resource. At PAB's recommendation, the Executive Coordinator is checking with the copyright holders of the Italian text to see whether they agree to the CLSA's usual arrangements for the copyright of the English text before proceeding with the project.

Publication Protocol

A copy of the CLSA publication protocol can be found on the CLSA website under the "Online Bookstore" tab. Key elements of the protocol are the following:

1. PAB will review all proposed publications at an early stage to make a recommendation to the BOG about the proposed concept as appropriate for the CLSA to publish.
2. The author/editor must submit the manuscript to the Executive Coordinator and PAB in Microsoft Word Windows (a format that will permit the Executive Coordinator to build up an electronic database of all publications).
3. PAB will arrange for peer review of the manuscript during its development or, at the latest, at the point of receiving the entire manuscript.
4. PAB will interact with the Executive Coordinator and make recommendations to the Executive Coordinator about the usual elements of publication such as formatting, size of the book, and design of the cover. All such technical decisions will be made by the Executive Coordinator in consultation with PAB.

Future Meetings

PAB accomplishes its mandate by monitoring all publications, working closely with the CLSA Office on all aspects of publication, making recommendations, when needed, to the Executive Coordinator and the BOG, and interacting with the R&D committee and other committees about activities that may result in publications. PAB's schedule during the current year will be as follows:

1. Meeting of PAB at the Chicago convention on Tuesday, October 9, 2012;
2. Chair's Report at the BOG meetings in January and April;
3. Conference Call in February to discuss budget assumptions for the next fiscal year;
4. Summer meeting to review all activities: date and place to be determined.

If members of the CLSA have comments or suggestions about the Society's publication activity, please feel free to communicate with any of the members of PAB, all of whose contact information can be found on the CLSA website.

Rev. Msgr. John Alesandro

****

Committee: Research and Development
Constituted: 2008
Mandate: *1. To initiate or cooperate in all Canon Law Society of America research projects such as seminars, symposia and special studies;*
2. To design and implement Think Tanks that will allow for diverse views on issues of ecclesial life having canonical implications;
3. To develop and recommend themes for the annual Conventions for submission to the Board of Governors for approval and subsequent referral to the Convention Planning Committee for implementation;
4. To maintain close communication with all the committees of the Society in order to facilitate needed research and discussion; (and)
5. To interact with the Publications Advisory Board in order to assess the current and contemplated publications of the Society and offer suggestions and guidance for publication planning.

Members: Chorbishop John D. Faris, *Chair*
Rev. John P. Beal
Very Rev. Patrick R. Lagges
Rev. Robert W. Oliver
Rev. John Vaughan, *ex officio*

Annual Report

The Research and Development (R&D) Committee held one meeting on October 12, 2011 and two conference calls on February 17, 2012 and July 17, 2012.

Regarding Mandates #1 and #2, the R & D Committee recommends that we consider the use of technology for Webinars, etc. Reduced budgets do not allow for travel and participation as in the past. We further note that there should be greater collaboration between the university faculties and the CLSA in sponsoring activities.

Regarding Mandate #3, the preliminary theme reflection for the 2014 St. Louis, Missouri convention was submitted to the BOG and approved. Given that the year 2014 is the 50th anniversary of the promulgation of *Lumen gentium, Orientalium Ecclesiarum,* and *Unitatis Redintegratio*, the theme is: "The Unity of the Church–Challenges and Prospects." The full theme reflection was drafted and revised by the Committee. It will be sent to the Executive Coordinator during the first week of August.

Regarding Mandate #4, the Committee decided that it will be more effective if certain committee members were assigned to liaise with certain committees and then report back to the R & D committee. The purpose of this arrangement is to ascertain from the committees what they were doing and had plans to do and to provide them with some input of the "brainstorming" of the R & D Committee. With the exception of one committee, this task has been carried out and proved to be beneficial.

Topics were suggested to the committees for further consideration (some of which are already being implemented through workshops): special faculties; canonical issues relating to foreign priests and seminarians; illegal immigrants; associations of the faithful; canonical and pastoral implications of unregistered parishioners.

Regarding Mandate #5, John Faris shared the substance of the minutes of the last PAB meeting with the committee to keep them updated.

Chorbishop John D. Faris

****

Committee:	Sacramental Law
Constituted:	2008
Mandate:	*1. To initiate as needed any projects pertinent to the study of canon law pertaining to the sacramental life of the Church of the implementation thereof;*
	2. To oversee projects referred to the committee by the Board of Governors;
	3. To oversee its subcommittees working on projects concerning the sacramental life of the Church;
	4. To offer suggestions to the Board of Governors for marriage topics for pre-convention workshops; (and)
	5. To collaborate with national organizations and other groups dealing with the sacramental life of the Church.
Members:	Sr. Victoria Vondenberger, RSM, *Chair*
	Rev. Msgr. Mark A. Plewka
	Ms. Amy Jill Strickland
	Rev. Bruce Miller
	Mr. James-Daniel Flynn

Annual Report

We are grateful for four months of work after the 2011 convention by John Foster, Margaret Gillett, and Michael Vigil who continued to serve on the committee until the Chair received formal notice of the new members of the committee in the February 28, 2012 response from the Board of Governors (BOG) to the Sacramental Law Committee (SLC) January report.

Pre-Convention

The Committee is pleased that Msgr. David Maria Jaeger, OFM will present the pre-convention workshop entitled *Making for a Better Fit: More on U.S. Tribunals and the Roman Rota.*

Research

From questions posed to members of the committee, there seems to be a need for canonical information about sacramental law to be made available in a popular format. Some issues are raised repeatedly on the list-serve and in phone call/email questions to canonists, especially those of us who have given presentations at provincial, regional, and national gatherings of canonists. The committee considered how to make helpful resources known to canonists: newer resources for those who studied canon law many years ago and basic resources for newer canonists or those changing ministry who need to handle part of the law with which they are not familiar.

This could be done by gathering questions about sacramental law from members of the Society and possibly from those on the canon law list-serve which committee members would consider for a set of frequently asked questions (FAQ). After choosing the questions, practical answers would be formulated, referring to key resources. The results would be posted on the CLSA website for quick reference (updated by the committee) and/or published in an inexpensive pamphlet. Amy Strickland and JD Flynn are beginning this effort by brainstorming questions with their colleagues to create sample questions and answers for the committee to review before deciding whether to submit a sample of this project to the Publications Advisory Board for approval to pursue the effort. If the project moves forward, we would seek questions through a CLSA newsletter and perhaps on the list-serve.

Sacramental Recordkeeping Subcommittee

A subcommittee created in April 2011 from members of the Sacramental Law Committee and the Laity Committee to "...review resources already available on diocesan websites, and then provide network access to the most helpful of those policies..." included Jay Conzemius, Chair, Margaret Gillett, and Mark Plewka.

In the January Sacramental Law Committee report to the Board of Governors, it was noted that the subcommittee was considering producing a DVD to provide instruction regarding sacramental record keeping which would be helpful particularly for parish secretaries who do the work without formal canonical training. In February, the BOG asked that the committee consider producing a webinar rather than the DVD. The BOG noted that perhaps the Canon Law Society would purchase the basic equipment, which could also be used by other committees. The subcommittee was directed to be in contact with the Publications Advisory Board and provide them with an outline of the content for any such webinar and then to contact the Office of Executive Coordinator about the details.

Jay Conzemius and Mark Plewka worked on finalizing the content about sacramental records. Bruce Miller said that USCCB has experience with webinars and Bishop Ron Herzog from his diocese who is a master at these things is willing to assist in this effort. We think it would be great to have a bishop involved in the webinar. As of July 2012, the Sacramental Law Committee has heard nothing about whether CLSA has purchased or intends to purchase the equipment needed to produce a webinar.

Rotal Jurisprudence
The committee is grateful for comments from the BOG about the *Rotal Jurisprudence* book being well done. The question remains open whether there will be future volumes of this work. The Editor and most of the translators are open to that possibility. The Committee has received a request from another publisher to handle future volumes of the book if CLSA decides not to pursue that effort.

Sr. Victoria Vondenberger, RSM

****

VARIA

SEVENTY-FOURTH ANNUAL BUSINESS MEETING
Chicago, IL
October 10, 2012

Minutes

Call to Order and Opening Prayer

Mrs. Rita Ferko-Joyce, President, called to order the Seventy-Fourth Annual Business Meeting of the Canon Law Society of America (CLSA), on October 10, 2012 at 11:00 a.m., at the Hyatt Regency O'Hare Hotel in Rosemont, IL. She presided over the meeting as Chair.

The Chair invited Rev. John Vaughan, CLSA Vice-President/President-Elect, to lead the assembly in an opening prayer.

The Chair then gave instructions on the voting procedures to be observed for the election of Officers and Consultants during the Business Meeting. The procedures were adopted as described by the Chair.

The Chair then reviewed the procedures for addressing the assembly, and the CLSA's practices for presenting resolutions. The procedures and practices were adopted as presented by the Chair.

The Chair then entertained a motion that Associate Members present at the meeting have the opportunity to address the assembly, as called for in Article 5.3 of the CLSA's *Constitution*. The motion was seconded and approved unanimously by the assembly.

The Chair then called upon the Secretary, Ms. Zabrina Decker, to read the Minutes of the Seventy-Third Business Meeting of the CLSA, unless there was a proposal to accept the Minutes as published in the 2011 *CLSA Proceedings*. A motion to accept the Minutes was presented. The motion was seconded, and approved by the assembly with two negatives given.

Election of Officers and Consultors

The Chair called upon Dr. Diane Barr, Chair of the Nominations Committee, to present the slate of nominees for Officers and Consultors. Dr. Barr announced the candidates for Officers and Consultors. No additional nominations were added to the slate, as is provided for in Article 9.5 of the CLSA's *Constitution*.

The Chair then read the provisions of the CLSA's *Bylaws* regarding elections. The active members of the CLSA were instructed to cast their votes. The tellers collected the ballots and retired to a separate room to count them. Later in the meeting Dr. Barr returned to the Business Meeting and informed the Chair of the election results. The Chair then announced that:

For the Office of Vice-President/President-Elect:
214 valid ballots were cast, with 107 votes needed for election. There was 1 abstention. The votes cast were:

> Reverend Phillip J. Brown, SS: 108
> Reverend Patrick J. Cogan, SA: 104

The Chair declared an election with Reverend Phillip J. Brown selected as Vice-President/President-Elect. The election was received with applause.

For the Office of Consultor:
214 valid ballots were cast, with 107 votes needed for election. There were 2 abstentions. The votes cast were:

> Reverend Patrick M. Cooney, OSB: 130
> Reverend John J.M. Foster: 125
> Reverend Gregory T. Luyet: 71
> Ms. Donna M. Miller: 89

The Chair declared an election with Reverend Patrick M. Cooney, OSB and Reverend John J.M. Foster selected as Consultors. The election was received with applause.

Reports

President's Report
The Chair referred the assembly to the written President's Report, which was found on pages 19-22 of the 2012 *Annual Reports Booklet* that was included in the registration packets for the convention. Since the membership had the opportunity to read the Report in advance of the Business Meeting, she called for any questions or observations on the Report. There were none.

Rita Joyce called the attention of the assembly to the fact that the membership of the Society numbers 1452 in 35 countries.

Rita Joyce then noted that Sister Sharon Euart would speak to the outcome of the resolution passed in Jacksonville, Florida at the 73rd annual convention which was to offer to the United States Conference of Catholic Bishops the assistance of the Society in formulating appropriate procedures for the conduct of investigations into the work of theologians in the United States.

The Chair indicated that the Canon Law Society had had a successful year and expressed her gratitude to the Office of the Executive Coordinator and all who made the year a success.

Executive Coordinator's Report
The Chair then invited Sister Sharon Euart, R.S.M., CLSA Executive Coordinator, to the podium to present the Executive Coordinator's Report. Sister Sharon referred to her written Report, which was found on pages 53-57 of the *2012 Annual Reports Booklet*.

Sister Sharon gave an update to the assembly regarding the resolution mentioned in the President's report to offer to the United States Conference of Catholic Bishops the assistance of the Society in formulating appropriate procedures for the conduct of investigations into the work of theologians in the United States. The resolution was sent initially to Cardinal Timothy Dolan, President of the United States Conference of Catholic Bishops, who forwarded the resolution to Cardinal Donald Wuerl, Chair of the Committee on Doctrine, which has competence in this area. Cardinal Wuerl wrote to the CLSA President in April suggesting a meeting of representatives of the Committee on Doctrine and the Canon Law Society of America. He indicated that he would consult the Chair of the Committee on Canonical Affairs and Church Governance regarding such a possibility. The CLSA was contacted following the June meeting of the Canonical Affairs and Church Governance Committee and invited to meet with the chairs and staff of the Doctrine and Canonical Affairs and Church Governance Committees on September 12 of this year (2012). Father Michael Joyce and Sister Sharon Euart attended the luncheon meeting for the CLSA and offered our assistance to Cardinal Wuerl and Archbishop Broglio whenever it would be helpful. Meanwhile, a new protocol for the Committee on Doctrine of the USCCB related to the investigation of the work of theologians has been published in *Origins*.

OEC Staff
On August 1, 2012 Colleen Crawford joined our staff as the new Executive Assistant. Colleen who comes from Hershey, PA is a 2011 *magna cum laude* graduate of The Catholic University of America. She has had to learn many functions quickly and is doing a great job.

Website Management and Development
The CLSA website continues to be a valuable resource for members and nonmembers alike. An increasing number of members are using the website for dues payment and event registration. With the development of the download avail-

ability of resources, the website has become an important resource for research by canonists throughout the world. There remain even greater uses we can make of the website for web-conferencing, committee interaction, and surveys.

Earlier this summer, Amy Tadlock completed the compilation of a data-based index of CLSA Advisory Opinions from 1984 to the present. The database lists each canon mentioned in the opinion, author, and volume wherein the opinion lies. The last CLSA newsletter had instructions on how to access the site.

Membership and Dues
Dues collection for 2011-2012 went way beyond expectations. We received 107.51% of the total income budgeted for dues for the fiscal year. This is a very positive response due in large part to the overwhelming number of new members since the beginning of the fiscal year. We had budgeted $7,000 for new member dues; we received $24,700. For the fiscal year we accepted seventy-seven (77) new members representing both U.S. and international active, associate, and student members. Many of our new members find the CLSA through access to the website and apply for membership online.

The OEC's office hosted a very successful open house for the canon law students from Catholic University of America. Our President, Rita Joyce, spoke with students at St. Paul. When the officers visit Rome, they also host a gathering of the Roman canon law students. Currently, there are have seventy-seven (77) student members: forty-seven (47) from The Catholic University of America, twelve (12) from St. Paul's, and seventeen (18) from other schools throughout the world.

Webinars
The OEC continues to move forward with planning for CLSA webinars in consultation with other local groups who have experience with this type of web-based meeting. The office has identified potential topics for the webinars. The timeline for having the project in place has been delayed due to the staff transition in the OEC this summer. The Executive Coordinator hopes to have the project in place by the end of 2012 or early 2013.

Publications
Earlier this year we received a request from LOGOS Research Systems, a digital library system, to include the CLSA *Code of Canon Law: Latin-English Edition* on its site. The request came via the USCCB which uses LOGOS for its bibles, *Catechism of the Catholic Church*, and *Adult Catechism*. The website is http://www/logos.com/catholic. After consultation with the USCCB and PAB, we proceeded to discuss the opportunities with LOGOS, which had already obtained permission to use the Latin translation from the Libreria Editrice Vaticana in Rome to publish both the Code and the CCEO in their digital library. The two codes will be

available together, always with the Latin, as stand-alone products or as part of the larger Catholic packages available from LOGOS. It will be available October 23.

The CLD electronic data base project, follow up to the 2009 convention resolution, is nearing completion. There is a detailed description of the project, referred to as the CLSA Research Database, in the report of the Publications Advisory Board. Reverend John Alesandro will demonstrate the potential of this site after the meeting.

Scholarships

The 2012 Scholarship Appeal was successful. The average per person donation this year is over $100 from 6 ½ % of the membership. Letters were mailed at the beginning of Lent and we continue to receive contributions with several being made in conjunction with annual dues payments. We are especially grateful to the Regional Conferences who have contributed to the fund: the New Orleans/Mobile Regional, Midwest Regional, and the Eastern Regional meetings.

Sister Sharon expressed her gratitude to the membership. She then opened the floor to questions. None were asked.

Treasurer's Report

The Chair next invited Reverend Gregory Bittner to provide the Treasurer's Report. Reverend Bittner noted that his written Report was found on pages 23-24 of the *2012 Annual Reports Booklet*.

He reported that last year, he had recommended to the BOG that it seriously consider a dues increase for the membership. The current dues are $200 per member. The last dues increase was in 2003. The BOG has discussed this and at the present time has deferred any action on this item.

Reverend Bittner noted that the figures that he would present do not match the figures in the supporting documents due to the fact that when he publishes his report, he does not have the most recent budget figures or the audit report.

The Publications unit posted a significant loss of almost $28,000 with gross profit of $64,000 and expenses of $92,000. Part of this loss is due to timing in the expenses incurred for books in one budget year and the corresponding income not received until the following budget year. The unaudited Balance sheet continues to be favorable, at $138,000, despite the loss.

In the convention unit, on pages 31-32, some line item notations do not match the line items. This will be corrected in Proceedings.

The Society's Investments continue, since 2008, in Christian Brothers Investment Services (CBIS). CBIS provides a number of investment vehicles. The

Society maintains two separate investment accounts, one for the General Operations unit and one for the Scholarship unit. Both investment accounts are with Catholic United Investment Trust (CUIT) Balanced Fund and have the same investment mix and objectives. The investment mix is generally 60% stocks and 40% fixed income. The fund return on our investments has underperformed relative to its benchmark and similar balanced funds over the last fiscal year, July 1, 2011 to June 30, 2012. This underperformance relative to benchmark was noted by our investment consultant with CBIS and is now being carefully monitored as we enter our new fiscal year. This does not mean we have lost money, only that our return was less than the benchmark by which it is compared. The fund return year to date relative to its benchmark has improved significantly. The bottom line is that the Society did not lose money. The Society is $73,000 ahead in our assets from the prior fiscal year to this fiscal year.

Reverend Bittner then called the attention of the Society to page 37 of the reports booklet. He indicated that this fiscal year we had a review, not a full audit. The review stated that our information was "fairly stated in all material respects in relation to the financial statements taken as a whole".

Reverend Bittner indicated that there has been a change in the way we balance our budget. The RAM along with the Accountant/Auditor has determined that we can list the Audited Prior Year Net Assets under the General Operations Income column in our Budget to assist in the Balancing of our Budget. You will see that figure ($24,012) in the General Operations Budget Summary for the current fiscal year 2012-2013. This is real money that we have accrued in that prior fiscal year. This allows us to utilize and to account for the Excess from the Difference between Income and Expenses which we have realized in the past few years and hopefully will continue in the future. Additionally, the financial guidelines for the Society found in the BOG Handbook state that the General Operations unit CUIT Balanced Investment Fund could be utilized to offset General Operations Expenses. It reduces the possible bottom line deficit. When those excesses stop, we can look at the investment account for general operations and tap a small percentage of the investment account.

Reverend Bittner reported that the BOG had passed a resolution to assist in the funding of scholarships. In the April Board of Governors meeting, the resolution was worded as follows: *The committee on Resource and Asset Management will establish a sum up to 5% of the total market value of the scholarship investment fund computed on the basis of a three year rolling quarterly average as of the December 31 immediately preceding the January Board of Governors meeting. This sum is to be made available for scholarship, administration, and fundraising efforts. This sum is to be transferred from the scholarship investment fund to a cash or cash equivalent account.*

Reverend Bittner then reviewed the 2012-2013 budget, which was found on pages 25-34 of the *2012 Annual Reports Booklet*. He thanked the members of the Resource and Asset Management Committee and the staff of the OEC for their assistance over the past year.

He ended his report by asking if the membership had any questions. None were asked.

Report on the Hyatt

Sister Sharon Euart then approached the podium once again to share information on the union and Hyatt situation. She reported that in 2010, the Society became aware of the issue with the workers union and the Hyatt. Over the past two years the Society has consulted various representatives including UNITE which represents workers and the management of the Hyatt. We did look at other venues for our convention but a review of our contract revealed that the Society would have incurred a severe financial loss if we broke our contract. At the time, the penalty was $140,000. Correspondence between the OEC and Hyatt demonstrated our commitment to social justice. We have been assured that our continued effort to support the workers has been helpful. We will not contract with Hyatt after the 2013 convention in Sacramento, California.

Nix staff has assisted us with media updates. In recent months, there has been coverage in sacred and secular press. In late August some members of the Society posted concerns and the OEC posted a response on the CLSA website and indicated that an update would be given at the convention.

Sister Sharon then elicited questions.

Reverend Sinclair Oubre – one of the members who raised concerns – expressed his appreciation to the Society for its efforts on behalf of the workers and the updates that had been given to the Society.

Resolutions

The Chair read the applicable CLSA *Bylaws* that governed the proposing of resolutions from the floor and asked if there were any such resolutions to be presented. There being none, she called upon Reverend Gregory T. Luyet, Chair of the Resolutions Committee, Susan Mulheron, time-keeper, and Reverend Michael Clark, to approach the podium and present the resolutions previously submitted to the Resolutions Committee.

The full text of the resolutions was projected onto screens in the hall. In addition, printed copies of the resolution were distributed to those in attendance.

Reverend Luyet thanked the presenters for submitting their resolution well in advance of the convention, and the members of the Committee on Resolutions for their service to the CLSA.

Resolution I: Honorary membership in the Canon Law Society of America for Rev. James A. Coriden

Proposed by: Board of Governors, upon the recommendation of the CLSA Committee on Clergy

Be it resolved that: The Canon Law Society of America's seventy-fourth convention approve Honorary Membership for Reverend James A. Coriden in recognition of his lifelong service to the Church, his numerous contributions as a teacher of Canon Law and adviser to Canon Lawyers, and his outstanding service to the Canon Law Society of America.

Implementation by means of: A certificate honoring James A. Coriden

Anticipated cost: $0

Rick Bass, Chair of the Clergy Committee, spoke in support of the resolution on behalf of the Clergy Committee and moved that it be accepted.

The Resolution committee moved the resolution

Catherine Gilligan of the Board of Governors spoke in favor of the resolution.

The Chair, Rita Joyce, then called the question.

In Favor: 214
Abstentions: None
Opposed: 4

The resolution was adopted.

A certificate was given to Reverend James Coriden. He gave a short response.

Resolution II: Accountability and Effectiveness of Diocesan Finance Councils

Proposed by: Barbara Anne Cusack

Be it resolved that: The Board of Governors assign to the Committee of Church Governance the task of studying U.S. dioceses to assess the use and effectiveness of Diocesan Finance Councils. The committee will report its findings and recommendations to the Board and the membership no later than the 2014 convention.

Implementation by means of: The Committee on Church Governance or a special subcommittee established by it Collaboration with other professional groups such as the DFMC could be considered in gathering the applicable data.

Anticipated cost: $4000

Cost supplied by: The CLSA Committee budget

The Resolution committee moved the resolution

Barbara Anne Cusack spoke in support of the resolution.

Reverend Tom Cronkleton of the Board of Governors spoke in favor of the resolution for the BOG.

The Chair, Rita Joyce, called the question.

In Favor: 218
Abstentions: None
Opposed: None

The resolution was adopted.

Resolution III: In Support of Non-Discriminatory Employment Policies

Proposed by: James A. Coriden

Be it resolved that: The Board of Governors of the CLSA send a letter to the President of the USCCB requesting that the conference leadership urge the U.S. bishops, in light of the unanimous decision of the Supreme Court of the United States, *Hosanna-Tabor Evangelical Lutheran Church and School v. Equal Employment Opportunity Commission* (January 11, 2012), to formulate and adopt personnel policies for the dioceses and Catholic institutions in keeping with Catholic social teaching regarding equality and non-discrimination.

Such employment policies shall urge full compliance with religious, doctrinal, and canonical requirements for the respective personnel positions, and not be construed or interpreted to be in derogation of them.

Further, that the Board of Governors of the CLSA send a similar letter to the President of The National Association of Church Personnel Administrators urging its member organizations to formulate and adopt similar policies for their respective organizations.

The Board shall promptly report the responses to these letters to the membership.

Implementation of means of: A letter to the president of the USCCB and other officers named above.

Anticipated cost: $10

Cost supplied by: The CLSA from unrestricted general operation funds.

This resolution was **not** moved by the Resolutions committee.

The Chair, Rita Joyce, asked Father Coriden if he wished to move the resolution, he did so and it was seconded.

Fr. James Coriden spoke to the resolution.

Fr. Sinclair Obure spoke in support of the resolution.

Fr. David Szatkowski spoke against the resolution.

Mary Santi, Chancellor of Seattle and member of NACPA, spoke against the resolution.

Marie Hilliard of the National Catholic Bioethics Center spoke against the resolution.

Mike Ritty of Canon Law Professionals spoke in favor of the resolution.

Brother Pat Shea spoke against the resolution.

A vote of the membership assembled was called by the Chair.

In Favor: 12
Abstentions: 16
Opposed: 190

The resolution was NOT adopted.

Old Business
The Chair opened the floor to discuss any Old Business of interest to the assembly. There was none.

New Business

The Chair opened the floor to discuss any New Business of interest to the assembly. There was none.

Varia

Greetings by Officials of Canon Law Societies

The Chair then invited visiting officials of other Canon Law Societies to the podium to address the assembly.

Rev. Monsignor James O'Cain, President of the Canon Law Society of Great Britain and Ireland (CLSGB&I), brought the greetings and good wishes of the CLSGB&I. He thanked the CLSA for its hospitality, welcome, and cordiality. He invited the assembly to the 13-17 of May 2013 convening of the CLSAGB&I in Galway, where he promised that the cordiality extended to him in would be returned in kind.

Sister Maria Casey, President of the Canon Law Society of Australia and New Zealand (CLSANZ), bestowed the greetings of the CLSANZ. She thanked the CLSA for its conviviality, hospitality, and cordiality. She also thanked the Society for the sharing of publications and our website. Sister announced that the CLSANZ's 2012 convention would be held September 10-13 in Auckland, New Zealand, and that its 2013 convention would be held September 2-5 in Adelaide, Australia. The 2014 convention will be held in Sydney, Australia, 2015 in Melbourne, and 2016 in Brisbane.

The Most Reverend Wayne Kirkpatrick, President of the Canadian Canon Law Society (CCLS), bestowed the greetings of the CCLS. He invited the assembly to the CCLS's convention in October from the 22nd to the 25th in Winnipeg with the 2013 convention being held in Sudbury, Ontario. Their 2015 convention will be held in Ottawa as they celebrate their anniversary as a society. Twenty-two percent of their membership is American with 14 bishops as members.

Rita Joyce then called Dr. Kurt Martens forward who gave us greetings from Monsignor Patrick Valdrini, President of the Consociatio Internationalis Studio Iuris Canonici Promovendo, expressing his regret at not being able to attend the CLSA convention. Professor Kurt Martens of the School of Canon Law at The Catholic University of America indicated that the Consociato will host its 2014 international congress from September 17 through September 21 at the School of Canon Law at the Catholic University of America. This will mark the first time that the Congress has been held in the U.S. The theme is penal law in the church.

Adjournment

There being no further business, the Chair thanked many and entertained a motion to adjourn the meeting. The motion was seconded, and passed unanimously.

At 12:55 p.m., Mrs. Rita Joyce formally closed the Seventy-Fourth Business Meeting of the Canon Law Society of America.

Respectfully Submitted,

Ms. Zabrina R. Decker
Secretary 2012

VARIA

REFLECTION AFTER COMMUNION
Rita F. Joyce

When You Do What You Do
In reflecting on what I would briefly share with you tonight I realized how much you symbolized for me the Servant Church and Christ as Servant. I rediscovered Cardinal Avery Dulles' *Models of Church*, an older book that most of us likely read while studying theology. He quotes Cardinal Chushing's 1966 pastoral letter, *The Servant Church*. He states: "Jesus came not only to proclaim the coming of the kingdom; he came also to give himself for its realization. He came to serve, to heal, to reconcile, to bind up wounds. Jesus, we may say, is in an exceptional way the Good Samaritan. He is the one who comes alongside of us in our need and in our sorrow; he extends himself for our sake. He truly dies that we might live and he ministers to us that we may be healed." (Richard Chushing, *The Servant Church*, [Boston, MA: Sisters of St. Paul] in Avery Dulles, SJ, *Models of Church*, [New York, NY: Image Books Doubleday, 1978] 6).

You symbolize the Servant Christ when you listen to the pain of a husband and wife experiencing the brokenness of their marriage, the shattering of their dreams. When you make a decision to declare a marriage null after you have reached moral certainty "with God only before your eyes," when you strive to uphold the sacred bond of marriage as the appointed defender, when you, through your judicial decision reconcile a man or woman back to the church, when you painstakingly probe the circumstances of a failed marriage, when you reconcile the petitioner and maybe on a very good day, even the respondent and perhaps even some members of their extended family back to the church, you are the Servant Church.

When you staunchly advance the bishop's position you give of yourself, often sometimes very painfully to uphold what the Charter for the Protection of Children and Young People demands of your bishop so that the church might be healed. When you agree to represent an accused brother or sister in ministry you serve like Christ the Good Samaritan. Those among us who represent the accused cleric easily will tell you that it is *very, very* difficult to bind up these wounds, but you do; you minister to protect rights so that here too the church might be healed.

When you draft decrees, when you merge one parish into another, when you alter a parish where generations of people have been baptized, married, received their sacraments and were buried, you walk along side the members of the parish in their sorrow, and you are the Servant Christ. When you are entrusted to secure and preserve the documents of the local church, when you preserve the history of the diocese, secure the archives, maintain the parish history and the sacramental records of our faithful you preserve our religious patrimony and show yourself as a Servant Christ.

When you teach our future pastors the law of the church in the seminary you are a Servant Christ. When you teach canon law in a program leading to the license or a doctorate you teach our legacy, to those canonists who follow in our footsteps and will do the work that we do, you are a Servant Christ.

When you give consultation to your bishops, or to the body of bishops, to your general councils or chapters, to pastors, to our church related institutions you advance the Servant Church. I realize that this above list is not exhaustive of what canonists do. When you prepare documents for transmittal to the Vatican, when you do all of the other routine things that you do, you act in the role of the Servant Church and the Servant Christ. For these reasons I am blessed and grateful to be your colleague in ministry. Thank you for what you do for the People of God day in and day out.

VARIA

ROLE OF LAW AWARD CITATION
Rita F. Joyce

Each year the Canon Law Society of America presents its distinguished Role of Law Award to an individual considered to be outstanding in the field of canonical science. The by-laws of the Society direct the Board of Governors to select a person who demonstrates in his or her life and legal practice the following characteristics:

Embodiment of pastoral attitude, commitment to research and study, participation in the development of law, response to needs or practical assistance, facilitation of dialogue and the interchange of ideas within the Society and with other groups.

These qualifications are a concise re-statement of the constitutionally-expressed purposes of the Society.

The person to whom this award is given is viewed by us as one who embodies all that we, as members of the Society, hold dear—as one to whom we can look for guidance and inspiration. Such an official statement alone is perhaps the greatest honor that can be bestowed on anyone—to be selected by one's friends and peers as outstanding among them.

This year's recipient of the Role of Law Award was ordained a priest in 1977.

Our honoree has generously served the Canon Law Society of America in many capacities. He was born in Buffalo, New York and had his final profession on August 15, 1976.

He holds a JCL from The Catholic University of America, a JCD/Ph.D from St. Paul University and the University of Ottawa—so both schools can claim him. He has been a member of the CLSA since 1982. This year's awardee has been the Promoter of Justice and the chair of a commission for the canonization for two individuals. He served diligently as a consultor, and before that as a member of the Clergy Committee. He is a prolific writer and editor, a frequent presenter, an author of at least seven advisory opinions, editor for *CLSA Advisory Opinions 1984-1993* and various other publications, as well as five books in the canonical field. He is currently an associate pastor. In his religious community he served as the Associate Director of the Ecumenical Institute and as Postulant and Novitiate Formation Director. He has taught on the faculty of Mount Saint Mary's Seminary in Emmitsburg, Maryland, as well as on the faculty of St. Paul University as Assistant Professor in the Faculty of Canon Law. He has served as the Chair of our Convention Planning Committee that has brought you such fine programs for the past several years. He served as the Executive Coordinator of our Society for seven years. He is the editor of *Canon Law Digest* Volumes 13 and 14, and he is a professed member of the Atonement Friars.

Tonight we honor a friend, a colleague, an educator, a parish priest, a past executive coordinator, and a fellow canonist. He is truly a Renaissance man of the Church. It my privilege to present the 2012 Role of Law Award, on behalf of the Canon Law Society of America and the Board of Governors, to Reverend Patrick J. Cogan, SA.

Varia

Role of Law Award Response
Reverend Patrick J. Cogan, SA

Last winter, when I received the telephone call from Rita Joyce about my nomination to receive the Role of Law award at this convention, I was stunned and inwardly I had a very deep emotional response beyond words. When I served in the CLSA office during the nineteen-nineties, the selection of the next recipient of this honor at the Board of Governors' meeting was like a solemn moment of discernment. There are so many worthy potential recipients – the challenge was not "who?" but "which one"? With heartfelt gratitude I wish to thank the Board of Governors and the entire CLSA membership for this honor. I am privileged to join the body of previous recipients. I will display this award proudly in my office so that it is clearly visible to all who enter, not so much for myself, but as a testimony to my cherished association with the CLSA. After more than a decade since my service in the Office of the Executive Coordinator, I still am very interested in how the CLSA is doing. My friends and family still ask me about the CLSA. One never knows when the CLSA will emerge in conversation. Once I was on an airplane, carrying a convention bag, when a passenger next to me asked if I was an optician! He saw the acronym CLSA and understood it to be the Contact Lens Society of America!

The title itself of this award, "Role of Law" offers a springboard for a very timely reflection. We are at both a sensitive and celebratory moment in the Church. A rapid scan of Catholic news and events in recent months signals the extended attention devoted to the fiftieth anniversary of the opening of the Second Vatican Council in October 1962, which day is tomorrow, October 11, also the beginning of the year of faith. An ecclesial golden jubilee! Various symposia, articles and books are celebrating this anniversary, especially with a focus on the continued reception of this great conciliar event, hardly a blip on the ecclesiastical screen as some might view it. Canonists are almost reflexively inclined to first think of January 1959 when John XXIII announced the convening of the Council, the revision of the 1917 Code, and a synod for Rome. But as canonists we are not disinterested parties for this observance of this fifty year anniversary of the Council. We know in a very real way what the Council has meant for canon law. After all, the revision of the 1917 Code is intrinsically associated with the Council's teachings; likewise the preparation of the 1990 Eastern Code. The first twenty-one of these fifty years were also about the revision of the 1917 Code, which only began in earnest after the conciliar documents were promulgated.

Often I have remarked that my own familiarity with the conciliar documents is very much owed to my canon law studies. Reading the conciliar text through a canonical lens is a very unique and necessary hermeneutic. Frequently I have observed to students that in the office of every canonist four books should be evident: the Bible, the 1983 and 1990 Codes, and the documents of Vatican II. In recent years, I even became more pro-active regarding which translation of Vatican II documents a student should use (preferably Tanner)!

The Code Commission was very aware of its task to give juridical expression to the conciliar teachings. What was immediately evident during the revision period was how the various *schemata* were scrutinized by canonists and theologians for their faithful reflection of conciliar teachings. This is clearly demonstrated in the CLSA evaluations of the various *schemata* and likewise in articles by various members. Often, when teaching, when a student was exegeting a canon in a research project or thesis, in addition to the standard commentaries and journals, I would direct them to these evaluations of the *schemata*.

There was a remarkable dynamic at work as the two Codes were being prepared: canonists, together with all the faithful, were still receiving and interpreting the Council. When the 1983 Code was promulgated, the many presentations (including at our annual conventions) and fresh commentaries would necessarily also involve teaching the conciliar foundations of the new law, and thus contributing to the reception of the Council. The law was and continues to be an important vehicle for this reception – if – it is good law. So the Council is and continues to be our standard. This occasion of the fiftieth anniversary of the opening of the Council thus offers an opportunity not only to revisit the conciliar texts, but also to once again examine the many laws which are born from these texts.

Other specialists of course were also deeply involved in the reception and actualization of the Council. Many CLSA members were collaborating with these other specialists. These arenas often involved canon law: a prime example is the renewal of the liturgy and the revision of liturgical law. I do not think it is an exaggeration to state that as regards the reception of the Council in the United States, canonists were often frontline actors as dioceses received both the law and Council and implemented new structures. The same is true for religious institutes in the revision of their particular law. As a long time observer of ecumenical dialogues, more than one ecumenist has observed that we will need the assistance of canonists to develop norms to implement various ecumenical agreements. Several CLSA members have been participants in various national and international ecumenical dialogues. Thus it is impossible to segregate the reception of the revised law from the reception the Council. So what I wish to highlight especially here is the role of the CLSA in this conciliar reception process and experience.

The post-conciliar arena, as a reflection of the ethos of the Council, is an area of continued CLSA activity. The CLSA has also anticipated the need to assist, not only canonists, but the entire People of God in their reception of the Council and also with the new laws issued post-promulgation.

I wish to raise up two examples that can be easily identified. In 1970 the CLSA proposed to the bishops the American Procedural Norms (APN), to assist in the timely processing of petitions for nullity. These norms served the People of God well, even if they were not totally incorporated into the revised legislation. A second example is when I was in the CLSA office, as part of the preparation for the bi-annual visits to the Roman Curia, I typically had a meeting with the CUA faculty to solicit topics for questions, clarifications, etc., to ask in Rome. I recall one such meeting when our sorely missed friend and mentor James Provost suggested that we ask at the Congregation for the Doctrine of the Faith how to understand the expression *"graviora delicta,"* in *Pastor Bonus,* art. 62. He already in 1996 had a sense that canonists need to be alert to what might be on the horizon. Unfortunately, we know only too well what those words mean! The CLSA subsequently has responded with resources for canonists and bishops to assist in the handling of these *graviora delicta* cases. And we continue to keep a high alert for further ways to serve the community of canonists and the Church.

We are already into another generation of canonists who have studied the law almost three decades after promulgation and even longer since the conclusion of the Council. Thus the experience and exhuberance of the Council is somewhat remote for this generation. But their learning about the law is also a good tutorial on the Council!

The golden jubilee of Vatican II is an occasion for celebration. It is also an opportunity to ask: what next? Where do we go from here? How do we continue as canonists "to read the signs of the times," the great conciliar clarion? It is of limited usefulness if we only look at the law with a certain retrospect as to how faithful the law is/was to the Council. Codes have a shorter life-span than ecumenical councils. (But it takes longer to revise a Code than to have a Council !)

Faithful observance of the law does not exclude a critical stance towards the law. It is our obligation as canonists to be ever alert to improvement of the law, when a law is not working well or is not responsive to new situations. The Legislator has invited recommendations for changes or improvements to the law. A most immediate example was the invitation to canon law faculties, conferences of bishops and others to comment on a proposed revision of Book Six – *De sanctionibus* of the 1983 Code. A recent visit of the CLSA officers to the Pontifical Council for Legislative Texts was also the occasion of such an invitation to revisit the law where appropriate. We cannot pass up this opportunity. And it is a task for which our track record says we do very well!

With increasing frequency, there are voices in the canonical literature about the future revision of the law, increasingly with specific recommendations, a "future" which perhaps is not too distant. One might wonder if this is an opportune moment in the history of the Church to revise the law, but maybe there is not always an ideal moment. Not every revision of the law has an ecumenical council as a beacon to inspire us! But we can be major participants in this endeavor.

I thank you again for this honor.

VARIA

U.S. TRIBUNAL STATISTICS
2011

Since 1975, the CLSA has published Tribunal Statistics annually in *Proceedings*. These statistics are provided voluntarily by participating tribunal offices in the United States. This year's statistical report was compiled similar to how they were compiled last year. Tribunals were asked to submit a copy of the report sent annually to the Apostolic Signatura, as well as some basic financial information, either by sending it to the CLSA office or by filling out the information online. This change was implemented last year, resulting in a more accurate comparison of statistics among U.S. tribunals.

Participation in the survey was down slightly compared to last year. This year, the CLSA received information from 151 tribunals, compared to 156 last year. This discrepancy should be considered when analyzing this year's data compared to previous years. Comparing statistics from the same tribunals from last year, however, does yield some usable data.

Included again in this year's report is the number of decisions found contrary to nullity from each reporting tribunal, with the percentage of negative decisions out of the total calculated. Following the same gradual trend as indicated in the past several years, the number of cases introduced and decisions made in American tribunals continues to decline, while expenses continue to rise.

The tribunals of the Archdioceses of Atlanta, Baltimore, Denver, Dubuque, Galveston-Houston, Miami, Mobile, Philadelphia, San Francisco, Santa Fe, Washington; and the Dioceses of Arlington, Boise, Charlotte, Covington, Duluth, El Paso, Fall River, Fargo, Juneau, Kalamazoo, Lafayette in Indiana, Lake Charles, Las Cruces, Las Vegas, Lubbock, Manchester, Orange, Salina, Venice, and Winona did not participate in the survey.

Five Year Comparison

Year	Documentary Cases	Formal Cases (Previous Year)	Formal Cases (This Year)	Cases Abated	Formal Decisions	Fees Received	Diocesan Subsidy	Total Expenses	Percentage of tribunals reporting
2011	3774	15775	15889	1515	14314	$4,569,371	$25,211,816	$30,372,513	81.62%
2010	4147	15368	16787	1284	14360	$5,193,872	$26,447,648	$31,612,970	83.78%
2009	12239	17457	19039	1846	17106	$4,980,461	$26,104,591	$31,123,946	88.11%
2008	14089	18704	19805	2002	18503	$5,551,648	$26,434,692	$32,465,062	88.11%
2007	12593	19168	19864	2451	18644	$5,411,389	$25,444,135	$30,950,916	86.49%

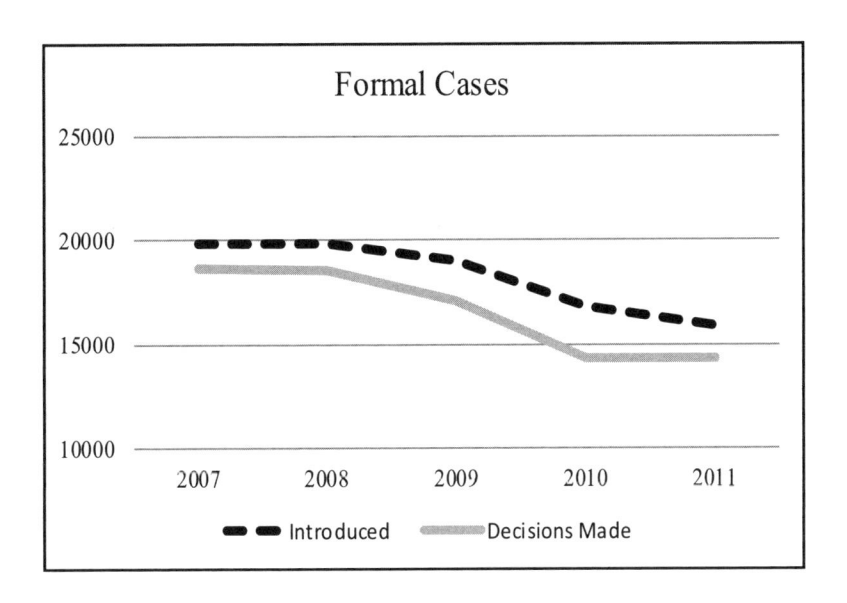

First Instance Statistics: 2011

(Arch)Diocese	Documentary Cases Closed	Formal Cases Held Over	Formal Cases Introduced	Sentence in Favor of Nullity	Sentence Contrary to Nullity	Total Formal Decisions (Affirm/Neg)	Percentage of Total Decisions Found Contrary to Nullity	Peremption/Renunciation	Total	Total Fees Received	Amount of Diocesan Subsidy	Total Annual Expenses
Albany		40	78	76	6	82	7%	3	85	$40,000	$225,000	$265,000
Alexandria		81	61	36	1	37	3%	2	39	$10,050	$170,405	$180,455
Allentown		155	146	142	0	142	0%	12	154	$63,000	$172,000	$235,000
Altoona-Johnstown	5	37	61	69	4	73	5%	15	88	$300	$71,000	$60,000
Anchorage	1	58	34	46	0	46	0%	1	47	$10,603	$113,305	$123,908
Austin	29	188	240	161	3	164	2%	7	171	$77,684	$250,701	$329,259
Baker		35	26	17	0	17	0%	3	20	$3,345	$115,307	$118,652
Baton Rouge	10	148	157	121	3	124	2%	12	137	$44,500	$208,807	$253,307
Beaumont	5	115	77	62	0	62	0%	7	69	$22,539	$159,228	$198,388
Biloxi		116	53	24	2	26	8%	3	29	$2,250	$156,372	$149,684
Birmingham	10	70	53	55	1	56	2%	0	56	$18,115	$165,876	$187,440
Bismarck	48	40	62	42	1	43	2%	4	47	$12,999	$201,230	$214,229
Boston		128	160	107	2	109	2%	12	121			
Bridgeport		26	62	45	0	45	0%	0	45	$29,305	$489,352	$518,658
Brooklyn		129	103	113	1	114	1%	9	123	$109,196	$330,104	$439,300
Brownsville	215	72	70	35	2	37	5%	24	61	$26,505	$51,547	$78,052
Buffalo	109	34	93	89	0	89	0%	1	90	$54,375	$201,343	$255,718
Burlington		56	46	54	4	58	7%	7	65	$0	$50,000	$50,000
Camden		94	49	61	1	62	2%	7	69	$44,375	$105,775	$150,150
Charleston	12	48	69	69	3	72	4%	7	79	$62,725	$313,759	$376,483
Cheyenne	8	33	55	31	2	33	6%	6	39	$22,376	$116,573	$138,949
Chicago	34	338	384	308	3	311	1%	34	345	$241,464	$734,022	$975,486
Cincinnati		185	272	210	34	244	14%	17	261	$77,877	$417,301	$488,263

410

(Arch)Diocese	Documentary Cases Closed	Formal Cases Held Over	Formal Cases Introduced	Sentence in Favor of Nullity	Sentence Contrary to Nullity	Total Formal Decisions (Affirm/Neg)	Percentage of Total Decisions Found Contrary to Nullity	Peremption/Renunciation	Total	Total Fees Received	Amount of Diocesan Subsidy	Total Annual Expenses
Cleveland	237	240	334	276	1	277	0%	17	294	$136,978	$531,908	$682,086
Colorado Springs	56	48	34	24	11	35	31%	8	51			
Columbus		151	206	158	3	161	2%	15	176	$0	$436,552	$436,552
Corpus Christi		106	183	73		73	0%	4	77	$30,280	$149,591	$179,870
Crookston		90	48	32	1	33	3%	8	41	$0	$133,149	$144,023
Dallas	36	236	274	120	12	132	9%	138	270	$0	$388,128	$388,778
Davenport	10	86	78	74	0	74	0%	8	82	$30,090	$108,406	$138,496
Des Moines	52	43	79	77	1	78	1%	2	80	$35,410	$111,292	$146,702
Detroit		35	429	373	7	380	2%	29	409			
Belleville	4	103	53	50	0	50	0%	3	53	$7,355	$52,457	$59,812
Memphis	14	45	90	67		67	0%	4	71	$0	$172,582	$175,582
Dodge City	2	3	32	32	0	32	0%	1	33	$3,971	$71,453	$75,424
Erie		68	159	114	1	115	1%	5	120	$37,745	$304,681	$342,426
Evansville		3	51	47	0	47	0%	5	52	$15,115	$174,485	$189,600
Fairbanks	1	18	9	8	0	8	0%	0	8	$2,100		
Ft Wayne-South Bend	106	54	72	42	21	63	33%	12	75	$20,160	$433,294	$458,294
Fort Worth	12	616	168	267	3	270	1%	16	286			
Fresno	214	140	183	132	0	132	0%	5	137	$82,427	$58,567	$140,994
Gallup		19	29	6	1	7	14%	6	13	$5,225		$28,380
Gary		170	68	56	2	58	3%	0	58	$26,395.00	$214,434	$241,154
Gaylord	3	33	42	22	8	30	27%	0	30	$0	$90,791	$90,791
Grand Island		49	44	37		37	0%	2	39	$3,725	$176,454	$180,179
Grand Rapids	75	130	153	103	1	104	1%	11	115	$0	$158,781	$158,781

(Arch)Diocese	Documentary Cases Closed	Formal Cases Held Over	Formal Cases Introduced	Sentence in Favor of Nullity	Sentence Contrary to Nullity	Total Formal Decisions (Affirm/Neg)	Percentage of Total Decisions Found Contrary to Nullity	Peremption/Renunciation	Total	Total Fees Received	Amount of Diocesan Subsidy	Total Annual Expenses
Great Falls-Billings	19			13	0	13	0%	1	14	$4,110	$111,715	$115,825
Green Bay		52	101	98	3	101	3%	0	101	$147,027	$110,267	$135,340
Greensburg		34	72	78	2	80	3%	1	81			
Harrisburg		271	176	210	13	223	6%	9	232	$100,659	$378,896	$479,555
Hartford		136	73	85	22	107	21%	27	134			
Helena	2	86	38	35	0	35	0%	1	36	$0	$100,000	$100,000
Honolulu	4	33	42	35	2	37	5%	7		$18,855	$140,517	$159,372
Houma-Thibodaux		28	42	40	1	41	2%	1	42	$10,885	$57,347	$68,232
Indianapolis	20	114	113	79	0	79	0%	7	86	$61,345	$333,278	$394,623
Jackson	3	22	46	44	0	44	0%	19	63	$0	$100,292	$100,292
Jefferson City	18	130	107	81	2	83	2%	11	94	$0	$163,924	$163,924
Joliet	13	66	158	202	13	215	6%	21	236	$73,060	$505,300	$574,300
Kansas City-St. Joseph	15	113	97	107	0	107	0%	4	111			
Kansas City in Kansas	134	262	283	198	4	202	2%	16	218	$68,274	$184,098	$252,372
La Crosse		58	150	153	2	155	1%	20	175	$42,580	$147,922	$190,502
Lafayette in Louisiana	6	293	147	107	23	130	18%	126	256	$48,565	$156,486	$166,577
Lansing	17	135	202	175	4	179	2%	9	188	$41,350	$357,256	$398,606
Laredo		27	27	20	2	22	9%	2	24	$11,450	$82,418	$78,566
Lexington	11	48	60	47	4	51	8%	4	55	$0	$280,385	$280,385
Lincoln		78	60	39	3	42	7%	10	52			
Little Rock	40	78	126	111	1	112	1%	24	136	$24,555	$139,295	$163,850
Los Angeles	29	530	422	530	0	530	0%	39	569			

(Arch)Diocese	Documentary Cases Closed	Formal Cases Held Over	Formal Cases Introduced	Sentence in Favor of Nullity	Sentence Contrary to Nullity	Total Formal Decisions (Affirm/Neg)	Percentage of Total Decisions Found Contrary to Nullity	Peremption/Renunciation	Total	Total Fees Received	Amount of Diocesan Subsidy	Total Annual Expenses
Louisville	8	23	123	122	1	123	1%	1	124	$27,265	$232,402	$259,667
Madison		41	62	31	0	31	0%	9	40	$33,000	$157,192	$190,192
Marquette	23	0	47	45	2	47	4%	0	47	$7,485	$29,889	$37,154
Metuchen		57	88	50	1	51	2%	2	53	$56,475	$243,165	$298,640
Military Services		287	110	90	1	91	1%	14	105	$34,380	$124,469	$162,249
Milwaukee		234	192	208	0	208	0%	20	20	$84,014	$412,299	$496,313
Monterey	66	55	30	33	10	43	23%	3	46	$22,500	$94,150	$116,660
Nashville	25	211	105	89	28	117	24%	3	120		$400,939	$400,939
New Orleans	6	228	129	86	13	99	13%	7	106	$58,545	$337,041	$395,586
New Ulm	22	28	25	22	0	22	0%	2	24	$5,161	$189,674	$194,835
New York	1	158	160	135	6	141	4%	7	148	$141,469	$1,166,683	$1,308,152
Newark	2	111	119	87	2	89	2%	26	115	$75,316	$450,637	$525,953
Norwich	3	39	33	26	3	29	10%	0	29	$16,000	$258,527	$274,527
Oakland	141	227	121	76	2	78	3%	17	95	$83,079	$399,374	$482,453
Ogdensburg		76	34	37	4	41	10%	21	62	$20,948	$86,228	$107,176
Oklahoma City	103	117	188	149	11	160	7%	0	160	$0	$145,000	$145,000
Omaha	131	141	157	124	12	136	9%	3	139	$42,568	279, 673	322, 241
Orlando		50	321	137	25	162	15%	16	178	$141,926	$272,077	$416,243
Owensboro	12	96	70	56	0	56	0%	8	64	$8,530	$234,745	$243,275
Palm Beach	12	63	97	94	4	98	4%	2	100			
Paterson		124	56	25	9	34	26%	14	48			
Pensacola-Tallahassee	84	25	69	62	1	63	2%	1	64	$0	$74,808	$74,808
Peoria		99	120	131	0	131	0%	4	4	$67,478	$356,367	$423,845
Phoenix		453	143	113	25	138	18%	14	152			

(Arch)Diocese	Documentary Cases Closed	Formal Cases Held Over	Formal Cases Introduced	Sentence in Favor of Nullity	Sentence Contrary to Nullity	Total Formal Decisions (Affirm/Neg)	Percentage of Total Decisions Found Contrary to Nullity	Peremption/Renunciation	Total	Total Fees Received	Amount of Diocesan Subsidy	Total Annual Expenses
Pittsburgh		143	191	216	1	217	0%	5	222	$162,230	$688,362	$850,592
Portland in Maine	94	105	89	118	0	118	0%	19	137	$26,500	$315,243	$341,743
Portland in Oregon	11	379	147	130	3	133	2%	7	140			
Providence		61	85	76	8	84	10%	2	86	$58,325	$249,380	$307,706
Pueblo	44	29	40	19	0	19	0%	12	31	$4,255	$37,214	$41,469
Raleigh	161	132	124	104	7	111	6%	12	123	$39,860	$179,138	$225,013
Rapid City	15	29	18	17	2	19	11%	6	25	$7,382	$72,966	$80,348
Reno		56	31	24	2	26	8%	2	29	$11,130	$121,024	$132,154
Richmond	14	101	191	162	7	169	4%	15	184			
Rochester	4	23	53	23	3	26	12%	8	34	$31,676	$190,841	$222,517
Rockford	134	60	162	193	4	197	2%	6	203			
Rockville Centre		261	263	194	0	194	0%	41	235			
Sacramento	17	274	124	87	19	106	18%	25	131	$75,769	$292,259	$368,028
Saginaw		43	81	83	1	84	1%	2	86	$2,530	$119,676	$121,630
Salt Lake City	15	10	72	63	4	67	6%	5	72	$12,575	$97,741	$110,316
San Angelo		36	47	40	0	40	0%	9	49	$5,960	$235,826	$242,286
San Antonio		64	263	263	12	275	4%	6	281	$106,850	$204,214	$311,064
San Bernardino	252	144	158	112	11	123	9%	12	135	$18,206	$336,926	$381,926
San Diego		232	204	211	3	214	1%	4	218	$60,539	$285,328	$345,867
San Jose	138	123	105	99	1	100	1%	1	101	$60, 984	$492,018	$553,002
Santa Rosa	33	18	38	32	0	32	0%	4	36	$19,266	$123,231	$142,497
Savannah		16	57	54	2	56	4%	10	66	$18,248	$208,929	$177,765
Scranton		105	140	154	2	156	1%	19	175	$84,965	$268,418	$353,383

(Arch)Diocese	Documentary Cases Closed	Formal Cases Held Over	Formal Cases Introduced	Sentence in Favor of Nullity	Sentence Contrary to Nullity	Total Formal Decisions (Affirm/Neg)	Percentage of Total Decisions Found Contrary to Nullity	Peremption/Renunciation	Total	Total Fees Received	Amount of Diocesan Subsidy	Total Annual Expenses
Seattle	30	212	161	163	4	167	2%	7	174	$78,309	$394,038	$535,714
Shreveport	6	56	37	33	1	34	3%	3	37	$13,300	$188,218	$174,918
Sioux City	1	66	67	67	3	70	4%	7	77	$22,985	$156,966	$179,951
Sioux Falls		38	86	71	6	77	8%	3	80	$28,135	$99,104	$119,054
Spokane	9	21	50	50		50	0%	1	51	$10,450	$14,712	$25,162
Springfield, Cape Girardeau	65	129	130	80	28	108	26%	18	126	$23,765	$194,811	$218,576
Springfield, IL	75	164	124	145	1	146	1%	4	150	$51,110	$151,185	$202,295
Springfield, MA	0	93	80	75	0	75	0%	10	85	$32,640	$189,513	$222,153
St. Augustine	20	103	93	86	0	86	0%	5	91			
St. Cloud		64	66	56	56	112	50%	2	58	$27,000	$117,790	$167,793
St. Louis	16	282	244	186	4	190	2%	25	215	$148,109	$334,597	$482,706
St. Paul & Minneapolis		249	216	105	46	151	30%	31	182			
St. Petersburg		44	219	192	9	201	4%	2	203			
Steubenville	4	29	44	45	0	45	0%	3	48	$10,525	$71,234	$81,759
Stockton	0	140	57	13	4	17	24%	9	26	$34,896	$177,030	$211,926
Superior	0	21	64	51		51	0%	0		$6,748	$98,890	$105,637
Syracuse	2	28	118	123	1	124	1%	4	128	$86,420	$25,762	$112,182
Toledo	163	92	160	149	0	149	0%	16	165	$37,979	$189,576	$227,555
Trenton	6	194	92	108	3	111	3%	9	120	$74,000	$298,350	$372,350
Tucson	7	131	72	39	1	40	3%	35	75	$37,907	$55,281	$93,188

415

(Arch)Diocese	Documentary Cases Closed	Formal Cases Held Over	Formal Cases Introduced	Sentence in Favor of Nullity	Sentence Contrary to Nullity	Total Formal Decisions (Affirm/Neg)	Percentage of Total Decisions Found Contrary to Nullity	Peremption/Renunciation	Total	Total Fees Received	Amount of Diocesan Subsidy	Total Annual Expenses
Tyler		35	75	32	11	43	26%	10	53	$9,640	$98,659	$108,299
Victoria		42	46	38	1	39	3%	0	39	$9,469	$31,250	$35,984
Wheeling-Charleston	10	182	58	77	8	85	9%	9	94			
Wichita	12	382	195	185	11	196	6%	13	209	$68,000	$40,000	$108,000
Wilmington		103	71	95		95	0%	1	96	$9,480	$104,977	$114,457
Worcester	2	24	41	56	0	56	0%	2	58	$33,300	$151,802	$185,102
Yakima		30	43	18	1	19	5%	0	19	$24,615	$87,401	$176,633
Youngstown	54	86	69	72	0	72	0%	2	74	$23,873	$307,100	$316,553

Second Instance Statistics: 2011

(Arch)Diocese	Second Instance Pending at Beginning of Year	Introduced	Closed	Decree Confirmation	Sentence in Favor of Nullity	Sentence Contrary to Nullity
Boston	12	246	251	239	6	3
Bridgeport	14	42	46	43	0	3
Camden	3	39	24	22	0	2
Cleveland	49	310	342	0	340	2
Davenport	0	44	43	43	0	0
Des Moines	0	47	47	47	47	0
Detroit	18	516	474			
Memphis	2	106	102	102	0	0
Fort Wayne-South Bend	27	31	43	26	6	9
Fresno	0	97	97	97	97	0
Gary	0	40	40			
Grand Rapids	2	256	233	233	231	2
Great Falls-Billings	9	24	14			
Green Bay		170	170			
Hartford	1	69	65	60	4	1
Indianapolis	48	37	60	59	59	0
Kansas City in Kansas	5	221	222	221		1
Lafayette in Louisiana	7	47	50		49	1
Lexington	33	52	81	77	0	4
Los Angeles	39	197	210	204	2	1
Louisville	11	103	100	100	100	0
Milwaukee	22	316	329	329	329	0
Nashville	4	67	61			
New Orleans	82	408	430	0	423	12
Newark	0	155	155	155	0	0
Newton, Eparchy of	0	8	8	8	8	0

(Arch)Diocese	Second Instance Pending at Beginning of Year	Introduced	Closed	Decree Confirmation	Sentence in Favor of Nullity	Sentence Contrary to Nullity
Norwich	1	43	44	40	0	1
Owensboro	13	54	49	0	49	0
Paterson	6	65	49	49	1	1
Philadelphia, Archeparchy for Ukrainians	0	4	4	4	4	0
Pittsburgh	45	136	280	280	0	0
Pittsburgh, Archeparchy for Byzantines	0	10	10		9	1
Portland in Maine	6	165	166	160	5	1
Portland in Oregon	140	230	230	230	0	0
Reno				29		1
San Bernardino	2	110	110	0	110	0
San Jose	9	124	112	112	0	0
Seattle	13	260	253	253	0	0
Sioux City	5	33	32	32	0	0
Sioux Falls	0	39	37	29	4	2
Springfield, MA	34	144	156	155	1	0
St. Cloud	9	42	30	30	30	
St. Louis	64	624	550	541	3	6
St. Paul and Minneapolis	170	322	344	322	24	13
St. Petersburg				188		
Steubenville	3	48	51	0	50	1
Stockton	57	157	163	132	0	0
Toledo	87	204	288	288		
Trenton	3	43	46	46	0	0
Wichita	3	242	245	245	3	4
Youngstown	0	101	101	101	101	0

VARIA

Contributors

Most Reverend Gregory M. Aymond, Archbishop of New Orleans, Louisiana

Reverend Monsignor Ricardo Bass, JCL, Pastor, St. Hubert Parish, Harrison Township, Michigan

Reverend Patrick J. Cogan, SA, JCD, Parochial Vicar, Christ the Redeemer Parish, Sterling, Virginia, 2012 Role of Law Recipient

Most Reverend R. Daniel Conlon, JCD, Bishop, Diocese of Joliet, Illinois

Chorbishop John D. Faris, JCD, Pastor, St. Louis Gonzaga Church, Utica, New York

Mark M. Gray, Senior Research Associate, Center for Applied Research in the Apostolate, Washington, District of Columbia

Doctor Eileen C. Jaramillo, JCD, Judge and Canonical Consultant, Diocese of Lansing, Michigan

Reverend Monsignor John G. Johnson, JCD, Judge, Diocese of Columbus, Ohio

Deacon Gerald T. Jorgensen, JCL, Judge, Archdiocese of Dubuque, Iowa

Rita F. Joyce, JD, JCL, General Counsel, Department for Canon and Civil Law Services, Diocese of Pittsburgh, Pennsylvania

Reverend Monsignor Patrick R. Lagges, JCD, Chaplain, Calvert House at the University of Chicago, Illinois

Sister Mary Paul McCaughey, OP, Superintendent of Catholic Schools, Chicago, Illinois

Very Reverend Mark O'Connell, JCD, Judicial Vicar, Archdiocese of Boston, Massachusetts

Reverend Monsignor Roch Pagé, JCD, Judicial Vicar, Canadian Appeal Tribunal, Ottawa, Ontario, Canada

Reverend Bruce Miller, JCL, Judicial Vicar, Diocese of Alexandria, Louisiana

Doctor Lynda Robitaille, JCD, Canonical Consultant, Vancouver, British Columbia, Canada

Sister Katarina Schuth, OSF, Endowed Chair for the Social Scientific Study of Religion, University of St. Thomas, St. Paul, Minnesota

Sister Marilyn Vassallo, CSJ, JCL, Director of the Office of Canonical Services, Diocese of Shreveport, Louisiana

Reverend Daniel J. Ward, OSB, JD, JCL, Executive Director, The Resource Center for Religious Institutes, Silver Spring, Maryland

VARIA

Participants

Joseph Abraham
  Reno, NV
Peter Akpoghiran
  New Orleans, LA
John Alesandro
  Rockville Centre, NY
Margaret Alokan
  Millen, GA
Krystyna Amborski
  San Francisco, CA
Arthur Anderson
  Chicago, IL
Thomas Anslow
  Los Angeles, CA
William Anton
  Lubbock, TX
Gary Applegate
  Kansas City, KS
Christopher Armstrong
  Cincinnati, OH
Das Arockia
  Lexington, KY
Anne Asselin
  Ottawa, ON
Joseph Augustine
  Romney, WV
Alberto Avella
  Grants, NM
Gregory Aymond
  New Orleans, LA
Renata Babicz-Baratto
  Lexington, KY
Paul Baillargeon
  London, ON
Marc Balestrieri
  Rome, Italy
Diane Barr
  Baltimore, MD

Mark Bartchak
  Altoona-Johnstown, PA
Mary Ann Bartolac
  Overland Park, KS
Virginia Bartolac
  Kansas City, KS
James Bartoloma
  Camden, NJ
Carlotta Bartone
  Philadelphia, PA
Ricardo Bass
  Detroit, MI
R. Paul Beach
  Louisville, KY
John Beal
  Erie, PA
John Bell
  Plano, TX
Iden Bello
  Laredo, TX
Charles Benoit
  Saint Benedict, LA
Richard Berube
  Colchester, VT
Barbara Bettwy
  Erie, PA
Kathleen Bierne
  Aberdeen, SD
Gregory Bittner
  Birmingham, AL
Mary Gen Blittschau
  Evansville, IN
Lucy Blyskal
  Rockville Centre, NY
Michael Boccaccio
  Norwalk, CT
James Bonke
  Indianapolis, IN

Marvin Borger
  Toledo, OH
Janelle Boyum
  New Ulm, MN
Michael Bradley
  Chicago, IL
R. Richard Brickler
  Rochester, NY
Barry Brinkman
  Salina, KS
Robert Brooks
  Atlanta, GA
George Brooks
  Chicago, IL
Max Brown
  River Forest, IL
Phillip Brown
  Washington, DC
Thomas Brundage
  Anchorage, AK
Michael Burchfield
  Fresno, CA
Marianne Burkhard
  Peoria, IL
Jesus Cabrera
  Milwaukee, WI
Steven Callahan
  San Diego, CA
Maria Casey
  Sydney, Australia
David Castronovo
  Atlanta, GA
Timothy Cavanaugh
  Madison, WI
Anthony Celino
  El Paso, TX
Martin Celuch
  Youngstown, OH

Deborah Cerullo
  Providence, RI
Charles Chaffman
  Los Angeles, CA
Margaret Chalmers
  Feura Bush, NY
Anna Marie Chamblee
  Fort Worth, TX
Cherry Clark
  Towson, MD
Paul Clark
  Harrisburg, PA
J. Michael Clark
  Owensboro, KY
Brian Clarke
  Scranton, PA
John Cody
  Columbus, OH
Patrick Cogan
  Garrison, NY
Daniel Condon
  Rochester, NY
R. Daniel Conlon
  Joliet, IL
James Connell
  Sheboygan, WI
Jay Conzemius
  Pittsburgh, PA
Patrick Cooney
  Saint Meinrad, IN
James Coriden
  Washington, DC
Paul Counce
  Baton Rouge, LA
Derek Covert
  Lake Charles, LA
Thomas Cronkleton
  Cheyenne, WY
Barbara Anne Cusack
  Milwaukee, WI
Jamin David
  Baton Rouge, LA
Zabrina Decker
  Milwaukee, WI

Robert Deeley
  Boston, MA
Jesus Del Angel Leon
  Fresno, CA
Frank Del Prete
  Saddle River, NJ
Robert DeLand
  Saginaw, MI
Louis DeNinno
  Pittsburgh, PA
John Dermond
  Trenton, NJ
Lawrence DiNardo
  Pittsburgh, PA
Francis Dolan
  Chicago, IL
Blake Dominguez
  Austin, TX
Robert Duesdieker
  Boonville, MO
Patricia Dugan
  Philadelphia, PA
Mary Edlund
  Dallas, TX
Peter Eke
  Gaylord, MI
Jace Eskind
  Lake Charles, LA
Sharon Euart
  Washington, DC
John Faris
  Utica, NY
Thomas Feeney
  Corpus Christi, TX
Karla Felix-Rivera
  San Jose, CA
David Fellhauer
  Victoria, TX
Christopher Ferrer
  Austin, TX
Victor Finelli
  Allentown, PA
Daniel Firmin
  Savannah, GA

Edward Fitzgerald
  Hanahan, SC
Terrance Fleming
  Los Angeles, CA
Robert Flummerfelt
  Las Vegas, NV
Debra Foreman
  Lake Charles, LA
Kenneth Fortener
  New Hope, KY
John J.M. Foster
  Washington, DC
Raphael Frackiewicz
  Chicago, IL
Thomas Fransiscus
  Reno, NV
Matthew H. Frisoni
  Albany, NY
Canuto Emeritus Fuentebella
  Aruba
Christopher Fusco
  Metuchen, NJ
Leonardo Gajardo
  Baltimore, MD
Engelberto Gammad
  San Jose, CA
Mark Gantley
  Honolulu, HI
Dennis Garcia
  Albuquerque, NM
John Gargan
  Dallas, TX
Elpidio Geneta
  Williamson, WV
Karen Giffin
  Seattle, WA
M. Margaret Gillett
  Dallas, TX
Catherine Gilligan
  Little Rock, AR
Garry Giroux
  Brasher Falls, NY
Matthew Glover
  Little Rock, AR

Raymond Goedert
  Chicago, IL
Paul Golden
  Denver, CO
James Goodwin
  Fargo, ND
Mary Ellen Goverts
  Rochester, NY
Mark Gray
  Washington, DC
Thomas Green
  Washington, DC
John Griffiths
  Chicago, IL
Janice Grochowsky
  Dodge City, KS
Robert Grosch
  Billings, MT
Ralph Gross
  Milwaukee, WI
Paul Hachey
  Atlanta, GA
Michael Hack
  Chicago, IL
Kathleen Hahn
  Grand Island, NE
Edward Hankiewicz
  Grand Rapids, MI
Stephen J. Harvey
  Milwaukee, WI
Mary Hauck
  Indianapolis, IN
Leo Hausmann
  Wall, SD
Robert Hayes
  San Jose, CA
Denis Heames
  Mt. Pleasant, MI
Robert Herbst
  Oakland, CA
Amy Hereford
  Saint Louis, MO
John Hergenrother
  Chicago, IL

Marie Hilliard
  Philadelphia, PA
Christina Hip-Flores
  Camden, NJ
Jordan Hite
  Harrisburg, PA
Thuan Hoang
  San Francisco, CA
John Hotze
  Wichita, KS
Christopher House
  Springfield, IL
Daniel Hoye
  Cape Cod, MA
Monte Hoyles
  Toledo, OH
James Innocenzi
  Trenton, NJ
Matthew Iwuji
  Austin, TX
David-Maria Jaeger
  Rome, Italy
Eileen Jaramillo
  Lansing, MI
Jolene Jasinski
  Beaver Falls, PA
John Johnson
  Columbus, OH
Bernard Johnson
  Vina, CA
Gerald Jorgensen
  Dubuque, IA
Saju Joseph
  San Jose, CA
Rita Joyce
  Pittsburgh, PA
Michael Joyce
  Memphis, TN
Vincent Juan
  Sacramento, CA
Dan Juelfs
  Eagle Butte, SD
Lawrence Jurcak
  Parma Heights, OH

Thomas Kadera
  Wheatland, WY
Thomas Joseph Kallikat
  Rome, Italy
Robert Kaslyn
  Washington, DC
Connie Kassahn
  Cheyenne, WY
Nicholas Kastenholz
  St. Louis, MO
James Kee
  Mobile, AL
Roger Keeler
  San Antonio, TX
Anthony Kerin
  Melbourne, Australia
Elaine Kerscher
  Joliet, IL
Rita Killackey
  Kansas City, MO
Adela Maria Kim
  Peoria, IL
R. Anne Kirby
  Sioux City, IA
Wayne Kirkpatrick
  Toronto, ON
Daniela Knepper
  Milwaukee, WI
Jose Kochuparambil
  Lubbock, TX
Robert Kolakowski
  Metuchen, NJ
K. Kopacz
  Fargo, ND
Barbara Kosinska
  Chicago, IL
Richard Kosisko
  Greensburg, PA
Michael J. Kotarski
  Flint, MI
Heidi Krupp
  Saginaw, MI
Francis Kub
  Chicago, IL

Christine Kub
  Chicago, IL
William Kulas
  Winona, MN
Michael Kurz
  Rockford, IL
Patrick Lagges
  Chicago, IL
Bonnie Landry
  Lake Charles, LA
James P. Lang
  Syracuse, NY
Kenneth Laverone
  Monterey, CA
Noeliva Le Blanc
  Roseau, Dominica
Richard Lelonis
  Pittsburgh, PA
Andres Ligot
  San Jose, CA
Judene Lillie
  New Orleans, LA
John List
  Lexington, KY
Douglas Loecke
  Dubuque, IA
Patti Loehrer
  Milwaukee, WI
Edward Lohse
  Rome, Italy
Douglas Lucia
  Ogdensburg, NY
William Lum
  Feura Bush, NY
Gregory Luyet
  Fort Smith, AR
Richard Lyons
  Metuchen, NJ
Jay Maddock
  Fall River, MA
Sandra Makowski
  Charleston, SC
Edward Malesic
  Harrisburg, PA

Michele Mangan
  San Jose, CA
Salvatore Manganello
  Buffalo, NY
Wojciech Marat
  Chicago, IL
Tomas Marin
  Miami, FL
Kurt Martens
  Washington, DC
Peggy Martin
  Englewood, CO
Ricardo Martin
  Racine, WI
Joseph Matt
  Kansas City, MO
Monica Mavric
  Chicago, IL
John McAllister
  Little Rock, AR
Robert McBride
  Newark, NJ
Jeremiah McCarthy
  Savannah, GA
Mary Paul McCaughey
  Chicago, IL
Rose McDermott
  Trenton, NJ
Wendy McGrath
  Manchester, NH
Fergal McGuinness
  Santa Rosa, CA
Kevin McKenna
  Rochester, NY
Maureen McPartland
  Dubuque, IA
Mark Mealey
  Arlington, VA
George Michalek
  Lansing, MI
C. Thomas Miles
  Charleston, SC
Bruce Miller
  Alexandria, LA

Donna Miller
  Arlington, VA
Christopher Moore
  Hagerstown, MD
Francis Morrisey
  Ottawa, ON
Susan Mulheron
  St. Paul, MN
John Mulvihill
  Chicago, IL
Henry Munroe
  Fall River, MA
Doni Needham
  Pueblo, CO
Martin Nelson
  Sour Lake, TX
Glenn Nelson
  Rockford, IL
Thu Nguyen
  Houston, TX
Kevin Niehoff
  Santa Fe, NM
Mary Judith O'Brien
  Saginaw, MI
James O'Brien
  Chicago, IL
Mark O'Connell
  Braintree, MA
Kelly O'Donnell
  San Diego, CA
James O'Kane
  Glasgow, Scotland
Robert Oliver
  Boston, MA
Timothy Olson
  Fargo, ND
Thomas Olszyk
  Washington, DC
George Oonnoonny
  New York, NY
Sinclair Oubre
  Port Arthur, TX
Roch Page
  Ottawa, ON

Carl Pallasch
  Chicago, IL
Duaine Pamment
  Laingsburg, MI
Thomas Paprocki
  Springfield, IL
Mark Payne
  Milwaukee, WI
John Payne
  New Orleans, LA
F. Stephen Pedone
  Worcester, MA
John Peiffer
  Irvine, CA
Joseph Perry
  Chicago, IL
Phu Phan
  Amarillo, TX
Anthony Pileggi
  Kansas City, MO
Robert Pine
  Austin, TX
Michael Podhajsky
  Dubuque, IA
Stanley Pondo
  Indianapolis, IN
Catherine Posch
  Edina, MN
George Puthusseril
  Miami Shores, FL
Liam Quinlan
  Bridgeport, CT
Gerry Quinn
  St. Louis, MO
Kevin Quirk
  Wheeling, WV
Angel Quitalig
  San Franciso, CA
Nicholas Rachford
  Lorain, OH
Steven Raica
  Lansing, MI
Marco M. Rajkovich, Jr.
  Lexington, KY

Margaret Ramsden
  Orange, CA
Noel Rankin
  Feura Bush, NY
Ann Rehrauer
  Green Bay, WI
Charles Renati
  San Francisco, CA
John Renken
  Ottawa, ON
William Reynolds
  Newton, IA
J. Patrick Reynolds
  Owensboro, KY
Mark Richards
  Sacramento, CA
Sheila Richardson
  Charlotte, NC
Thomas Richstatter
  Saint Meinrad, IN
George Rigazzi
  Oklahoma City, OK
Kenneth Riley
  Kansas City, MO
J. Michael Ritty
  Feura Bush, NY
Lynda Robitaille
  Vancouver, BC
Marie Roldan
  San Jose, CA
Meg Romano-Hogan
  Ft. Worth, TX
Eloise Rosenblatt
  San Jose, CA
Charles Rowland
  Charleston, SC
James Ruef
  Columbus, OH
Patricia Ruiz
  Fresno, CA
Alfred Samoranski
  Atlanta, GA
Mary Santi
  Seattle, WA

Edward Schaefer
  St. Rose, IL
Mary Schaumber
  Alma, MI
Joseph Scheib
  Pittsburgh, PA
J. Gerard Schreck
  Savannah, GA
Katarina Schuth
  St. Paul, MN
Gilbert Seitz
  Baltimore, MD
John Sekellick
  Passaic, NJ
Balappa Selvaraj
  Atlanta, GA
Donetta Shaw
  Kansas City, MO
Patrick Shea
  Cleveland, OH
Langes Silva
  Salt Lake City, UT
Robert Sinatra
  Camden, NJ
Jaroslaw Skrzypek
  New Madrid, MO
H. Roberta Small
  Seattle, WA
Daniel Smilanic
  Chicago, IL
Rosemary Smith
  Convent Station, NJ
Harry Snow
  Ogdensburg, NY
James Socias
  Woodridge, IL
Michael Souckar
  Coral Springs, FL
Richard Stansberry
  Oklahoma City, OK
Amy Strickland
  Silver Spring, MD
Therese Sullivan
  Cleveland, OH

David Szatkowski
  Nesbit, MS
Amy Tadlock
  Washington, DC
Joseph Taphorn
  Omaha, NE
Charles Thompson
  Evansville, IN
Maurice Thompson
  Milwaukee, WI
Allison Townley
  Kansas City, MO
Luc Tran
  San Bernardino, CA
Gregory Trawick
  Sturgis, KY
Francis Tse
  Hong Kong
Ann Tully
  Indianapolis, IN
Silvana Usandivaras
  New York, NY
Benedetto Vaghetto
  Pittsburgh, PA
Irene Valles
  Las Cruces, NM

Jan van der Loos
  Hague, Netherlands
Marilyn Vassallo
  Shreveport, LA
John Vaughan
  Owensboro, KY
Andrew R.J. Vaughn
  Milwaukee, WI
Desmond Vella
  New York, NY
Siobhan Verbeek
  Washington, DC
Manuel Viera
  Cincinnati, OH
Adam Voisin
  Hamilton, ON
Victoria Vondenberger
  Cincinnati, OH
Richard Wahl
  Houston, TX
John Ward
  Baltimore, MD
Daniel Ward
  Silver Spring, MD
Rosanne Warner
  Rochester, NY

Hildegard Warnink
  Leuven, Belgium
Lynn Marie Welbig
  Sioux Falls, SD
Rick Wells
  St. Petersburg, FL
Daniel Welter
  Chicago, IL
Robert Wendelken
  Cleveland, OH
Mary Catherine Wenstrup
  Covington, KY
Paul Wienhoff
  Belleville, IL
Philip Wilson
  Adelaide, Australia
Thomas Wisniewski
  Darby, PA
William H. Woestman
  Chicago, IL
Joseph Wolf
  Davenport, IA
Nicholas Wolfla
  Jonesboro, GA
Emmanuel Zamora
  Lexington, KY